France 1815-1914

France 1815-1914:
The Bourgeois Century

Roger Magraw
University of Warwick

New York · Oxford
Oxford University Press
1986

Oxford University Press

Copyright © 1983 by Roger Magraw

Originally published in Great Britain in 1983 by William Collins Sons & Co.
First published in the United States in paperback in 1986 by
Oxford University Press, Inc., 200 Madison Avenue, New York, New York 10016

Oxford is a registered trademark of Oxford University Press

Library of Congress Cataloging-in-Publication Data
Magraw, Roger.
  France, 1815-1914.
  Originally published: London : W. Collins, 1983.
  Bibliography: p.
  Includes index.
  1. France—History—19th century. 2. France—Social conditions—19th century.
3. Middle classes—France—History—19th century.
I. Title.
DC252.M27   1986   944.06   85-21811
ISBN 0-19-520510-3
ISBN 0-19-520503-0 (pbk.)

Printing (last digit): 9 8 7 6 5 4 3 2 1
Printed in the United States of America

For my Mother and Father
and my daughter Nathalie

Contents

Acknowledgements

Since this is essentially a work of synthesis rather than of original research, the debt I owe to the countless historians whose works and ideas I have pillaged should be obvious on every page. Frequently I felt stimulated most by those, such as Eugen Weber or Peter Stearns, with whom I have disagreed the most strongly.

I would like to thank the University of Warwick for granting me sabbatical leave in which to complete the manuscript. Professor Douglas Johnson has been a friendly and approachable editor and the staff at Fontana have been helpful and considerate. I owe a good deal to Alan Bainbridge for making valuable comments on several chapters, to Norma Bainbridge for undertaking the bulk of the typing, and to both of them for their generosity and friendship to me over the years. Chris and Françoise Read and Mike and Angie Wilson gave much-appreciated personal support during the writing of the book. Susan Newton and Sue Threadgold rendered valuable typing assistance in the last frantic days before completion, and Olwen Greenhalgh kindly helped turn my indecipherable writing into legible prose. My colleague and friend Dr Gwynne Lewis kindly accepted the chore of reading the manuscript, made countless valuable suggestions and tried to curb the worst excesses of style and content. Those idiosyncrasies, errors and weaknesses which remain are all my own.

Roger Magraw
University of Warwick

Foreword

In October 1882, Maupassant published in *Le Gaulois* a short story which was to become well known under the title *Aux champs*. This was situated in Normandy and revolved around two country hovels, inhabited by families each of which had four children. They lived so close to each other that there was confusion in the minds of the fathers, who could never remember the names of their respective offspring. They were all poor, surrounded by mud, living on soup, potatoes and fresh air, except for the great occasion of Sunday, when a small quantity of meat was served in each family. Into this hamlet, one summer afternoon, there came a carriage, driven by a young woman who was accompanied by her husband. We learn that she was called Madame Henri d'Hubières, and she was instantly attracted by the sight of the children, especially by one of the little ones. After several visits she and her husband go to see the parents, whose name is Tuvache. They explain that they have no children, and that they would wish to adopt the little boy, Charlot. They offer advantageous financial terms, but la mère Tuvache is indignant ('C'est-i permis d'vouloir prendre un enfant comme ça!') and they are told to go and never to come back. As they leave, Madame d'Hubières sees that there is another little boy playing outside, so she visits the neighbouring couple, his parents, who are called Vallin. They turn out to be much more receptive to the same proposal, and once they have succeeded in putting up the monthly *rente* from 100 to 120 francs on the grounds that the boy would have been working within a few years, then a bargain is struck and Madame d'Hubières triumphantly carries the child off ('comme on emporte un bibelot désiré d'un majestie').

Charlot Tuvache was nearly 21 years old and still living with his parents and slaving away in the fields when, one morning, a smart carriage arrived. Out got an elegant young man, accompanied by an elderly woman. He went into the dwelling-place of the Vallins and hailed the couple as his mother and father. Once the initial shock was past, they were pleased and moved to see their son again, and they proudly took him to show him off to the mayor, the *curé* and the *instituteur*. Charlot Tuvache watched all this enviously. He knew the story of how his parents had refused to sell him. Otherwise he would have been like that elegant young man. He could not bear it. That evening, as he heard the Vallins continuing their rejoicing, he told his parents that he could no longer stay with them. 'Manants, va,' he shouted, and went out into the night.

This story tells one much about nineteenth-century French history. There is the backwardness, the poverty and the rapacity of the French peasantry. There is the childlessness, the wealth and the pretension of the French bourgeoisie. The rivalry between town and country is made all the more telling since the name Tuvache is the same name that Flaubert had given to the mayor of Yonville in *Madame Bovary* and the name D'Hubières suggests a false nobility. Even the most backward peasants seem to know how to call upon the services of the *notaire*, to use the mayor as a witness and to drive a bargain. And within this calculating self-interest there is the supposedly noble sentiment of Madame Tuvache that it is not right to sell one's child, a sentiment that meets with general approval in the *pays* so that Charlot Tuvache grows up with the idea that he is superior to his contemporaries in the village, since, after all, he was not sold. Then, when he is face to face with the reality of what he might have been and what he is, he breaks with his parents. 'Manants' he calls them, using an ancient opprobrious, possibly Norman word for the peasantry and the backward, although he himself is precisely such a peasant, 'un manant'. It is a rupture of like and like, and it is explained by an all-knowing but distant, cynical narrator.

Because this story carries within it certain of the themes of modern French history, it would be easy to say that it suggests certain patterns of French history. But there are many who would object to this. Not only is a simple story being made to carry too heavy a burden, but they would also object to the way in which French history has been presented in terms of patterns. They would object to historians who believe in a recurrent pattern, whereby the cycle of revolution, reaction and restoration is repeated until it works its way out some time in the twentieth century. Put in human terms this means that there were those who sought for major political reform and for social change, while there were those who resisted the pressure for change or who desired only limited, or partisan, rearrangements on the political or social scene. The context of this pattern is usually seen as one of a developing economy in the early stages of social modernization. Another way of describing this recurrent pattern is to speak of an oscillation in political terms, whereby France is divided into two sections, the one consisting of those who wish to maintain the social status and authority that they possess and which is allied to certain traditional French values, the other consisting of those who believe in progress and change and who, in their turn, are able to invoke certain particular French precedents for their beliefs and actions. This oscillation between 'les deux Frances', which has a geographical as well as a statistical constancy, is necessarily set in a context where economic and demographic change are limited. All such patterns, it is maintained, are necessarily false and represent a composed and artificial form of history.

It is also suggested that to see the history of France in terms of such, or other, patterns is to wish to endow French history with privileged characteristics, as if French history could not be like the history of other countries, as if the revolution of 1789 set France upon a path that was unique. But it is more likely that the desire to establish a pattern in French history arises from the uncertainties that prevail about the nature of that history, and the consequent desire of historians to strengthen their interpretations by making them all the more general. These uncertainties arise from the endless controversy over the revolution itself. Was it a series of events which succeeded in establishing a certain form of society but which failed to establish any political system? Or was it a political event, inaugurating a whole series of further political events, all of which have had political consequences? Guizot, in the 1820s, had seen European civilization as being characterized by diversity and by its refusal to accept any one exclusive principle, and he believed that in France this characteristic was most fully developed. Prévost-Paradol, writing in 1868, had seen a France that could be rendered powerless by the clash of ideological extremes. Ernest Renan explained the defeat of 1870 by the materialism of French society, and, writing in the 1950s, Charles Morazé explained the decline of France by the adoption (in the course of the nineteenth century) of a passion for theory and abstract thought.

If historians have been impressed by the power of the French state and of the centralized bureaucracy, they have also been struck by the weaknesses of that state, by its vulnerability to those who could conquer the streets of Paris, by the diversity of those who worked the bureaucratic machine. Since it became obvious that the history of France was overdominated by Paris, historians have plunged into histories of regions and localities and have revelled in discovering further complexities. A preoccupation with the national leaders and the theoreticians of the working-class movement is no longer allowed to obscure the actions of French workers. The historians of village history suggest a double evolution in village societies, as they move from the traditional to the progressive in political life and from folklore to modernity in everyday life, but they point out that these phenomena did not take place at the same time, so that rural societies moved at different speeds and in different ways.

Thus the history of France in the nineteenth century demands constant revision. The traditional approach of seeing French history through the histories of French governments, remains as necessary as ever. More recent approaches, of examining French social, economic and cultural history are more vital than ever. The following pages seek to bring together something of these different methods and to present an assessment of the present state of studies.

Douglas Johnson

Introduction

Despite recent attempts by French, British and American writers to reinterpret the French Revolution, the only plausible, coherent analysis remains that of scholars who, in the tradition of the great French historian George Lefèbvre, see it as a 'bourgeois revolution'. If one looks beneath the surface of the conflicts and chaos which shook French society between the 1780s and 1815 it becomes evident that the 'bourgeoisie' has been the major beneficiary of those changes which occurred. It was they who were ideally positioned to monopolize posts in the bureaucracy and army vacated by the aristocracy, as careers became 'open' if not to talent, then at least to men of wealth, education and initiative rather than to birth alone. It was the bourgeoisie who acquired the bulk of the *biens nationaux*, that 10 per cent of the land of France confiscated from the church in 1790 and auctioned to the highest bidders. Equally important, the revolutionary legislation created the framework within which French capitalism could subsequently develop. Guilds, which had protected artisanal craft production, were abolished, thereby permitting merchant-manufacturers the option of utilizing machines and cheaper unskilled labour. The obstacles to the enclosure of villagers' communal lands were removed. The Le Chapelier Law of 1791 forbade trade unions. Paternalistic governmental policies, designed to protect local consumers by limiting freedom of the grain trade, were abandoned, though both the Jacobin government of 1793 and Napoleon in 1811–12 revived controls briefly in crisis years. Internal customs barriers were abolished.

Yet if the history of nineteenth-century France was to show that the triumph of the bourgeoisie was both incomplete and precarious, the explanation can be found in the 1789–1815 period. For the bourgeoisie had defeated the 'feudal' ancien régime only with the aid of peasant and urban artisan revolts. By 1794 it appeared that the bourgeoisie, having made use of their lower-class 'allies', had effectively crushed or controlled the potential threat from autonomous popular movements. Yet the memory of years when 'the people' had dared to aspire to participate in politics could not be erased by police repression. In Paris and many provincial towns artisans continued to dream those egalitarian dreams which the revolution's rhetoric had encouraged. The growing threat to artisanal trades from new capitalist forms of production accentuated their social grievances and served to keep alive their political aspirations of 1789–94. The active participation of peasants in the upheavals of 1789–93 had ensured the abolition of seigneurial dues and thwarted attempts to impose payment of 'redemption fees' similar to those imposed on 'emancipated' Russian serfs after 1861. Although many peasants were angry at the bourgeois domination of church land-purchase and felt threatened by the legal abolition of communal rights, their struggles during the early years of the revolution had established their right, exercised through the nineteenth century, to stay on the land. This created problems for the bourgeoisie which encountered village communities determined to resist the extension of capitalist practices into the countryside and which discovered that a sizeable peasant sector was a potential obstacle to agricultural modernization and to the growth of a domestic consumer market.

The bourgeois leaders of 1789 yearned for a constitutional system on the British model, with government controlled by a parliament dominated by men of property. Louis XVI's refusal to play the role of constitutional monarch thwarted such aspirations in the years 1789–92. The need to rally popular support to defend the revolution against internal counter-revolution, backed by the aristocracy, and foreign invasion produced a brief phase of Jacobin radical government in 1793–4. Once the counter-revolutionary threat had been neutralized, and the Parisian popular movement emasculated, the bourgeoisie jettisoned the Jacobins, and the Directory government (1795–9) sought to consolidate the bourgeoisie's political control in order to safeguard its socio-economic gains. However, continued war and urban and rural popular unrest, arising from peasant and artisan dissatisfaction with the outcome of the revolution and frequently incited either by 'Jacobin' democrats or by agents of the aristocracy, made political stability increasingly elusive. The bourgeois 'victors' of the revolution could secure their gains only by restricting the franchise to a narrow, propertied elite and by striking out, in turn, at 'radical' or 'counter-revolutionary' enemies. A general election held under universal suffrage would, almost certainly, have swept them from power and restored the Bourbons. Finally their quest for law and order drove them into the arms of a man-on-horseback, General Bonaparte, one of the revolution's most successful generals.

For several years after 1799 Bonaparte carried out his function of consolidating the bourgeois revolution. The bourgeois *notables* who helped put him into power were gratified to see him establish a Bank of France and introduce the *Code Napoléon* which consolidated the post-1789 legislation. Prefects were appointed to run each of France's eighty new departments to strengthen state bureaucratic power. A secular state system for secondary and higher education was established, headed by the *Université* in Paris and including grammar schools (lycées) and exclusive Parisian *grandes écoles*, designed to train army officers and state bureaucrats. The Concordat of 1801 with Rome served to undermine the support which the clergy had given, since 1790, to the counter-revolution, while the Organic Articles, appended unilaterally to it by Bonaparte, restricted contacts between the French clergy and the papacy.

However, reliance on a military dictator proved costly for the bourgeois elites. Bonaparte, driven by the logic of military dictatorship and the economic war against Britain, developed evergrowing dynastic dreams. The character of the war altered. In the 1790s France had been mobilized to defend the bourgeois revolution and to challenge the growing British domination of overseas and colonial markets. As warfare became a permanent feature and a tool of the emperor's insatiable ambitions, its 'rational' goals were forgotten, and the bourgeoisie began to harbour doubts. Certainly thousands of ambitious young men found an outlet for career promotion in Bonaparte's administration. War profiteers flourished, and some industrial sectors prospered as French political hegemony on the continent allowed the systematic weakening of rival industries in Italy or Germany. However, British naval supremacy led to a blockade of the French coastline, colonial and Latin American markets were lost, and west-coast ports whose eighteenth-century dynamism had fuelled the bourgeoisie's ascent to power went into steep decline. Even before Napoleon finally over-extended his military power by invading Russia (1812), many of those bourgeois *notables* who had supported his coup d'état were losing faith in him.

As the empire began to disintegrate the central problem for these elites was how to end the war and introduce a new regime which could guarantee political stability, safeguard post-1789 gains, without falling victim either to renewed popular revolt or to the threat of the return of the old aristocratic and clerical elites who might turn the clock back a quarter of a century by restoring the ancien régime. Such a threat did not appear too far-fetched. If the Concordat had rallied some priests to the post-revolutionary settlement in which they had become salaried servants of a state-church, the ongoing disputes between empire and papacy had re-enforced the hostility of many clergy to the new order and encouraged nostalgia for the lost world of church estates, tithes and Catholic religious domination. With the old 'Gallican' tradition of French Catholicism now identified with acceptance of the revolution's religious settlement, those clergy who rejected this tended to adopt a more pro-papal, 'ultramontane' stance. Despite Bonaparte's encouragement of exiled aristocrats (*émigrés*) to return to France and to integrate themselves with the new elites into a broad class of *notables*, memories of lost land, prestige, seigneurial rights and of guillotined relatives made any rapid 'rallying' of the nobility to the new France unlikely.

As Bonaparte's final military defeat became inevitable after 1812, crucial political questions emerged. What regime would follow the empire? If, as appeared likely, the victorious allies restored the Bourbons to the French throne, would the bourgeoisie's revolutionary gains be secure? Even if the Bourbons themselves were to recognize that some compromise with the revolutionary bourgeoisie was necessary, could their aristocratic and clerical supporters be restrained from viewing Bonaparte's fall as an opportunity to take their revenge for twenty-five years of humiliation?

Part One

The France of the *Notables*

Chapter 1

The Indian Summer of the Aristocracy (1815–30)

In April 1814, faced with military disaster, Napoleon abdicated. In the baggage train of the victorious allied armies, the Bourbons returned to France after a gap of twenty-two years. Louis XVIII, the new ruler, appeared from the outset to feel that the success of his regime depended on the achievement of a satisfactory compromise with the revolutionary bourgeoisie. The Constitution of 1814, the *Charte*, guaranteed most of the post-revolution changes. France was to be a constitutional monarchy, with royal ministers dependent on support from a parliament elected by men of property who paid more than 300 francs per year direct taxes. The land-settlement was maintained, as was religious toleration.

This settlement appeared to be threatened by the episode of Napoleon's 'Hundred Days', in the summer of 1815, during which he escaped from Elba, returned to France and attempted to rally support by claiming that he alone could prevent a return to the ancien régime. After Napoleon's defeat at Waterloo there followed a period in which Louis XVIII's government proved unable, or unwilling, to restrain the desire of its provincial-extremist followers from exacting revenge on those who had rallied to Bonaparte. After four years (1816–20) during which the chances for reconciliation appeared to improve, tensions began to mount again during the 1820s. By 1830 many bourgeois who, initially, had been prepared to give the Bourbons a fair chance, had been provoked into supporting a new revolution, a brief replay of 1789. In part their disenchantment stemmed from the replacement of Louis XVIII in 1824 by his more 'reactionary' brother, the comte d'Artois, who became Charles X. However the fundamental cause relates to the attitudes, behaviour and position of the old aristocratic and clerical elites in post-1815 society.

I The Survival of the Aristocracy

Undeniably the revolution delivered a severe blow to the political power, economic interests, social authority and prestige of the nobility. Aristocrats had borne the brunt of forced loans of the 1790s and were now subject, like other landowners, to the 16 per cent land tax. The abolition of seigneurial dues cut aristocratic income in the Charente by 50 per cent while average noble income in the Toulouse region fell by 35 per cent between 1789 and 1830. Possibly one-quarter of noble families had been involved in emigration, of which some 10,000 had lands confiscated by the state and sold. Losses were heavy in the Bordelais where profitable wine estates had been snapped up by port merchants, eager to diversify investment as English naval blockades disrupted overseas commerce. Around Toulouse the nobility were less vulnerable to bourgeois competition: they had kept a low profile by remaining on their estates, and their losses were fewer. If the aristocracy had owned one-quarter of French land in 1789, they had lost perhaps 20 per cent of this by 1820.

Although lost land could, as in the Sarthe, be subsequently repurchased, this resulted in heavy indebtedness. Sadly for indebted nobles, the Napoleonic Code protected creditors, and the 1825 indemnity, voted to compensate for revolutionary losses and benefiting some 12,500 nobles, reiterated this liability for debt. The Code's emphasis on the division of legacies among all heirs threatened the integrity of noble estates, and fuelled family feuds. Prime Minister Villèle was to attempt, vainly, to restore primogeniture in the 1820s. Loss of their monopoly of higher posts in army and bureacracy accentuated the weakening of the aristocracy's position. Equally important, if less tangible, was the weakening of bonds of deference and respect on which the ancien régime elite had relied, symbolized by the loss of seigneurial jurisdiction.

In all regions aristocratic families had suffered major losses. M. Agulhon estimates that 78 of 235 noble families in Provence in the 1780s were virtually 'inactive' after 1815. T. Beck's analysis of the electoral lists of the 1830s suggests that 40 per cent of the 25,000 noble families of 1789 had 'disappeared' half a century later –

though in the west many may have been too impoverished to meet the electoral tax-qualification. The Burgundian dynasty of Saulx-Tavanes epitomizes precarious survival. 2780 acres of arable and pasture land, iron forges, and even the château furniture, had been auctioned off in 1794–5 to a rising bourgeoisie of notaries, iron-masters, and large tenant-farmers who became local mayors. The retention of 5000 acres of forest gave the tough duchess hope for a revival of fortunes, for 'the old ideas have still great power'. Her hopes were unrealized. Family cohesion was disrupted by feuds over inheritance. The family paid the price for its earlier failures to become actively involved in commercial agriculture, its over-reliance on sinecures from the ancien régime court for its conspicuous consumption. The family failed to master new skills for survival in a new world. There was 'an atrophy of favours from above, respect from below, and family solidarity from within' (R. Forster). The duchess felt a sad, alienated figure in her declining years, 'like the daughters of Jerusalem, I mourn the miseries of Zion in a strange land.'

Yet if the nobles were, along with the clergy, the clear losers from the revolution, French history in the nineteenth century is incomprehensible if one fails to appreciate the strength which they retained. They had survived with their own distinctive politics, interests, marriage patterns. They had not simply dissolved into the broader world of the *'grand notable'*. The precise extent of their economic power is not easy to calculate for article 71 of the 1814 Charter permitted parvenu Napoleonic nobles to retain their titles and the bourgeois snobs in the nineteenth century were as liberal in their appropriation of the *particule* as the father of one recent president. R. Gibson has shown that in the years 1820–1900 the percentage of ancien régime nobles on the Dordogne elected departmental council (*Conseil Général*) fell from 29 per cent to 4.3 per cent, yet in 1900 15 per cent still prefixed their name with *de*. Most estimates agree, however, that the nobility owned at least one-fifth of French land after 1815. Departmental studies in the Pas-de-Calais, Calvados and Rhône suggest aristocratic ownership of between 16 per cent and 21 per cent of the land. Nearly two-thirds of the richest group of taxpayers in Calvados in the 1820s were aristocrats. Despite losing one-third of their lands in the Vendée, they still controlled 24 per cent and above 30 per cent in the Pays de Retz. By 1824 they had regained nearly two-thirds of the 10 per cent which they had lost in Mayenne, though at the price of heavy capital outlay, which left them short of ready cash. In south-west Sarthe the nobility lost little land; in Franche-Comté, Brélot argues, their wealth was reduced but by no means destroyed. In all, prefects estimated that 60 per cent of the richest 670 families in France in the 1820s were ancien régime aristocrats, including 90 per cent of the 500 richest landowners.

A variety of strategies had permitted this successful riding of the revolutionary rapids. In the west many had virtually maintained seigneurial dues by renaming them and writing them into sharecroppers' leases. Some had actually bought up church lands. *Émigrés* had utilized 'straw men' to buy up their own confiscated property and noble ladies had divorced *émigré* husbands to avoid confiscation. In royalist heartlands like the Vendée tax agents of the Directory, working in 'enemy territory', had been intimidated or misled into massive underestimation of the extent of noble sharecropping farms. Some had prospered in new ways, like Chapt-de-Rastignac in the Dordogne who removed the *fleur de lys* from his château, purchased a forge and made ammunition for Bonaparte's armies.

While many departments retained islands of aristocratic dominance, the heartlands were the west, north-west, south-west and areas of the Lyonnais, Burgundy and the Massif-Central. They were weakest in the east. Their power was strongest in regions away from roads and commercial agriculture, ports and industrial towns, in areas of hamlets, rather than villages, where the urban bourgeois was alien and ties of deference persisted, and where landownership perpetuated controls over sharecroppers, labourers and dependent tradesmen. One noble near Toulouse maintained 'feudal' traditions of labour service into the 1840s, using the *curé*'s sermon to tell villagers when his château required stones carried from the quarry. Aristocratic domination of the north-west was accentuated by the economic decline of the commercial bourgeoisie of Nantes, for the loss of colonial markets undercut much of the industry of the hinterland. In Mayenne and in Brittany some businessmen switched their investment to land, became 'feudalized', assimilated Catholic-royalist opinions and accepted noble domination. Such men saw social stability and the defence of property in post-revolution society as best achieved under a restored monarchy.

It would be an error, however, to reduce noble influence to the power of economic intimidation over their dependants. They enjoyed a measure of genuine popular – and populist – support. The map of Cathlolic-royalist domination in western France after 1815 does not simply coincide with that of aristocratic land-holding. Quarrymen, woodcutters, charcoal burners, rural textile- and nail-makers were often the sociological base of 'undeferential' communities in an otherwise conservative western countryside. Yet A. Siegfried, who argued that a property structure which permitted big noble landowners to dominate deferential sharecroppers was *the* key to rural royalism, was forced to confess that parts of the west were 'elusive political terrain' where his categories were meaningless. In western Sarthe, western and eastern parts of Ille-et-Vilaine, and in areas of the Vendée, small peasant owners exhibited persistent loyalty to Catholic-royalism. Mythology attributed this to the devotion of simple peasants for king, priest and lord of the manor (*châtelain*).

However, this allegiance was, in part, a negative one. Where the revolution had seen the triumph of urban-based lawyers and textile merchants, who had monopolized purchase of church lands and control of new municipal offices, the end product had been the disappointment of peasants' land-acquisition dreams and a 'counter-revolutionary' peasant backlash against taxation and conscription demands from the Jacobin state. Peasants felt traditional religious practice threatened and the relative autonomy of eighteenth century village community challenged by the intrusion of an alien bureaucratic state. While some market-orientated peasants such as Loire valley wine growers acquired church lands and welcomed the revolution, peasants in subsistence farming areas such as the Mauges experienced the revolution as an economic and cultural disaster. The old noble and clerical elites, often unpopular in 1789 because of seigneurial dues and tithes, acquired an unprecedented popularity as a lesser evil. Patterns of political and religious loyalty set in the 1790s often persisted across the nineteeth century – although it has been argued that rival neighbouring 'royalist' and 'republican' villages of the nineteenth century had often been on opposite sides in the sixteenth-century war of religions!

In south-eastern France the old aristocracy succeeded in harnessing populist anti-capitalism. In the Gard and the Ardèche the main beneficiaries of the revolution had been a Protestant elite of financiers, silk merchants and coal owners who came to dominate the Languedoc economy, ousting smaller Catholic entrepreneurs and trapping peasants and artisans into a cycle of indebtedness. They used the revolution to achieve political control commensurate with their economic hegemony, thereby provoking an alliance of declining noble and clerical elites with threatened Catholic peasants, artisan and petty bourgeois elements. This aristocratic-populist alliance was to use the restoration of 1815 to seek revenge for two decades of humiliation in the 1815 'White Terror' which witnessed the sectarian murder of several hundred Protestants. One typical victim was Antoine Teste of Bagnols, widely loathed as the legal defender of rapacious grain merchants, and for selling church lands cheap to his friends while forcing Catholic priests into hiding. Catholic nobles orchestrated these murders. Royalist deputy Trinquelaque appointed his own man, Vidal, to run the police, and acted as the paternalistic defender of small-scale miners against Protestant big business near Uzès. Another grass-roots organizer was Froment, a minor Catholic *notable* whose career as a church-revenue collector had been wrecked by the revolution. Catholic ultraroyalism was, thus, not simply the tool of the most 'reactionary' nobility but a populist anticapitalist movement – albeit one manipulated by elites.

Royalist populism existed in those numerous towns whose ancien régime economy had been based on church, *parlements* and aristocratic town houses (*hôtels*). Here the revolution was an economic disaster for the poor, for declining aristocratic and clerical fortunes implied the collapse of charity and of orders to artisans for luxury goods. In Toulouse, the revolution benefited a narrow legal and commercial elite, while precipitating an economic decline which created among the poor a 'selective nostalgia' for 'the good old days' before 1789. In the surrounding countryside, the nobility maintained tight control over dependent sharecroppers, an economic domination idealized as an organic social relationship by young royalist romantics who eulogized the suckling of aristocratic babies by sturdy peasant wet nurses!

With 80 per cent of the Toulousain *biens nationaux* appropriated by the bourgeoisie there was little peasant sympathy for a revolution viewed as urban, anticlerical and 'northern'. The aristocracy used the clergy to channel the 'Spanish' religiosity of Toulouse artisans into penitent societies which doubled as royalist political leagues. The Rights of Man were no substitute for food and jobs in Toulouse, a city which remained 'an offence to the liberal mind' (Rémusat). The aristocracy cultivated the myth of a lost golden age of independent *parlements*, church splendour, ceremony, regional independence, full employment, guild loyalties and paternalist social welfare – a myth challenged only by a small liberal bourgeoisie and some markedly undeferential riverside workers of St Cyprien. The local aristocracy, epitomized by Villèle, prime minister in the 1820s, who stayed on his estates during the revolution, used intermediaries to repurchase his confiscated property, and shrewdly incited popular conscription protest in the declining years of Bonaparte. Wellington was welcomed as a saviour in Toulouse in 1814. Paramilitary bands known as *verdets*, recruited from luxury artisans, terrorized the countryside and sabotaged compromise between the restored Bourbons and the liberal bourgeoisie. The moderate prefect, Rémusat, was boycotted, the pulpits resounded to bloodthirsty sermons, and Paris found it impossible to impose central authority. Nobles flooded back to monopolize local administration and the courts. Prefects were suspect as tools of Parisian centralization, for the Toulouse aristocracy advocated a decentralization of power into the hands of 'natural' local elites (i.e., themselves) in 'organic' regions. Though royalist writers waxed lyrical about an idyllic Germany of small princes and medieval *Schloss*, Midi ultraroyalists were not simply political romantics, obsessed by a feudal never-never land, but had specific local objectives.

The religious factor unites these areas of royalist populism. In Languedoc Catholicism was a rallying force against Protestant capitalists. In the upland regions of the southern Massif, the Catholic peasantry of the Aveyron and the Lozère felt alienated by a revolution espoused, in the main, by the Protestant merchants and artisans of small towns like Rodez.

In the Vendée the defence of local priests against their 'persecution' by revolutionary authorities in the 1790s had crystallized the hostility of peasants to urban intervention in subsistence farming areas where the *curé* had been the sole intermediary between the hamlet and the outside world. In Toulouse artisan royalism was organized into religious *confréries*. Despite the real progress of de-christianization among strata of the bourgeoisie, city artisans and the peasantry in some regions, religion remained central to the community life and seasonal routine of much of rural France. Pillaging of churches, persecution of priests and local acts of sacrilege, such as the destruction of the Black Madonna of La Dourade near Toulouse, had served to generate a martyrology in many areas. In departments as varied as the Pas-de-Calais and the Sarthe, self-righteous peasants were fired by envy of an anticlerical bourgeoisie which had monopolized purchase of church lands, which they had coveted. One should however beware of universal crude correlations between high religious practice and royalism. In the diocese of Rennes, as Lagrée has emphasized, religious practice was generally high. However, in the south-east of the diocese the population was Catholic without being clerical and a 'blue' republican tradition had emerged, while the east of the diocese, the most strongly royalist, appeared less pious in terms of religious vocations than western cantons where royalism was less monolithically strong.

The Restoration aristocracy strove to manipulate such religiosity for its own political purposes. Nearly 80 per cent of episcopal appointments after 1815 were aristocratic. Many church organizations relied on aristocratic financial patronage. Many *curés* were expected to be virtual servants of the *châtelain* – even to the extent of eating in the kitchen with the domestic staff. In those dioceses where liberal-Gallican bishops survived, the younger generation of ultramontane clergy were incited against their superiors by local royalist elites. The financial benevolence of the Restoration, which increased the religious budget to 175 per cent above its 1815 level, helped foster a religious revival which saw ordinations swell from 900 to 2550 per annum, seminaries increase from 50 to 80 and nuns double to 25,000. The depletions in clerical ranks caused by the revolutionary 'persecution' were rapidly made good. Diocesan studies, notably in the west and the Midi, emphasize a widespread – if often ephemeral – religious revival marked by increased vocations and higher church attendance in the years after 1815. Revivalist missions, travelling political variety shows, spread royalist propaganda. Stendhal noted wryly of a spectacular mission procession in Eastern France that 'such a day undoes the work of 100 Jacobin newspapers'. Zealots burned copies of Voltaire, and Midi clergy revived penitent groups and religious fêtes after the revolutionary hiatus. The *Université*, which directed public education, was placed under Mgr Frayssinous, and 33 per cent of its personnel were clergy by 1830. Chairs of political economy were abolished, attempts were made to rescue the souls of college students from enlightenment heresies, and royalist departmental councils, as in Mayenne, placed regular clergy in control of village schools. Diocesan catechisms frequently insisted that non-payment of tithe, abolished in 1790, was a mortal sin!

Religion was central to royalist ideology. De Bonald and De Maistre, the high theorists of counter-revolution, were virtual theocrats for whom 1789 was an atheistic revolution, regicides were deicides, politics was a Manichean struggle in which good would triumph only if the sins of the enlightenment were washed away by veneration of pope and Bourbon. Liberal fallacies of human progress were heretical. Man was born in sin – and kept in line only by fear of God and of the executioner. The extended family was the bastion of society – threatened by the revolution's introduction of divorce, a reform duly abolished by the Restoration. At its worst the writings of these two men express that paranoid hatred of ideas, intellectuals, *déracinés*, which produced the notorious 1825 sacrilege law introducing the death penalty for blasphemy. At his most lucid De Bonald hinted at an interesting organic critique of the harsh new world of laissez-faire, in which peasant communities and artisanal skills were being destroyed by capitalist greed. De Bonald, in particular, catches something of that desperate alienation experienced by royalism's populist clientèle in the face of the advent of capitalism.

Royalism's major bastions were in peripheral regions such as Brittany and Languedoc, marked by vigorous cultural and linguistic particularism. Brittany had been notably undertaxed and underadministered in the eighteenth century – and the benefits of growing bureaucratic centralization appeared dubious, its disadvantages severe. Paris-made laws, northern bureaucrats, tax collectors and conscription sergeants, the French language itself were seen as alien. Royalism cultivated a strain of right-wing 'anarchism'. Aristocratic deputies in 1816 urged financial and administrative independence for local assemblies and expressed a rhetorical distaste for the agents of the centralizing state, stressing instead the virtues of 'natural' elites. In the Toulouse region, some nobles toyed with the idea of using the *Conseil Général* as a weapon of devolution against 'Parisian' prefects, viewing Louis XVIII's feeble acceptance of parliament and of the Bonapartist bureaucratic structure as a betrayal.

The aristocracy thus retained a powerful landed base. Anticapitalist populism, popular religiosity and regionalism provided access to wider mass support. Too often ultraroyalist nobles are dismissed as simple-minded anachronisms, their potential influence underestimated. Some aristocrats hoped to utilize these strengths to turn the tables on the bourgeoisie, and overthrow the revolutionary settlement. Yet the very factors which gave them populist support posed awkward policy dilemmas. David Higgs has argued that the aristocracy's key mistake after 1815 was the failure to expand from their landed base by coming to terms with capitalism, modernizing their estates and diversifying investment into industry. Instead of making an alliance with bourgeois elites, they ostracized *biens nationaux* holders, condemned speculative investment, criticized usury, and adopted an agrarian antimodern posture which proved their undoing.

Certainly examples of such attitudes can be found. In the Mayenne, M. Denis portrays returned *émigrés* wasting their energies on hunting, or studying local insects, while the profits of increased yields went to the estate managers who ran their farms, and agricultural improvements were dominated by bourgeois liberals like Sebastian Guichard. Yet this thesis needs careful qualification. Many aristocrats *were* involved in capitalism, agrarian or industrial, as coal and forge owners or wine producers. Having lost much arable land many made full commercial use of forests which they retained. Yet such activities raised a central dilemma. For, if their popular influence rested on a paternalist-anticapitalist-populism, one consequence of the espousal of capitalist practices might be the erosion of their support among peasants and workers who would see them as indistinguishable from bourgeois exploiters. The image of Toulouse aristocratic paternalism was dented during the 1816–17 grain crisis, when noble landowners insisted on their right as property-owners in a post-1789 laissez-faire world to maximize profits by exporting grain from the region. Conversely, the royalist elite in the Gard, less involved in cereal production, strengthened its influence in the same crisis by charitable food handouts.

The Restoration aristocrat was a man caught uncomfortably between two sets of values. As an ancien régime nobleman he despised the parvenu revolutionary bourgeoisie. Frequent expressions of contempt for *biens nationaux* holders precluded easy merging of old and new elites. Yet, as a property-owner in a new world of laissez-faire, he could be seduced by the temptation to make profits. The grain riots of 1817 proved as offensive to Toulousain aristocratic landowners as to bourgeois grain merchants. As a social-Catholic paternalist, Villeneuve-Bargemont voiced concern with the social problems of Lille cotton workers. As prefect of the Nord in 1827 he used police against working-class protestors. The ultraroyalist aristocracy's rhetorical denunciation of the bureacratic state combined with a willingness to use police, army and prefectoral powers against social disorder. The artisan and peasant upheavals of the 1790s were sufficiently recent to produce alarm. Royalist strongholds, such as eastern Ille-et-Vilaine, were often areas of endemic popular 'anarchy' – poaching, tax and conscription evasion. It was this which restrained the aristocracy from playing the populist electoral card. The post-1815 franchise, based on payment of 300 francs per year in direct taxes, produced a narrow electorate of some 90,000 property-owners, the majority bourgeois. One ultraroyalist deputy saw this system prostrating France before 'the aristocracy of wealth, the most insolent of all aristocracies' and suggested abolishing the tax-qualification to drown liberal bourgeois in the waves of loyalist peasant voters. Yet, faced with liberal electoral gains in the 1820s, the eventual strategy was a cautious one of narrowing the franchise to the largest, hopefully royalist, taxpayers. Similarly, the aristocracy came to take over and colonize the Bonapartist prefectoral corps which, their rhetoric had suggested, required abolition. By the mid-1820s the odd anti-bureaucratic ultraroyalist voice in parliament was crying in a wilderness.

A further area of ambivalence among royalist aristocrats and their clerical allies was in their attitude towards popular culture. They posed as the benevolent protectors of traditional culture, ceremonies and festivals against the kill-joy puritanism of Jacobins. Yet popular culture was an unruly beast. Festivals could get out of hand and lead to violence. Many aristocrats came to share 'bourgeois' distaste, and to express the need to impose tighter controls. The clergy's enjoyment of the apparent revival of popular religiosity was tempered by the neo-Jansenist disapproval of younger clergy for the 'superstitious', unruly and drunken accretions of religious festivals. In Provence, in 1814–15, popular royalist fervour was influenced by hopes that a Bourbon restoration implied the end of the *droits-réunis* (wine taxes). The tax riots which followed the realization that they were not to be abolished converted local royalists to the need for tough policing policies. One central dilemma lay at the heart of royalist politics. If the aristocracy were the enemies of the revolutionary bourgeoisie, should they be prepared to dabble in populist politics, to arouse the artisan and peasant victims of capitalist change? If so, this meant allying, as in the Midi, with a quasi-anarchist popular royalism which hated taxes, conscription and the police. Yet aristocrats were men of property. As such, did their interests lie in accommodation with bourgeois property-owners to defend 'law and order'? There was a basis for such synthesis. Mercantile groups in cities like Marseille had royalist sympathies. Aristocrats like de Solages owned mines, just as many bourgeois owned land. Many liberals accepted the idea of an aristocracy. However, when pragmatic royalist politicians like Villèle attempted to develop such a conservative coalition of old and new elites, atavistic family memories, traditions and hatreds thwarted him. On the eve of the 1830 revolution one perceptive liberal journalist contrasted Villèle's moderate 'capitalist' royalists with those, led by Polignac, representing bankrupt aristocrats with less to lose from populism and extremism.

The failure of the Restoration aristocracy to resolve this dilemma is illustrated, in microcosm, in the politics of the Mayenne. Here many bourgeois lawyers and businessmen rallied to the new regime because of weariness with endless war, only to be alienated rapidly by the arrogance of the ultraroyalist aristocrats who monopolized the local administration. In one *arrondissement*, one-third of mayors were ex-seigneurs. One ultraroyalist sub-prefect placed the entire financial burden of allied troop occupation on to *biens nationaux* purchasers. Yet, while pushing the bourgeoisie into the liberal opposition, the aristocracy simultaneously failed to satisfy their popular clientele, ex-*chouans* who wanted rewards from the Restoration for their counter-revolutionary militancy, in the form of jobs or exemption from taxation conscription. Even in the 1790s the bands of counter-revolutionary peasants, so called *chouans*, had been difficult to control, with aristocratic landowners among their victims – an awkward fact obscured by subsequent royalist mythology. They wanted a genuine counter-revolution, revenge on *biens nationaux* holders. Their apocalyptic expectations were fuelled by the preachings of some of the clergy. They viewed the Charter of 1814, which accepted the revolution's land settlement, as a betrayal. The aristocratic elite fêted them, while attempting to muzzle them. They were thanked for their efforts by a few handouts, a few jobs in the local police, tossed a few bones. Yet, essentially, they were disarmed, incorporated into the National Guard, soothed by Benedictine mission preaching. In Mayenne the aristocracy, in short, had alienated the bourgeoisie while failing to satisfy its own popular clientele.

II The Politics of Reaction (1814–30)

Restoration politics was to be marked by alternating periods of moderation and ultraroyalist reaction. The liberal periods-1816–19, 1828–9 – were, however, brief and failed to establish the dominant tone. Efforts at a synthesis between old and new elites were, thus, undermined as the regime steadily forfeited the confidence of an initially not unsympathetic bourgeoisie.

Prospects for a viable compromise appeared promising in 1814. Bonapartist support had waned steadily since 1811 in the face of endless war, economic blockade and growing burdens of taxation and conscription. Mercantile port elites were hit by the collapse of overseas trade. Peasant conscription evasion, army desertion and tax protest grew rapidly. Submission to the empire in the Midi and the west had been, at best, reluctant. 'Rallied' aristocrats in the Bonapartist bureaucracy retained latent Bourbon sympathies and many Bonapartist officials, sensing impending disaster, were prepared to desert the sinking ship. The returning Bourbons were thus greeted enthusiastically in Toulouse, but also with cautious sympathy by a Parisian upper bourgeoisie which preferred the prospect of a constitutional monarchy to the threat of a Jacobin revival, saw in the Bourbon's ally, Britain, a hopeful example of the fusion of old and new elites, and who were willing to accept the assurance of Talleyrand that the advent of Louis XVIII would mean that 'nothing has changed in France except that there is one more Frenchman!'

Sadly, Louis's entourage did not exactly encourage optimism about the prospects of a negotiated compromise. His brother, d'Artois, was spoiled, obstinate, illiberal and a recent convert to ultramontane Catholicism. De Berry, with potential army and popular appeal, was unstable, and subject to fits of rage. D'Angoulême, ecstatically greeted when he 'liberated' the Midi, had simple courage, but even loyal pilgrims from the west were appalled by the banality of his conversation and his wife, Madame la Rancune, was snobbishly anti-bourgeois. Louis did something to offset the disadvantage of his appalling relatives. Egotistic and fat, he nevertheless concealed his private divine-right prejudices behind tactful phraseology to appeal to bourgeois audiences. 'I do not wish to be king of two peoples,' he claimed.

The chances of the new regime were improved when, in the Treaty of Paris (May 1814), the victorious allies imposed neither a military occupation nor a war indemnity on the defeated French. The central provisions of the Charter (4 June 1814) were acceptable to the bourgeoisie, although some were alarmed by the notion that the constitution was a 'concession' made in the 'nineteenth year' of Louis's reign. There were guarantees of the revolutionary land settlement, religious freedom, civil rights and press freedoms – although undefined abuses were to be controlled. The king, as the chief executive, had law-making initiative, but parliament had to vote laws and accept budgets. If article 14 ominously permitted the crown to make ordinances necessary for state security, nevertheless it appeared a constitution which balanced royal power with bourgeois interests.

The first measures of the new regime appeared conciliatory, with two-thirds of prefectoral appointments made from ex-imperial officials. Yet the First Restoration provided a miniature preview of the conflicts which were to be replayed over the next fifteen years. The arrogance of returning *émigrés* and clergy offset the studied moderation of the government, and caused the widening of opposition which had initially been confined to disgruntled Bonapartist NCOs, Parisian students, and patriotic areas of the east. Snobbish *émigrés* snubbed *nouveaux riches*. Savage cuts in the bureacracy and army left 15,000 officials jobless and 12,000 officers on half pay. Over-zealous clergy insulted *biens nationaux* purchasers, denounced married ex-priests, threatened obligatory Sunday rest and preached the moral obligation of tithe payment. In Rennes, students and troops rioted at the announcement of indemnities for counter-revolutionary brigand leader, Cadoudal. It was to this growing mood of alarm at the possible return of the ancien régime that Bonapartist propaganda made its appeal during the Hundred Days. Napoleon presented himself as the defender of the revolution against a seigneurial-clerical revival.

After Waterloo, the Second Restoration faced a dilemma. Ultraroyalists argued that support for Bonaparte's Hundred Days had been possible only through excessive leniency. 1815–16 was a violent period. In Burgundy and Dauphiné allied troops raped, requisitioned, pillaged – thus providing republican politicians across the nineteenth century with a peasant clientele deeply resentful of the Bourbons who had returned 'in the baggage train' of such barbarous foreign invaders. The violence in the Midi stemmed from ultraroyalism's internal logic. Fifty Bonapartists were massacred in Marseille, General Ramel killed as he tried to control ultraroyalist paramilitary *verdets* in Toulouse. The majority of the Bonapartist garrison in Nîmes was slaughtered after being persuaded to surrender.

Bertier de Sauvigny, a learned apologist for the Restoration, interpreted the wave of murderous violence as a 'spontaneous' popular vengeance, ignoring the way in which artisan and peasant murder gangs were controlled by the local elites in touch with d'Artois. Local ultraroyalist organizers like Lavondes had influential contacts, who interceded at court to get him freed when arrested for intimidating his creditors. Protestant sympathy with the Hundred Days permitted Froment to implement orchestrated terrorist plans, with the complicity of deputies like René de Bernis. The sub-prefect of Uzès (Gard), who reported to Paris that popular excesses were uncontrollable, was himself implicated in Catholic murder gang activity. The newly arrived prefect of the Gard, d'Arbaud-Jouges, was obliged, under pressure, to side with the ultraroyalists. His police chief, Vidal, rigged tax-lists to disenfranchise Protestant bourgeois, while Vidal's son was implicated in a plot to kill General Lagarde who tried to protect a Protestant temple from Catholic rioters, and was then acquitted at his trial when the prefect packed the jury. Catholic aristocrats 'regularized' their paramilitary gangs by incorporating them into National Guard units which stood by to watch Protestant voters murdered at polling booths. The royalist elites in the Midi relied on this popular violence to intimidate their Protestant rivals and achieve local hegemony. Once in power they found that sectarian violence could not be turned off like a tap. Continued atrocities became an increasing embarrassment for they drew Paris's attention to the region.

Away from the violent Midi, terror was more legalistic. Fifty thousand officials were purged. There were 3476 political convictions, 3382 arrests without trial. Ex-Bonapartist police chief Fouché proved his loyalty to his new masters by naming 54 for exemplary execution: 'He has forgotten none of his friends,' noted Talleyrand on viewing the list. La Bourdonnaye called for mass executions to end all plots. Widespread electoral intimidation allowed the ultraroyalists to achieve a parliament in which 90 per cent of deputies were royalist, and which was 50 per cent noble, 20 per cent *émigré* in composition. The *Chevaliers de la Foi* group, active in anti-Bonapartist plotting, before 1814, gave royalist deputies some organization. A national network stretching from d'Artois, via the prefects, to local National Guard units gave ultraroyalism a powerful position.

However Prime Minister Richelieu, not unsympathetic to ultraroyalists ideas, was sufficiently pragmatic to view this as 'madness' which was alienating the bourgeoisie and the staunchly pro-Bourbon Wellington. In September 1816 the irony of a royal dissolution of the ultraroyalists' parliament occurred, followed by governmental pressure for election of a more moderate assembly. This pushed some ultraroyalists, paradoxically, into defending parliament against the 'despotism' of a 'liberal' king. In the new chamber the ultraroyalists were reduced to 90 deputies out of 238, mainly from the west and the Midi. The years until 1820 marked the highpoint of a liberal Restoration in which the flexible Décazes sought to appease the liberals, who made electoral gains until 1819. Leading business figures like Laffitte and Casimir Périer were sympathetic to the studious middle course between 'reaction' and 'democracy'. Rapid payment of war indemnities accelerated the withdrawal of allied troops to silence jibes that Bourbon rule meant foreign occupation. Press laws were liberalized, and the St Cyr army reforms maintained competitive examinations for entry to the officer corps.

Yet reconciliation proved difficult. Attempts to woo pragmatic ultras, like Villèle, foundered as the *Chevaliers de la Foi* exerted pressure on him. Ultraroyalist extremism in the Midi persisted, if more muted than in 1815–16. Prefect Jouques was sacked in the

Gard for complicity with agents of the White Terror and in 1817–19 ultraroyalist plans were reduced to theatrical plots to capture Louis XVIII and impose policy on him. The new prefect of the Gard, Dargout, found his attempts to reconcile the aristocracy with the Protestant bourgeoisie fruitless: 'They all detest me in the most polite manner possible, Protestants and Catholics alike. The former believe I have not done enough for them, the latter think I am a Jacobin.' Dargout's attempts to break the ultraroyalist monopoly of the National Guard aroused tensions between the aristocracy and their popular clientele, who looked to the National Guard for jobs. The aristocracy 'are not loved,' insisted Dargout. The ultraroyalist rank and file 'had no desire to be exploited for the benefit of the nobility alone'. With its patronage threatened, the Catholic elite stepped up its sectarian propaganda, using Catholic festivals as the occasion for anti-Protestant riots. After three years of liberal policy, the Midi was still close to civil war. 'A single shot, a sign from Nîmes, and the whole department would be in flames,' the prefect warned.

Liberal election gains in 1819, and the murder of d'Artois's son, the Duc de Berry, by a Bonapartist fanatic in 1820, were taken by the ultraroyalists as justification of their warnings of the dire consequences of Décazes's policies. The dagger which killed de Berry was, Nodier claimed, 'a liberal idea'. Under right-wing pressure, Richelieu tightened press controls, introduced a double vote for the richest quarter of the electorate, manipulated tax qualifications to eliminate liberal voters. The 1824 election reduced the liberals to nineteen seats.

Villèle, who presided over the shift to the right in the 1820s, was a complex politician. While he shared many of the ideals of Toulouse ultraroyalism, and had been mayor of the city during the massacres of 1815, he lacked the emotional extremism of his followers, 'disdained the vaporous passions of *occitan* royalism' (Rémusat). The taste for order and economy which he exhibited on his own estates he brought to state finances. His uncharismatic low-key pragmatism found its expression in his careful balancing of state budgets, and development of rules of parliamentary financial accountability – though sceptical liberals noted that he kept consumer taxes high, and that shrewdly calculated land tax cuts served to disenfranchise some liberals while aiding noble grain producers hit by the price slump of the early 1820s.

Nevertheless, either through conviction or inability to control his extremist allies, Villèle tolerated a series of government measures which alarmed liberal opinion. In response to calls by Abbé Liautaud for reduction in the numbers of licensed printers, toleration only of an official press printing 'facts' and weather reports, and a return to the good old days when 'one had to publish Voltaire in Amsterdam', the regime tightened press censorship by prosecuting articles for their 'general tendency'. French troops did the dirty work of the Holy Alliance by crushing Spanish liberals – and the opposition deputy Manuel was evicted from parliament for daring to remind the Bourbons of the consequences of war in 1792. The transition from the sceptical, cynical Louis XVIII to the 'dévot' Charles X in 1824 was marked by an ostentatiously medieval coronation at Rheims Cathedral, during which the archbishop denounced the Charter. The 1825 sacrilege law, symbolically reintroducing capital punishment for blasphemy, was both highly provocative and virtually inapplicable.

Even when Villèle attempted conciliatory policies, the vehemence of his ultaroyalist backbenchers and growing liberal alarm combined to produce heightened emotion. An indemnity bill of 1825, compensating victims for losses sustained during the revolution, may have been intended to reassure *biens nationaux* holders as a final settlement of the vexed land question, and did, indeed, help to raise the value of ex-church property by reducing uncertainties surrounding it. Yet, the violent rhetoric surrounding the debate meant that the indemnity was seen as an insult, a fine to punish the nation for the 'crime' of 1789. Ultra-extremists blurred the purpose of the bill with demands for the overthrow of the entire revolutionary property settlement. While the impact of the 630 million franc compensation on rural landholding was small, the aristocracy's critics commented that loyalist *vendéen* peasants received none of it, while bourgeois monied interests were angered because the scheme was financed by a 40 per cent cut in interest rates on state bonds.

Factional in-fighting rashly sabotaged Villèle's apparently impregnable parliamentary position. The assault on Villèle by Chateaubriand's constitutional royalists, Montmorency's '*dévots*', and La Bourdonnaye's ultra-extremists stemmed, in part, from a Namier-ite squabble for the spoils of office. 'Believe me, find posts for all the royalists, after that the whole future is yours',

Chateaubriand had advised Villèle. La Bourdonnaye was disappointed in his quest for ambassadorial posts for his kinsmen. However, the suicidal political indiscipline within the aristocracy was exacerbated by cultural and ideological incompatibilities between crusading ultramontane zealots, and the more reserved, neo-Gallican Catholicism of heirs of the old *parlement* tradition such as Montlosier. Such feuding lost Villèle the support of the most vigorous royalist newspapers.

His fall came in 1827, when the upper house, which still contained liberals from the 1816–20 period, rejected tighter press controls and Villèle's attempt to restore primogeniture to check the fragmentation of aristocratic estates. Thrown off balance by anticlerical demonstrations by Parisian petty bourgeois National Guards, Villèle rashly called for fresh elections and, to his surprise, lost heavily. One hundred and eighty liberals were elected as the *Aide-toi, le ciel t'aidera* society mobilized a bourgeois electorate, particularly in northern and eastern France, alarmed by recent governmental trends and by deepening economic crisis. Liberals won 50 of 75 by-elections held in 1828–9.

Villèle's fall forced Charles X into a brief and insincere volte-face. Under the Martignac government of 1828–9 press laws were liberalized and an attempt made to halt the rising anti-clerical tide by a series of Gallican measures, including a ban on Jesuit teaching and a limit on seminary school pupils. These concessions were largely cosmetic. The events of 1829–30 illustrated the king's lack of elementary political caution. Not content with replacing Martignac with a ministry of ultraroyalists, he chose to confront the liberal-dominated parliament with three of the most provocative figures of the aristocratic right. Polignac was an ex-*émigré*, son of a favourite of Marie-Antoinette. Boument was an ex-*chouan*, who had rallied to Napoleon, only to betray him on the eve of Waterloo. La Bourdonnaye had been calling for blood since 1815. Rumours of an immiment coup circulated, though the mystical Polignac and the windbag Bourdonnaye were scarcely the men of action to engineer an efficient one. In the face of a hostile liberal majority of 221, Polignac dissolved parliament – only to find that a fresh election increased liberal strength to 274. Bourbon election management, successful in the early 1820s, was disintegrating. Hitherto, the regime had relied on a double vote for the wealthiest 20,000 electors, which alone allowed it to win any seat at all in eastern France. Above all, it had manipulated tax assessments to disenfranchise liberal voters, and used prefects to systematically falsify electoral lists and bribe voters with favours and banquets. The electorate had thus fallen from 110,000 to 79,000 between 1817–1829. Now, however, the determined efforts of the *Aide-toi* electoral organization secured the reinstatement of bourgeois voters, 46 in the Douai region alone in 1830.

Polignac was driven by the election disaster to a desperate last throw. The new parliament was dissolved, press freedom ended, and the electorate reduced by 75 per cent by elimination of all but the richest landowners, among whom the ultras could hope to find a majority. The measures were justified constitutionally by article 14 of the Charter, allowing the king to act in exceptional circumstances – and justified tactically by Polignac's celestial vision prophesying success in the venture! Sadly, much of the army was involved in a colonial conquest of Algeria designed to win the regime belated prestige – and no attempt was made to prepare metropolitan troops to meet the inevitable liberal backlash.

III The Revolution of 1830

In July 1830 three days of Parisian street fighting sufficed to overthrow the Bourbons. Analysis of the sources of the opposition to the fallen regime is essential for any understanding of the nature of its successor. Grievances were ideological as well as material, popular as well as middle-class – though the bourgeoisie were to confiscate the fruits of victory.

'1830' was a revolution of frustrated careerists. Once in power, ultraroyalists had colonized the state bureaucracy rather than seeking to dismantle it. 'A bishop, an army commander, a prefect, a public prosecutor, a police commandant – if these are for God and King I will answer for the rest,' Chateaubriand had asserted. Seventy per cent of restoration prefects, and 40 per cent of sub-prefects nominated had been from the old nobility, so that by 1830, 45 per cent of the corps were aristocrats. For the only time in the century the aristocracy dominated the commanding heights of the state machine. The superiority of benevolent impartial rule by gentlemen-amateurs from the natural elite was lauded. Job seekers learned to begin application forms with an outline of family genealogy. Bureaucratic careers gave aristocrats salary and status to compensate for the loss of seigneurial rights in a period of shrinking job opportunity after 1815, but neutralized the efforts of Décazes to achieve a *modus vivendi* with bourgeois liberals. By the 1820s there was a growing number of aspiring, jobless, educated bourgeois for whom the Napoleonic empire became a lost golden age of career opportunity. The Bonapartist cult was strong among Restoration liberals. Koechlin, a leading Alsace liberal, who had his house constructed on the model of Napoleon's St Helena residence, had lost his post as mayor of Colmar after 1815. Similarly Côte d'Or liberalism was headed by Hernoux, the dismissed mayor of Dijon. The Jura opposition leader, Cohn, was a lawyer sacked from his *procureur-général* office in 1815. The proportion of the prefectoral corps under 40 years of age fell from 46 per cent to 23 per cent, in a population where life expectancy was thirty-six years. The 1789 myth of a career open to talent was in jeopardy. After July 1830 leading liberal politicians were deluged with demands for bureaucratic posts.

Similar tensions existed within the army. The Restoration had purged 15,000 Bonapartist officers in 1815–17 and replaced some with *émigrés*. St Cyr's 1818 reforms had attempted a balanced synthesis, permitting promotion by merit and a trained reserve containing Bonapartist veterans. As the regime lurched to the right, after 1819, St Cyr was dismissed, aristocratic favouritism grew and NCOs and ex-officers began to flirt with liberal secret societies, culminating in garrison revolts in Saumur and La Rochelle. Liberal propagandists emphasized the humiliation of Waterloo, the sad contrast between the glories of the 'anti-feudal' crusading armies of 1792–1814 and the renewed aristocratic ethos within the army. In 1823 over 24 per cent of reservists failed to respond to the call-up, and many of those who did, expressed a desire to fight for, not against, the Spanish liberals. The reserve was abolished. But the army remained open to liberal propaganda, and secret society recruitment. Much of this unrest was careerist rather than ideological. Pay was low. An École Polytechnique graduate could quadruple his salary by leaving the officer corps for industry. Promotion was slow – one third of 1816 captains held that rank in 1830. The tedium of provincial garrison life made troops susceptible to café politics. Aristocratic promotions aroused jealousy, chaplains were viewed as royalist spies. In July 1830 there were mutinies, NCOs sped to Paris to secure National Guard posts, 20 per cent of the troops deserted. Many officers, hedging their bets, kept contacts with liberals. Officers were denounced as 'Carlists' by men aspiring to their jobs. One prime task of the new regime was to satisfy some of these career grievances while restoring discipline in order to smash the wave of popular unrest which exploded in the power vacuum which followed the July days.

Secret societies provided a permanent if largely ineffectual opposition to the Restoration. The Carbonari, which organized the 1820–3 risings, was an epilogue to Jacobinism and a seedbed for the subsequent resistance to the Orleanist regime. It was 'anti-aristocratic' but otherwise ideologically heterogeneous, containing future republicans and socialists, alongside men like Dupont de l'Eure, who became pillars of the subsequent Orleanist establishment. Carbonarism hoped that secret-society plotting could engender a coup, which would destroy aristocratic control and return France to '1789' – or '1793' – as well as avenging the 1815 national humiliation. Twenty-three per cent of known members were serving troops, 17 per cent retired *demi-soldes* resentful of their dismissals and of police harassment. Eleven per cent were students, disgruntled at clerical education and declining career prospects. Another 35 per cent were bourgeois – ranging from Alsace industrialists to provincial tavern-keepers, Parisian lawyers to travelling salesmen. Wider popular recruitment occurred in eastern frontier areas, which resented '1815', and in the small towns of the west where artisans feared clerical-royalist rural domination. By 1821 it may have recruited 60,000 members in sixty departments. Its organization was on masonic lines – and freemasonry was a common denominator of many liberal leaders. The abortive summer rising won artisan, wine grower and Loire boatmen's support in an area won over to the republic in 1792. However, Carbonarism suffered from a certain narrow elitism, made a ritual of secrecy yet was infiltrated by police, relied overmuch on vague coup plots in a period of the early 1820s when the economy was healthy and the bourgeoisie not yet totally alienated from the regime.

The Charter's guarantee that *biens nationaux* were inviolable failed to reassure many of their holders. In the Mayenne, clergy railed against such owners until the 1860s. They had been the principal target of the White Terror of 1815–16. Areas with *biens nationaux* purchasers provided islands of anticlericalism in the largely religious Pas-de-Calais countryside. As Leuillot shows, leading Alsace liberals like Koechlin and Hartmann of Mulhouse had been prominent acquirers of local Benedictine abbeys. The endemic frictions between such men and returning *émigrés* emerge in the distaste of one western noble for the local mayor – 'an imbecile, coarse illiterate peasant, whose only property is the débris of my fortune which he uses to get drunk . . . with people of his type. He never ceases uttering *"Vive l'Empereur"* and "Down with the royalists".' Anticlericalism provided an ideal issue for bourgeois liberals, keen to attract a popular following without emphasizing socio-economic issues which might expose latent frictions between bourgeoisie and masses. In Nantes the embryonic hostility of workers to the mercantile elite was diverted by their common fear of the clerical-royalism of the rural hinterland. In St Pol and Arras (Pas-de-Calais) peasants and bourgeois landholders alike lived with a fear of an ultraroyalist triumph which would restore the ancien régime and the church lands. They were regularly abused in sermons or denied absolution.

Restoration clericalism took diverse forms and offended many interests and susceptibilities. In Provence, refusal of church burials to old republicans offended villagers. Diocesan catechisms alarmed peasants by stressing the 'mortal sin' of non-payment of tithe. Lycée students rioted against imposition of mass attendance by clerical headmasters. The blatant utilization of Catholic missions for royalist propaganda outraged the future anarchist Proudhon in Franche-Comté. The fervour of the crusade of younger clergy against dancing became the target of P.-L. Courier's widely read pamphlets, with their titillating exposés of sexual misdemeanours of hypocritical *curés*. The extremism of ultramontane clergy prompted an instinctive Gallican backlash among royalists, who argued that fewer priests had produced a more genuine religion in the eighteenth century. The increased religious budgets of the 1820s fuelled a backlash against the *parti-prêtre* which became the main target of the liberal press by 1828–9. Restoration support for Spanish royalism evoked images of the Inquisition. A rape in Vaucluse gave opportunity for salacious press coverage of a priest's trial. In 1830 Brissaud was jailed for publishing Courier's articles on the prying of the clergy in the confessional into the sex lives of married women. The sacrilege law of 1825 gave the regime a theocratic, obscurantist image confirmed by ultraroyalist passion for saints' relics and the bishops' support for Polignac. Clerical electoral inference in the 1830 elections was flagrant. The liberals were able to create a potent and flexible myth with which to manipulate broader popular grievances. In 1830 the clergy were to be a prime target of popular violence – both in Paris and the provinces. In the Orléanais in 1830–1 priests were afraid to wear clerical garb in the streets.

As in 1789, the revolution occurred in a context of economic depression. In itself this did not make revolution 'inevitable'. The 1816–17 slump had triggered substantial popular anti-tax riots, but of an uncoordinated, localized nature and in a context in which the bourgeois elite retained confidence in the regime and in which bourgeois National Guards were prepared to restore order. The 1826 depression evolved in the classic pattern, as poor harvests drove up food prices, reduced consumer purchasing power, and produced textile unemployment. The freeing of the grain trade provoked widespread attacks on grain convoys in western and central France. Wheat prices rose 66 per cent in eastern France between 1826 and 1830. The 2½ million population growth since 1815 accentuated demographic pressures. A credit crisis led to panic, bankruptcies and unemployment. The 1827 electoral swing to the liberals reflected the erosion of business confidence. The prefects became unanimous in the viewing the business classes as won over to liberalism. In the Pas-de-Calais 249 of 331 business electors, 75 per cent, were liberals – although liberals could win seats only because over 55 per cent of landed voters there had also abandoned the government. Economic debates dominated parliamentary discussion in 1828–9. Peasant grain and tax riots swept the provinces, accompanied by widespread rural arson in Normandy. In Paris the petty bourgeoisie, which lacked the vote, had been angered by the abolition of its National Guard in 1827, and found the threat of bankruptcy adding economic to political grievances. The 'clerical' Paris police chief Mangin alienated shopkeepers by a ban on Sunday trading, and prostitutes and their clients by a ban on soliciting, while Polignac's threat of wider press censorship threatened jobs in the sizeable Parisian printing trades. Paris building wages fell 30 per cent in 1825 and poor housing, sewerage and overcrowding made the Parisian death rate 40 per cent above the national average.

Business confidence was shaken by the slump and by the threat of widespread popular unrest. Residual business sympathy for the regime was steadily eroded. Many businessmen had initially welcomed the Restoration, which had ended the war and the crippling economic blockade which had wrecked port economies. There were pro-royalist strata among merchants, industrialists and financiers like Mallet, who opposed the Hundred Days. Villèle's balanced budgets and the prosperity of the early 1820s sustained this mood. The Anzin Coal Company found the government responsive to its appeal for anti-Belgian tariffs, and recorded 40 per cent profits. Gradually, however, ultraroyalist policies sabotaged initial hopes of a unity of possessing classes. Business mayors like Poillard at Port-Brillet were ousted. Merchants were eliminated from electoral rolls, or met hurtful snubs in Paris salons. The inflexibility of tariff policies worried manufacturers reliant on raw cotton imports. Economic depression produced a wave of business failures in cities like Lyon and Bordeaux, and even large financiers, such as Laffitte, were worried by the fall in share values. In Limoges, industrialists spearheaded vigorous protest movements. The city felt neglected by the aristocratic mayor, de la Bastide, permanently absent riding horses on his estates and able to find funds to build roads to his château, apparently unavailable for Limoges' own desperate road and sewerage needs. The local bishop supported the sacrilege law, sponsored missions and advocated press censorship – provoking stink bombs at religious ceremonies and large crowds at the funeral of an anticlerical comedian denied burial by the clergy. Industrialists resented the lack of government aid in the depression and the failure to develop the region's transport network. Alluaud, the liberal leader and post-1830 mayor, was a porcelain manufacturer with bitter memories of the bullying of non-aristocratic pupils by his Catholic schoolmasters in the 1780s. Here, as elsewhere, Polignac's threat to disenfranchise business was the last straw to businessmen who saw themselves as producers, aristocrats as parasitic.

Liberal financiers did not want a revolution, had a horror of mass insurrection. Yet, Laffitte and Hottinguer became convinced that only by contriving a change of regime could real revolution, and consequent 'anarchy', be avoided. The *deus ex machina* was the Orleanist prince, Louis Philippe, who offered the *via media* of a constitutional monarchy avoiding the twin perils of reaction and anarchy. Louis Philippe had fought for the revolution's armies in 1792. Opposition politicians, with their developed taste for historical scholarship, found precedents in 1688. Charles X was James II, Louis Philippe, William of Orange. 'Let us enlist him without consulting him,' Thiers urged.

Journalists organized the final assault by orchestrating the anti-clerical crusade and exposing the regime to damaging caricature. Liberal newspaper circulation exceeded that of a royalist press, hopelessly split by internecine rivalries. In Paris the liberals had 50,000 subscribers, the royalist press a mere 15,000. Casimir Périer's financing of *Constitutionel* epitomized big business support for the liberal press. The ephemeral relaxation of censorship in 1828–9 satisfied no one, for ultras were outraged while liberal martyrs were still being created, as Béranger was jailed for his caricatures on 'Charles the Simple' and his gerontocracy. Polignac's arrival was greeted as a return to medieval feudalism, the end of the phoney war. Despite the emergence of a few radical papers, the general tone was liberal-constitutionalist with admiration expressed for British-style moderation *à la* 1688. Planned resistance to 'illegal' taxation recalled seventeenth-century England. The opposition press succeeded in its aim to lock the Bourbons in the Charter and get them to escape by jumping out of the window!

The distinctive feature of '1830' was the success with which the bourgeoisie incited and manipulated popular unrest to oust the regime, and then turned to repression of artisan and peasant agitation. A royalist newspaper found it 'astounding' that 'wealthy men, bankers and industrialists, who . . . belong in their country mansions, do not hesitate to play on popular passions!' How did bourgeois politicians succeed in making Polignac's disenfranchment of a few wealthy middle-class electors into an issue for which Parisian workers were prepared to fight? Analysis of the 2800 victims of the July days shows that the fighting was done overwhelmingly by the Parisian artisans. Yet only a minority of popular insurgents voiced radical-republican ideas. Many had been exposed to liberal anticlerical propaganda. Some had been wooed at evening classes at the *Conservatoire des Arts et Métiers*. Doubtless, printing workers could respond to their employer's concern with 'liberty', because press censorship spelled a threat to their employment. Some employers shut down their workshops, even armed their workers. Liberal papers, circulating in popular cafés, portrayed deputies like Manuel as martyrs opposed to clerical-feudal tyranny. A groundswell of populist anticlericalism could be tapped by cheap editions of Voltaire or Molière's *Tartuffe*. In Paris, and in Rouen, episcopal palaces were prime crowd targets – a useful diversion of mass frustrations against peripheral enemies which left bourgeois economic interests unscathed. Urban popular classes, hit by the depression but politically unorganized, were intoxicated by liberal rhetoric and carried through a revolution on behalf of their exploiters.

It is difficult to avoid a cynical assessment of '1830'. Despotism shifted from château to Stock Exchange. The new elite represented narrowly oligarchical interests, extended the franchise only marginally to 200-franc taxpayers, indulged in a quest for bureaucratic posts and sought to annihilate those popular forces which put them in power.

Of course, limited liberalization occurred. Polignac's 'feudal reaction' was defeated. The new king swore his oath in parliament and accepted the tricolour and the gains of 1789. Article 14 of the Charter was abolished to check arbitrary executive power. Jury trial was introduced for press offences, and the municipal franchise was widened considerably. Yet the revolution was not, as sometimes portrayed, a mere coup executed in Paris and passively accepted by the provinces. It had aroused widespread expectations, and was followed by several years of popular disturbances, peaking in August 1830 and early 1832, in which workers and peasants tested the ability, and discovered the unwillingness, of the new regime to satisfy their grievances over wine taxes and forest rights, grain prices, unemployment and the threat of machines.

Economic change was the essential factor which fuelled the political and social unrest which undermined the Restoration. The ultraroyalist attempt to create a stable regime on the basis of land, religion, hierarchy and deference proved futile because a period of peace allowed the acceleration of changes in market-relations, technology and organization of production which the laissez-faire legislation of the 1790s had encouraged. In the ultraroyalist stronghold of the Gard the rapid growth of coal, silk, woollen textiles and wine-monoculture rendered abortive the efforts of the Catholic-royalist elites to turn back the clock. Economic development boosted the strength of the bourgeoisie, multiplied the numbers of cafés where politics were discussed, generated a demand for education among the petty bourgeoisie and popular classes. The Gard was precocious in its economic development, 'atypical' because of the Protestant presence. But it was not unique. The weight of 'dynamic' France tipped the scales against ultraroyalism.

Chapter 2

The Triumph of the
Grande Bourgeoisie? (1830–48)

I The Debate on the Nature of the Orleanist Regime

The nature of the Orleanist regime, once a matter of general consensus, has become the subject of heated debate. Historians once accepted contemporaries' assessment that the 'Bourgeois Monarchy' saw France run like a joint-stock company by a narrow oligarchy. The liberal Stendhal had agreed on this with Catholic-royalist fellow-novelist Balzac, the liberal-conservative aristocrat de Tocqueville with Marx. Prime Minister Guizot, indignantly repudiating the aspersions of selfish materialism expressed by such critics, nevertheless claimed bourgeois dominance over aristocracy and masses as the regime's proud justification. '1830' was seen as complementing '1789', ending the aristocratic revival, permitting the bourgeoisie to capture the bureaucracy and, by extending the vote to 200-franc taxpayers, guaranteeing its electoral control, so as to enjoy the profits of capitalist expansion.

Whereas French historians analyse new evidence within this accepted framework, some recent Anglo-American historiography has suggested a very different model for interpreting the nature of the ruling elite, and has questioned the performance of French capitalism in these years. A portrait of a sluggish, undynamic, economy has been drawn to 'prove' that the Orleanist ruling elites were conservative landowners, indistinguishable from the aristocracy they had allegedly replaced. Their ideal remained that of the ancien régime, of a 'bourgeois living nobly' as an idle rentier from landed income. 377 of the 512 richest tax-paying *notables* of the 1840s were landowners, only 45 merchants or bankers, 26 industrialists. Landowners dominated departmental *Conseils Généraux*, and remained the dominant group in the electorate. A mere 5 per cent of Parisian bourgeois investment was in industry, as against 40 per cent in land and 20 per cent in state bonds. Guizot defended cereal protectionism on the grounds that landed property remained 'the very foundation of society, the source of its grandeur, security, morality and force, more consonant than any other with the nature of man.' Once the landed base of the elite is acknowledged, Cobban argued, 'it does not matter whether we call it an aristocracy or a bourgeoisie.' Pinkney questions the idea that the revolution marked the advent of a new class to political power. '1830' represented a victory for lawyers, bureaucrats and ex-Bonapartist officers, who swarmed to occupy posts vacated by supporters of the Bourbons, but this was a change in personnel, not in social class. Obsession with public office-holding continued the ethos of the ancien régime, where purchase of office was a key to social status. The secondary and higher education system remained geared to the training of bureaucratic rather than economic elites. The baccalauréat led to the *grandes écoles* which trained administrators and officers. Bureaucratic careers were prized above those in business. For a modest outlay on secondary schooling, families could acquire secure and prestigious posts for their sons. Of sixty Orleanist ministers, thirty-six were bureaucrats, only seven businessmen.

Revisionist historians also argue that the '*bourgeoisie*' was too heterogeneous to form the ruling class of the orthodox myth. Intra-class tensions were manifold. Protectionist iron, coal and cotton groups clashed with free-trade silk, wine and shipping interests, able to compete in overseas markets. West coast cane-sugar importers and refiners clashed with the sugar beet interests of the agri-businessmen of the north, who had dominated the internal market during the pre-1815 blockade. Political conflicts were sectional and inter-regional. An advanced north stood out from a stagnant south-west. Parisian financiers clashed with provincial *notables* over control of local railways. River steamboat owners like Bonnardel of Lyon resented the advent of railways. There was no clear industrial-agrarian split, for cereal growers shared the protectionism of cotton owners, wine growers the free-trade preference of silk manufacturers. The Parisian bourgeoisie, defined by A. Daumard as that 15 per cent of the city's inhabitants which could afford to pay for their own funerals, was a complex hierarchy ranging from a narrow elite of financiers with national interests, via a *bonne bourgeoisie* of prosperous traders to an amorphous *bourgeoisie populaire* of retailers, clerks and minor functionaries, distinguishable from the masses more by function than income. T.

Zeldin portrays a world in which doctors, notaries and bureaucrats are distinct groups, each with their own ambitions, and where criteria for bourgeois status relate to life style, manners, classical education and patterns of eating, rather than to economic function. Among industrialists, there was little similarity between northern family textile firms and large, heavily capitalized, metallurgical firms. A mythology which sees France dominated by an alleged oligarchy of two hundred families fails to encompass the complex reality of this fragmentation.

Yet such reductionist demolition of the concept of bourgeois class dominance is, ultimately, unconvincing. Having detailed the internal fragmentation and squabbling of the '*notables*', Tudesq emphasizes that such intra-class feuding was possible in the early 1840s precisely because bourgeois rule appeared secure, in the absence of immediate challenge from aristocracy or masses. Internal division faded in face of popular revolt in 1848. Tudesq's exhaustive analysis of Orleanist *notables* illustrates, also, that in the Nord, Normandy, Lyonnais and Alsace the ethos was one of work, thrift, energy – not of rentier idleness. Lyonnais families pushed reluctant sons into economic careers.

Other planks of the revisionist platform are equally precarious. French economic growth was delayed less by the 'non-bourgeois' nature of '1830' or the non-capitalist values of its elites than by the loss of colonial wars with Britain, which deprived France of Caribbean and Latin American markets. After 1815, France had only 10 per cent of Haitian trade, now dominated by Liverpool. Investment in wine-estates was a rational capitalist response for Bordeaux merchants seeking stability after the pre-1815 blockade, not an atavistic taste for land *per se*. The internal divisions within the elites were not unnoticed by Marx, the implicit target of revisionist historiography, who perceived genuine friction between an 'Orleanist' financial and railway elite, which controlled legislation and public office, and an embryonic industrial bourgeoisie which was a minority in parliament. The latter's interests in cheap credit and cheap rail tariffs caused frictions which led them to flirt with the moderate opposition. Yet this polarization must not be exaggerated. Leading Orleanists Delessert and Sellier were simultaneously financiers and industrialists. The Périer family illustrate the artificiality of neat distinctions between landed, legal and business groups, and the reality of the power of the '*dynasties bourgeoises*'. Already Dauphiné lawyers and landowners, the Périers acquired *biens nationaux* and diversified into soap, glass and coal in the 1790s. Casimir Périer became regent of the Bank of France and the prime minister who, after July 1830, brutally denied that any 'revolution' had occurred. Four of his brothers were deputies, his son became a minister in the 1860s, his grandson a president of the Third Republic.

A constant osmosis between industry, finance, land and bureaucracy marked the Orleanist elite. Gironde *notables* included Bordeaux shipowners and Médoc wine growers. Yet they agreed on free trade. The city's Protestant mayor, the merchant Johnstone, had large estates in the hinterland. M. Dambreuse, the banker in Flaubert's *Sentimental Education* bequeaths an archetypal Orleanist fortune in stocks and shares, factories, farms and 'the forest of Crancé in the Yonne'. Northern landowners ran sugar refining plants. Décazes, head of the *Conseil Général d'agriculture* in 1840, was a metallurgy owner who tended to subordinate the council's agricultural interests to those of industry. It is absurd to talk of an Orleanist 'landed elite' indistinguishable from an ancien régime aristocracy. The agrarian capitalism of the 1840s was not the seigneurial system. Land was a commodity, the grain trade was free, communal rights in decline. Landed wealth was not exclusively that of inert rentiers. The heirs of eighteenth-century land agents and lawyers, the 'worms in the seigneurial fruit', had acquired church lands and were keen on agricultural innovation. In Mayenne a new class of 100-hectares bourgeois owners was in the vanguard of scientific breeding. In the Paris basin there were new dynasties of 'industrial farmers', like Potel-Lecouteaux in Créteil, who began as farm managers and developed mechanized threshing, sugar refining and deeper ploughing. The mayor of the Denain (Nord) was a coal owner yet owned 430 hectares of land and a distillery. Burgundy landowners were involved in local iron forges and Dijon banks channelled agricultural profits into industry. Landowners invested heavily in Paris real estate and building. Landowners with forests, grain, wine or sugar-beet interests were as 'capitalist' as textile manufacturers. Over half the 160 directors of the fifteen largest firms in the 1840s were designated on electoral lists as *propriétaires*.

Pinkney's analysis of the alleged similarity between the parliaments of the 1830s and those of the late-Restoration is disingenuous. By his own statistics, the proportion of business deputies rose from one-seventh to one-sixth between 1829 and 1831, while landowners fell from 31 per cent to 23 per cent. Beck has shown that the percentage of noble deputies in 1827–31 fell from 44 per cent to 14 per cent. Aristocratic domination of the prefectoral corps was broken. Thirty-three of the 112 mayors who resigned in Dordogne in 1830 were nobles; only one of their replacements. Pinkney lays great store by the legal and bureaucratic domination of parliament in the 1830s, yet the alleged division between legal and business elites is a red herring. Businessmen lacked the inclination and training to waste time in parliament – though they provided the bulk of mayors of major towns. What they needed was effective spokesmen for their interests. Lawyers were trained to speak, and relied on economic elites for patronage. Le Havre consistently sent lawyers to parliament to defend its shipping interests. Thiers, the Midi lawyer who became an Anzin director, was the archetypal member of the professional bourgeoisie, who succeeded by 'singing for his supper' in defence of capitalist interests. Businessmen wanted a political framework for their economic activity, not to be politicians themselves. Counting the heads of business deputies is less relevant to an analysis of the relations between Orleanism and capitalism than asking what the bourgeoisie required from the state, and ascertaining whether they obtained it.

II Orleanism and Capitalism

The French bourgeoisie expressed considerable alarm about rapid industrialization. While Duchâtel in parliament in 1837 claimed that France could achieve 'grandeur, power, dignity and independence' only by emulating British industrial power, many, including the Bank of France governor Argout, were worried about the unacceptable face of British capitalism. Visions of the disintegration of stability, moral values and physical health, of the family disruption and class war of smoke-filled industrial cities, fed by the reports of French consuls in northern England, haunted French elites. The debates on liberalizing joint-stock company law (1838) and rail policy were beset by worries about the social and moral consequences of unfettered capitalism. Growing social unrest within France itself during the 1839–40 slump augmented such fears.

The tone of much recent historiography was, indeed, established by Anglo-American economic historians who emphasized the major obstacles to rapid French industrialization, denying that any 'take-off' in the French economy occurred in these years. The revolution certainly benefited long-term capitalist development by ending 'feudalism', secularizing church lands, abolishing internal tolls, lifting guild restrictions, freeing the grain trade and unifying the legal and currency systems. However, the Orleanist years may be viewed as a transitional period, in which surviving obstacles to economic growth were only partially overcome. Market deficiencies have been invoked as one explanation for this. The naval blockade and colonial losses of the Napoleonic years deprived France of Latin American and West Indian markets. The decline of shipbuilding, sugar-refining, and textiles in the west-coast ports and their hinterland resulted in actual de-industrialization, with port elites transferring investment into land. In Port-Brillet (Mayenne) forge owner Pailland-Dubignon shifted capital into grain production, and the Laval tulle industry declined. A similar decline in Mediterranean markets led to a 75 per cent fall in Marseille industrial production between 1789 and 1815.

Poor internal transport, the survival of a quasi-autarchic peasant economy and relatively slow demographic growth burdened French entrepreneurs with weak internal markets. The road system was constructed with military priorities, and concentrated on linking Paris with the frontiers. River transport was hampered by meandering rivers, flooding and irregular water levels. A journey on the Loire from Nantes to Paris could take six months. Bridges were rare, secondary roads poor, slow-moving carts meant heavy fodder costs. In the south-east, coal was moved from Allevard by mule, while Mulhouse cotton masters paid 40 francs per ton to transport raw cotton from Le Havre. France remained, it is claimed, a series of fragmented markets – a large land mass with a patchwork of local economies.

The survival of a large peasant sector raised further obstacles to capitalist development. The French bourgeois revolution had relied in part on peasant revolts to dismantle the ancien régime – but then paid the price in the nineteenth century, for peasants owned nearly half the land, and farmed most of the remainder as tenants or sharecroppers. Many historians portray the peasants as semi-subsistence farmers, growing their own food, purchasing little, failing to supply a viable internal market for French entrepreneurs. By clinging tenaciously to the soil, the peasantry forced French industrialists to import Belgian or Swiss immigrant labour. Many French workers, like the miners of Carmaux (Tarn) were quasi-peasants who disappeared at harvest time. Small peasant owners, reluctant to subdivide their farms, are also held responsible for the low rate of demographic growth. The British population doubled between 1800 and 1850, the French rose by only 30 per cent. 1830–50 saw the birth rate fall from 3.2 per cent to 2.7 per cent, accentuating the sluggishness of internal demand. American historians have defined a characteristic French entrepreneurial mentality and ascribed to it much responsibility for allegedly modest economic performance. Having no faith in market expansion, French entrepreneurs doubted that lower prices meant wider sales. Investment in plant and machinery to boost productivity seemed risky and unnecessary. Fohlen argued that textile owners viewing demand as inelastic, concentrated on profit per unit of production. Jealous protection of the home market led the large Anzin mine company to delay transport improvements in northern France, lest they facilitate Belgian coal sales to Paris. Northern textile dynasties allegedly venerated family independence, shunned reliance on outside capital from shareholders or banks and avoided the risk of expansion. Debt was viewed with distaste. Motte-Bussut reluctantly put up capital for a giant mechanized spinning plant for his son, but saw such ventures as immoral, and refused to enter the new factory! Fragmentation remained the norm. Rouen in 1835 had 450 cloth manufacturers, 300 spinners, 60 dyers and 60 textile printers. The low prestige and high risk associated with industrial enterprise caused a constant haemorrhage of capital into land, for security and status.

Three further factors are cited by 'pessimists' to explain French 'retardation'. Banking, dominated by the conservative and cautious *haute banque*, emphasized state loans above the provision of industrial capital and made investment decisions on the basis of habit and inertia. Industrial investment was viewed as risky. Banking remained geographically fragmented, more commercial than industrial. Long-term industrial loans were avoided. Control of credit was tight. The formation of joint-stock industrial companies was limited to a mediocre average of ten per year by tight state supervision. This check on the development of limited liability allegedly discouraged industrial investors. Finally, France's raw material resources were either mediocre, or poorly located. Limited coal resources were often in scattered outcrops in southern France, away from expanding northern industry. Seams were thin, much of the coal unsuitable for coking, and poor transport made prices at the point of consumption in some cases up to 800 per cent higher than at the pithead. Substantial forest resources thus encouraged the survival of archaic charcoal forges.

Recent 'pessimists' thus deny that a true 'industrial revolution' was occurring. Prices and profits were low for three decades before 1848. Fifteen of the twenty modern forges collapsed in the 1826–32 depression. Much of the growth in textile production occurred in rural outwork in the Normandy countryside, and even the 'Gallic Bradford', Roubaix, retained twice as many hand looms as power looms. The 'rail boom' of the 1840s was a mere flutter, capital investment barely one-fifth that of subsequent decades, and there was little multiplier effect on heavy industry. A few industrial giants were emerging – but islands in a sea of small firms cushioned by protectionist tariffs.

Yet this image of an undynamic capitalism and cautious capitalists is seriously distorted. Recent historiography has begun to redress the balance. Many French entrepreneurs, faced with very real obstacles, did not react simply as status-conscious, tradition-bound rentiers. Britain had massive coal resources, control of imperial and world markets, and a technological lead which made it difficult to beat her at her own game. Yet imaginative efforts were made to evolve strategies to maximize France's own potential advantages. Quantitative analysis has suggested overall economic growth of 3.5 per cent per annum in the 1825–34 to 1835–44 period, reaching 5.6 per cent per annum in key industries. Industrial production was 30 per cent higher in 1835–44 than in the previous decade. In the framing of economic policy one can sense the growing influence of business interests on Orleanist government. It is misleading to view the bureaucracy as hostile to economic interests. Only 17 per cent of deputies in the 1838 parliament were businessmen. Yet this is less relevant than asking what policies industrialists demanded from government and enquiring if they succeeded in obtaining satisfaction.

If landowners and rentiers still made up 40 per cent of the 1842 electorate, nevertheless the more 'modern' section of the bourgeoisie had a powerful voice in framing key legislation. The bankruptcy laws were eased in 1838, making prison less likely for investors. Relaxation of state control allowed joint-stock companies to emerge in the rail sector, and encouraged the habit of industrial investment. The regime tended to override local small business opposition to 'monopolies', encouraging the *Compagnie des Mines de la Loire*, which came to dominate the St Étienne coalfield. Laffitte's *Caisse Générale du Commerce et de l'Industrie* hinted at more flexible industrial banking strategies – and, as Lévy-Leboyer shows, even the *Haute-Banque* was more 'progressive' in this field than once thought. Industrialists found the regime sympathetic to their needs for a tough anti-strike policy, for in a labour intensive economy wage control was essential to French capitalism's efforts to become competitive by reducing unit costs. When the Rhône prefect intervened in 1831 to urge silk employers to accept wage increases, Lyon capitalists successfully pressured Casimir Périer to sack him – and troops put down the ensuing rising. Anti-union laws were tightened in 1834, industrial tribunals (*conseils des prud'hommes*) remained employer-dominated, capitalists retained the right to be sole judges of the quality and weight of the product of outworkers.

Half the government's tax revenue came from indirect consumer taxes, facilitating the accumulation of profits by undertaxed elite groups. Transport policy was coordinated by a new breed of technocratic bureaucrats in the commerce and public works ministries, epitomized by Legrand of the *Ponts-et-Chaussées*, trained at the *École Polytechnique*. This keen advocate of transport modernization was willing to confront deputies and local *notables* who obstructed rail developments. Humann, finance minister in the 1840s, was a Strasbourg merchant who typified the advent of business interests to key ministries. The Restoration's balanced budgets had hampered a positive transport policy. Transport budgets increased 50 per cent in the 1830s, and laws of 1836–7 obliged municipalities to maintain local roads and allowed prefects to increase departmental taxes for this purpose. 2500 kilometres of canals were completed, including key Rhine-Rhône and Paris-Nord links. The Restoration had built 399 kilometres of road per year; the July Monarchy built 1326 kilometres per year. Internal steamboat traffic enjoyed a brief pre-railway golden age. The 1842 act encouraged rail expansion, and provided handsome guarantees for investors. The state purchased land and provided stations and tracks, while private capital provided rolling stock and was promised long-term concessions and profit levels.

The presence of financial giants, such as Hottinguer, as directors of rail companies opened the regime to charges of surrender to financial feudal barons. Fifty per cent of shares in the Paris-Lille company were held by four men, and Paris-based financiers tended to elbow out local interests. Vested interests among steamboat and coaching firms delayed rail-building, but the pro-rail lobby triumphed despite the fears of opposition deputies that the government would use rail routes as electoral bribes or threats, and of the threat of state interventionism implicit in Legrand's activities. There existed a potential incompatibility between the 'national interest' in transport modernization, which required the use of cheaper imported iron and coal, and vested interests of powerful domestic heavy metallurgy and mining lobbies. Orleanist tariff policy remains contentious. The 1831 ministry of commerce enquiry found businessmen critical of inflexible Restoration tariffs, keen for low duties on raw materials, but in favour of prohibitive duties on products likely to undercut domestic industry. By 1836 iron tariffs stood at 100 per cent. Lobbying sabotaged plans for a customs union with Belgium, and governmental free-trade flirtations were ruthlessly quashed. Some see in this the *grande bourgeoisie* at its most cynical, incapable of surmounting short-term vested interest, even for goals of economic modernization which it favoured. Charcoal forge owners slowed rail development by insisting on use of their own pig iron. The free-trade efforts of commerce minister Passy (1834–6) were thwarted, and the coal-textile lobby would have jettisoned Guizot had he insisted on the 1841 treaty with Belgium. Free trade had support from Saint Simonians* like Chevalier, the economist J. B. Say, and export industries like wine and silk. Some industrialists shared the conviction of their Lancashire counterparts that ending cereal duties would mean cheaper bread and lower wages. Yet, it is significant that in the Aube or the Côte d'Or, where free-trade wine and protectionists iron interests coexisted, it was the industrial interest, *not* the agricultural lobby, which controlled the departmental *Conseil Général*.

* See page 103.

Did myopic protectionism retard French industrialization? Many entrepreneurs justifiably feared that free trade would wreck embryonic French industries. Possibly only guaranteed high internal prices provided the incentive for capital investment in heavy industry.

The harsh criticisms of French entrepreneurial performance require careful qualification. Lévy-Leboyer has argued, plausibly, that French entrepreneurs, aware of the impossibility of competition with Britain in cheap mass production, adapted imaginatively to world markets by concentration on quality products such as silk, gloves, porcelain, reliant on skilled labour. It remained economically rational for Normandy and Picardy textile entrepreneurs to utilize the pool of cheap rural outworkers rather than investing in machinery. Round St Quentin, there were still 75,000 rural textile workers in the 1830s. Family firms were not necessarily inefficient, many adapting quickly to changing fashions. Lyon silk manufacturers, faced with militant artisan protest, adopted an effective strategy, mixing mechanization with rural dispersal. Even Landes, the foremost critic of French entrepreneurship, has conceded the dynamism of the Motte textile dynasty in the Nord. Labour productivity in French industry may, O'Brien claims, have been higher than in Britain.

The stereotype of the cautious, traditionalist businessman is misleading. The dynamism of certain heavy metal, coal and textile firms shows that a genuine industrial bourgeoisie was being formed. Rail development, if still under 2000 kilometres in 1848, encouraged economies of scale in metallurgy. Charcoal forges were, themselves, boosted briefly by the early 1840s expansion, but the percentage of coke-produced pig iron rose from 14 per cent to 45 per cent between 1836 and 1850, while the ten largest firms increased their market shares from 24 per cent to 37 per cent. Since a coke-forge cost eight times the price of a Catalan wood forge, auto-finance declined, and Le Creusot became linked with the Seillier bank, while Dufaud at Fourchambault used *École Polytechnique* graduates as managers.

Improved transport, and rising wood prices, made coal a viable fuel for Paris, production trebled to five million tons between 1830 and 1850, and concentration accelerated so that ten coal companies came to control 71 per cent of production. Glass production began to cluster at the coalfields, as at Rive-de-Gier and Carmaux.

Directors were frequently financiers with diverse economic holdings, who left local control to salaried managers.

Textiles remained highly diverse, marked by uneven development. Lace, linen and hemp were in decline. In the woollen sector the mechanized spinning centres of Rheims and Roubaix gained ground, as older Midi centres like Lodève declined. Cotton was more dynamic, with mechanized spinning producing bottlenecks which required weaving mechanization in the 1840s. Cotton, printing and chlorine bleaching were already technologically advanced. The Protestant dynasties of Alsace, with their access to Swiss capital and capacity for innovation, scarcely fit the Landes's stereotype. The number of handlooms in Alsace fell 50 per cent from 1830–44, and emphasis on quality production boosted Mulhouse exports. In Lille the number of looms per mill rose by 135 per cent, and the number of mills fell from 50 to 27. By the 1840s the average size of a French cotton plant was fully comparable with its British counterpart. Alsace averaged 290 workers per plant. The offspring of the Dollfuss dynasty received scientific training in Paris, entrepreneurs like Koechlin entered the national elite, and access into the textile dynasties became closed to outsiders.

Stearns has emphasized the positive labour control strategies adopted by many dynamic industrialists, faced with the problems of the lure of the land for peasant workers, the need to train key workers and the habitual indiscipline of early industrial labourers who kept 'St Monday', talked and drank, worked slowly to avoid lay-offs, and proved unresponsive to wage incentives. Labour policy used the stick of tighter discipline, foremen, fines and subsidy of local troop garrisons, as at Fourchambault. But it mixed with this the calculated generosity of more 'paternalist' schemes and spent a fixed percentage of its outlay on welfare schemes. Le Creusot established schools to indoctrinate and socialize future workers; Decazeville housed half its workforce, ran company pensions, and mutual aid schemes designed to produce healthy, disciplined, loyal workers – liable to lose pension or homes if militant. Labour turnover was reduced at Le Creusot. Here, as elsewhere, the French entrepreneur emerges as more innovative than often portrayed.

III Orleanist Ideology

Orleanism's critics accused it of cynical opportunism, doubting that politicians like Guizot understood any first principles other than bourgeois supremacy. Yet ideologues produced a theory of 'middleingness' to cloak the economic interests of the elites. Expounded by learned men, with some sophistication, this gave the regime its veneer of intellectual respectability. An elaborate ideology, involving theories of sovereignty, representation and freedom in history, justified constitutional monarchy. Significantly its exponents, such as Broglie and Guizot, often represented Normandy constituencies, just across the channel from English Whigs whose '1688' mythology and defence of the golden mean of 'liberty' with 'order' they admired. D. Johnson's study of Guizot, the history professor who was education minister in 1833 and prime minister after 1840, emphasizes Guizot's Protestantism, his 'Victorian' attributes and his links with the liberal *Edinburgh Review*. With reciprocal admiration Lord Russell praised the doctrinaires as 'French Whigs', resisting extremes of revolution and reaction. The equation was misleading, for time had healed the wounds of '1688', Catholic-royalism and neo-Jacobinism were more dangerous beasts than their English equivalents. Wellington was no Polignac, Francis Place no Blanqui.

As a Protestant from the Gard Guizot had reason to abhor ultraroyalism and Jacobinism. His father was guillotined in the year II, his fellow Protestants massacred by ultras in 1815. 1789–92 epitomized the 'good' revolution. Sovereignty, safe neither with divine-right monarchs nor with the brutal masses, should rest with Reason tempered by Reasonableness – embodied in the Charter, civil liberties, religious toleration. Sadly, prudential men, on whom this relied, were rare in France. Extremists made the constitution their battlefield, sought within this peace treaty for arms to renew a war. '1830' was no reassuring victory, for it was achieved by popular violence, not by sweet reason. Guizot, among the conquerors, confessed that victory was 'sad indeed'. Delacroix's 'Liberty leading the People', evoking the working-class barricade fighters, embarrassed the regime and was locked away from public view.

'Reason' was involved as being above persons and classes, a

denial of further conflicts. Like Burkean Whigs, Orleanists emphasized experience, tradition, history rather than abstract rationalism. The 'authentic' France comprised the supporters of '1789/1830', together with those who, sick of chaos, yearned for order. Factious troublemakers sought either to reject 1789, or to extend its egalitarian implications. Since most men were weak or corrupt, reasonable men should impose their reasonableness. Public opinion was volatile. Politics was too complex for the uneducated. Government by the propertyless would be government by crime. 'After 1830,' Guizot claimed, 'we had no support save the middle class. I should not have had the slightest objection to . . . extending the franchise if it promised to strengthen our cause, but it promised nothing except danger.'

Reasonableness was unevenly spread through a society which, itself, was the sum of rights and legitimate interests, represented by parliament. Everyone had *civil* rights. However, *political* rights were distributed according to 'natural inequalities which it pleases providence to establish among men.' Political participation required 'capacity', ability to act according to reason. Personal wealth established the presumption of such capacity and of political judgement. A minority, transcending mass passions, thus represented all legitimate interests. Parliament, an assembly of such superior beings, represented the 'general reason of the whole'. The bourgeoisie was the repository of all genuine interests. As an historian, Guizot emphasized the heroic role of the Third Estate in the battle against feudalism, culminating in the triumph of a class which synthesized all valuable attributes. Class war, the motor of History, was now over. Bourgeois electors protected the valid interests of men below them. All interests found 'natural representation' in a bourgeoisie which monopolized useful virtues, for aristocracies attempted to dominate, while ignorant masses lacked all 'capacity'. However Guizot's notorious advice to the non-enfranchised, 'Get rich!', implicitly emphasized that the bourgeoisie was an expanding elite, closed only to the 'dull, lazy, licentious'.

Guizot's claim that 200-franc taxpayers, who had the vote, represented all other taxpayers, remained unconvincing to any in the lower strata of the middle class, who came to see Orleanism as defending only a narrow, oligarchic elite of *grand bourgeois*. The notion that the bourgeoisie incarnated all true values was undermined by the continuing schizophrenia of elites poised between the old taste for rentier idleness and land and the growing emphasis on entrepreneurial dynamism and the work-ethic. The historian de Tocqueville, who had broken with his aristocratic family by accepting '1830' as a *fait accompli* and becoming a deputy while retaining a certain aristocratic distaste for middle-class upstarts, argued that exclusive upper-bourgeois rule caused the Orleanist elite to appear as a selfish plutocratic oligarchy. Orleanism singularly lacked a mobilizing, crusading image to sell itself to excluded strata of the population. In 1830 the battle against Charles X had been fuelled by rhetoric about press freedoms. After 1830 such 'freedoms' ceased to be absolutes. Principles were an early casualty of the battle to safeguard the *juste milieu* from extremism. Royer Collard's brilliant speeches against press censorship were quietly buried. The 1835 press law filled St Pélagie jail with radical journalists, forcing Daumier to retreat from his open caricatures of Louis Philippe to indirect satire on 'Robert Macaire', the archetypal bourgeois swindler.

Free trade could never play the crusading role which it performed for English liberals, who could utilize the Anti-Corn Law League to mobilize working-class support for cheaper bread against the Protectionist landed oligarchy. Since most French industrialists were protectionists, Orleanist laissez-faire stood exposed in its full hypocrisy, unguarded by any Cobdenite rhetoric of a world of international trade, peace and cheap food. Guizot claimed that attempts to intervene in the economy to improve social conditions were 'chimerical and disastrous' philanthropic dreams. Yet, apparently, his government was free to guarantee rail profits or impose tariff restrictions, for 'all responsible government' had the duty to protect established interests from 'vicissitudes of unlimited foreign competition'. Anti-association laws outlawed trade-union organization yet ignored employers' associations. Guizot's social laissez-faire exuded the odour of stern Calvinism. The lazy and the stupid failed to prosper. He showed no empathy for the plight of factory workers. Tudesq's analysis of debate on the 1841 factory act, which regulated child labour, shows how this mentality was shared by the bulk of the elite. 'Pauperism' was dismissed as due to 'constantly exaggerated and growing needs', rather than actual want, a product of drink and gambling. Recruited from 'the lazy vagabonds . . . vicious and corrupted beings whom society repels yet tolerates, pauperism had made itself an organized right.' The remedy lay in religion and improved morality. A few employers admitted paternalistic responsibility for their workers, but, like Imbet-Desgranges from Dauphiné, insisted that 'if I do something for my workers, I want them to be grateful.' The 1841 factory act, passed only because military experts emphasized the declining health of army conscripts, met outraged protest from industrialists who, like Guy Lussac, saw factories as 'sanctuaries as sacred as a father's house'. Did not a thirteen-hour day teach children salutary habits of industriousness and obedience? Nord deputies expressed sorrow for proletarian families deprived of the wages of their seven-year-old offspring. The lack of an effective inspectorate rendered the act virtually worthless.

Since religion and education are twin pillars of the hegemony of ruling elites, continued friction between Catholicism and anticlericalism weakened Orleanism. The regime included Voltaireans, deists and Protestants, united by distaste for Restoration clericalism. Many Orleanist *notables*, still engaged in local feuds with pro-Bourbon clergy, were understandably dubious about utilizing religion as a bastion of the *status quo*. Yet the situation evolved, for Orleanist anti-clericalism was always Gallican and nuanced, never vulgar or extreme. V. Cousin, the Orleanist philosopher and idealogue, attempted a *modus vivendi* with the church via his eclectic amalgamation of spiritualism and rationalism. The mood of late-romanticism increased the susceptibility of bourgeois audiences to the sermons of the fashionable Dominican preacher Lacordaire. The emergence of 'liberal Catholicism' advocated by the aristocrat Montalembert, who had imbibed British constitutional ideas while in exile in London and dreamed of reconciling the Church with the principles of 1789, encouraged hopes of a compromise. Prefect-bishop relations improved after many initial tensions. In the Nord, as Trénard shows, the drift of the liberal bourgeoisie back to the church as a bulwark of social order was occurring *before* 1848.

Orleanist primary education policy reflected some compromise with the church. Protestants like Guizot, rejecting old fears that any education expansion would multiply the numbers of semi-literate *déraciné* subversives, claimed that schooling would 'moralize', calm social unrest. As schools opened to inculcate bourgeois values of sobriety and thrift, so prisons would close. The 1833 Guizot law insisted on a school in every village, a teachers' training college in every department. Pupils increased from 1.9 to 3.5 million between 1833 and 1847; conscript literacy grew from 47 per cent to 60 per cent. Yet there were narrow limits to Orleanist reformism. Few industrialists emphasized the case for a literate workforce. Schooling was neither free nor compulsory, for the economy relied on child-labour, and *notables* were reluctant to pay extra taxes. Above all, it was emphasized that school fees encouraged ambitious, thrifty parents to save to educate their offspring, opening education to those who espoused the regime's values. A strong religious component was envisaged. Municipalities could engage clerical teachers, provided they had a teaching certificate. Catechism and religious texts anchored the school curriculum. Christian resignation was eulogized as the prerequisite for deference and acceptance of inequality. Yet, as traditionalist conservatives had warned, education acquired a momentum of its own. Trainee teachers, 75 per cent of them peasants' sons, were educated in a pious, conservative atmosphere. Yet by 1848 many made resentful by low salaries and daily subordination to the village *curé*, were infected with radical ideas which they transmitted to their pupils.

Persisting conflicts between old and new elites were more intense in secondary education. The *Université*, heir to the laic values of the 1790s, saw its role as cementing national unity via a dominant state education system. Educationally it was conservative, preferring classics to science, arguing that the pseudo-Roman values which it imparted were necessary counterweights to a materialist age. It was not 'atheist', for it espoused an eclectic spiritualism.

Yet it was politically 'liberal', frowned on Catholic colleges, insisted on its right to inspect Catholic schools, to maintain limits on the number of Catholic pupils, to restrict *petits séminaires* to training priests. Faced with such firmness even liberal Catholics like Montalembert protested the rights of Catholics in a free society to run their own schools.

Education helped perpetuate existing class divisions. The few scholarships for secondary and higher education were designed for bourgeois orphans not the clever poor. Petty-bourgeois and peasant boys could study in the lycées, but took 'practical' courses and rarely entered the baccalauréat stream. Only 4 per cent of 100,000 secondary pupils in the 1840s studied for the baccalauréat. The Parisian *grandes écoles*, which produced a stratum of progressive technocrats, influenced by St Simonian ideas, were recruited, as Terry Shin shows, from a narrow elite whose domination they legitimized and perpetuated. In the *École Polytechnique*, whose graduates began to monopolize the upper-bureaucracy, 60 per cent of places went to sons of the *haute bourgeoisie*. It remained the fief of a class, in the interests of that class.

IV Orleanist Politics

In 1840 two-thirds of the 459 deputies paid above 1000 francs in direct taxation, placing them among the richest eighteen thousand Frenchmen. Parliament was monopolized by Tudesq's *notables*, established families with solid regional roots, influence, prestige, security and leisure. Though only 10 per cent of deputies in 1846 were businessmen, and though the regime's 'bankocratic' image waned slightly after the early pre-eminence of Laffitte and Casimir Périer, capitalist groups retained ample means to defend their economic interests. Marshal Soult, introduced to Guizot's cabinet to provide a military facade for a pacific regime, was a Tarn coal-mine director. The proportion of business voters on the electoral rolls in Arras increased from 15 per cent to 35 per cent between 1830 and 1848.

The narrowness of the political system deserves emphasis. After 1832 Britain had one elector for every twenty-five inhabitants; France had one for every 170. Only 27 constituencies had above 1000 voters; 30 per cent of deputies were elected by under 200 voters. Wealthy Normandy had five times as many electors *per capita* as impoverished mountain departments. Politics in Haute-Alpes, where one constituency had 150 electors, consisted of the efforts of prefects to bribe or bully a handful of voters to support the governmental candidate against an 'independent' fellow landowner. Loyal voters were, then, rewarded with government favours. Unsurprisingly, poorer departments returned the fewest opposition candidates. The unrepresentative nature of the system was highlighted in the west, a largely rural region with pro-Bourbon (Legitimist) sympathies, which produced many 'liberal' deputies elected by the 'blue' urban bourgeoisie.

Conflict in this circumscribed world was rarely ideological. Many rivalries were personal rather than political. The personal preferences of the king, such as his distaste for Broglie, often explained ministerial reshuffles in the ephemeral cabinets of the 1830s. The endemic ministerial instability of 1835–9 may have reflected, paradoxically, the increasing stability of the regime. The defeat of legitimist, republican and working-class protest by 1835, the upturn in the economy, and the advent of a solid bloc of governmental deputies allowed the elite a psychological security which permitted internal squabbling. The absence of real electoral disagreements produced a Namierite obsession with the spoils of office, as deputies abandoned ministers who failed to deliver expected sinecures and favours. De Tocqueville, who, as a deputy, moved in this world, yet as an aristocrat preserved a certain aloofness from it, disdainfully dismissed Orleanist deputies as heirs involved in sordid squabbles over the division of an inheritance. The limited franchise and the 'internal exile' of many aristocrats left 'ideological' parties, legitimist and republican, as a tiny minority in parliament. Most deputies were part of a depoliticized consensus, in agreement on most fundamental issues. Only a spasm of alarm during the socio-economic and foreign policy crises of 1839–40 disturbed a decade of apparent complacency.

Issues which did arise, such as the debate over protectionism, were rarely party or class quarrels. Both free-trade and protection lobbies included industrial and agricultural interests. Legitimist industrialists were protectionist, legitimist wine growers, free traders. The conflict over Catholic education was not a clear fight between legitimists and Orleanists but, rather, split the Orleanist bourgeoisie between Voltaireans and a growing *bien-pensant* element.

Parliamentary politics until 1839 was marked by apparent ministerial instability. The king, reluctant to be a mere figurehead, wished ministers to administer not frame policies and preferred the cabinet of the capable but politically weak bureaucrat Molé to stronger cabinets under Guizot or Thiers. 1839 witnessed a revolt of 'excluded chieftains' against royal personal government. Yet this was essentially a battle between 'outs' and 'ins' – 'all because M. Guizot and M. Thiers wish to be ministers', Metternich observed cynically. Guizot's pacific view of foreign policy was closer to that of Molé, whom he ousted, than to Thiers, his 'ally' in this ministerial coup.

Thiers dominated a second, short, phase in 1839–40. As a ruthless parvenu he had earlier made a ferocious law-and-order interior minister. Now, however, he cultivated a 'liberal' image as a defender of parliament against crown, a sympathizer with Spanish liberals. This gained him a certain popularity with nationalist elements of the urban petty bourgeoisie, for whom his rise from obscure provincial lawyer to Anzin mine director provided a rags-to-riches legend. The social unrest provoked by the 1839 economic slump called his bluff. Faced with strikes and petty-bourgeoisie franchise reform demands, he consulted the king, broke the strikes and rejected electoral change. His big business connections resulted in extension of privileges for the Bank of France and concessions to the railway companies. However, his rash flirtation with a dynamic nationalistic foreign policy proved his undoing.

Indeed the aftermath of the 1839–40 foreign policy crisis was to prove significant for the regime's future popularity, for both parliamentary and extra-parliamentary oppositions were to make Orleanist diplomacy a central target of their criticism. Since 1830 the twin foundations of foreign policy had been good relations with London and the avoidance of a bellicose stance. Europe had been alarmed in 1830 by the prospect of a resurgence of Bonapartist or neo-Jacobin expansionism. Republicans denounced the 1815 settlements and urged export of revolution to Belgium and Italy. However, in August 1830 the new regime rejected such adventurism, seeking to avoid war without appearing deferential towards the Holy Alliance. Louis Philippe had no wish to revive the ghost of Jacobinism and made no effort to aid the revolt of the Poles against their tsarist oppressors. The decision of the London Conference (1831) to establish an independent, neutral Belgium was accepted. France made no territorial claims, refusing also a Belgian offer that one of Louis Philippe's sons should take the Belgian throne.

Such moderation won British approval, and prospects for an entente between the two 'liberal' powers, who shared an interest in obstructing Russian expansion into the Mediterranean, appeared good. However, Palmerston remained deeply suspicious of France: protectionist interests in the French parliament obstructed progress towards free trade desired by British coal and textile producers, and British commercial penetration of Spain alarmed French businessmen. Tensions finally exploded over France's role in

Egypt, where French military advisers, teachers and engineers in the service of Mehemet Ali, its modernizing ruler, were reviving Bonapartist dreams and hinting at French control of an expanding raw cotton sector and of a projected Suez canal. Thiers hoped to use his protégé, Mehemet Ali, to carve out territorial gains in Syria at the expense of the declining Ottoman Empire and, playing for high stakes, rashly rejected Palmerston's compromise suggestion whereby French influence in southern Syria would be recognized. London reacted by achieving a European guarantee of Turkish integrity (15 July 1840). When Thiers whipped up war fever by rebuilding the Paris fortifications and uttering bellicose noises, Palmerston called his bluff by bombarding Beirut and forcing Mehemet Ali's withdrawal. The king, alarmed by France's diplomatic isolation and influenced by business fears that war would worsen economic dislocation and social unrest, accepted Thiers's resignation.

His successor, Guizot, viewed the episode as a major error, which risked returning France to the revolutionary upheavals of 1830–4. He lacked empathy with French nationalist dreams. France ought to cease to posture and utter threats to the *status quo*, for the 1815 settlement was not unfavourable to her. Jacobin-Bonapartist policies were anachronistic. France had no interests in helping to create nationalist German or Italian states on her frontiers. France's true role was as the 'fixed star' not the 'flaming meteor' of European politics. She should cultivate peace and trade. War over Beirut was even less justifiable than war over Bologna. And, despite General Bugeaud's continued brutal repression of native resistance in Algeria, Guizot showed little enthusiasm either for the numerous ambitious projects for the colonization and economic exploitation of North Africa, nor for the claims of writers like Dubergier de Hauranne that colonial wars were a welcome proof of French virility.

Guizot envisaged a solution to near eastern tensions via negotiation rather than unilateral French action. As a committed Anglophile, he attempted to cultivate close personal ties with London. However, he overestimated the efficacy of such contacts in reducing fundamental rivalries between Britain and France. His efforts to rebuild the entente aroused bitter hostility in France. West-coast shipping deputies like Billault denounced his concession to the British navy of the right to combat the slave trade by searching French ships off the African coast as a threat to French trade. Opposition parties used this accusation in the 1842 election. The granting of a financial indemnity to a British missionary, expelled from Tahiti during colonial skirmishings in the Pacific, fed accusations that Paris was subservient to London. Even 'success' in the 1846 Spanish marriage affair proved illusory. Guizot hoped for a friendly constitutional monarchy in Spain, for a regime neither revolutionary, nor under British control, nor Carlist, for fear of a 'Vendée' on France's southern frontier which might support Midi legitimist counter-revolutionaries. Though he succeeded in thwarting a British-supported Coburg marriage by arranging a marriage of Louis Philippe's younger son to the childless Spanish queen's younger sister, this coup was perceived in France as more a dynastic than a French triumph. At the same time it wrecked hopes of an entente with London.

To escape from diplomatic isolation, Guizot then concentrated on friendship with the Habsburg Chancellor Metternich, which attracted accusations of obsequiousness towards reactionary foreign powers. Guizot saw the solution to unrest in Italy as judicious administrative reform, not national unification, and shared Metternich's obsession with checking the activities of radical Italian nationalists in Switzerland. Faced with civil war in Switzerland between 'radical' Protestant centralists and conservative Catholic federalists, Guizot found himself, embarrassingly, on the same side as Metternich and the Lucerne 'Jesuits'.

Guizot's intractible problem was the schizophrenia of the French political classes, aspiring simultaneously to sleep, well-fed and well-clothed, in comfortable beds and yet to be 'on the march, barefooted and starving, engaged in the conquest of Europe' (X. Doudon). He was denounced for a pacific foreign policy by critics like Lamartine and de Tocqueville who, once themselves in office after 1848, pursued an almost identical course. His chief parliamentary opponents, the Dynastic Opposition, had little real intention of taking France to war. To that extent, as Douglas Johnson argues, the conflict was 'artificial'. Guizot's essential failure was one of imaginative empathy. Personally immune to Anglophobia and to post-1789 nationalism, he viewed such sentiments as anachronistic, failing to comprehend their hold on his compatriots. De Tocqueville warned in 1839 that Orleanism needed to pursue an activist foreign policy, could not survive on the 'ruin of national honour'. Merruau, with that cynical pragmatism shared by at least one modern European government, observed that 'a little war, carried out aptly and in good conditions' could give a powerful boost to the flagging popularity of conservative regimes. Instead Guizot found himself caricatured as 'Sir Guizot', a bastard Englishman.

Guizot had claimed that the 1839–40 crisis had emphasized the danger of permitting popular passions to intrude into policy-making. It had left France isolated, revived the threat of social revolution, and bequeathed a budget deficit because of military preparations. With the rail boom of the early 1840s easing economic pressures, Guizot posed as the champion of peace and stability against the war and chaos threatened by Thiers's adventurism. The ministerial instability of the 1830s posed, Guizot argued, a real threat to Orleanist survival. Yet his goal of strong, homogeneous cabinets, based on stable governmental parliamentary majorities, proved elusive. His own supporters, the 'Doctrinaires', united in their respect for constitutional monarchy, comprised only forty deputies and were fragmented by personal animosities. Critics emphasized that the sordid charade of 1839, when Guizot himself allied with politicians like Barrot, whom he frequently denounced as quasi-Jacobin, to oust the conservative Molé, set a poor example, for it weakened respect for parliamentary integrity and undermined future attempts to form a stable conservative ministry. In his memoirs Guizot hinted that he may, indeed, have made a blunder. Personal animosities between himself and Molé were not healed until after 1848, despite the essential similarity of their political ideas. Thiers, despite losing ground because of the 1840 fiasco, and despite his 'unplumbed depths of shallowness' (D. Johnson), remained a formidably quick-witted opponent, capable of dramatic speeches and resounding calls for an unspecified, 'active' policy. Passy's Third Party and Barrot's dynastic opposition, the permanent 'outs' in the parliamentary spoils game, indulged in similar shrill condemnation of foreign policy and, as Guizot's ministry extended from months into years, flirted opportunistically with electoral reform.

Guizot was, consequently, obliged to cobble together a slim majority by enlisting Marshal Soult into the cabinet. Soult's protégé Teste, who became minister of public works, was to contribute to the regime's growing notoriety for corruption when he was exposed as accepting bribes from the rail companies, while the Marshal's incessant quest for sinecures for his family became a source of constant embarrassment. Guizot emerged from the 1842 election with a slim majority of forty-five, many of whom were lukewarm supporters who needed wooing with 'favours'. The art of governing, as Koepke argues, took precedence over the substance of good government, obsession with maintaining narrow majorities obscured positive policy-making. Protectionist opposition obstructed a customs-union with Belgium. Feuds between Catholics and anticlericals over control of secondary education left Guizot, who sympathized neither with the Jesuits nor with Michelet, trapped in the crossfire.

However, Guizot's position appeared strengthened by the 1846 electoral victory, achieved by claiming credit for economic expansion and by blatant but effective government 'pressure'. Prefects threatened government employees and offered jobs or favours in return for votes. Half of Guizot's majority were salaried administrative officials. One Midi voter captured the mood of the election by expressing his willingness to vote for the prefect's horse provided the railway passed through Pézenas! At last, a secure majority had, apparently, been secured by an alliance of conservative ex-liberals, rallied legitimists, bureaucrats and local *notables* eager for government favours. The disheartened parliamentary opposition appeared fragmented. Barrot's one hundred dynastic opposition deputies, mainly from the patriotic east and the 'blue' bourgeoisie of the west, urged an adventurist foreign policy which alarmed Passy as too risky and worried de Tocqueville by its Anglophobia. Guizot repudiated accusations of electoral corruption by insisting that his critics, made bilious by sour grapes, had their own 'rotten boroughs' and were envious careerists, concerned only with their exclusion from the political gravy train. Thiers, who had rejected petitions for electoral reform in 1840, had no right to pose as an electoral reformer.

However, in making such self-righteous self-justifications, Guizot exhibited a myopic disregard for a genuine and growing malaise. He had, as Johnson observes, a puritanical sense of martyrdom, a conviction that, if everyone criticized him, he must be right. Above all, he failed to appreciate that the ground rules of the political game were changing, as economic depression fuelled social grievances and emerging political demands among broad strata of the population excluded from the political system. It was self-evidently true that his parliamentary opponents were as corrupt and careerist as his own supporters. But for the millions of Frenchmen outside the cosy, tiny world of Orleanist electoral politics, that was irrelevant. Lamartine, for once, captured the mood of the real France, when he proclaimed that 'Guizot, Molé, Thiers, Passy and Dufaure' were 'five ways of saying the same word. They bore me. Let the Devil conjugate them as he will.'

The electoral triumph, thus, proved a Pyrrhic victory, engendering in Guizot a complacency, derived from his dominance of the narrow parliamentary world, which blinded him to external dangers. In January 1848 de Tocqueville, having come to view Guizot's *immobilisme* as suicidal, warned his fellow deputies that revolution was imminent. He subsequently confessed that the correctness of his own prophecy had taken him by surprise. Why was it that a regime that had sailed confidently through the storms of 1830–4 and 1839–40 sank without trace within hours in February 1848? De Tocqueville, who was no determinist, insisted that certain unfortunate 'accidents' contributed to the disaster. The stubborn king rejected all electoral concessions. Guizot's supine foreign policy was widely disliked by a French public which was not accustomed to see its government walk quietly and carry a small stick (G. Wright). Tudesq argues that the financial and sexual scandals which beset the Orleanist elite in 1846–7 convinced broad strata of the middle and petty bourgeoisie of the deep-seated corruption of the ruling oligarchy. Yet, even as a liberal historian, de Tocqueville was forced to concede that 1848 could not be explained away as the consequence of a chapter of accidents. His claim that a growing proletariat, infected by socialism, was determined to destroy the privileges of wealth, just as 1789 demolished those of birth, contained elements of truth, yet failed to explain the hostility of broad strata of the middle-classes towards Orleanism. As ever, revolution was possible only because of deep fissures in the propertied classes.

Economic depression, too, played a key role in precipitating political crisis – a factor which de Tocqueville, persuaded by the half-truth that revolutions are caused by rising expectations, largely overlooked. Having demanded credit for the 1840–5 economic boom, Guizot's government paid the price by receiving blame for the ensuing cyclical slump. Disastrous grain and potato harvests doubled food prices. Declining expenditure on consumer goods engendered a textile slump and mass unemployment. When the government was obliged to use its resources to import grain there followed an acute shortage of liquid capital and a credit crisis. The depression spread to the building and rail-construction programme, leaving the Bordeaux-Sète railway abandoned uncompleted. Bankruptcies in 1847 ran at double the level of already disastrous 1846. A major Le Havre bank collapsed. Municipalities, burdened by poor relief expenditure, sent frenzied appeals for governmental aid, producing a budget deficit of 258 million francs, the largest since 1815. Death rates soared; the birth rate fell. 'Traditional' patterns of food-rioting, attacks on grain-convoys, assaults on 'hoarders' spread through northern and eastern France. There were strikes and worker demonstrations, rural arson, Luddism, invasion of the forests. Alarm at the extent of social unrest eroded business confidence and investment fell.

Guizot responded with an extraordinary lack of urgency. Viewing the economic depression as ephemeral, he was reassured by signs that it was 'bottoming out', that improved harvests in 1847 were lowering food prices. He insisted that opposition criticism reflected 'blind passions', that minor concessions which modified the *status quo* would simply provoke demands for wider change. He failed conspicuously to put his extensive knowledge of English history to good use, for the English oligarchy, faced with a comparable crisis in 1830–2, had survived through electoral concessions which satisfied middle-class protesters, thereby splitting the alliance between the popular movement and bourgeois reformers. Worried progressive conservative 'wets' in Guizot's parliamentary majority urged electoral concessions to appease the lower-middle class. Some even argued that the unacceptable face of French capitalism needed modifications, that government action was needed to counter the recession, that only reform of the banking system could prevent further liquidity crises. However, bills to enfranchise 100-franc taxpayers and to ban the system which allowed public officials to be deputies were defeated. Guizot's prudish self-righteousness aroused increasing distaste. Hugo claimed that Guizot was 'personally incorruptible, yet he governs by corruption. He has the effect on me of an honest woman who runs a brothel.' After 1846 there were approximately two hundred deputies who simultaneously held public posts as officers, magistrates, diplomats or state engineers. They comprised half or more of the members of parliament in forty departments. The system's defenders could argue that such deputies were technically efficient, skilled at parliamentary committee work and that they had expertise in many fields. The strengthening of the technocratic element could be interpreted as signifying a move away from the world of landed *notables* towards a bureaucratization of politics better suited to the needs of an industrial society.

However the system clearly was ideal for the government in office. It secured Guizot his large majority. Several *députés-fonctionnaires* who dared vote against Guizot over the Tahiti affair lost their jobs. Thirty-four of them voted for Rémusat's 1847 reform bill, but 129 against it. Loyal support for the government boosted a man's career prospects and those of his family. It was no coincidence that G. Réal, appointed sub-prefect at the age of twenty-three, had a father who was a deputy and a councillor of state. The shrewd *député-fonctionnaire* was adept at using his contacts for electoral purposes, at ensuring that village churches were repaired on the eve of polling-day, or that his town was blessed with the establishment of a branch of the Bank of France. Offers of a post in the magistracy could win over opposition leaders, as in Bar-sur-Aube in 1846.

Unsurprisingly Orleanism's critics viewed this as 'corruption'. The bulk of legitimists and republicans had been purged from the administration by 1835. The presence of a large block of officials in parliament, whether 'experts' or careerist opportunists, robbed parliamentary debate of the vitality of ideological debate. The interpenetration of the bureaucratic and political worlds led to accusations that the narrow political oligarchy were monopolizing public office. In 1847 the Sorbonne professor and conservative deputy, St Marc Girardin, argued that independence was the first requisite of a deputy, subordination the prime quality of an official – and that the two roles were thus mutually exclusive. He shared the awareness of conservative-liberals like de Tocqueville and Rémusat of the damage which was being done to Orleanism's image by this system.

By 1847 the dynastic opposition was playing the role of sorcerer's apprentice. Its campaign of decorous political banquets, sponsored by *notables* demanding minor electoral adjustments, began to spin out of control as radicals began to address artisans and peasants in Burgundy and the north on the necessity of universal suffrage and social reform. The radical leader and barrister Ledru-Rollin began to awake the Jacobin ghosts of 1793. By February 1848, when the intransigent Guizot attempted to ban a political banquet in Paris, the parliamentary opposition were terrified by the monster which they had helped to create. For the crisis revealed starkly the feebleness of Orleanism's hold on broad strata of the propertied classes, who failed to rally to it in its hour of need.

V Divisions Within the Elites

The Legitimist Right

1830 was a severe blow to the nobility. Its control of the state machinery was badly shaken. Over 80 per cent of the prefectoral corps and of public prosecutors were either purged, or resigned. The proportion of aristocratic army officers fell from around two-thirds to one-third. Attempts at armed counter-revolution petered out after the fiasco of 1832 when the Duchesse de Berry failed to awake a new 'Vendée' in the Midi and the west. The young Legitimist pretender, the comte de Chambord, son of the duc de Berry, was the object of mystical hagiography and frequent pilgrimage, but provided no clear political strategy. Old families like the Ségurs were split, as some of their young, frustrated by the endless tedium of salon-existence, rallied to the new regime.

Yet the landed power of the nobility remained intact. Tudesq claims that 238 of the 512 richest *notables* in France were aristocrats. In the Pas-de-Calais over 60 per cent of taxpayers paying above 1000 francs per year were nobles. Beck has shown that whereas 64 per cent of titled noble electors paid above 1000 francs tax, this was true of only 7 per cent of bourgeois electors. Many returned to their estates after 1830 and, like Forbin Jeason, became progressive farmers. In the west, where their relative power was accentuated by the decline of local industry, clashes of protocol were frequent, with sub-prefects humiliated by the absence of the tricolour at local agricultural shows. Nobles' arrogance was undiminished. In Aquitaine sharecroppers of the Comte de Commignes were caned for failure to doff their caps in the presence of their lord. When the Comte de la Tour d'Auvergne was visited by the village mayor rather than the Aude sub-prefect to reply to his complaints of local electoral irregularities, he wrote to complain as 'an individual who, without excessive pride . . . believes that he has acquired rights to consideration which nothing can destroy.'

Was their power undermined by a failure to adapt to the emerging capitalist economy? In 1837–9 two-thirds of noble deputies were landowners or officers, whereas two-thirds of non-noble deputies were in business or law. Beck found that a mere 4 per cent of noble electors were in business, as against 28 per cent of non-nobles and that over 40 per cent of *arrondissements* lacked a single 'business' noble. Yet such evidence needs careful qualification. Nobles were prominent in major industries and non-agricultural enterprises – in the Carmaux and Anzin mines, the forges of Alais, Midi rail companies and insurance. Legitimism had support in the legal and business communities of many southern towns. Nobles were agrarian capitalists, developing Languedoc wine estates and enclosing Provençal forests. Yet such capitalist enterprise added to their schizophrenia, made their political strategies less, not more, coherent. Economically, such nobles were difficult to distinguish from their Orleanist-bourgeois opponents. Root-and-branch hostility to the regime, including flirtation with popular protest, was thus unlikely. Balzac, a Catholic-royalist with no illusions about the possibility of an aristocratic revival, lamented that 'under the Restoration the aristocracy has become economical, careful, provident; in fact, bourgeois and inglorious. Now 1830 has completed the work of 1793. In France, henceforth, there will be great names but no more great houses. Everything bears the stamp of personal interest. The wisest buy annuities with their money. The family has been destroyed.' Yet ideology, family tradition and religion, kept them apart, slowed the development of a united class of *grand notables*. Their salons were often exclusive – even if they did tolerate Legitimist lawyers like Berryer, and Stendhal's Lucien Leuwen gains an entrée in pursuit of a beautiful aristocratic lady merely by faking deep Catholic piety. Tudesq found that only 8 per cent of 146 marriages among a sample of twenty aristocratic families between 1800 and 1860 was with a bourgeois partner.

In the Nord, where legitimists were involved in industry and commerce, the growth of worker protest led to a *de facto rapprochement* with Orleanism to defend law and order. Legitimists became conservatives rather than reactionaries; their opposition to the regime focused on 'peripheral' issues such as education, their political strategy electoralist rather than populist or insurrectionary. Yet in the Gard or the Tarn, where the business elite was Protestant-Orleanist, legitimism still posed as the populist defender of the Catholic masses, advocating universal suffrage and flirting with popular tax and conscription protest. Abbé Genoude argued that legitimism was the champion of 'those who have been robbed, against the thieves!' Sectarian conflicts in Nîmes in August 1830 left forty-four dead or wounded. Legitimist nobles drilled paramilitary squads on their estates, distributed charity during economic slumps, and gave jobs on Camargue land-reclamation projects to their Catholic popular clientele. Yet, even in the Midi, there were limits to Legitimist populism. The *Gazette du Midi* was forced to tone down its attacks on Orleanist capitalism because Benoit d'Azy, a leading legitimist iron and coal manufacturer, was among the paper's financial backers. Midi legitimists were becoming involved in capitalist forest enclosures, wine and grain production.

A similar dilemma appeared in the contortions of legitimist 'social Catholics' who espoused a benevolent paternalism, including a rhetorical critique of heartless, soulless laissez-faire capitalism. There were 282 *St Vincent de Paul* groups in France by 1848, dispensing charity to soften the burden of providential inequality. Yet the Lyon silk weavers revolt of 1834 exposed the hollowness of their rhetoric. Mgr de Bonald, legitimist archbishop of Lyon, was tempted to use the silk weaver's plight as a stick to beat Orleanism. Yet local legitimist businessmen yearned for law and order in the face of workers' revolt. Villeneuve-Bargemont, the prominent northern social Catholic, critical of modern industry, insisted that 'revolt is never permitted', for he was also a railway director. Even populist legitimists in the Gard refrained from backing the silk weavers.

Should legitimists espouse a popular alliance with artisans and peasants against the victors of '1830', or should they accept a *de facto* compromise with Orleanist elites, whose economic interests paralleled their own? Local men with local roots often clung to an intransigent *politique du pire*, flirting with popular protest. Parisian legitimists, politicians and those with business interests were less disposed to endanger their wealth. Many rallied to the regime. Sixteen per cent of the nobles analysed by Beck were in state service

– in the army, magistracy. Yet the loyalty of such men to Orleanism in the 1846–8 crisis was often lukewarm. De Tocqueville, who broke with his legitimist family tradition to become a deputy, penned in his *Recollections* some of the most eloquent denunciation of the greedy, selfish materialism of the Orleanist elite. He feared revolution which might lead to socialist anarchy, yet shed few tears for the departing regime, whose vices he dissected with aristocratic disdain.

Another aristocratic 'liberal', Montalembert, was active in the field of education, where internecine elite squabbling made political unity impossible. Orleanism defended the *Université* and insisted on strict state limitation of Catholic education. 'Unauthorized' religious orders were still officially banned; Catholic secondary pupils restricted to twenty thousand; *petits seminaires* restricted to training priests. Montalembert urged that Catholics should combat such Gallican secularism in the name of Orleanism's own 'liberal' principles – demanding the right to teach and to open schools, petitioning for parental choice in education. The violence of local conflicts which this engendered made any Orleanist-Catholic *modus vivendi* difficult. Gontard has illustrated the bitter feud between Mgr Mazenod of Marseille and the Aix University rector, Defougères, who had been sacked from a teaching post in 1821 by a clerical inspector. The rector resisted the Catholic 'invasion' of education, which he saw as a counter-revolutionary threat, fought the Jesuits who returned in 1839, tried to limit the number of seminary pupils, forbade the *petit séminaire* to teach pupils for the baccalauréat, and blocked primary teaching by unqualified nuns. Mgr Mazenod denounced the 'atheism' of *Université* philosophy teaching and exploited a scandal in which state college pupils were discovered in a brothel, to justify establishing a Catholic college. The rector was forced on to the defensive, confessing that as a seaport, Marseille was forced to admit to its college 'Negroes, Creoles, Spaniards, Jews, Greeks . . . different in language, religion, even colour', foreigners whose primary schooling had been 'vicious' and who had acquired 'depraved tastes' and 'shameful habits' abroad – a fine example of Orleanist liberal rhetoric! Education minister Salvandy, aiming to appease such local conflicts, ignored the rector's calls for tough suppression of Catholic primary schools.

Despite the widely documented drift of the Orleanist bourgeoisie back to the church before 1848, such fierce divisions within the elites must be viewed as a major source of the regime's weakness, for many Catholics, whether liberal or legitimist, could welcome its fall as a chance for relaxation of education controls. The correspondence of L. Watelot, of the legitimist *Gazette de Flandre*, illustrates the central dilemma facing the old elite. Many of his friends rallied through boredom, via dabbling in industrial or rail speculation, or because bourgeois Orleanism became less anticlerical, allowing a meeting ground in 'liberal Catholicism'. Yet his sister remained intransigent. The Protestant-atheistic *Université* was held responsible for crime increases. The lower clergy were often legitimist hardliners. The presence of a Catholic college in Boulogne made education a contentious local election issue in 1846. Many Catholics thus welcomed revolution in 1848 for introducing universal suffrage, which allowed the Ternois nobles and clergy to mobilize peasant voters to defend Catholicism and end Orleanist domination of local politics.

An Alienated Bourgeoisie?

Paradoxically Orleanism's Achilles heel was its unpopularity among broad strata of that very middle class whose values it purported to enshrine. In part this is explicable in simple socio-political terms. The urban petty bourgeoisie, which manned the National Guard units which kept 'order' during the 1839–40 social unrest, was excluded from the franchise. As early as 1840 National Guardsmen greeted Louis Philippe with shouts for electoral reform. Also, as Daumard emphasizes, the Parisian class structure was becoming more rigid as the upper bourgeoisie hardened into a closed caste, reducing upward mobility. The 1845–8 economic depression exposed the vulnerability of small businesses with limited access to credit. As bankruptcies increased, Ledru-Rollin warned the regime that 'inflexible monopolies' were threatening small workshops and petty traders to the point that 'all those retailers, who were your supporters, will rise against you'. As the rail slump threatened the shares of small investors there was anger against 'swindlers' in the big rail companies.

By publishing accounts of sensational cases of fraud and corruption, 'apolitical' newspapers such as the *Gazette des Tribuneaux* disseminated an image of Orleanism as a rotting plutocracy, while titillating petty-bourgeois readers with the sexual scandals of the elite. Daumier, denied the opportunity by the 1835 press law to continue his assault on the person of the monarch, directed his savage caricatures against 'Robert Macaire', a swindler who epitomized the regime's ethos.

As in the 1820s frustrated careerism fuelled antigovernment feeling. One Orleanist bureaucrat claimed that 'it isn't the workers one should fear, rather it is the *déclassés*, doctors without patients, lawyers without briefs, all the misunderstood, the discontented, who, finding no place at the banquet-table . . . try to overturn it. In Paris of every 1200 reading for the law, 20 achieve fame, 80 fortune, 200 a modest living – the rest vegetate.' If Stendhal's Julien Sorel had seen the returning *émigrés* as the threat to his career prospects, Balzac's heroes discover that the education system continued to overproduce aspirants to legal and bureaucratic careers. The young men in Balzac's *Lost Illusions* 'under all circumstances desire places'. Sadly, as Albéric Second remarked, there remained 'twenty times more lawyers than suits to be lost, painters than portraits to paint, soldiers than victories to gain, doctors than patients to kill'. Porch emphasizes that careerist frustration continued to stimulate republican sympathies among junior officers and NCOs. Since Paris acted as a magnet for the ambitious, the problem's political implications were multiplied by concentration. Orleanism was reviled as a senile gerontocracy, neglecting the 'flower of that admirable youth so much sought after by Napoleon'. In turn, fear of a 'floating mass of unemployed and inconstant persons who form an army always available to the instigators of revolt' informed Guizot's hostility to the extension of post-primary education which, by diverting 'a great number of young men from their natural situation' created 'perturbation', produced 'a multiplicity of restless people . . . who trouble society without obtaining fortune or reputation to which they vainly aspire'. Then, as now, the unemployed, *déraciné*, arts graduate inhabited the nightmares of the ruling elites.

The souring of the ideals of 1830 generated disillusionment which fuelled a generational rebellion among middle-class youth. One expression of this was a cultural bohemianism which scorned Orleanism's dominant philistine utilitarianism. Paris developed a subculture of eastern exoticism, drugs, dabblings in pseudo-religion, experiments in sexual liberation and in community living. This subculture thumbed its nose at an official ethos which idealized the family while licensing a massive, carefully regulated and policed system of brothels for bourgeois husbands. The cult of artistic beauty, the rejection of materialism, could be 'non-political'. Gauthier perceived no difference between the 'Sabre, the Holy-Water Sprinkler and the Umbrella', the symbol of the Bourgeois monarch, and expressed astonishment that men quarrelled over 'the choice of cudgel to administer the blows'. Some of this counterculture was a youthful sowing of wild oats. The arch-bohemian and improbably named Philothée O'Neddy became a bureaucrat. Many St Simonians abandoned their sexual and community experiments to become the technocratic servants of the Second Empire. Much adolescent 'revolt' was little more than a desire to shock the bourgeoisie, as with de Nerval's celebrated Parisian promenades with a lobster on a lead!

Yet authentic cultural protest did reflect a genuine sense of alienation. Aspiring writers clashed with pragmatic fathers who viewed artists as idlers, buffoons or subversives. Vigny's cultivated refinement reflected a rejection of modern industry as ugly and soulless. With ancien régime art patronage dead, writers faced acute dilemmas. They needed an audience, both for their own self-esteem and to earn a living. Yet they professed to despise 'philistine' bourgeois readers, resented selling their souls to commercial publishers or press magnates, who treated literature as a saleable 'product'. Stendhal, whose finances never recovered fully from the loss of his Napoleonic bureacratic job in 1815, needed money from his writings, resented writing for the market and expressed irony at the small size of his audiences, yet felt a certain bitterness at the commercial successes of vulgar rivals like Paul de Kock. Having savaged restoration clericalism in *Scarlet and Black*, he was rapidly disillusioned by Orleanism. His *Lucien Leuwen* is the saga of a hero too sensitive to be properly bourgeois, yet too bourgeois to be heroic. Lucien, the son of an Orleanist *notable*, seeks fulfillment as an army officer, only to find his active service limited to breaking strikes. Despite his contempt for materialism, he accepts a bureaucratic post to maintain his standard of living after his father's death, only to discover that his task is that of bribing electors. Like all great French novelists of the nineteenth century, Stendhal found it impossible to create an authentic 'bourgeois hero', since authenticity appeared incompatible with success in the new capitalist world. Stendhal viewed Louis Philippe as the most crooked of rulers, despised Orleanist plutocracy, yet, like many ageing armchair radicals, was ironically aware of his own fear of violent revolution.

Balzac, coarser and more energetic, was more prepared to hurl himself into the jungle of commercial publishing, to write serialized stories for newspapers. Yet fascination with material success coexisted with anger at the distortion of his art by financial pressures. His adopted stance of bloody-minded Catholic-royalism expressed a paternalistic distaste for the ethos of a society ruled by 'the holy, venerable, solid, gracious, beautiful but ever-young, almighty franc'. His perception of the role of the cash-nexus attracted Marx's admiration. Orleanism he assessed as an 'insurance contract drawn up between the rich against the poor'. Its brave new world was personified by his character Vautrin, simultaneously criminal, ex-convict, business swindler and policeman. Balzac's Paris is a jungle where young careerists 'kill each other, like spiders in a jar'. The young writers in *Lost Illusions* either starve in garrets or sell out to commercial journalism. In *César Birotteau*, Balzac attempted to portray the 'tragedy' of an 'honest' small businessman who falls into the jaws of financial sharks. Yet Birotteau's story is mock-heroic. Like the middle class which he epitomizes, Birotteau is fatally flawed by greed, the lure of expansion and wealth, which negate his solid virtues.

A third great novelist, Flaubert, became a disillusioned romantic turned cynic, whose *rentier*-status, concern for order and distaste for vulgar mediocrity distanced him from the left. Yet his *Sentimental Education* is more than a scathing dissection of the delusions, lack of realism and self-interested hypocrisy of the young romantic radicals of the 1840s, epitomized by Deslauriers, whose 'republicanism' masks careerist ambition. For Flaubert did not disguise his greater distaste for the Orleanist elite. His industrialist M. Dambreuse is a craven Vicar of Bray, truckling to Empire, Restoration, Orleanism and the republic in turn to safeguard his investments, a hypocrite who describes his demand for tariff-protection for his coal company as 'patriotism'. Despite his scorn for socialist utopias, Flaubert insisted that he was 'harder on the reactionaries, because they seem to be more criminal.' For all the 'apolitical' cynicism of his later years, the Flaubert of 1848 had, almost certainly, welcomed the revolution.

Equally important for the analysis of anti-Orleanist sentiment is evidence drawn from the nature of less exalted literature and of its audience. J. S. Allen has emphasized the important expansion of the petty bourgeois reading public in these years, with Parisian press circulation trebling as cheaper printing processes and advertising revenue cut newspaper prices. The city had 472 bookshops, and *cabinets de lecture* multiplied. With publishers competing to find bestsellers, writers published in the 1830s were markedly younger than those of the Restoration. Styles and themes from elite romanticism were popularized. Many authors followed the shift of romanticism from 'right' to 'left', its abandonment of aristocratic dreams, medieval castles, introspective melancholia and private angst for 'social' themes. Eugène Sue utilized the format of the serialized *roman feuilleton*, in newspapers like *Journal des Débats*, to evade the 1835 press laws and disseminated a thinly veiled political message. *Le Juif Errant* (1844) accentuated the violent anti-Jesuit feelings which surfaced during the debate over Catholic secondary education, emphasizing that anticlericalism, waning in the Orleanist elite, remained strong among sectors of the petty bourgeoisie. His exposé, in *Mystères de Paris* (1844), of the underworld of criminality and prostitution reached a wide audience which was both fascinated and appalled. De la Hodde's *romans feuilletons* in *La Réforme*, eulogizing Boulogne-based anti-British pirates of the Napoleonic period, tapped that groundswell of Anglophobia which found Guizot's 'pacifism' distasteful.

Excessive claims for the political message of such literature should be avoided. One could argue that Sue dabbled in cheap utopias for the workers – and pocketed the proceeds. He was a dilettante, roaming the streets around Les Halles in disguise to glean titbits of popular culture to excite his petty-bourgeois readers. His hero, Rodolphe, is an implausible knight errant dispensing justice to the Parisian poor. 'Social romanticism' tended to confuse socialism with charity. George Sand's artisan heroes tend to marry aristocrats. Hugo was furious at crowds who jeered at carriages leaving charity balls, for did not the rich put money into circulation to benefit the poor? Doubtless many petty-bourgeois readers were more conformist and conservative than bourgeois intellectuals. Yet such literature publicized inequalities, gave a human face to poverty, portrayed the regime as oligarchic and hinted that the wealth of the few came at the expense of the many. Chateaubriand claimed that these authors struck a 'mortal blow' at Orleanism. The vogue for romantic history, still powerful in the 1840s, overlapped with the professional history of academics like Michelet, who were reviving a Jacobin-populist interpretation of the 1790s, hinting that it was 'the people' not the bourgeoisie alone which constituted the real France. In short, popular romanticism marked a clear stage in the cultural and political evolution of the urban lower-middle classes.

Republicanism provided one expression of middle-class anti-Orleanist sentiment. Marx correctly emphasized the difficulty of analysing republicanism simply as the ideology of a definable socio-economic class. Leaders like Carnot or Godeffroy Cavaignac derived their political creed from family traditions, for they were sons of Jacobins. Carnot claimed that he imbibed his beliefs 'in my cradle'. Neo-Jacobin nationalists deplored Orleanism's refusal to aid radical-nationalist movements in 1830–1 and its craven subservience to Metternich.

Republican membership in the early 1830s was dominated by lawyers and doctors such as Raspail and Trélat, students, NCOs and small businessmen, hit by the 1826–3? depression. They reluctantly accepted '1830' only because they felt 'not strong enough' (Cavaignac) to do otherwise. However, they made a sustained attempt to exploit the socio-economic unrest of 1830–4. The legalistic *Aide-toi* society was outflanked by the *Société des Droits de l'Homme* (SDH) which demanded universal suffrage, free education, trade-union liberties, cheap credit, tax reform and democratization of the National Guard. Its subscription rate was lowered to broaden the social base of its recruitment. Its network of cells was strongest in Paris, east-central France and the south-east. Its populist social reform programme attracted some 4000 Paris artisans and even small wine growers in Burgundy. Côte-d'Or had 1000 members in sixty-seven sections.

However, flirtation with working-class revolt in Lyon and Paris provoked government repression. The September 1835 press laws banned direct attacks on the regime or the monarch or direct mention of the republic. There were 2000 arrests in 1834–5, including a show trial of 164 leaders. An alleged garrison plot in Lunéville was uncovered, republicans in the judiciary purged. Daumier, who had caricatured Louis Philippe as a pear (*poire* means both 'pear' and 'idiot') and as a gross monster seated on a chamberpot throne swallowing the material produce of his poverty-stricken subjects and defecating it as pensions for his courtiers, was jailed.

Tactical and ideological divisions then plagued republicanism for a decade. A minority took to secret society plotting, culminating in the abortive 1839 coup attempt. A moderate wing became, in Godeffroy Cavaignac's words, 'pacified and soft', attempting to work within the system in conjunction with the dynastic opposition. Its paper, *Le National*, offered a decorous programme of electoral and educational reform. The group round *La Réforme* rejected insurrectionism but urged social reform to combat 'industrial feudalism'. They espoused income tax, secular schooling, financial aid for artisan cooperatives and the right to work, opening their columns to reformist socialists like Louis Blanc.

Republicanism on the eve of 1848 was a real but limited force. It had ten deputies. The combined circulation of its two major newspapers was barely 6000. It was weak in rural France. The premature death of Godeffroy Cavaignac, who was moving to the left, robbed it of its most dynamic leader. Revolution in 1848 took the movement by surprise. Yet it had a broad, if amorphous appeal. Many Paris students idolized the great republican historian Michelet, though few of them appeared on the barricades in February 1848, and their only casualty there was one who accidentally fell off! Republicanism tapped the deep-seated Anglophobe nationalism and anticlericalism which Orleanism failed to satisfy. It appealed to provincial businessmen envious of Parisian financiers, small traders hit by the depression, St Simonians keen on economic planning, pragmatists like Dupont-White who saw Guizot's rejection of electoral reform and refusal to intervene to alleviate economic depression as a recipe for violent revolution. Above all it could express the distaste, widespread in the middle class, and a product both of idealism and jealousy, for the 'corruption' of the narrow Orleanist oligarchy.

Part Two

The Challenge from Below

Chapter 3

The Growth of Popular Protest

I The Making of the French Working Class?

Many historians have argued that, until 1848, there was minority politicization but mass apathy among French workers, that the fertility of utopian socialist ideas cannot obscure the feebleness of working-class organization. Nevertheless, there is a strong case for locating the origins of an authentic working-class consciousness in the years after 1830. Joseph Benoît, a Lyon silk weaver, recounts in his memoirs that the minority of Lyon workers who in 1830 questioned the Orleanist settlement were isolated 'as if in a desert', and threatened by the crowds for chanting *'Vive la République!'*. Yet fifteen years later Lyon workers found the republicanism of F. Arago much too anaemic for their advanced tastes. The July Monarchy witnessed insurrectionary upheavals in Lyon and Paris, an abortive coup attempt in 1839, the multiplication of mutual aid societies, strikes organized by 'resistance societies', the first worker newspapers, and producer and consumer cooperative experiments. 'Utopian' socialism not only fascinated or horrified bourgeois observers, but secured a sizeable worker audience.

The bitterness of worker protest was accentuated by the sense of betrayal experienced when the hopes of 1830 were dashed by the harshness of bourgeois class rule. A law of 1834 made any association of five people potentially illegal. The Code insisted that in disputes between employers and workers the word of the former should be accepted. Employers and foremen had a built-in majority on industrial disputes tribunals (*Conseils des prud'hommes*). Workers were obliged to carry a passbook (*livret*) which detailed their employment record and made it impossible for sacked militants to secure alternative jobs.

If the French 'working-class' did not enter the period of its 'making' devoid of craft traditions or political experience, these could contribute as much to disunity as to solidarity. Small journeymen's associations (*compagnonnages*) which survived among artisan trades, notably in the building sector, fostered mutual aid and craft pride, yet their divisions into separate organizations fostered rivalries, undercutting of wage rates to secure contracts and endemic street brawling. While Agricol Perdiguier hoped that a reformed *compagnonnage* movement, freed from internecine feuds, might function as the foundation of a new labour movement, realists viewed their obsession with ritual and hierarchy as an obstacle to unity. Political traditions were diverse. Artisans in cities such as Toulouse or Marseille often looked back nostalgically to ancien régime guilds, spoke patois, organized their social life around religious penitent societies, and retained Catholic-royalist sympathies. Neo-Jacobinism survived among Parisian craftsmen, though two decades of incessant police harassment had, as Richard Cobb shows, effectively dismantled the remnants of the popular movement of 1793–4. In Nantes embryonic conflict between workers and the mercantile bourgeoisie was obscured by their common fear of the legitimist rural hinterland.

Which workers were most likely to participate in protest movements? Historians have offered two contrasting models to answer this question. The first, an 'uprooting' thesis, argues that rapid urbanization produced social dislocation and political instability as ties of religion, family and locality were disrupted. Violent protest among marginal uprooted groups ensued, until new integrative norms and values and institutions emerged. Louis Chevalier's portrait of Paris as a monstrous jungle typifies this approach. The city's population doubled to over one million between 1800 and 1846, as peasants and village artisans flooded in from the overpopulated countryside. Housing, sewerage, water supply and employment opportunities failed to keep pace with this demographic explosion. Between 1831 and 1846 the population rose by 34 per cent, housing by 22 per cent, landlord incomes by 72 per cent. Despite the emergence of the La Chapelle locomotive works, Paris remained a pre-industrial city, offering little factory employment. Fifty thousand migrants lodged up to thirty to a room in the cheap *garnis* of central and eastern Paris, segregated geographically from the elites who moved to spacious western *faubourgs* to escape the fetid stench of open sewers and refuse dumps of the popular *quartiers*. Cholera epidemics accentuated the class gulf, as bourgeois fled the city while disease ravaged worker neighbourhoods. Sexual tensions and prostitution resulted from the weakened family ties produced by predominantly male immigration. Illegitimacy rates rose above 30 per cent, and homeless, jobless adolescents prowled the city. Structural unemployment and cyclical crises drove the immiserated masses into endemic criminality, equated with imminent social revolution by terrified bourgeois.

Chevalier's vivid portrait reflects the elite's perception of the danger of social revolt more than reality. Correlations between uprooting, criminality and radical protest are weak. Unskilled navvies and porters participated in food riots, much less in political industrial protest. The victims of the July days were, as Pinkney shows, artisans, not adolescents or recent rural migrants. Chevalier confuses individual antisocial behaviour with collective social protest. His image of Paris bears a certain affinity with an hysterical analysis of modern Britain threatened by black muggers and Trotskyite football hooligans. It was the stability of social groups and relationships, not the instability of mass uprooting, which provided the seedbed of radicalism. Barely 16 per cent of 'political' arrests in 1831–4 were of unskilled labourers. The main characteristics of the Parisian workforce were skill and high literacy – above 80 per cent. Nor is Chevalier's thesis of Parisian uniqueness entirely convincing. In rapidly expanding Lyon, unskilled migrants provided 56 per cent of 'criminal' arrests while silk weavers who comprised over 50 per cent of those arrested for radical protest, constituted only 20 per cent of 'criminals'. In Marseille, unskilled migrants, 50 per cent of whom were illiterate, represented 17 per cent of the population, produced 40 per cent of convicted criminals yet only 10 per cent of militants recorded on police files in the late 1840s. Chevalier's evocative thesis is based on dangerous biological metaphors describing Paris as a 'sick' city, with a 'pathological' population. The implied linking of crime, disease, illegitimacy and political revolt mirrors the hysteria of contemporary elite observers, keen to label socialism as the foul doctrine of depraved criminal classes. Yet in 1848 when Parisian crowds invaded the jails, they freed political prisoners, but not criminal convicts.

If the big city poor make unconvincing revolutionaries, can radicalism be plausibly located in the new factory proletariat, whose deplorable material conditions were lamented by social observers such as Villermé? Lille had 15,000 cotton workers in 34 large mills together with 14,000 linen and tweed workers in smaller plants. The working day could be as long as sixteen hours. The exhausting pressure of piecework led to frequent accidents as workers cleaned moving machinery. Workers were victims of fraudulent measures of their work by foremen. In the Rue d'Étaques, families, deprived of elementary sanitation, were crowded into single-roomed cellars. Bronchial diseases were endemic, while child labour produced deformed, stunted growth which rendered half the conscripts from the Nord unfit for military service.

Yet, militancy was almost totally absent. Lille's 1839 riots were a solitary instance of resistance to employer fraud. The 'modern' industrial sector generated only 10 per cent of strike activity during the Orleanist period. The Nord textile sector generated only two strikes in eighteen years. Those which occurred were defensive, protests against wage cuts, spontaneous, unorganized, lacking strike funds and brief. Cyclical business slumps made it unlikely that strikes would succeed. 'Archaic' food riots remained the most common form of protest, as in 1845–8 when they spread from rural outworkers in the Cambrésis to the mill towns, where workers spent 40 per cent of income on bread even in good years. In Normandy, where modern mills were rarer, and water power widely used, outworkers still attempted to preserve domestic production units and the symbolism of protest demonstrations resembled peasant riots more than wage strikes. The ruthless Rouen *patronat*, which imposed wages without negotiation, and refused workers the right to keep a tally of piecework production, was delighted with their apparent passivity in the 1845–6 slump. Fear reinforced factory discipline; sackings for insubordination fell 75 per cent below normal levels. The Tourcoing chamber of commerce expressed a similar incredulous delight at the quiescence of their workers during the slump.

Older textile centres such as Lodève (Herault) were more militant. Here artisan workshop production, under guild control, had been destroyed in the 1770s as a new employer class first undermined the master weavers by dispersing production to the countryside, then reurbanized the industry with mechanized factory production. By the 1830s, the new proletariat was fighting back. Rural migrants had been assimilated and intermarried with Lodève workers. There were twelve strikes between 1821 and 1848.

Sophisticated tactics emerged – including focusing strikes on mills with heavy order books, then attempting to generalize wage gains to other mills. Blacklegs had to be imported from outside the region because of the degree of local class solidarity achieved. The combativity of Lodève workers highlights the docility of Nord textile workers, recently recruited from a Catholic countryside, lacking as yet, traditions of urban solidarity and organization. Unskilled workers were easily replaced if they attempted to strike. Forty per cent of the one million workers in plants with more than ten employees were women and children. One study of 23 Rouen textile mills showed that 34 per cent of workers were women, 20 per cent children, and that three-quarters of them were on exhausting piecework. Nord employers manipulated the religiosity of Flemish mill-girls through a network of factory chapels, and Catholic clubs. There was more militancy in 1847 than in 1830 in towns like Elbeuf and Lille, but usually confined to skilled male cotton spinners or wool combers whose higher wages permitted savings for strike funds.

Child factory labour produced literacy rates in mill towns below the levels of surrounding rural areas. In 1846, 75 per cent of Mulhouse was illiterate, barely one-quarter of Lille children attended school and Rouen school attendance was 40 per cent below the average for the neighbouring Dieppe rural *arrondissement*. The industrial Nord was, thus, less receptive than older artisan centres to radical newspapers. Exhausting labour and low wages permitted industrial workers little energy to plan strikes, or cash to finance them. Collective protest, when it occurred in the Nord, was likely to take the form of xenophobic attacks on Belgian workers. And, as Stearns comments, if some strikes were born in bars, many more were drowned there.

Although some coalmines, such as Carmaux, still employed a quasi-peasant workforce, strikes were more frequent among miners. Some older coalfields already possessed an hereditary workforce. Strikes in 1834 and 1846 at Anzin, and 1837 at Rive-de-Gier, generated demands for wage-increases which were rare in textile strikes. The 1840s strikes against the *Compagnie des Mines de la Loire* (CML) monopoly, exhibited a degree of planning and coordination rare among proletarian workers. Blacklegs were intimidated and café owners collected strike funds. However, miners proved relatively indifferent to socialist propaganda, and the CML fostered discord between pits by paying different wage rates.

Militancy in the proletarian sector was, thus, at best embryonic. The French working class was born in the workshops, not the factory, among artisans whose immediate experience in the July Monarchy were reflected through values lodged deep in their culture-norms, profoundly antagonistic to the ethos of the capitalist emphasis on profit maximization. Ninety per cent of strikes were by artisans and 2000 mutual aid societies, which often collected funds for strikes, were exclusively artisanal. Despite their nostalgia for the ancien régime and internecine feuds which made them, too often, 'warriors, rival armies . . . who dreamed only of crushing one another' (*Perdiguier*), *compagnonnages* provided a language of solidarity, an emphasis that jobs should go to qualified men. 'Working-class' solidarity was filtered through the prism of old corporatism. *Compagnons* were prominent in six major Parisian carpenters' strike between 1822 and 1845.

Radicalization of the artisanate occurred most spectacularly in Lyon, where the silk industry, which produced one-third of the value of French exports, employed 50,000 in a city population of 180,000. Several hundred merchant-manufacturers (*fabricants*) put out orders and provided raw silk for weaving and marketed the finished product. Production was done in the workshop-homes of several thousand master craftsmen (*chefs d'atelier*), who were aided by wives, journeymen and apprentices. Many *fabricants*, vulnerable in fluctuating world markets to Swiss and German competition, looked to structural rationalization as a panacea, to the detriment of the masters, weakened by abolition of the guilds which sent them defenceless into a laissez-faire world. *Fabricants* had the right to regulate cloth quality. Workshop masters were subject to the *livret*. Jacquard looms, too tall for the old workshops and too costly for the masters, were introduced, and production moved from the Croix-Rousse quarter into the suburbs or the countryside. Between 1825 and 1850 the proportion of Lyonnais looms located in the countryside increased from 25 per cent to 50 per cent.

The silk weavers (*canuts*), proud of their independence as well as of their skill in producing brocaded cloth, were prepared to resist. They viewed the merchants as parasites. The word *fabricants*, Joseph Benoît argued, was a misnomer, for they produced nothing. Success for the masters depended on persuading journeymen that they shared common interests. They worked, lived and drank together, and journeymen harboured aspirations of establishing their own workshops. Despite inevitable frictions, an alliance emerged, with journeymen viewing masters more as 'mistreated workers' than as employers.

Thus, paradoxically, a hierarchic craft group achieved a degree of solidarity. Relative, if threatened, affluence and a sense of community and professional pride made them the vanguard of worker resistance movements. They founded the first two worker newspapers on the continent – *Echo de la Fabrique* and *Echo des Travailleurs* – which coordinated wage information and planned strike tactics. Mutual aid societies collected funds for their own strikes, and exhibited a wider class solidarity by sending funds to aid Anzin miners. The 1831 insurrection was triggered by the government's sacking of the prefect, whose intervention to guarantee a minimum price (*tarif*) had outraged local *fabricants*. After troops reconquered the city from insurgent workers, the weavers resorted to selective strikes against intransigent merchants, and efforts to increase their say in the *prud'hommes*. In 1834, an eight-day strike for a new *tarif* was broken by arrests of strike leaders. The army took six days to crush the ensuing revolt. Lyon became the symbol for a new working-class threat, its risings compared to St Domingo slave revolts by terrified Orleanist bourgeois.

After 1834, the decline of production of quality *façonnes* and the dispersal of cheaper *unies* cloths to the countryside inexorably eroded the sik weaver's position. Benoît claimed that artisans could only secure orders by slashing their prices or by allowing their wives to sleep with *fabricants*. The female population suffered catastrophically from the decline of the old economy. Hitherto, girls had married journeymen at the point where they could hope to establish a workshop together. Now, some were driven to live with men without marriage, risking being left with illegitimate children. Others lived alone on wages from new factory employment, but found prostitution the only way to make ends meet. A third option was to work in 'convent workshops', boarded in barracks, disciplined by nuns who supervised dormitories, and marched girls to church. These unpleasant institutions, designed to undercut male artisan wage rates, were the target of attacks in 1848.

The plight of Lyonnais silk-girls throws serious doubt on the views of optimists like Edward Shorter that the job opportunity offered by early capitalist industrialization accelerated female social and sexual 'liberation'!

Yet militancy persisted in Lyon. Proudhon claimed to have encountered there 'a more enlightened fanaticism than I have ever known'. Seven worker newspapers emerged between 1831 and 1845, and were read aloud in workshops and cafés. J. Benoît, who rejected the illusion of an alliance with the progressive bourgeois and urged workers to rely on their own efforts, held adult classes in the woods outside the city, praised the workers 'insatiable' thirst for knowledge, and disseminated socialist propaganda. He hailed Buonarrotti's account of Babeuf's 1796 conspiracy as 'our bible', viewed history as class struggle, criticized the Jacobins for their lack of understanding of capitalist developments, but cautioned that revolution would be premature until workers were more educated. Propaganda stressed the difference between the workers motto, 'to live by working', and that of the *fabricants*, 'to live well'. The master journeyman alliances held firm, for only 11 per cent of strikes in the 1830–40s were by journeymen against masters. Masters like Greppo and Benoît, who became 'socialist' deputies in 1848, were a respected elite in *quartiers* lacking a resident bourgeoisie. Recent migrants from the Beaujolais or Dauphiné were assimilated rapidly by the workers' community. As mechanized competition forced artisans to accept longer hours and lower rates, Flora Tristan found desperate weavers willing to risk all by further insurrection. Producer cooperatives were one alternative to such violence. Four profit-sharing cooperatives existed by 1847, their professed goal to wrest control of the market from 'parasitic' merchants. The mutualist ideas of Proudhon bear a close resemblance to this silk weavers' dream.

Indeed, this cooperative dream was the focal point of artisan aspiration and utopian socialist theory. Tailoring, shoemaking and cabinet-making were prominent crafts under threat less from mechanized factory production, as yet, than from new organization of marketing and production which permitted artisans to survive only under deteriorating conditions. Division of labour reduced level of skill in the expanding ready-made tailoring sector for all except an elite of cutters. The trade became overcrowded by the influx of foreign and rural migrants. Instead of producing for individual customers, tailors found themselves reliant on off-the-peg standardized products for new department stores like *Bonhomme Richard*. This growing *confection* sector of the trade captured 40 per cent of the market by 1848, and its workforce was two-thirds female, paid at half male wage rates. Whereas a master tailor had normally employed four artisans, *confection* employers like Parissot employed up to thirty, utilizing cheap materials, and aiming at petty-bourgeois customers. Tailors were skilled, reflective, literate, deeply resentful of the changes in their trade. Master tailors resisted shoddy competition by reasserting the need for quality regulation and apprenticeships, but clashed with their journeymen when they tried to cut wages in the bespoke sector to meet the *confection* threat. Journeymen turned to federalist trade socialism. Their strike in 1840 sparked off a wider Parisian strike wave. In Toulouse, where 214 masters were bankrupted between 1844 and 1848, masters and journeymen combined to fight for a minimum *tarif* and socialist leaders of the Second Republic like Gaillard emerged from the ranks of master tailors. During the 1848 revolution, warehouses of ready-made *confection* employers in Paris were to be burned down by artisan tailors.

The problems of Parisian tailors were duplicated in other trades and other cities. Retail stores were replacing direct orders from artisan cabinet-makers in the Faubourg St Antoine, where three-quarters of Parisian furniture was made, provoking strikes in 1840 and 1847. In Marseille, Sewell has contrasted the passivity of the unorganized, unskilled labourers – often Italians – and the Catholic-royalist sub-culture of local labour aristocrats like the patois-speaking stevedores, who passed jobs from father to son, with the militancy of 'open' artisan trades such as shoemakers who were skilled, literate, ran mutual aid societies, yet whose trade was being 'diluted' and overcrowded. Real wages fell, while the port's bourgeoisie prospered from Algerian trade. Migrant artisans who came to the city broke down the inward-looking insularity of traditionalist values, spoke French, not Provençal, weakened religious practice, and espoused cooperative socialist ideas. In nearby Toulon, radical tailors and shoemakers found allies with the influx of skilled metalworkers into the naval dockyard and arsenal which diluted the Catholic traditionalism of native dockyard workers, and led to the impressive 1845 strike there.

Producer cooperatives were not the utopia of intellectual

dreamers, nor simply the attempt of an elite of small masters to achieve entrepreneurial status, but a widely diffused idea aimed at freeing threatened crafts from the wages system. It was hoped that cooperatives would pool resources into collective capital, introduce machinery without the mass redundancies of the free-market system. The printers who participated in the July days of 1830 rapidly broke with their liberal allies and attacked new printing machines. The printer-socialist Leroux launched a print cooperative in 1833. Tailors turned to cooperatives after the 1833 strikes, in part to avoid police harassment of trade unions. Cooperation was a 'home-grown' artisan panacea for the threat of 'sweating', division of labour, competition from outworkers, convent and prison workshops, the decline of apprenticeships and the glutting of the labour market. Workers with craft skills were confident of their ability to organize their trade without 'parasitic' merchants and middlemen.

Different writers accentuated various nuances of cooperativist ideology. For Louis Blanc one prerequisite was universal suffrage, which could produce a social-democratic republic to assist cooperatives with cheap credit and state orders. He envisaged a unified cooperative structure in each trade. The social-Catholic artisans of the newspaper *L'Atelier* shared Blanc's republicanism, but envisaged pluralistic, 'fair' competition between cooperatives and a lesser state role. Blanc wrote for the radical newspaper *La Réforme*, for republicanism espoused 'associationist' ideas, either through a genuine desire for a petty-producer democracy, or as a cynical strategy to divert worker energy away from revolutionary paths into peaceful, harmless utopianism. Proudhon differed in his rejection of 'politics', and his contempt for the Jacobin tradition. He claimed that political revolutions simply replaced one elite by another, that neo-Jacobin politicians would dupe the workers. His 'mutualism' envisaged an autonomous movement of craftsmen controlling their own workshops and exchanging products without state interference, views stemming both from Proudhon's own experiences as a failed small printer, and from his contact with the Lyon master silk weavers. With considerable foresight he was deeply sceptical about universal suffrage, foreseeing the way in which elites could manipulate 'democracy'.

The parallels and contrasts between Proudhon and Corbon of *L'Atelier* are instructive. For Corbon, Catholicism purged of its ancien régime connections, of notions of God-given inequality, and of original sin, represented the moral basis of a socially just society. Proudhon, retaining vivid memories of the royalism of the revivalist mission of his youth in Franche-Comté, saw Catholicism as wedded to pernicious and patronizing ideas of charity in an age when workers sought justice. He had little sympathy for the thick fog of religiosity which enveloped utopians who viewed socialism as applied Christian fraternity. Yet both men shared a certain artisanal austerity and moral puritanism, an awareness that cooperative socialism required self-discipline which workers might not sustain. '*L'Atelier*' was an austere journal, read by an artisan elite. Making few concessions to popular readership, its circulation was only 1700.

By contrast, Étienne Cabet became the most popular of utopian socialist writers, channelling artisan grievances into an embryonic political party. His *Populaire* newspaper had 4500 subscribers and, read aloud in cafés and workshops, may have reached an audience of 200,000. It featured readers' letters, serialized stories, human-interest tales illustrating social injustices, and simple slogans. Cabet's clientele lay in older craft towns, among threatened trades such as tailors, shoemakers, cabinet-makers and handloom weavers – sedentary, thoughtful family men who disliked violence. The arrest of strike leaders and the crushing of their strikes in the 1830s led them to seek new tactics. Cabet won support among Lyon silk weavers, persuaded by the smashing of the 1834 rising of the futility of armed insurrection, and from handloom weavers in Rheims and Vienne threatened by wool mechanization and by a 50 per cent wage decline. Cabet's role as defence lawyer in the 1843 Toulouse trial of tax rioters won him support in the south-west.

Cabet's theory was minimal, his utopia (*Icaria*) a direct democracy based on civic education, censorship and modern technology. Two features distinguished his movement. It rejected violence, claiming that socialism would arrive through the conversion of the bourgeoisie by peaceful propaganda, for men of good will were susceptible to appeals to their reason and sense of justice. Those Lyon workers who dared question this social pacifism were excommunicated by Cabet, who saw them as a threat to his hopes of making socialism respectable. Religiosity was Cabetism's second characteristic, for many artisans remained responsive to the message that socialism was practical Christianity. The readers' letters in the *Populaire* which portrayed *Icaria* as a promised land suggests that the movement functioned as a substitute religion.

By 1846, however, Cabet's belated and reluctant realization that the bourgeoisie remained impervious to socialist persuasion contributed to the movement's crisis. Economic depression heightened class tensions and shattered dreams of class collaboration. Unwilling to admit the inevitability of class war, Cabet retreated into escapism, urging his followers to emigrate to model communities in America. In the 1848 crisis, Cabet offered no strategy other than flight. Cabetist membership fell from 2000 to 600 in Toulouse after 1846. His net influence was unfortunate, for it seduced sections of the young labour movement with the siren song of impossible class collaboration followed by escape to a Texas never-never land.

Relations between the labour movement and republicanism were complex. After 1830 republicans had tried to recruit workers as allies against Orleanism and expressed interest in cooperative ideas. The SDH recruited several thousand Parisian workers and had been active, if ultimately ineffectual, in the 1834 Lyon rising. Possibly the links weakened in the following decade. In Toulouse, where republicans pursued electoralist tactics and introduced blackleg labour to smash a printers' strike on their newspaper, *L'Emancipation*, socialist workers were sufficiently angered to boycott the funeral of a republican leader. However, by 1846–8 Duportal revived links with the workers, reemphasized republicanism's sympathy for cooperatives and used local sexual scandals involving Catholic teachers to whip up anticlericalism. For the city's popular Catholic royalism was in retreat. Luxury artisans in the city centre remained dependant on aristocratic clients and patronage. Yet, although legitimism could still boast 1000 workers in paramilitary groups in the 1830s, the old social relations between aristocracy, clergy and workers, organized around *confréries*, charity and deference were crumbling. The mechanism of assimilation broke down as the aristocracy failed to extend its hegemony to the rowing *faubourgs*. Mutual aid societies threw off clerical patronage. Aristocratic charity was inadequate to meet the scale of 1846–7 unemployment. Legitimism's temptation to play the populist card against Orleanism was reduced by fear of strikers and the unemployed. But workers were tempted to ally instead with a republican movement dominated by law students, unenfranchised small doctors and local medium-scale businessmen hit by the depression and northern economic competition. Fifty-one per cent of republican activists, by 1838, were workers, 12 per cent small masters.

Relationships between worker militants and bourgeois intellectuals were similarly ambivalent. Followers of that eccentric prophet of industrial society Saint-Simon, who had died in 1825, were given the opportunity by the brief relaxation of censorship after 1830 to reach a wide worker audience with an ideology which emphasized the need to replace the rule of parasites, such as clergy and large landowners, with a technocratic elite committed to industrial expansion, where each would contribute according to his capacity in a society held together by a religion of humanity. Martin Nadaud claimed that this message was above the heads of most workers. Vinçard of *La Ruche Populaire*, extracted the socialist element of the St Simonian gospel, while stressing the need for workers to be independent of arrogant patronizing from such religious mystics and elitist technocrats. Yet Vinçard was not immune from flirtation with benevolent bourgeois writers like Eugène Sue. In Toulon, as Agulhon emphasizes, workers responded to the vague social rhetoric of the progressive wing of the local borgeoisie, merchants and naval engineers influenced by St Simonianism. A clear class-conscious ideology was slow to emerge in a period when even the revolutionary theorist and conspirator Blanqui, unique in rejecting all utopias and insistent on the need to smash the bourgeois state in an armed coup, led by a small revolutionary elite, had no clear definition of 'proletariat' – using the term to describe those thirty million Frenchmen who did not belong to the ruling oligarchy. Ambiguities in attitudes are captured in the memoirs of Martin Nadaud, though these must be treated with care since they were written in the Third Republic, when their author had become a pillar of the moderate radical establishment.

Nadaud was the son of a Creuse peasant who followed his father into seasonal stonemasonry work in the Paris building sector. His account illustrates both the growth of worker consciousness and its continued ambivalences. In the 1830s the migrant labourers, lodged twelve to a room in filthy *garnis*, despised as 'chestnut eaters' by native Parisians, were usually fatalistic and divided by feuds between Limousins and Auvergnats which frequently resulted in dance-hall

brawls. Such quarrels weakened worker solidarity, Nadaud claimed
– though he himself acquired his reputation as a leader partly
through his fists. Yet fatalism and internecine rivalries waned.
'Bitter disillusionment' after the 1830 betrayal, resentment at the
repressive legislation of 1834 and at the cavalry charge which
dispersed a peaceful meeting of 7000 strikers in 1840, fostered
militancy. Nadaud, who taught evening classes to fellow workers,
read them revolutionary texts, saw growing literacy as producing a
more questioning working class,* and argued that a growing group
of skilled militants provoked the rank and file out of their apathy.
Yet Nadaud himself had aspirations to become a small building
contractor. If he admired socialists like Blanc, he also praised
workers who sent a delegation to thank the republican deputy
Arago for raising the 'social question' in parliament. He was
grateful to the courteous bourgeois student who complimented him
on his reading skill, to republican lawyers who defended workers
in court, to Cabet for welcoming workers *en blouse* into his family
home. He admired worker-poets like Poncy for 'doing honour to
our class'. His preoccupation was with worker dignity. Workers
should acquire education, show decent virtues, wear responsible
clothes, thus forcing the bourgeoisie to respect them. In short,
Nadaud remained precariously balanced between class militancy
and the dream of an alliance with the liberal bourgeoisie.

It would be futile to deny the weaknesses of a still embryonic
labour movement. Despite stirrings of militancy among Loire
miners, Toulon dockyard workers or La Chapelle locomotive
workers it attracted artisans rather than proletarians or rural
outworkers. 'Aristocratic' luxury trades remained politically
moderate. Friction between masters and journeymen weakened
the common front against merchant capitalists. Workers' religious
attitudes varied widely, from the militant anticlericalism of
Proudhon or the Lyon silk weavers who attacked convent-

---

* Recent studies of Parisian popular education in the July Monarchy are rather less
optimistic. While municipal education expenditure did increase after 1830, and
teacher training improved, financial resources remained inadequate, rapidly
growing *quartiers* like Belleville and La Chapelle were entirely deficient in public
schools, barely 50 per cent of children attended classes and nearly 90 per cent of
these left before the age of twelve. An 1835 survey showed that only 7 per cent
of the pupils in the ten-to-twelve age groups could do simple dictation. Over half
of pupils attended overcrowded Catholic schools, where classes could be as large
as 120.

workshops, via the religiosity of Cabetists or the unorthodox social Catholicism of *L'Atelier*, to the piety of Flemish mill-girls in the Nord and the militant Catholic-royalist populism of Nîmes. Yet, if religion was sometimes the opium of the workers, republicans could, equally, manipulate anticlericalism to divert workers from attacks on capitalism. If workers were more responsive to utopian socialist ideas than some historians have admitted, these ideas were frequently contradictory. Cabet welcomed an alliance with progressive bourgeois which Proudhon and Blanqui saw as a trap. St Simonians praised new technology and factory production which alarmed and appalled skilled artisans like J. Benoît. The emphasis on model community building among Fourierists and Cabetists was denounced by others as diverting the movement into escapist dreams. Puritans like Proudhon had no sympathy with the emphasis on pleasure and sexual emancipation among the followers of the eccentric visionary and commercial traveller Fourier. Writers who emphasized the desirability of producer cooperatives were divided about the role of the state.

The 'working class' was thus neither sociologically nor ideologically homogeneous. Despite gestures of solidarity when artisans collected funds for striking miners, it proved impossible to channel the disparate grievances of factory workers, outworkers, big city poor and the threatened artisans into a coherent movement. The self-educated artisans who edited *La Ruche* oscillated between writing of 'workers' and 'the people', between denouncing the new 'bourgeois aristocracy' and viewing the bourgeoisie as productive in comparison with the parasitic aristocracy. The autodidacts who dominated the worker-press ran the risk of becoming respectable, high minded and austere, anxious to moralize the workers to make them fit for the franchise – in short, of losing touch with the bitter violence of much worker protest. A final problem for the movement was that raised by the issue of female labour. As mill-girls in the Nord, sweated garment-workers in Paris, Jacquard-loom operators or raw-silk preparers in the Lyonnais, women played a crucial role in new work processes. Yet if Saint Simonians and Fourierists gave priority to female emancipation, and a small feminist press emerged, many artisan militants, threatened by 'dilution' of their crafts, shared Proudhon's male chauvinist call for confining women to the home. *L'Atelier* saw male voters as 'representing' women – just as Guizot had argued that large taxpayers 'represented' small!

L. Strumhinger correctly emphasizes that the silk weavers' insistence on attempting to destroy the new female-operated mills rather than to organize women workers was a major weakness in the Lyon labour movement.

And yet by 1848 Orleanism was facing a serious challenge. While alarmed bourgeois denounced the savagery of the *classes dangereuses*, equating socialism with criminality, many workers were developing the idea that they were the truly productive class. Lyon workers insisted that they would 'live working' or 'die fighting'. Workers assimilated the new slogans of the 'Right to Work' or 'Property is Theft', although few, as yet, faced up to the central problem of how to act if the bourgeoisie rejected their insistent pleas for social justice.

II The Crisis of Peasant France?

The 1840s marked both the apogee and the crisis of French peasant society. Never before – nor since – had the countryside been so populous, for the French population grew from 27 to 35 million between 1800 and 1850 and, despite some rural exodus, the bulk of this increase occurred in rural areas. With the villages still full of young people, the folklore culture of carnival, dance and folk song still flourished. Yet the spread of the capitalist market economy, and demographic pressures, created an acute crisis, accentuated by the harvest failures of 1845–7. Behind the 'archaic' peasant response of food, tax and forest riots and rural arson, some have discerned a growing 'political' awareness, accelerated by the widening of the municipal franchise in 1831 and the advent of universal suffrage in 1848. The complexity of peasant behaviour in the 1840s can only be understood with reference to rural social structure, landholding patterns, the nature of the rural economy and, as recent historians have persuasively argued, peasant culture, historic memory and '*mentalités*'.

P. Vigier's comment in his study of five alpine departments that there was not *a* peasant problem, but *several*, can be applied to France in general. For rural France was a varied world, a crazy patchwork quilt of large bourgeois or aristocratic estates and tiny peasant holdings, of modern capitalist market production, peasant cash-drop farmers, and subsistence agriculture. Patterns of ownership and exploitation varied widely, as did interests, traditions and types of village community. The old myth of contented, Catholic, conservative smallholders needs careful qualification. Approximately half the land was owned by 2.7 million peasant proprietors. Yet the post-1845 crisis showed that many of these were far from 'satisfied'. The other half of the land was held by large- and medium-scale noble and bourgeois owners. 0.6 per cent of owners controlled 20 per cent of France. These estates were leased to 0.9 million tenants, 0.5 million sharecroppers, and worked by 3.3 million agricultural labourers and farm servants.

One broad, but useful, generalization is that 'capitalist hierarchies' with large estates, big tenant-farmers and day-labourers were much more prevalent to the north of the Loire. The existence of large urban markets such as Paris and the textile towns of the Nord and of Normandy, together with easy communication along navigable rivers across flat terrain, tended to encourage precocious market specialization, particularly in grain in the Île-de-France, livestock in Normandy and sugar beet in Flanders. Clout has emphasized that the three regions of the north, north-east and north-west produced more grain than the seven other regions combined. An agricultural revolution was occurring in the Île-de-France, Brie and Soissonnais, as big tenant-farmers introduced fertilizers and threshing machines. Normandy produced 11 per cent of French agricultural wealth with only 6 per cent of the nation's acreage. The Elbeuf and Louviers region specialized in meat and dairy produce for the growing Paris market, and the bulk of the 50 per cent increase in horses and cattle in France between 1812 and the 1830s was in the north. The 1789 revolution in the Nord, as Lefèbvre showed, benefited bourgeois church-land purchasers and large peasants, *coqs du village*, who quickly undermined the communal rights of the remaining small peasants. Despite the bitter resistance of the rural poor there was a similar erosion of communal rights in Alsace, as large farmers turned to commercial maize and tobacco. In Champagne and Burgundy urban bourgeoisie bought their way into newly prestigious wine houses.

Capitalist enclaves also existed to the south of the Loire, in the wine estates of the Bordelais and of lower Languedoc, as in the grain area round Toulouse. Here a quasi-capitalist aristocracy raised yields and profits by replacing the sharecroppers with *maitres-valets*, who were hired by the year, and paid in kind, yet under tight control of estate managers who took 75 per cent of the crop. As Armengaud illustrates, the power of the rural elites was strengthened by internal divisions within the rural poor, with *solatiers*, hired to work the estates by the year and allowed their own plots, holding their own separate dances and fêtes distinct from those of the despised *brassiers*, hired by the day.

Yet, three-quarters of French farms were below five hectares. Small owners, though found throughout France, were more typical of the south and centre. However, the term 'small peasant proprietor' suggests a spurious uniformity. One could distinguish, perhaps, three types of peasant farming in these years. Firstly, peasants in isolated areas such as the central massif, the alpine upland and the Pyrénées, remained quasi-subsistence farmers. These areas were largely untouched by the canal- and road-building programmes of the 1830s. It is from such regions that Eugen Weber drew much of the evidence for his brilliantly evocative but unbalanced portrait of pre-railway peasant France. He described a world untouched by commercial farming, without market contacts. Agricultural methods remained those of the seventeenth century. Diets were dominated by chestnuts and black bread. The metric system and the franc still took second place to ancien régime measurements and coinage. The distant state, encountered only through tax collectors and conscription, was widely hated. A variety of local patois were still spoken; French was still the alien tongue of bureaucrats and hated town dwellers. Low literacy was accompanied by a total lack of interest in education, for peasant children began to tend sheep at the age of six. It was a world marked by brutality towards the very young and the old, and hatred of 'outsiders' – even those from the next village. A deep-seated religiosity was heavily tinged with superstition. Priests, who rang church bells to ward off thunderstorms and led processions to magic fountains to pray for good crops, were witch doctors who shared local respect with sorcerers and *sage-femmes*. Such peasants, Weber concluded, had no knowledge of or interest in 'politics', for their frame of reference was too localized.

Yet at the opposite pole to such subsistence peasants lay a group of large *kulaks*, peasant market producers who had the capacity to produce a sizeable cash-crop surplus, and to achieve reasonable prosperity. The Beauce grain growers are examples of this category. Many more peasants, however, comprised an intermediate stratum of small scale, cash-crop market producers, typified by the wine growers of Burgundy, lower Languedoc and Provence, or the hemp and raw-silk producers of the Rhône Valley and lower Alps studied by Vigier. Such peasants were drawn into the market economy by taxation pressures or the needs of local industry, where communications permitted, as in the Saône Valley or on the Mediterranean coast. The small size of farms, lack of capital and vulnerability to price fluctuations made such peasant market production highly precarious. Yet its steady emergence during the July Monarchy throws doubt on Weber's stereotype of autarkic, isolated subsistence farming. As Margadant has shown, steady 'proto-urban' development was occurring. By 1841 there were 981 bourgs of between 1500 and 3000 inhabitants in France, functioning as small market towns and centres of local commercial farming networks. Twenty-two per cent of the Provençal population lived in such communities – as against a mere 8 per cent of Bretons. There were some 3000 weekly markets and 7000 fairs in rural France.

Historians of the French peasantry in these years have tended to be divided between 'optimists' and 'pessimists'. Weber and Vidalenc portray a rural society locked into extreme material poverty by poor transport, subdivision of land, poor agricultural techniques, illiteracy, routine and lack of capital. Meat was a rare festive treat, bread itself a luxury in many regions which survived on buckwheat or chestnuts. Malaria, goitre, digestive and deficiency diseases such as rickets were endemic. The economist A. Blanqui claimed that many animals were better housed than peasants who lived in single room hovels, in darkness in order to avoid window tax.

Others have suggested that such monolithic pessimism is excessive. A 33 per cent rise in food production between 1790 and the 1830s allowed France to feed a population which grew at 330,000 per annum between 1821 and 1846. Agricultural change preceded the railway revolution. Road and canal construction enabled Burgundy and Midi wines to reach the north. Land-reclamation rescued sizeable areas from heath and moorland. Average wheat yields increased by 70 per cent per hectare, from 8.59 to 14.7 hectolitres, between 1815 and 1835, and wheat gained at the expense of rye and buckwheat. Market gardening appeared in the Paris region, Loire Valley and Brittany, while intensive cultivation of commercial crops such as silk and vines, producing high profit per hectare, sustained high population density in the south-east and Alsace. Fodder crops allowed a 50 per cent increase in livestock between 1815 and 1835, increasing manure, and thus crop yields. The introduction of maize to the south-west produced a minor revolution by cutting fallow land and sustaining a rising population. Potato production rose by 60 per cent, notably in the north-east and south-west, and became a staple food rather than one merely fed to pigs. Military conscription records suggest that rural conscripts, at least from northern France, were coming healthier and taller.

This revisionism is a useful corrective to an excessive stress on rural misery.. Such evidence prompted Newell to discern an embryonic agricultural revolution, and Margadant to suggest rising peasant living standards. Yet, the very real economic 'archaisms' persisted; poor transport still limited whole areas of the central Massif, Pyrénées, inland Brittany to a quasi-subsistence agriculture. It made the food surpluses of the more fertile areas difficult to transport, in crisis years, to needy regions and maintained wide regional price differences. Threat of famine obliged all areas to grow cereals, however unsuitable the soil. Seed-yield ratios in parts of the Midi were 70 per cent below those of the well-manured north. Southern livestock was scarce, breeding unselective, overworked draught animals scraggy and diseased. Midi ploughs were thus light and often inadequate for breaking hard soil. Meat-eating was a northern and urban luxury, providing under 3 per cent of the calorie intake in the Alps. Regions like the Périgord subsisted on chestnuts, and even the affluent Beauce subsisted on black bread. Even in good years, there was a 'hungry' France.

Vidalenc emphasizes, too, that food resources were coming under strain from demographic pressure, a rural exodus was beginning in some overpopulated departments. The 1845–7 crisis showed the continuing vulnerability of the system to harvest failure. Since some of the highest population growth had occurred in 'backward' departments, the balance of population and resources was becoming as precarious as on the eve of 1789.

Peasant communities had developed survival strategies for coping with inadequate agrarian resources. The Limousin sent thousands of migrants to work annually in the Parisian and Lyon building sector, from which they returned in winter with cash to prop up their small farms – but also with new clothes, sophisticated habits and radical ideas. They were 'agents of progress and civilization' (M. Nadaud), in the villages, monopolized storytelling in the winter evening gatherings (*veillées*), had first choice of brides. Pyrenean villages produced *colporteurs*, who travelled France selling books and almanacks, as well as touring entertainers. A tame performing bear was a frequent item in local dowries! Aquitaine upland peasants did harvest work in the lower Languedoc coastal vineyards; in the wooded Morvan, wet-nursing was a major source of income for peasant women, who suckled offspring of Parisian petty-bourgeois families. In the central Massif, women sold their hair.

Population growth swelled the numbers of small peasant-proprietors, although to circumvent the provision of the Code, which required subdivision of property among offspring, it was common for one son to buy out the inheritance of his brothers and sisters. In the alpine region, peasant owners were increasing by 1 per cent per annum in the Orleanist period. In their eagerness to acquire viable farms, or to cash in on market booms such as that for raw silk in the Lyonnais, peasants resorted to borrowing money at high interest rates from 'usurers', often small-town *notaires*. Nadaud recounts that 30 per cent interest on a loan necessitated by a combination of bad harvests, a daughter's dowry, and medical bills, reduced his father to tears. Endemic indebtedness in much of rural France made tens of thousands of peasants vulnerable to the threat of expropriation during price slumps. Balzac's *Les Paysans* (1844) provides a graphic illustration of why the 'usurer' was replacing the *'seigneur'* as the most hated man in peasant France. The peasants of the novel nibble away at a Burgundian noble estate – yet can acquire cash to purchase extra land only by falling into the clutches of Rigoult, the local money lender. Marx correctly valued this novel for showing how the illusory victory of the peasantry over feudalism inexorably played into the hands of the bourgeoisie. In 1848 seventeen of the forty-five cantons in the Isère saw anti-usurer riots. In one Pyrenean canton, a self-made usurer, who loaned money to entire villages, left over 500,000 francs in his will.

Excessive subdivision of land was avoided in some regions by sending children into the church, or by late marriage. In Corrèze, the average male marriage age was thirty-one. Elsewhere, birth control proved the logical solution. Small wine growers in the southern Paris basin had practised this since the 1770s. By the 1820s Midi clergy were denouncing 'the detestable crimes of Onan, knowledge of which has penetrated even into peasant cottages.' In 1800, the French birth rate was 3.8 per cent; by 1850 it had fallen to 2.6 per cent. 'Catholic' Brittany maintained much higher birth-rates, while elsewhere contraception was facilitated by weak religious practice and, in turn, fostered peasant-*curé* conflicts.

The decline of rural industry compounded the demographic problem. Rural outwork in textiles, pottery and shoemaking alone sustained the viability of many inadequate farms. The peasantry of the Marlhes adjusted to the mechanization of ribbon-making by switching from rural outwork to a strategy of sending their daughters to work in the Stephenois mills to earn money, which was channelled back into their farms. The development of the Nord textile mills undermined rural weaving in Picardy, linen declined in rural Normandy, clogmaking in the Yonne. In Alsace, where the population density of 124 km^2 was double the national average, factory employment failed to mop up surplus rural manpower which began to seek an outlet in emigration.

Erosion of communal rights presented a more serious threat to peasant communities. The 1827 Forest Code facilitated the selling of communal forest lands to private owners and iron forge owners and tightened the control of state forest officials over grazing and wood-collection rights. This was a potential disaster for thousands of marginal small owners in central, southern and eastern France, dependent on the forests for supplementary resources – firewood, grazing, mushrooms and rabbits to sell in local markets. In 1834, when unemployed vineyard workers in Mèze (Hérault) invaded the local forest, the police blamed the 'spirit of anarchy' engendered by the Lyon weavers' revolt, which allowed 'enemies of public order' to persuade 'ignorant populations that the republic was going to be proclaimed, along with common ownership of land.' This may have been overreaction by nervous authorities, but there was certainly potential in the forest issue for a politicization of village communities. Prolonged conflict developed in the Ariège in the Pyrénées, a department with a perennial grain deficit and a 37 per cent population increase between 1801 and 1846. As iron forge owners excluded the peasantry from the forests, impoverished villagers launched a revolt involving theft of wood, illegal grazing, assaults on forest guards and ritualistic mobilization of the 'folklore' practice of *charivari* to humiliate the guards and owners. The rebels were know as '*demoiselles*' because they adopted the carnival practice of dressing themselves in female clothing. One village in Quérigut took its case to court at Foix in 1832 and won, only to have the decision overturned in 1833. In 1841, troops had to be sent to the village to protect forest guards against assaults. In 1844 there were 2400 convictions for forest offences in the Ariège. The *demoiselles* continued their activity, sporadically, until 1872. The canton of Quérigut was still fighting its legal battle in 1973! Similar conflicts were, as Agulhon shows, endemic in Provence, where one-sixth of the land was forest. In Côte-d'Or, the loss of 4000 hectares of communal land to private pasture threatened the ability of small peasants to keep their traditional '*vache du pauvre*'.

Wine-tax collectors were as hated in wine growing areas as the forests guards in the Pyrénées. Small Burgundy winegrowers blamed the wine taxes for reducing sales to Paris. Protectionist tariffs, designed to aid northern industry and livestock, hit exports of Alsace and Franche-Comté wine to south-west Germany and Switzerland. Tax officials became scapegoats, visible local targets for peasant dislike of the policies of a distant government. There were violent protests in the early 1830s at the failure of the new regime to abolish the tax. In lower Languedoc republicans were more successful in manipulating these than were the legitimists. Mathieu Mayneau, leader of the protests near Béziers, was from an old Jacobin family. In 1833–4 there were daily demonstrations and clashes with police, and in this once Catholic-royalist region there was evidence of growing anticlericalism. Rioters in Béziers, about to set fire to the home and library of the local wine-tax collector, withdrew when the shout went up, 'Respect the books! They were the works of Voltaire, friend of the people!'

There was, thus, ample cause for peasant unrest in these years. Demographic pressure, subdivision of small farms, lack of access to credit and indebtedness to usurers, state taxation and the erosion of communal rights by capitalist legislation all posed a threat to the viability of peasant agriculture. There was no single reaction to economic pressures, however, in part because response was mediated through a complex and varied peasant culture formed by local history and folk memory, community and religion.

In central and southern France, especially but not exclusively in areas of concentrated habitat, the village community remained strong and resistant to that fragmentation which had occurred in the more 'capitalist' north, where peasant solidarity had crumbled as a minority of *kulaks* reaped the benefits of post-1789 laissez-faire legislation, while the small peasants lost their communal rights and sank into the rural proletariat. Village youth groups (*corps de jeunesse*) supervised the sexual behaviour of young couples. Transgressors against village norms were treated to 'rough music' – serenaded with ironic songs, tied backwards on donkeys. Such transgressors could include older women who aspired to marry younger men, outsiders who dared to presume to marry village girls. A profound suspicion of outsiders could produce intervillage violence at local markets, or hatred of Jewish clothes dealers in Alsace. Yet there could also be a high degree of communal solidarity, fostered in the scattered hamlets of the Limousin by evenings passed together in *veillées* – weaving, mending tools and telling stories. In the large Provençal villages, with their shoemakers, blacksmiths, barrel-makers and cork workers, mutual aid societies developed. The involvement of parts of the Midi and east-central France in market economies meant less of that antiurban sentiment which existed elsewhere, and which E. Weber mistakenly attributed to the peasantry as a whole. Many villages retained practices of a shared communal shepherd, or of agreed dates to begin harvesting, or community memories of resistance to tax collectors and seigneurs. In the Jura, there were thriving communal cooperative wine and cheese storage associations (*fruitières*).

Linguistic factor accentuated the gulf between much of the peasantry and the French bourgeois state. It was not only Basques, Alsatians, Bretons and Flemings who found French a foreign tongue, but the peasantry of central and southern France who spoke a variety of Provençal or Languedoc patois. The prefects, police, tax-collectors, forest guards and conscription sergeants were alien agents of a foreign power, apparently interested only in taking the village community's land, cash and sons. Many peripheral regions appeared to be suffering the pains of capitalist development – decline of rural industry, erosion of communal rights, higher taxes – with few of its compensations. In turn 'northern' bureaucrats viewed the Midi, in particular, as violent, rebellious and anarchic.

Religion, which remained a dominant element in peasant culture, retained many pre-Christian elements. The village *curé* often acted as official witch doctor, sharing local prestige with unofficial rival sorcerers. His key function was to protect crops and livestock, to ring church bells against thunder storms, tie garters to church bell ropes to make women fertile and to lead processions to holy fountains. Religious festivals were the occasion for collective social and psychological release, holidays more than holy days, accompanied by meat-eating, wine-drinking, dancing and other rare carnal pleasures.

Yet, formal religious practice had become highly uneven. If the west, the central Massif and Flanders remained areas of monolithically high church-attendance, conversely, extremely low church-attendance had become the norm in much of the southern Paris basin, the centre and, increasingly, the Midi and parts of the south-west and the Limousin. Some of this pattern of 'de-Christianization' can only be explained with reference to pre-1789 history. The area round Saintes had been a Protestant enclave, unreconciled to its forcible reconversion to Catholicism after 1685. The Sens diocese had been a notorious centre of Jansenism, and rural anticlericalism there may have owed its origins to peasant resentment at puritanical, interfering Jansenist clergy. Anticlericalism round Cluny in Burgundy, or in parts of the Montpellier diocese, may have been rooted in hostility of the eighteenth century peasantry to tithe-appropriating monasteries. Conversely, Hilaire claims that high practice in Flanders was due to the efficiency of seventeenth century counter-reformation missions. The consequences of the revolution were widely felt. The 'armées révolutionaires' had, as Cobb shows, provided a crash course in ritual demystification for some rural areas. The absence of priests from many villages for a decade or more broke habits of churchgoing, lengthened baptism delays, began the practice of civil marriage. Clashes between juror and non-juror priests produced bitter local feuds in villages in Dauphiné, Provence and the centre.

Many dioceses suffered from a continued shortage of priests after 1815. The Yonne had 180 vacant parishes, Aude 148, Nièvre 94. C. Marcilhacy's study of the seminary of the Orléans diocese confirms the impressionistic portrait in Stendhal's *Scarlet and Black*, that many priests were ill-educated peasant boys who entered the church as a comfortable alternative to agricultural toil. The increase in vocations after 1815 produced more quantity than quality – though Mgr Leblanc de Beaulieu said that he preferred 'ploughing the Lord's vineyards with asses to leaving them fallow'! Where, as in the mid-Loire valley, peasants had acquired church lands in the revolution, fear of the restoration of these to the clergy persisted for decades. Sociological patterns can provide a useful key to rural religiosity. River valleys and villages along main routes with active mobile populations of wood-floaters, boatmen, travellers, and with numerous cafés, tended to have low practice. Marcilhacy's study of the Orléanais contrasted a practising Sologne, isolated and dominated by aristocratic landholders, with anticlerical areas like the Val de Loire, with its boatmen and winegrowers, the Beauce, where a prosperous middle-peasantry had acquired church lands and made their farm servants work on Sundays, and the wild Gatinais, with its poor exploited woodmen. By 1848 only 11 per cent of the inhabitants of the diocese attended church, the bulk of them women. In the Val-de-Loire, male attendance was only 2 per cent, peasants saw confession as humiliating. First communion came to signify the end of catechism, childhood and of religious practice.

The clergy's behaviour fuelled rural anticlericalism. In Burgundy, where the seigneurial system had been onerous, the clergy's legitimism perpetuated peasant fears of a return to the ancien régime. In Provence, Agulhon has illustrated the anger produced in Var villages when liberal-Voltairean lawyers, who defended communal forest rights in court, were refused burial by legitimist priests. Peasants had a 'cult of the dead', believing that all men, practising or otherwise, had the right to a decent funeral. The communal pride of Midi villages was frequently offended by the meddling efforts of clergy to run municipal affairs.

Friction was accentuated by the efforts of younger, more zealous clergy to eliminate the elements of drinking and dancing from religious festivals. Sober northern bishops in the Montpellier diocese led a crusade against the crude profanities which marked the religious practice of *pénitent* groups. But if drink, dancing and protection of livestock were the function of religious fêtes and of village priests, then the *curé* who censured such practices lost his *raison d'être*. When one Var priest boycotted the traditional St Eloi Day blessing of the livestock because of the debauchery which habitually followed, the villagers sent a delegation. 'Come, monsieur le curé, all the donkeys are waiting: you alone are missing.'

The greater tolerance of the Breton clergy for these elements of 'popular religion' may have contributed to the continuing strength of religious practice in the west. The cadres of village anticlericalism were provided by the rural petty bourgeoisie of café-owners, vets, village artisans and minor government officials, who were not infected by the drift of the Orleanist upper bourgeoisie back to the church. The emergence of the schoolteacher, after the 1833 Guizot law, gave them a valuable new ally. The spread of rural education may have been an element in growing anticlericalism, though there is no simple correlation of literacy and de-Christianization. Catholic Doubs had 83 per cent conscript literacy in 1827, anticlerical Corrèze a mere 14.9 per cent. Gradually teachers, from being a badly paid and ill-regarded group of social misfits, drunks and ex-NCO's, who doubled as gravediggers, bell-ringers and village barbers, began to develop an *esprit de corps*. In 1830, there were thirteen *écoles normales* (teacher's training colleges); by 1837, seventy-four. Only 3000 villages lacked a school by 1847. Many municipalities were too poor to finance adequate schooling, many landowners viewed the prospect of literate sharecroppers or labourers as a threat, a step towards insubordination or rural exodus. Many *curés* insisted that their favourite parishioners were the god-fearing illiterates. The tone of *école normale* training remained conservative and Christian, and, once in the village, the teacher often reflected rather than moulded opinion. Subsistence peasants saw little need, as yet, for literacy. Yet, illiteracy *was* declining, bilingualism increasing in patois areas, and the teacher, sometimes a subscriber to the radical *Echo des Instituteurs*, was a potential new culture-broker in the village, a latent rival to the old *notables*.

On the eve of 1848, the relationship between 'culture' and rural politics was complex. The correlation between 'traditional' culture and conservatism is plausible in the Catholic west, but less so elsewhere. Literacy was highest, agriculture most 'modernized', the old culture weakest, in northern France. Yet the rural north, dominated by big estates and large commercial tenant farmers, witnessed only sporadic grain riots, rural Luddism and arson, as in the Normandy fires of 1830. Protest was more generalized in the centre and Midi, where capitalistic legal changes and market relationships threatened surviving peasant communities. In fighting these pressures, peasants had the possibility of mobilizing their culture, as in the case of those Ariège mountain-dwellers, who utilized the *charivari* and the disguises of carnival in their battles against the forest guards.

Peasant response to the agrarian crisis of 1845–7 was, thus, diverse. Grain and potato harvest failures exposed the precarious inadequacy of transport and food systems in a countryside under demographic pressure – though the crisis peak of grain prices remained one-third below that of 1816–17. The victims were agricultural labourers, adversely affected by high food prices and unemployment, rural outworkers hit by textile depression, wine growers who grew no grain, and small peasants whose poor crops forced them to become grain purchasers. Large capitalist farmers made big profits on their surpluses. In Côte-d'Or, the authorities suspected large owners of holding back grain supplies to drive up prices. Paternalistic efforts to combat rural misery with charity schemes were, as Dupeux illustrated for the Loir-et-Cher, largely cosmetic and ineffectual. As in 1787–9, 1816–17 and 1828–30, bands of vagrants prowled the countryside in search of food.

The troubles in Buzençais (Indre) epitomize the nature of rural unrest. In this market town rural artisans and agricultural labourers alarmed by the spectacle of the export of grain from their locality, rioted, halted grain convoys, and, in the presence of the municipal council, sold the grain at pre-crisis 'just' prices. Threshing machines were destroyed in the fields. Cavalry was used to break up bands of up to 150 vagrants. The old hostility to the château was replaced by new hatreds of landowners and grain merchants. Five flour mills were pillaged to cries to 'Kill the bourgeois!' A local 'usurer' was killed after he had shot two men who presented him with a petition urging sale of grain at lower prices. The Orleanist authorities determined to make a sharp example of the accused, and to prove that there was a subversive political plot. Three of twenty-six accused received the death penalty, with the judge arguing that café frequentation by the prisoners proved that they were neither poor nor hungry! Pleased with the verdict, the regime gave it wide publicity. But the case aroused widespread distaste. George Sand commented that the really disgusting spectacle was men 'gorged with money [refusing] necessities to fellow men, and [rubbing] their hands, saying it was an excellent year for making good grain profits.' The defence lawyer in the trial was to be a democratic-socialist deputy in 1849.

Behind the archaism of sporadic rural violence lay the latent possibility of the emergence of a radical-populist political response to the agrarian crisis. Already in 1830–4, Orleanism had been alarmed by republican involvement in wine-tax protests in Languedoc and Burgundy. The 1831 widening of the municipal franchise permitted an embryonic peasant democracy in some southern villages. The 1830 revolution had illustrated how a national political upheaval could stimulate the expression of peasant grievances. Some preconditions existed for the politicization of peasant protest as literacy grew, republican lawyers aided Provençal peasants in forest rights disputes, migrant building workers put the Limousin hill-farms in contact with urban ideas. A banner bearing the Lyon silk weavers' slogan, 'To live working, or die fighting', was hoisted there during a riot in 1840. Anticlericalism was eroding rural deference. Wine growers had deep-seated grievances against the regime's taxation policy. Forest communities hated the forest code. Whether, with the advent of mass suffrage in 1848, the left had the rural knowledge, experience or policies to tap such grievances was an open question.

Chapter 4

Revolution and Reaction
(1848–51)

I The Elites and the Advent of the Republic

That astute observer of Parisian life, Daumier, warned in June 1847 that though a purely proletarian revolt would be suppressed easily enough, the shopkeepers of the Rue St Denis were unhappy: 'If the middle classes are mixed up in it, things are serious.' As Marx emphasized, the revolution of February 1848 was the product of an ephemeral alliance between the non-ruling elements of the bourgeoisie and the workers. The sources of anti-Orleanist sentiment have already been analysed.* However the insurrection which toppled the regime was, in itself, an 'accident'. Radicals refused to obey the government ban on a planned reform banquet, though O. Barrot's dynastic opposition, mistrustful of popular pressure and desiring only minor franchise adjustments, tried to wash its hands of this protest. Workers mingled with the protesters; petty-bourgeois elements in the National Guard, sympathetic to reform, not only refused to quell the demonstration but, by fraternizing with the army, confused troops who were reluctant to fire on middle-class demonstrators. Demoralized army units simply melted away. The small republican movement had made no plans for this contingency. Ledru-Rollin, fearing a confrontation would be suicidal, had urged calm. Flocon, of the radical *La Réforme*, had written an editorial warning against an insurrection which he subsequently justified as a spontaneous defence of popular sovereignty.

Pitchforked into prominence by these events were the moderate republicans of *Le National*, who favoured a 'republic with provisos', an apology for revolution, a period of delay followed by a constitutional referendum. Working-class pressure in the Paris streets pushed them into conceding universal suffrage and four

* See chapters 2 and 3.

cabinet places to socialists and radicals. Members of the dynastic opposition and republicans alike were shaken and alarmed by their own 'triumph'. De Tocqueville recalled seeing Barrot wearing the expression of a man about to be hanged. Success via popular insurrection was a dangerous path to power. The middle class welcomed the vote, blessed trees of liberty, praised dignified, heroic workers who had overthrown Orleanism with so little violence, and talked of a new social harmony based on the alliance of bourgeoisie, people and clergy. Yet beneath the façade of this 'beautiful revolution' (Marx) there were undertones of terror. The urban masses could also be dark, brutal, barbarous criminals. Men of property feared for order, foresaw 'excesses' and prudently converted their investments into ready cash. Republicans in the Provisional Government began to recruit and train a *Garde Mobile* to keep the peace. As Tim Clark comments, we have no real artistic image of the February revolution. Daumier began a picture of workers and bourgeois united on the barricade and – significantly – never completed it.

The Provisional Government reflected the contradictions of the social forces which had elevated it to power. It made tactical concessions to appease worker agitation, flirted with slavery abolition, primary education reform, even contemplated selective rail nationalization to revive railway construction and mop up unemployment. Yet it was in an economic straightjacket. The revolution worried businessmen; investment dried up, share values fell 55 per cent, Bank of France reserves declined 70 per cent in three weeks. Lille industrial output fell by 66 per cent in three months. Metallurgy and mining, relatively sheltered in the 1846–7 depression, slumped. The agrarian crisis continued. Government tax revenue was falling sharply, just as it came under pressure to increase welfare programmes for the urban unemployed. Radicals urged a package of income tax and inheritance tax to finance welfare and public-works projects. Instead, as good laissez-faire liberals, the Provisional Government clung to financial orthodoxy. To bolster their flagging financial credit they appealed to the Bank of France. A regime born from a revolt against the Orleanist 'bankocracy' found itself hostage to the goodwill of the *Haute Banque*. Experiments with progressive taxation or deficit financing became impossible.

To balance their budget the republicans were pushed into a fatal error. A 45 per cent increase in the land tax imposed the bulk of the burden of the state deficit on the shoulders of a peasantry already hit by acute agrarian crisis, which had seen, for example, the purchasing power of Loir-et-Cher winegrowers fall by 25 per cent since 1847. Many peasants had welcomed the change of regime. Forest riots, protests against the wine taxes, rural Luddism, had multiplied in March 1848 as village communities looked to the republic for sympathy. At a stroke potential peasant goodwill was lost. Widespread tax-revolt broke out, which was to occupy some 50,000 troops for the remainder of 1848. Protest was most violent in the poorer polyculture regions of the south-west and western Massif, where cash shortage was acute. Royalist elites were handed an electoral trump card against the new regime.

Yet the Provisional Government remained a schizophrenic beast. While taxation policy sabotaged republic chances of securing peasant support, Interior Minister Ledru-Rollin was attempting to 'democratize' rural France. Prefects were replaced by 110 *commissaires*, whose task was to 'guide' the April elections. Barely one-quarter of these were radicals. Many faced formidable tasks, confronted by hostile royalist *notables* and disappointed peasants. Attempts to fill key posts with loyal republicans were only partly successful. Many Orleanist officeholders retained their posts through a prudent tactical conversion to republicanism. Too many republican *commissaires* mixed the rhetoric of vague fraternal goodwill with a disconcerting absence of clear political analysis. In Loir-et-Cher, G. Sarrut announced that he had come to introduce biblical equality and liberty on earth – then gave six key posts in Blois to Orleanist *grand*-bourgeois. Even neo-Jacobins like Delescluze in the Nord, sympathetic to Anzin miners against the coal companies, were forced to suppress Luddism, to maintain 'order'.

Nevertheless Education Minister Carnot's schemes for educational reforms, which included open examinations for the bureaucracy, and plans for railway nationalization, were denounced by conservatives as creeping socialism. The Parisian elites were alarmed by the appointment as Paris police chief of Caussidière, a veteran of the radical secret societies who had been jailed for involvement in the 1834 Lyon rising. Caussidière was not a socialist, and urged Paris tenants to pay their rents. But his *garde rouge*, recruited from unemployed barricade fighters, excluded unpopular *sergeants de ville* from the Orleanist police, and elected its own lower officers. Caussidière refused to spy on workers' clubs. His organization outraged the propertied classes, who perceived it as the 'dangerous classes' in uniform.

The *notables* had responded to the February insurrection with weeks of panic. Many looked to the Provisional Government for salvation from a return to the horrors of the Year II. Many tried to appease workers by wearing red buttonholes, like Montalembert, or by donations to the February victims, like Rothschild. Flaubert's banker Dambreuse becomes a populist, claiming 'we are all workers now.' Many fled from the cities to their estates or, where rural unrest flared, from their estates to the nearest town. A château was pillaged in Loir-et-Cher. One Languedoc royalist ordered servants to stop ringing the château dinner-gong, lest the sound provoke his hungry tenants! Daumier's series of cartoons, *The Alarmists*, portrayed timid bourgeois alarmed at every group of children in the streets, every knock at the door, every rise in the price of fish. Their world appeared to be full of *jacqueries*, threats of railway nationalization or of army mutinies. Ominously the sub-commisioner appointed in Riom was the son of Babeuf, the primitive communist whose 1796 conspiracy had represented the most radical phase of the Great Revolution.

In the Provisional Government only Lamartime, a romantic Catholic landowner, a sentimental republican who disclaimed any intention of spreading Jacobin revolution to Europe, reassured them.

Yet the elites' panic was shortlived. In provincial towns they kept their heads down for a few weeks, then gradually re-emerged unscathed. Full-scale municipal council purges had occurred only in industrial cities like Lyon and Limoges. In the Gironde only seventeen of 544 municipalities changed hands. The jabbering, incoherent Thiers of February regained his nerve and began plotting. *Notables* formed electoral committees. Clergy, who sympathized with the revolt against 'Voltairean' Orleanism, had been alarmed by outbursts of popular anticlericalism into demands for order. The April elections gave the conservatives the opportunity to restore their class rule through the manipulation of universal suffrage in a still-rural France. They hoped to scare peasant proprietors with talk of Jacobin *commissaires* and urban *partageux*, to infuriate them with images of idle Parisian socialists living on the dole. They blamed the republic for the land-tax increase and continuing agrarian depression. The election became an unequal battle between Ledru-Rollin's *commissaires*, and the teachers, mobilized by Carnot on the one side and the greater power of the traditional *notables* and clergy on the other – although only sixteen of seventy clerical candidates were elected, and a minority of clergy supported the republic. De Tocqueville, unsympathetic to the republicans, claimed that there had been few revolutionaries in history more stupid, for they had gratuitously alienated the peasantry. Of the republican *commissaires* only Pierre Joigneaux in the Côte-d'Or appeared sufficiently familiar with peasant grievances to suggest a persuasive radical agrarian programme.

The result was disaster for the republicans. Of 900 elected deputies, barely 270 were republicans. Only 80 were radicals or socialists. Over 500 were crypto-royalists, though most stood simply as 'conservatives'. *Notables* and the middle-bourgeoisie dominated the assembly, though 30 workers were elected. De Tocqueville claimed that the new assembly contained more gentry, landowners and clergy than the Orleanist parliament. In the Nord legitimists and Orleanists patched up an alliance in face of worker unrest. In the west, legitimists, with clergy support, stood alone in their rural fiefs. In eastern France, conceding the shadow to retain the substance of power, *notables* hid behind moderate republican lawyers, and in Paris they voted for social Catholics like Buchez to keep out the far left. Only in 23 departments, south of a line from the Ain to the Gironde, did the left make a real impression.

The new government was dominated by moderates, with Ledru-Rollin as the token radical. Electoral success gave the *notables* the self-confidence to contemplate confronting the threat from the workers. Faced with a common enemy, legitimists, Orleanists and republican moderates like Marrast buried their differences. Thiers, that scourge of the Jesuits, became an improbable ally of the clergy in Seine-Inférieure. 'Liberals' became counter-revolutionaries, while legitimists rallied to conservative liberalism. A *rue de Poitiers* group, headed by Baraguey d'Hilliers, sacked for brutality in Algeria, helped coordinate strategy. The rhetoric against idle 'red' scroungers was accentuated, pragmatic republic proposals to stimulate rail-building by selective nationalization was greeted by

Montalembert as creeping socialism. The way to revive business confidence, claimed rail-director Rothschild, was simple – break up strikes and end labour unrest.

II The Republic and the Workers

The spring and early summer of 1848 were dominated by the determined efforts of urban workers to achieve a social republic. No amount of talk about 'universal fraternity' could erase the bitter memory of the betrayal of 1830, evoked even by the moderate artisans of *L'Atelier*. Working-class crowds in February imposed the republic, and forced the Provisional Government to include the socialist writer Louis Blanc. They demanded rights as workers, not merely as citizens – forcing the rhetorical concessions of the 'right to work'. Piecemeal and token concessions were made to appease a mobilized, restive working class and to buy time. Within weeks the political uncertainty created by the revolution undermined fragile business confidence and, as the weak economic recovery foundered, Parisian unemployment rose rapidly to 60 per cent of the city's 340,000-strong workforce.

Faced with demand for a ministry of labour and state aid for cooperatives, government moderates felt impelled to give the impression of activity. They created 'national workshops', little more in practice than the charity workshops utilized to aid the jobless in 1830–1. It was hoped that this would both calm worker agitation and, because of the overtones of Blanc's 'social workshops', serve to discredit socialist ideas. Interior Minister Marie hoped to use them to organize and discipline workers. In March, jobs were arranged for workshop members to keep them away from Blanquist demonstrations for an election postponement to allow the left time to propagandize provincial France. In April they were paid to distribute antisocialist election propaganda. However, artisans rapidly grew bitter at performing menial unskilled navvying tasks for under half their normal pay – and public works engineers expressed alarm at the 'contamination' of their own employees by workshop militants.

As a substitute for a ministry of labour the workers were offered the palliative of the Luxembourg Commission, in which elected delegates from Parisian trades were to debate industrial problems.

Marx insisted that, since it lacked a budget and real power, this was doomed to impotent rhetoric. However, it did function as a focus of worker organization, urging worker unity transcending craft divisions. Vinçard's *Journal des Travailleurs* insisted that the 'right to work' meant not the outdoor relief of the national workshops, but the right to receive the fruits of one's labour from exercising one's own profession, which alone guaranteed dignity. The Commission also became the nucleus for producer cooperative experiments in which 50,000 Paris workers became involved. Philippe Bérard's tailors' cooperative won orders for National Guard uniforms. The Luxembourg helped workers to realize that they should act as producers, not as atomized voters. Sceptical of Blanc's patronizing insistence that they should rely on the goodwill of a benevolent republic, workers came to stress self-emancipation. Small masters and journeymen took problems over apprenticeships, 'dilution' and sweating to the Luxembourg and won great workers' presence on the *conseils des prud'hommes*. A committee was set up to coordinate worker candidates for the April elections, and the craft corporations whose members swelled the political demonstrations of the Parisian spring had their hopes fired on the Luxembourg.

Levels of worker militancy in provincial France varied enormously. In smaller Nord textile towns, Luddism and anti-Belgian xenophobia were the main activities. Company towns were generally quiet – at Decazeville the manager told assembled workers that *he* remained more powerful than any distant republican government. In Nantes, surrounded by a hostile Catholic countryside, workers put their trust in the anticlerical republican, Dr Guepin, who assured them that class violence was unnecessary, that the elites would not resist reform, and refused to purge Orleanists from the municipal council. Militancy was similarly defused in Vienne and Rheims by Cabetist social-pacifist leaders. Striking miners in Anzin won wage concessions with aid from neo-Jacobin *commissaire* Delescluze, but Loire miners' initial enthusiasm for the revolution was unsustained.

However, the Parisian labour movement did not lack allies. Government orders for silk flags from the Lyon silk industry were a minor palliative which failed to calm agitation in the city. Convent-workshops were assaulted, and 8000 workers enrolled in 167 clubs. Propaganda among the garrison led to a troop mutiny in

March, and the Croix-Rousse became a 'no-go' area for the authorities, with a worker's militia (the *Voraces*) patrolling the streets, even delivering mail. Lyon *canuts*, Limoges porcelain-workers, Marseille tailors, all demanded financial aid for cooperatives as an alternative to navvying tasks. However, financial limits made it impossible for the Marseille authorities to afford a major port renewal project. Entry of workers into the National Guard provoked tensions in Limoges, Toulon and elsewhere. The worker-republican alliance disintegrated in Toulouse, where a 'liberal' councillor told the unemployed that 'men who know how to die, weapons in hand, in defence of liberty . . . know how to die of hunger out of respect for order!' By April, Joly's municipality was resisting strikes and demonstrations for worker access to the militia. Paris workers did have potential allies – though undoubtedly the worker movement was deficient in national coordination.

Much attention focused on the April elections, for which the most effective mass mobilization machine proved to be the Parisian club movement. Flaubert provides an unflattering image of large, noisy, disorderly gatherings of the unwashed, doctrinal babels, distinguished by a profusion of absurd messianic hopes. Male chauvinists of the left, like Daumier, shared Flaubert's contempt for 'unnatural' feminist demands. P. Amann's analysis is, however, more sober. He sees the clubs' goal as pragmatic – the provision of a crash course in political education for a mass audience. At their peak, 200 clubs had 75,000 members. When George Sand locked herself out of her apartment, all three locksmiths in her *quartier* were absent at club meetings. A 75 per cent Parisian turnout in the elections testifies to some success in registering voters. They succeeded in popularizing slogans, in hammering home the distinction between a purely formal and a 'social' republic. Revolutions are about *power* and, more than the cooperative movement, the clubs attempted to exercise 'dual power' – to be the soviets of 1848. However, their deficiencies were serious. They were cumbersome, no substitute for a revolutionary party. Their debates and resolutions, electoral lists and demonstrations, failed to add up to a political strategy. The 250 delegates sent to propagandize the provinces included key militants who would have been more effective in the capital. Their links with the craft cooperatives were weak. They put up too many obscure election candidates, and were fragmented by personal rivalries between Blanqui and fellow socialist club-leader Barbès, accentuated by fraudulent government evidence that Blanqui had acted as a police spy.

Election defeat halted the momentum of the worker movement. Even in Paris, the socialists won only six of 34 seats. In Limoges, where porcelain-workers had challenged the elites by demands for producer cooperatives and access to the National Guard, 3000 troops put down an insurrection provoked by the drowning of the urban socialist vote by the anti-republican, anti-tax vote of the Haute-Vienne peasantry. In Rouen, where tension between the elite and radical Commissaire Deschamps had been growing over the cost of workshop relief for 7500 unemployed, and over his 'leniency' towards Luddism, post-election bitterness escalated into rioting, which left 39 dead. A new savagery was entering social relations, captured by a Daumier cartoon, described by Baudelaire, in which arrogant uniformed Rouen bigwigs assemble, whilst a judge with shark-like teeth scratches a bullet-ridden corpse with his claws, murmuring, 'Ah, that Norman! He's only shamming dead to avoid answering to justice.'

Workers became grim and sullen as hopes faded. Parisian clubs declined by two-thirds in the month after the election. On 16 May bourgeois National Guards' units smashed an ill-planned, unarmed demonstration which had invaded the assembly in support of the Polish cause. The government, claiming that this was an attempted coup, seized club records, sacked radical police chief Caussidière, and arrested Blanqui, depriving the left of a potential leader for the forthcoming confrontation. Unlike Blanc, Blanqui had had no faith in the ability of the republic to bring socialism, and had warned that premature elections would hand France back to the elites. He had learned the lesson from his 1839 fiasco that a coup could only succeed in conjunction with a broader mass movement, and thus bided his time in 1848 until the workers' early illusions had been shattered. Sadly for this revolutionary Hamlet, he delayed too long, and was again in prison when the conflict exploded.

The elites were now eager for a showdown. De Tocqueville claimed that he had never harboured any hope of a peaceful settlement. The socialist peril could only be 'stopped all at once by a great battle'. His memoirs provide a vivid insight into the class prejudices of a French 'liberal'. Socialism is ascribed to greed not need, for workers' conditions, allegedly, were improving. Workers, whose slogan was 'the right to work', in protest against unemployment, are seen as demanding 'remedies against that disease which has afflicted man since the beginning of his existence, work'! His account of the invasion of the assembly is pervaded by a deep-seated aristocratic distaste at the sight and smell of alien beings from a different world. As a prison reformer, de Tocqueville should, perhaps, have connected Blanqui's appearance as an ashen-faced 'mouldy corpse' with the fact that he had just spent nine years in jail after the 1839 coup attempt!

As McKay shows, conservatives, infuriated by images of scroungers idling on street-corner at taxpayers' expense discussing socialism, shared de Tocqueville's taste for a decisive confrontation. Troops were moved towards Paris, and placed under General Cavaignac– a republican, but a man brutalized by a colonial war in Algeria and outraged at leftist plans to put Algeria under civilian rule. The involvement of 14,000 national workshop men in the 15 May demonstration confirmed conservative opinion that these had outlived their usefulness, and should be closed, even if this provoked insurrection. Socialist victories in a Paris by-election on 4 June appeared to confirm a shift to the left in the city. On 22 June the workshops closed; Cavaignac's troops waited while barricades were raised before intervening.

Fifty thousand workers took up arms, of whom some 1500 were killed, nearly twelve thousand arrested. Though the rising had no formal leadership, 80 per cent of those arrested came from the clubs, National Guard or workshops which provided a loose organizational framework for the insurgents. In essence, the assertions of Marx and de Tocqueville that this was a 'class war' are clearly true. The issue at stake was clear. Recent historians have provided nuanced social analysis of the insurrection. Among the insurgents were café owners and wine merchants from popular quarters, and tenants whose focus of hatred were landlords. Rent arrears had built up since February, and many tenants were arrested after landlords tipped off the forces of order. Many small masters fought alongside their journeymen, out of hatred for merchant capitalists who controlled market outlets and accelerated the division of labour. In general the workers involved were skilled men – though groups like tailors involved in cooperative projects were underrepresented, while engineering workers from large plants, such as Cail or La Chapelle locomotive works, were heavily involved. Building workers and metalworkers were the most prominent groups among those arrested, whereas unskilled and unorganized groups such as the transport workers were under-represented. The victors included 25,000 regular troops and National Guard units from western Paris. These included some luxury artisans, building workers dependent on big contractors for jobs, and some workers who saw the republic as threatened. However, most were shopkeepers, clerks, landlords and commercial travellers. Though Baudelaire fought for the insurgents, the confused, idealistic young intellectuals and students who had been liberals in the spring became, as Flaubert observes, the pessimistic, disillusioned champions of 'order' in June. Flaubert chronicles the savagery of reprisals against the prisoners, including summary executions. Property had been elevated to a religion; socialists were atheists, cannibals; the massacre was a holy war for civilization.

The artistic masterpiece of '1830' had been Delacroix's *Liberty Guiding the People* in which an Amazon figure leads bourgeois and worker together across the barricade. The masterpiece of June 1848 was, as Tim Clarke observes, Meissonier's *The Barricade*, a heap of corpses lying in a dark street, a sombre warning on the bloody reality of civil war to dissuade future rebels.

Twelve thousand *gardes mobiles* provided the most notorious element in the repression. Neatly turning paranoid bourgeoisie theories of the criminal and dangerous classes on their head, Marx called them lumpen-proletarians, 'scum' from the dregs of the poor, unleashed to fight for 'civilization' against honest, decent, socialist working men. Recent research has qualified but not destroyed this insight. Only 3 per cent of identifiable *garde mobiles* were from 'lumpen' trades; only 13 per cent were illiterate. They were distinguished largely by their youth – on average at twenty-one years of age they were thirteen years younger than the average insurgent. They were from the bottom of the skill hierarchy, youths who would have been apprentices were it not for the depression and the technological threat to the artisan trades. They lacked craft tradition or solidarity, had been exposed to heavy unemployment and, in consequence, had been easily recruited by prospects of food, uniforms, rifles and the chance of licenced violence against older, married skilled workers.

Trapped in the middle, in impotent agony, were the Montagnard radicals. Marx's accusations that the June days saw them 'betray' the proletariat is slightly unfair. Men like Flocon and Joigneaux had spent time in Orleanist jails. They were neo-Jacobins, seeing themselves as allies of the *petit peuple* against exploiters. They favoured social reform and associationist 'socialism' in a democratic republic. When suffrage produced a reactionary majority, which proceeded to confront the workers, they were trapped on sterile middle ground, sympathizing with the workers but not with an insurrection against an elected government. They did not, however, become 'reactionary'. They had urged workers to be patient, to wait until the next election, and not to be provoked into a suicidal rising. They now pleaded in *La Réforme* for clemency, and for social reform, to stop the workers being a pariah class.

The workers' movement was now in retreat – a process accelerated by tightening repression and growing weary disillusionment. In 1848 Daumier had drawn a fat bourgeois Parisian eyeing in amazement a worker eagerly reading a political newspaper. By 1850, Daumier's Parisian workers sit cynically on a wall criticizing all deputies as idlers on 25 francs a day. Their hopes and militancy had turned sour. As Merriman has shown, an embryonic police state gradually dismantled the urban left, and its capacity to coordinate national movement. The powerful Limoges's labour movement was stifled – its press prosecuted, its cooperative dissolved as 'secret societies'. A bourgeois militia patrolled worker suburbs and an increased garrison had its troops changed regularly to avoid seduction by militant porcelain-workers. The radical deputy for Toulon, Suchard, was exiled and in the naval dockyard foremen supervised election voting and sacked 'reds'. Lyon, the 'Rome of socialism', elected artisan socialist deputies in May 1849, but a rising in June against French support for the papacy, in which 120 insurgents died and 1200 were arrested, signalled a state of siege which persisted until the coup d'état of December 1851. Police reports from the city continued to read like despatches from 'colonial administrators in some violent, exotic, vaguely understood territory', but the estimated 25,000 socialists were reduced to activity within a still extensive cooperative movement.

Indeed the post-June days labour movement's main refuge in unfavourable circumstances now lay in producer and consumer cooperatives. In so far as this had a 'leader', it was Proudhon. He had been ill-at-ease in the politics of 1848, with no faith in the Jacobin republican tradition either in its Blanquist revolutionary form or in Blanc's state socialist reformism. February was soon 'lost in the emptiness of words'. He wandered the streets in a daze during the June days, sympathizing with the workers but seeing insurrectionism as futile. Political strategies could not achieve social goals, he insisted. Paradoxically he had been elected a deputy in June 1848, and won the hatred of a vengeful right and the reluctant admiration of the Montagnards of the left by daring to propose a bill, within days of the June insurrection, calling for a wealth tax to finance cheap credit schemes for cooperatives. Typically, his disappointment when the bill lost by 693 votes to two was due to the fact that his had not been the solitary vote in its favour!

His paper, *Le Peuple*, advocated cheap credit schemes in the form of a 'People's Bank' whose artisan members would use exchange notes, circulating as money on the strength of commodities already produced. The scheme, for all its deficiencies, attracted wide artisan support, symptomatic of a deep hatred of 'parasitic' financiers and a concern with a society based on the mutualist collaboration of small producers. Sadly, such a vision was a 'utopian' sidetrack which ignored harsh political realities. Across France, however, deprived of government sympathy, cooperative ventures struggled on. In Paris, the Clichy tailors' cooperative, in Lyon 22 producer-consumer cooperatives, and in Toulon cooperatives, communal restaurants, mutual aid societies and song groups, all survived. In Rheims, despite harassment from police and private entrepreneurs, Dr Bressy coordinated a broad movement, including producer cooperatives, bakeries and grocers. In Nantes, a cooperative bakers' enterprise was dissolved by the police for corresponding with Proudhon.

Such repression was to reduce the possibility of worker resistance to the coup. To some extent, a limited recovery in the industrial sector had already defused some workers' protest. Unemployment fell in the Nord from 1849, meat consumption rose, the death rate in Lille fell. There was a tentative revival in Paris construction. Marx saw this cyclical boom as spelling the end of the European revolutions, yet it remained a fragile growth, with fear of the 1852 elections sapping business confidence.

III The Resurgence of the Right (June 1848–51)

The government of General Cavaignac, which followed his repression of the June days, was, claimed the radical Catholic Lamennais, 'assuredly not the republic, but around its tomb the saturnalia of Reaction'. Recently, however, F. de Luna has made a valiant effort to salvage the general's reputation as a liberal republican. He argues that it was the conservative majority in parliament which repeatedly sabotaged Cavaignac's reformist measures. Efforts were made to implement Carnot's plans for free primary education, even after Carnot himself had been jettisoned to appease the right. Republicans remained sympathetic to associationist schemes, appointed social Catholics, like the artisan-deputy Corbon, to parliamentary committees, voted three million francs to subsidize cooperatives, and rejected doctrinaire laissez-faire. Public relief expenditure on the unemployed continued, if at reduced levels. State subsidies were given to public works projects and to Algerian colonization schemes designed to ease metropolitan unemployment. If the 'right to work' was abolished and income tax rejected this was only because republican deputies were outvoted.

Such revisionism is rather too kind to Cavaignac. His initial cabinet included the orthodox financier Goudchoux, a firm opponent of the national workshops, and Sénard, the *procureur-général* responsible for repression in Rouen. In heavily garrisoned Paris, clubs were suppressed and press freedom circumscribed. A parliamentary enquiry blamed the peaceful Louis Blanc for the June insurrection, forcing him into exile. 'Pure' republicanism was exposed as a hollow ideology, lacking a coherent social base in a France polarized by economic crisis and class-hatreds, in which defenders of 'order' yearned for strong government, and sections of republicanism's potential petty-bourgeois and peasant clienteles, faced with bankruptcy, felt the pull of political extremes. The centre of French politics could not hold.

The involvement of National Guards units from 53 departments in the suppression of the June days delighted de Tocqueville, basking in the rediscovered harmony of landed elites and 'their' peasants in the face of the socialist urban scum. Breton and Norman peasants kept guard on their fields to ward off assaults by mythical bands of communists. With the press thundering against proletarian 'cannibals', the right's confidence flooded back. They seized the initiative, hounded Carnot from office, denounced republican prefects like Marc Dufraisse in the Indre as crypto-communists. Autumn municipal elections apparently confirmed the drift to the right, with a mere ten *Conseils Généraux* headed by republicans, and 50 per cent of July Monarchy mayors re-elected. The savage mood of the conservatives was epitomized by the oratory of Thiers in his parliamentary assaults on an anodyne bill designed to prevent rich parents purchasing replacements for conscripted sons. Anyone who criticized the existing system as inegalitarian was a communist. The poor welcomed such opportunities to earn money. An army officered by the elites, commanding conscripts from the masses, mirrored that 'natural hierarchy of society which one cannot change'.

Thiers remained a key figure in the 'rue de Poitiers' group which coordinated conservative strategy. Faced with the socialist peril, legitimists and Orleanists buried atavistic squabbles over the dynasty or the role of Catholicism in education. Landowners and businessmen, 'nobles' and bourgeois discovered material interests in common. They would stand or fall together. Paradoxically only a republic offered a framework for political unity in the short term, for suggestions of a restoration would merely revive dynastic rivalries. Intra-class ideological feuds were shelved. The liberal-Catholic Montalembert allied with ultramontane Veuillot. The Voltairean Thiers praised Catholic education. The title of one Thiers pamphlet, distributed in its thousands throughout France, epitomized the basis for these reconciliations. It was called 'On Property'.

Yet presidential elections, scheduled for December, posed problems for the elites. Selection of a Party of Order candidate against Cavaignac ran two major risks. Any candidate with a royalist background might rekindle dynastic divisions. Above all the peasantry, however disillusioned with the republic's tax policy and neglect of their grievances, would not necessarily, except in the legitimist heartlands, vote for a royalist. With Cavaignac viewed by most *notables* as too 'liberal', the right's dilemma was acute.

The dark horse in the campaign was Louis Napoleon. Two mock-heroic invasion attempts by the great Napoleon's nephew during the July Monarchy had ended in farce. When he returned to France in 1848 many *notables* scorned him as a buffoon. Yet his name, a vague reputation as a social reformer, an astute feel for public opinion and opportunistic political manoeuvre and shrewd propaganda won him a populist following. During the June days Bonapartist slogans had mixed with socialist demands. While the political significance of his campaign remained vague and ambiguous, he had the advantage of appearing as a fresh candidate, untarnished by the failures of Orleanism or the republic. *Notables* feared his populism and warned that Bonapartism might mean war, which could radicalize the revolution. And yet, scared of the radical Ledru-Rollin, unenthusiastic about Cavaignac and aware of the danger of fielding their own candidate, most rallied reluctantly to Louis Napoleon.

Marx commented acidly that, because he was nothing, Louis Napoleon could appear to be everything. Guizot gave a reluctant admiration to a candidate who stood as guarantor of order, revolution and national glory – locating him simultaneously on the right, on the left, and 'above' party politics. He capitalized on the multifaceted, ambiguous resonance of the Napoleonic myth. He stood for law and order against the red peril – and for the peasant gains of 1789 against 'feudal reaction'. Catholics valued the 1801 Concordat, while bourgeois Protestants recalled that Bonapartism had sheltered them from the White Terror. Urban workers, for whom Cavaignac was the 'June butcher', were not unresponsive to propaganda emphasizing Bonaparte's social concerns and his lack of ties to the economic elites. His rural propaganda avoiding the right's stale rhetoric of religion and the family, hinted at agrarian reforms and tax cuts, appealing to a volatile peasantry devastated by agrarian crisis, indebtedness, low crop prices and involved in widespread tax resistance against Cavaignac's troops. With Orleanism linked with 'usurious' financiers, legitimism with the threat of a return to the seigneurial system, republicanism with the 45 per cent land tax increase and socialism implying confiscation of farms, Bonapartism appeared the logical repository of a peasant protest vote. Two leading politicians of the Second Republic, Nadaud and Joigneaux, from rural backgrounds in the Limousin and Burgundy, both stressed in their autobiographies that they derived their radical politics in part from their fathers. Yet the elder Nadaud, a peasant-stonemason, and the elder Joigneaux, a wine-carter, were both fervent admirers of Napoleon I.

Louis Napoleon simultaneously wooed the elites with promise of 'order' and hints of aid for Catholic education and the papacy. He was the one candidate who could offer a charismatic name, a populist urban and rural appeal together with assurances for the propertied classes. The result was a sweeping election triumph, in which only parts of the Midi and the west and some towns resisted the Bonapartist landslide.

In much of rural France Bonaparte was embraced not as a 'conservative' but as a charismatic messiah, offering hopes of agrarian reform. In one Alsace village voters trooped behind a figure dressed in Napoleonic uniform to reclaim communal forest lands. In Loir-et-Cher Bonapartist peasants drank and fired guns in church on polling day. Many marched to the polling-booths chanting 'Death to the rich!' or 'Aristocrats and usurers to the guillotine!', scarcely the usual rhetoric of the Party of Order. 10 December was thus, as Marx observed, a peasant revolution by proxy. Peasant France, devastated by agrarian crisis, yet too dispersed and unorganized to produce its own national political party, put its trust in a saviour, a resurrected legend, a name made famous since 1815 in the villages by the stories of army veterans in the *veillées*, by lithographs, by the iconography of the *images d'Épinal*. In congratulating themselves on the defeat of Ledru-Rollin most *notables* failed to perceive the mood of latent rural revolt which had fuelled the Bonapartist vote.

The elites' complacency was accentuated when Louis Napoleon chose his first cabinet from the Party of Order. They eagerly sought and achieved a rapid dissolution of parliament, in the confident expectation that fresh elections would eliminate the remaining radical deputies. In the May elections they had the advantage of lavishly financed propaganda orchestrated by the Rue de Poitiers. Interior Minister Faucher, a sometime critic of Orleanist 'corruption', disclaimed any intention of exerting administrative pressure. Yet radical local officials were sacked, left-wing propaganda impeded, opponents intimidated by house searches. With no assurance of a secret ballot, tenants and sharecroppers could be intimidated by landowners, tradesmen by wealthy clients, workers in company towns by employers. Yet the right's electoral triumph proved oddly muted. The republicans slumped to 11 per cent of the poll. The right, with some 50 per cent of the poll, won a clear majority in parliamentary seats. Alarmingly, however, a 'democratic-socialist' radical alliance polled nearly 40 per cent, 2.3 million votes. Its sweeping success in rural areas of central and southern France shook the conservatives' naive trust in the peasantry as a solid anti-socialist bastion. Exorcized from the cities, the red spectre began to haunt the countryside. Within two years, predicted an alarmed *Journal des Debats* as the left made substantial by-election gains in 1849–50, France might face a legally elected 'socialist' majority.*

The rhetoric of religion permeated the political discourse of the right in these years. In the summer of 1849, contravening article 7 of the constitution, the government committed the apostasy of sending troops to crush a sister republic in Rome to restore papal tyranny. The left's disgust, expressed by protest demonstrations in Paris and Lyon, provoked a state of siege in sixteen departments and the exile of leading radical politicians. In 1850 the Falloux Law extended clerical education controls by placing bishops in the *Université* and on departmental education councils, abolishing restrictions on Catholic secondary pupil numbers, and by permitting the religious orders to teach without a teaching certificate (*brevet de capacité*). Teacher training colleges were placed under tight supervision, radical teachers and anticlerical academics like Michelet sacked. Leading Catholic laymen Montalembert and Falloux became key spokesmen of the Party of Order. The former insisted that France was the scene of a Manichean conflict, in which the only remaining choice was between Catholicism and communism. Men of property were survivors of the shipwreck of civilization, clinging to a life raft in a hurricane. He justified the law of 30 May 1850, which disenfranchised some 30 per cent of voters, including migrant workers who lacked a fixed residence and anyone with a police record, as a 'moralization' of the electorate, an 'internal Roman expedition'.

During the 1840s liberal Catholics, led by Montalembert himself, had sought to reconcile Catholicism with '1789', claiming rights for Catholic schools in the name of liberal pluralism. Catholic democrats like Lamennais exposed the cause of subject Poles and Irish. Social Catholics like Ozanam and Maret, if critical of state collectivism, urged that Catholics support social reform, for the

---

* For the significance of peasant 'socialism' see pages 141–55.

masses had rights as well as duties. Catholic artisans of *L'Atelier*, like Corbon, espoused cooperative socialism, a social gospel which rejected resignation. Socialists like Leroux emphasized the links between socialism and the equality, fraternity and justice of primitive Christianity. Jesus the Carpenter stood for the dignity of manual labour. Christianity implied social justice, not a charity which humiliated its recipients, social solidarity not laissez-faire selfishness. Despite outbursts of popular anticlericalism, notably in Lyon, there was less hostility to priests in the spring of 1848 than in 1830. They were less tied to the fallen regime. Many *curés* appeared willing to bless trees of Liberty.

Yet this strange alliance of religion and liberty proved predictably fragile. Clergy supported conservatives in the April 1848 elections. Montalembert denounced schemes to nationalize the railways as creeping socialism, and was outraged, on inspecting prisoners among the defeated June insurgents, that 'not one had the air of being morally beaten, contrite or humiliated.' Veuillot, editor of the right-wing Catholic newspaper *L'Univers*, insisted that these rebels were 'reptiles and street vermin', suffering from 'pride not hunger'. For such bulwarks of Catholicism the church was a hierarchy, the pope a king. It was thus blasphemous that socialists should claim Christ as the 'author of their odious heresies'. Man was a brief traveller in a vale of tears, here to suffer. The poor, always with us, should be grateful for charity. The attitudes of such Catholic leaders towards work were firmly confident if self-contradictory. Work was man's punishment for original sin, insisted the 'liberal' Mgr Dupanloup. However there was no 'right to work', since society owed the workers nothing.

Such rhetoric was sweet music to the one-time Voltairean Thiers, who eagerly embraced the Catholics as allies and helped prepare the Falloux Law – though the intransigent Veuillot rejected this as involving a compromise with the 'atheist' *Université*.

The Catholic democrats were submerged by this torrent of reactionary verbiage. The progressive social-Catholic paper *L'Ère Nouvelle*, which had supported progressive taxation and social reform, collapsed. The handful of radical priests were hounded by the hierarchy; the warning of the Catholic radical deputy Arnaud de l'Ariège about the dangers of tying Catholicism to political reaction was ignored. Corbon was driven to abandon a church by which he felt betrayed. The subsequent ferocity of republican and socialist anticlericalism had its origins in the clergy's apostasy in these years. Proudhon demanded whether there remained a single honest man in France who did not ask himself, 'Shall I die without killing a priest?', and, in semi-seriousness, offered to forgive Louis Napoleon 'one-third' of his coup d'état if he allowed him to make war on the church. Nadaud claimed that he would die happy 'to the sounds of the churches crumbling under the hammers of the people'. Even de Tocqueville, who shared Montalembert's aristocratic background and conservative-liberal views, warned that religious extremism was generating an anticlerical backlash. 'For a long time I have thought,' he wrote, 'that after Voltaire, the greatest enemy that the church has in France is Montalembert.'

In the months after its narrow victory in the 1849 election the right became increasingly nervous about its precarious position. It remained dangerously fragmented. The bonds of common material interest in the defence of capitalist property relations could not obscure the divisions caused by history, family memory and dynastic loyalty. The intransigence of the exiled legitimist pretender, Chambord, sabotaged any deal with Orleanism. The legitimists' popular support only accentuated policy dilemmas. With their Catholic peasant and artisan clientèle in the Midi in deep economic distress, some legitimists were tempted to abandon Party of Order conservatism for a populist programme for their own ends. The *Droit National* faction argued that a radical-populist posture was necessary to retain popular support. The ensuing split between orthodox and 'populist' legitimists allowed the '*Dem-Socs*' to win a key by-election in the Gard in January 1850. Legitimist-Orleanist squabbling permitted the left to win a seat in the Gironde. The prefects and *procureurs-généraux* expressed alarm, and irritation with royalist politicians whose internecine feuds threatened their own class interests. The *PG* of Nîmes insisted that dynastic rivalries and friction between president and Party of Order caused uncertainties which prevented economic recovery and, hence, nurtured socialist extremism. Prefects argued that only a constitutional revision, to permit Bonaparte to stand again for the presidency in 1852, could guarantee stability. Yet, in the west and the Midi, legitimists' hatred for Bonapartism let them reject this strategy. Gradually the propertied classes grew impatient with their own squabbling politicians. The *PG* of Besançon denounced Jura *notables* who were haunted by the red spectre, yet unable to resolve their own feuds.

French elites remained uncertain on the best political strategy to adopt to defend their class interests. In 1850–1, as in 1799, faced with internal instability and renascent threats from the left, the authoritarian option appeared attractive. Defence of vested interests required the end of constitutional rule of law. Capitalism could function only with a strong bureaucracy given a free hand to restore 'order' and transcend party and class conflict. The upper bureaucracy, purged of the modest republican lawyers of 1848, was dominated by ex-Orleanist careerists. A few *PG*s retained residual liberal qualms about an authoritarian solution, but, as Forstenzer emphasizes, most came to view themselves as frontline soldiers, standing between civilization and anarchy. The Rhône *PG* endlessly denounced 'soft', unthinking civilian politicians. An incident in Toulouse, when Interior Minister Faucher sacked the prefect Maupas for a blatant attempt to plant evidence in a political trial, illustrates the nuances within the right. Louis Napoleon consoled Maupas by assuring him that his behaviour merited praise not reproach, promoting him to Paris Prefect of Police. Yet Faucher, the 'liberal', was a firm supporter of the idea of ending universal suffrage, and accepted the 1851 coup d'état as necessary to defeat socialism.

Louis Napoleon played his cards skilfully. There was an unobtrusive purge of overscrupulous prefects. The army was assiduously wooed with decorations and pay increases; the Bonapartist Saint-Arnaud replaced royalist Changarnier as war minister. He scared conservatives with rumours of the 'red peril', laying blame for dangerous uncertainty on assembly politicians. He cultivated the church, juggled with his cabinets. When the conservative parliamentary majority, alarmed at leftist by-election successes, disenfranchised over 30 per cent of the electorate with the law of 30 May 1851, he preserved his populist image by keeping aloof from such 'reactionary' measures. His provincial speeches were shrewdly varied. He flattered the church in the west, deplored the new suffrage law in the republican east. Yet he failed to secure a sufficient majority in parliament to revise the consitution to allow him to stand again for the presidency. Only a coup could prevent the end of his presidential career.

IV The Republic of the Peasants (1848–51)

In older histories of the Second Republic the period 1849–51 was neglected, viewed as a tedious interlude between the left's defeats of June and December 1848 and Louis Napoleon's inevitable promotion from president to emperor, and marked only by skirmishings between him and the royalist elites. Recent historiography has redressed the balance. For the left, exorcized from the cities, reorientated its effort to the countryside, developing an extensive peasant press and imaginative propaganda. Having gained nearly 40 per cent of the votes in May 1849, they won 21 of 30 by-elections in 1849–50, mainly in rural departments. Fear of a possible, if improbable, left-wing victory in the 1852 election provoked the May 1850 electoral law, which disenfranchised 30 per cent of the electorate and, finally, the December 1851 coup d'état – resisted by a major rural rising in central, south-eastern and south-western France.

One explanation for this radical mobilization has emphasized the *Dem-Soc*'s success in attracting small peasant cash-crop producers during an agrarian depression marked by the collapse of price levels. Ownership of their own small farms gave peasant proprietors some basis for independent political action denied to agricultural labourers or to sharecroppers. Economic insecurity bred dissatisfaction, while regular urban market contracts provided access to ideologies which explained the contradictions of existing society and offered alternatives. In the Jura, cheese and wine producers round Dôle and Poligny borrowed money to purchase land in the 1840s, then, hit by a 30 per cent price fall, fell into debt. Encouraged by local watchmakers, they became attracted to cooperative ideas. In the Alpine region wine, raw silk and hemp producers had, similarly, borrowed heavily to purchase extra land to exploit the pre-1845 price boom. Rising expectations were then rudely shattered. The Drôme silk crop fell 60 per cent in value between 1847 and 1848. Prefect Ferlay, reporting 70 per cent of owners to be in debt and fearing expropriation, stressed that this was the key to the left's gains. Propagandists addressed mass meetings in the bourgs denouncing businessmen who made millions 'from the misery of Alpine peasants'.

Margadant has attempted to minimize the role of indebtedness in securing an audience for the *Dem-Socs*, claiming that 'only' 100 of 7000 households round Crest, a centre of the 1851 insurrections, had been expropriated. His case is unconvincing. Nine of the 90 known leaders of the revolt in central Drôme had been expropriated. JPs in future insurrectionary areas had commented more frequently in the 1848 Agricultural Enquiry than colleagues elsewhere on the 'usury' problem. Margadant plays down the extent of official concern over the issue, implausibly denies the link between indebtedness and the popularity of the left's cheap credit proposals, and ignores the psychological impact which a handful of expropriations could have on tight-knit village communities. P. Levêque's study of Burgundy emphasizes that much peasant indebtedness went unrecorded in the notarial records on which Margadant relies. 'Usurers' advanced peasants money to pay off 'official' debts, but charged higher interest on the new 'unofficial' loans. In the Limousin, where JPs emphasized the debt issue in 42 of 52 cantons, one prefect confessed, 'I don't like to say this, but usury is one of the causes of socialist success.' In Bejuat (Creuse) one 'usurer' lent to the entire village, pastured his herds on peasants' land and acquired their crops at 50 per cent below market prices. In the Ardèche where antimoneylender sentiment was traditionally expressed in the hatred of the Catholic peasants for Protestant financiers, the Rhône prefect portrayed a peasantry 'enslaved by a despotism as onerous as that of feudal times . . . the despotism of money. Lyon merchants acquire raw silk at cut-price rates from peasants to whom they lend money.' In 1849 *Dem-Soc* propaganda against the 'bloodsuckers of the Ardèche' redirected atavistic sectarianism into class politics, winning seven seats by attracting Catholic votes. In 1851 the peasant rebels marched on Privas to 'burn the prefecture, mortage office and tax bureau'.

Dem-Soc newspapers, like the *Feuille du Village*, made 2 per cent credit a central electoral pledge, portrayed Bonaparte as too tied to financiers to fulfil his December 1848 promises, and patronized cooperative schemes, a sort of agrarian Proudhonism in which Jura peasants received credit from local traders on the security of produce stored in local cooperative cellars.

Small wine growers in Burgundy, the Mâconnais, the Jura and the Midi were among the left's rural converts. The manifesto of the left in lower-Languedoc, began 'the vine is the purest product of the love affair between soil and sun . . . wine is the old man's milk, the consoler of the afflicted, the support of the weak . . . !' Hérault wine prices in 1848–51 were 70 per cent below 1830s levels. Export prospects suffered from protectionist tariffs designed to safeguard industry. The *droits réunis* sales taxes reduced urban consumption, while flat-rate taxes discriminated against cheap *vin ordinaire* produced by small wine growers. With wine a labour-intensive crop, vineyard areas were densely populated and *vignerons* tended to live in large villages alongside wine-related groups of café owners, barrel- and cork-makers, and carters. For all its life-enhancing qualities, man cannot live by wine alone. Wine growers needed to market their crop to purchase food. *Dem-Soc* propaganda promised abolition of wine taxes, portrayed tax officials ('*rats de caves*') as bogeymen, and emphasized the solidarity of *vigneron* interests with those of urban artisans – for only if the latter had decent wages could they afford wine.

Wine regions provide the only, partial exception to the general rule that peasant smallowners dominated rural radicalism. Agricultural labourers were isolated, subject to landowner pressure and, if in work, benefited from the low grain prices, which prevented repetition of the grain riots of 1845–7. However, as Margadant emphasizes, day labourers outnumbered peasant owners round the radical stronghold of Béziers (Hérault). The crucial factor in this precocious militancy of vineyard workers was, however, their close relationship with local small *vignerons*. Many smallowners, or their sons, did part-time day labouring on the big estates, and labourers and *vignerons* lived alongside each other in the large villages of the Mediterranean coastal plain.

Sharecroppers, too, were little touched by radicalism. E. Guillaumin's *La Vie d'un Simple* vividly evoked the deference of Allier sharecroppers, faced with short leases and the ever-present threat of eviction. The hero's father removes him from school when the '*maître*' expresses disapproval of education. Sharecroppers tended to be involved in quasi-subsistence polyculture farming, lacked market contacts, and during the price slump of 1848–51 were cushioned by paying rents in kind. Rural protest in the Allier was dominated by smallowners and lumbermen. Garrier has emphasized the political passivity of dependent winegrowing sharecroppers in the Beaujolais, although similar groups in the Mâconnais were to be roused by *Dem-Soc* propaganda in 1849.

This propaganda was an adaptation of artisanal 'associationist' socialism. Pierre Joigneaux's *Feuille du Village*, which circulated widely in central and eastern France, preached a 'fraternal' ideology, which advocated aid for the old, elimination of middlemen, rural cooperatives to store produce and avoid rapid sales on depressed markets. 'Association' could, it was stressed, resolve difficulties produced by the division of land. 'Small resources will be pooled and become powerful.' Joigneaux insisted that the authentic values of village culture were collective not individualistic. Like Russian *narodniks*, he perceived in the traditional practices of the countryside, such as Breton village dances which flattened the soil for house-building, evidence of an age-old doctrineless village communism, the seeds of future socialism. Police repression of cooperative associations, as in the Cher in 1851, helped heighten peasant political consciousness.

Margadant, while acknowledging the 1848–51 price slump, insists that agrarian depression cannot be used as a blanket explanation of rural radicalism. Grain areas of northern France suffered from low prices yet remained 'conservative'.* With wine growers and rural artisans, as consumers, benefiting from low food prices, there was no repetition of the subsistence crisis of 1846–7. Although Margadant pushes his case too far, ignoring the extent to which alarmed prefects correctly emphasized that rural distress was feeding radical recruitment, it is certainly true that no crude economistic model alone can provide the key to rural politics.

The peasantry's response to the economic crisis was mediated through their culture. Historians such as Weber and Bercé have argued for an 'archaic-primitivist' model, in which the alleged 'politicization' of the countryside in these years is portrayed as merely a traditional peasant *jacquerie*. The tax revolts in south-western France in 1848 witnessed an age-old pattern in which village columns, summoned by church bells and drums, marched on the nearest bourg, where they burned tax records exorcizing the mysterious power of the written word, pillaged cafés, got drunk and went home. Such 'pre-political' behaviour is viewed as posing no

---

*One could explain the greater 'conservatism' of the northern cereal-growing countryside by emphasizing the scattered habitat of the north, the fact that cereal growers had fewer tax and tariff grievances against the government, and by greater rural-urban friction. Barrel-makers and cork workers in Midi small towns shared a common interest in the wine trade with *vignerons*. Northern factory workers and cereal-growers shared no such mutual interest – and were potentially hostile as grain consumers and producers.

serious threat to the social order. E. Weber, whose pre-railway rural France is isolated, autarkic, lacking in market-relationships, sees the very idea that patois-speaking, superstitious peasants, conscious of the distant state only via the tax collector, could be involved in national politics as absurd. At best they knew the name of Bonaparte. Alleged evidence of class war in rural France is thus dismissed as a mere extension of paranoid feuds between town and countryside, exemplified by the peasant invasion of Crest (Drôme) in December 1851. The peasantry was too fragmented to be a class 'for-itself'. Much peasant mobilization continued to occur, as in the brief June 1849 Brande des Mottes rising in the Allier to protest at Bonaparte's Rome expedition, out of deference to a radical local *notable*. In the Alps 'politics' was, in effect, feuding between rival clans of 'red' and 'white' landowners. In the southern Massif, Jones has, similarly, portrayed the peasantry as the pawns in feuds between Catholic conservative rural elites and the 'neo-Jacobin' Protestant merchants and artisans of small towns like Millau and Rodez.

Baudelaire once cooled the ardour of a Dijon bourgeois radical by terrifying him with a vision of a 'ferocious bestial socialism of fork and scythe'. Yet this primitivist model of peasant protest is the rural equivalent of the 'dangerous classes' myth – and was to be cultivated by Bonapartists to justify repression after the December 1851 coup. Round Clamécy (Nièvre) the wood-floaters and peasant rebels of 1851 were told by their leader, Milletot, that 'probity is the first virtue of a republican', and kept strict discipline. The brutality came from the troops, who behaved 'as if in Africa' in smashing the rising. Weber's portrait of market isolation and antiurbanism fits areas of the south-west better than it does radicalized regions of the Midi or the centre, where links between countryside and the towns were close. If the 1848 south-western tax revolts *were* more concerned to retreat from the state than to capture it, only nine of the 300 tax-revolt centres rose in 1851. 'Antiurbanism', in the form of peasant fear of urban socialism, was stronger in conservative Normandy than in the Midi.

Indeed, in pardonable over-reaction against such 'archaic' models, Margadant has emphasized cultural 'modernization'. Radical areas were 'proto-urban', with expanding economic horizons and rising expectations. Falling birth rates denote use of contraceptive practices. Market contacts made education valuable.

Literacy rates rose from 40 per cent to 67 per cent in the Var in 1837–50, accentuating generational conflict as educated youths contested their elders' traditional authority and wisdom. This explains the ferocity of Thiers's attack on lay schoolteachers, for in Weber's traditionalist countryside the teacher would still have been a marginal figure. The degree of involvement of teachers in leftist politics varied widely. In Basses-Alpes the majority kept a cautious low profile after Carnot's dismissal, and only sixteen (4 per cent) were arrested after the coup. Yet a teacher was elected as *Dem-Soc* deputy in the Nièvre; in Burgundy prefects expressed anxiety at teachers reading radical papers to the peasants in cafés. In Clavreux (Jura) there were demonstrations in support of sacked teachers.

Nevertheless, this cultural 'modernization' thesis requires careful qualification. Radical Jura was less literate than neighbouring Catholic-conservative Doubs. In the Loiret, royalist Sologne and the radical Gâtinais forest area shared low literacy levels. The cultural roots of peasant militancy have been exposed most convincingly in M. Agulhon's brilliant analysis of the complex interplay of 'archaism' and 'modernity' in the Var. Provençal peasants involved in a cash-crop economy of wine, olives and cork, were politicized through the 'cultural brokerage' of rural artisans and petty bourgeois, who were their neighbours in the large villages and small towns – not alien 'urban' intruders. Papers read aloud in cafés enabled ideas to circulate in a region of modest literacy. The rural bourgeoisie, here as elsewhere, were an ambivalent social force. As 'usurers' or bailiffs they were targets for peasant hatreds. Yet key figures in the politics of rural radicalism were, precisely, city-educated sons of middle peasants who maintained contacts with their village roots. The storm at the Paris salon of 1851 over Courbet's masterpiece, *Burial at Ornans*, arose, as Tim Clark emphasizes, from the painting's oblique suggestion of this complex rural social structure, which was deeply disturbing to conservatives who idealized a world of rustic tranquillity, remote from urban class conflicts. In the Var, bourgeois social clubs (*cercles*) were copied by peasant *chambrées*, which acted as the focus of village sociability, subscribed to newspapers, functioned as mutual aid societies and tried to evade the wine tax.

A complex dialectical process of continuity and change occurred. Elements of the traditional culture acted as a medium for the transmission of a new consciousness. In the Midi the 'folklore' culture permeated village life, integrating peasants with the community from cradle to grave. Villagers shared the duties of parenthood, adolescents entered the village youth group, which utilized *charivaris* to punish offenders against communal norms. There was an annual cycle of festivals and carnivals, bonfire dances at St Jean, blessing of the livestock at St Eloi. Unilinear 'modernization' theories which dismiss such practices as a barrier to politicization are inadequate, for their very vitality provided a medium for expressionist protest. Attachment to the village community gave peasants something to defend, while 'cultural brokerage' injected political language and perspectives, and gave the goal of a 'social republic' rather than a simple hatred of a distant northern state.

Charivaris, carnivals, farandole dances became protest vehicles. The vigorous tradition of protest songs against thieving millers or feudal seigneurs was directed against new targets. In the Midi, wedding guests began to carry red flowers. Radicals at Collioures (Pyrénées-Orientales) appropriated Mardi Gras festivities. *Mannequins*, ritually burned or beheaded at the climax of carnival, began to appear dressed in royalist white, or to resemble the local prefect. One prefect was made to dismount from his carriage and dance a farandole into the centre of a Var village. When police reacted by trying to harass or prevent such festive activities they became branded as enemies of cultural traditions of which the left became the defender.* Fêtes had always been periods of tolerated licence during which the elites patronizingly permitted a 'world turned upside down', secure in the knowledge that the remainder of the year would return to the world of hierarchy. 'At this privileged moment of time, two innocences were united – that of politics just beginning, that of the fête reaching its apogee,' wrote one French historian, with pardonable exaggeration.

Instead of abandoning peasant culture to the right, the *Dem-Socs* made a conscious effort to encourage and exploit peasant 'atavisms'. The journalist Pierre Joigneaux attempted to synthesize communal traditions with 'socialism', praising the oral, collective culture of work and community. The *veillée*, the evening gathering

---

* Basque nationalists made similar use of the Pamplona bull-fighting festival in Franco's last years.

in the barn, was praised as an ideal vehicle for transmitting ideas in areas of scattered habitat like the wooded, hilly, Morvan (Nièvre). The conversion of remote, barren Creuse to the left can be attributed in part to the influence of migrant peasant-stonemasons, 428 of whom were arrested in the June days, who brought to their villages an interest in literacy, birth control, socialist newspapers and a lack of deference. Yet elements in the local village culture allowed radical ideas to take root – an egalitarian social structure, fierce communal solidarity expressed in riots in 1849–50 against loss of communal rights, the *veillée* socialibility which allowed ideas to circulate without police control. Many prefects became alarmed as the left revamped *almanachs*, the staple diet of *veillée* reading matter, by augmenting their normal agricultural and medical tips with simplified *Dem-Soc* ideology. Ledru-Rollin pipes, statues of Christ the Worker, the songs of Pierre Dupont such as the *Chant des Vignerons*, flooded the countryside to rival Bonapartist iconography. Anti-conscription feeling, endemic in a society in which peasants relied on their sons' labour, was encouraged by propaganda against the 'parasitic' standing army, and the ritual inter-village brawls which traditionally marked the conscription-day drawing of lots in market towns, frequently metamorphosed into concerted attacks on the police.

Margadant's denial that the left were able to channel forest rights disputes from the sporadic wood-seizures of spring 1848 into electoral politics in 1849 or resistance to the 1851 coup is not totally convincing. The ongoing *révolte carnavalesque* of the Ariège *demoiselles* against the forest guards was translated into an 1849 electoral victory for the *Dem-Socs*, though bureaucratic repression of radical municipal cadres demobilized the left there before 1851. Round St Sauvier (Allier) perennial disputes over forest rights, marked by the assassination of the aristocrat forest-encloser de la Romagère in the 1830s, lay at the root of *Dem-Soc* gains. In the Ain and in Burgundy police reported forest invasions, accompanied by flags and socialist slogans. Forest expropriation by nobles in the Ardèche helped weaken Catholic-royalism. Twenty of the 48 Var villages with forest conflicts before 1848 witnessed risings in 1851, though politicization of such disputes was easier, where, as in Provence, they were adjacent to cash-crop peasant farming, than in the remote Pyrenees.

In Zola's *La Terre*, Jésu-Christ, the village 'red', is also the local poacher. The hero of E. Le Roy's *Jacquou le Croquant*, set in Périgord, is a young peasant who swears vengeance on the local landowner after his father has died in prison, convicted of poaching. The *Dem-Soc* press idolized poachers as village culture-heroes, as courageous Robin Hood figures. They demanded the abolition of the 25-franc hunting licence. Shoot-outs between poachers and police in Ardèche led to declaration of a state of siege there in 1851. Villagers' sympathy with poachers was cited as evidence of the 'depravity' produced by 'deplorable ideologies' by one Burgundian prefect. The 'anarchy' of forest regions was accentuated by the presence of independent-minded non-peasant elements. Lumbermen in the central departments, Yonne clog-makers and cork-workers in Provence were all active in rural radicalism. The wood-floaters of Clamecy (Nièvre), who floated logs down the River Yonne to Paris, were a constant source of alarm to local police. The threat to their trade from the depression and from railway competition, the efforts of the wood-merchants to disperse log-assembly away from Clamecy, and their occupational contacts with Paris made them a *Dem-Soc* vanguard. It is important to remember that the *Dem-Soc* movement became *rural*, but not exclusively 'peasant'.

Merriman's claim that the emerging 'police state' of 1848–51 effectively broke the back of the *Dem-Soc* movement, echoes Marx's assertion that bureaucratic repression inevitably demoralized a politically immature peasantry. Election meetings were banned. By December 1850, 185 newspapers had been prosecuted. Leftist by-election gains provoked the May 1850 law disenfranchising over 30 per cent of the electorate, including migrants and 'criminals', meaning in the village context, anyone with a poaching or forest conviction. Mayors were dismissed, municipal councils and National Guard units dissolved, teachers sacked. The purge extended down to the Allier postman, whose dog's red collar and white tail ribbon was taken to symbolize the victory of socialism over royalism, and to the Yonne school-gardener sacked for growing red flowers! Links between the national, departmental and village cadres of the *Dem-Soc* movement were broken. With Limoges heavily garrisoned, dozens of mayors sacked, radical politicians hounded by the police, the Limousin, which had voted heavily for the *Dem-Socs* in 1849, failed to resist the 1851 coup. In the Ariège, where the left had translated endemic forest conflicts into electoral success, persecution of municipal radical cadres snapped the tenuous ties with the national leadership.

Yet neither the Limousin nor Ariège were 'typical' of *Dem-Soc* rural bastions. Ariège was isolated and poorly integrated into the market economy. Limousin lacked concentrated habitat, and the militancy of its peasant-stonemason migrants was weakened by the Paris building upturn of 1850–1. The scale of resistance to the 1851 coup, with above 100,000 insurgents in twenty departments, suggests that Merriman over-estimates the effectiveness of repression. Suppressed newspapers re-emerged under new names. Police lamented their inability to control *colportage* of *almanachs*. Attempts to erode the political rights of newly enfranchised peasants provoked anger. Villagers resented persecution of their elected municipalities. In the Jura, where 75 per cent of mayors were 'agents of disorder', suspended mayors were re-elected. The mayor of Mèze (Hérault) returned from jail to a reception of bands, flowers and weeping women. In the Midi there was a positive correlation between municipal purges of 1849–50 and involvement in the 1851 rising. Mayors refused to draw up the revised restricted electoral lists after the May 1850 law, and the success of a mass petition, attracting over half a million signatures in protest at this law, contradicted the prefects' claims that peasants were congenitally indifferent to abstract political issues. A growing chorus of prefects and *procureurs-généraux* urged Paris to return to governmental appointment of mayors.

The regime had sufficient power to intimidate rural opposition, but not to suppress it. Village constables (*gardes-champêtres*) sometimes shared the radicalism of fellow villagers. One in the Ardèche was shot while dancing the *Ça Ira* on a café table! The *Procureur-Général* of Dijon saw the Saône-et-Loire local police as 'dangerous to use for political purposes'. Eighteen thousand paramilitary gendarmes were insufficient to attempt more than exemplary missions. Policing mixed arbitrary oppression with absurd ineffectuality. Police commissioners in the Gers were instructed that 'the times we live in do not permit neutrality between good and evil.' One was sacked for admitting that he reasoned with local socialists: 'I talk to them man to man, as if to humans not to horses.' A second was dismissed for expressing an 'attachment to the proletariat' by suggestion that unemployment boosted socialist support. Arbitrary arrests of café-owners, dismissal of mayors, police harassment of weekend dances antagonized Gers peasants and village artisans. The pragmatic PG of Nîmes deplored provocative policing strategies. Why send fifty troops to an Ardèche village when a red scarf was found on a tree? Why ban village fêtes when, 'unless the countryside is placed under a state of siege', this would merely 'incite disobedience and bloody the soil of every village in the *arrondissement*?' The net result was that 'men who are . . . harmless find themselves treated as if guilty. In their irritation they enter the general current of opposition to government.' In Vaucluse there were arrests at 29 funerals where mourners wore red ties. In Hérault over half of the 12 per cent of villages which resisted the coup had suffered such local arbitrary persecution. Midi juries, attached to local customs, tended to acquit those arrested at fêtes, so that bureaucrats came to view the jury system as incorrigibly flawed. As Marx noted sardonically, the red peril caused 'liberals' to come to perceive the rule of law itself as 'socialist'. Prefects cast envious eyes at Lyon, where a state of siege was permanently in force after June 1849. By 1851 four further departments had emulated this.

Repression drove the *Dem-Soc* underground. A network of some 700 secret societies coordinated the 1851 insurrection. In the Yonne electoral gains in 1849 had been spearheaded by the artisans and petty-bourgeoisie of towns like Joigny. But as urban cadres were persecuted, the centre of gravity shifted to the foresters, wood-floaters, clogmakers and peasant smallholders of the wooded Puisaye. The secret societies were led by village artisans, peasants, even day-labourers. Weber's argument that the *Dem-Soc* movement simply reflected the loyalty of villagers to republican *notables* is misleading. Agulhon shows how these latter lost control of the movement in Provence. In Canet (Pyrénées-Orientales) P. Mcphee has illustrated that the local republican landowner, Cassanyes, heir of a dynasty of *biens nationaux* purchasers, alarmed by a growing secret society militancy among the vineyard labourers which he was unable to control, came to welcome the 1851 coup together with his traditional legitimist rivals, the Lazermes family. The secret society movement adopted a quasi-Carbonarist ritual, involving oaths to defend the 'social and democratic republic' sworn at night, blindfolded, over crossed daggers. It was prepared for armed resistance, suggesting that not all the left shared that 'parliamentary cretinism' of which Marx accused them.

Margadant is thus correct in seeing in this movement evidence of a genuine politicization of a peasantry angered by police harassment and determined to defend their new political rights. And, for all their paranoid fantasies of plots and armed risings, the prefects and PGs did not cynically 'invent' a red peril to justify a coup. That peril existed, if, in part, of their own making. Their reports, as Forstenzer argues, were chronicles of their frustrated impotence to control the 'occult army of socialism', a 'disease' based on greed and envy which was spreading like a plague. The imagery of the language of their official reports is revealing. Cafés 'seduced' their customers. The peasantry in radical areas had 'gangrene'. Poaching, forest offences and *Dem-Soc* voting were symptoms of a deep-seated moral crisis. radical bourgeois leaders were physically and morally deformed *déclassés* who had roused the naturally apathetic masses. Yet, the masses were 'female'. They could be intimidated as well as seduced – but only by a Bonapartist coup.

The coup of 2 December occurred with the active participation of the army and the upper bureaucracy, for Bonaparte had carefully promoted his supporters into command posts during the previous months. The legalist scruples or royalist preferences of many subordinate officials were thereby neutralized by loyalty to their superiors. Radical politicians and known militants were arrested in their homes. Many conservative *notables* who felt little personal enthusiasm for Bonaparte reluctantly accepted the coup as necessary to end threat from the left. Only a few legitimist loyalists protested openly. Stock exchange shares rose rapidly. The clergy, with the exception of a handful of legitimists or convinced democrats, joyfully sang *Te Deums* to give thanks for the nation's deliverance from the spectre of socialism. Parisian workers, unwilling to take up arms to defend a conservative assembly, responded with a small insurrection in the eastern *faubourgs* when they heard of the arrest of *Dem-Soc* deputies. Twenty-seven soldiers were killed in repressing this. Possible protest in radical cities like Lyon was cowed by a massive show of military force.

The coup wrecked hopes, viewed by Marx as naive and millenial, of some *Dem-Soc* leaders that 1852 would bring electoral triumph. In seventeen departments of the centre, south-east and south-west more than 100,000 insurgents took up arms against it. With their national leaders arrested, mobilization occurred through the village secret-society network, whose contingency plans were activated. Towns like Béziers (Hérault) roused the surrounding countryside. Local leadership fell to peasants and village craftsmen. In the Drôme and Ardèche peasant columns marched on local market towns. However, faced with regular troops, with imprecise purpose, they began to lose heart when they realized that heavily-garrisoned cities had failed to rise. The Protestant peasants of the Cévennes found the Nîmes radicals already crushed by military occupation.

Contemporary political interpretations of this insurrection correspond, in an odd way, with those of recent historians. In order to win over liberal or royalist sceptics among the elites, Bonapartists described it as a primitive, brutal *jacquerie*, marked by rape and pillage. Guizot wrote to Morny of his approval of a coup which had saved France from such savages. The Drôme prefect, Ferlay, claimed that bourgeois republicans had been terrified to march at the head of such barbarians. Republican propagandists like Tenot in the 1860s portrayed the insurgents as sober, principled republicans, outraged by the violation of the constitution. Atrocity stories were a Bonapartist fabrication, at most the insurgents, led by republican bourgeois, stole weapons. The Third Republic enshrined this mythology by granting medals to the survivors in 1880. Socialist synthesized elements from these two interpretations, though, paradoxically, by emphasizing the social grievances of the insurgents, came closer to the Bonapartist thesis. While agreeing with Tenot that there were political motives, they emphasized that the goal was a 'social' republic. Insurgents were mobilized by economic grievances, peasants tried to seize estates, lumbermen held employers hostage. The secret societies frequently had cooperative and mutual aid functions. Political and social aspirations were intertwined, for the *Dem-Socs* had channelled dreams for a world without taxmen or usurers into a political programme.

1851 was, thus, as much the precursor of later rural socialism as of the bourgeois Third Republic. In the Haute-Alpes the 'pure' political republicans among the Protestants of Ventavon stood aloof from the rising, because their society 'which was formed only for the defence of universal suffrage, could have become a society for vandalism and brigandage'. This alarm on the part of bourgeois republicans was echoed, as Goujon shows, near Chalons in Saône-et-Loire. In Cuers (Var), Agulhon emphasizes the growing alienation from radical activities of republican elites, as local control was assumed by barrel-makers and *vignerons*. Yet the Aix PG was forced to confess that the Cuers rising had not been an undisciplined *jacquerie*, for its peasant and artisan leaders had maintained discipline, 'a certain moderation . . . a certain legality. Help me to find the correct word.'

The nature and extent of subsequent repression had major political consequences. At least 27,000 were brought to trial, probably many more. In some rebel departments only half those arrested were actually tried. Others were killed, wounded, or fled abroad – from the Jura into Switzerland for example. 9500 were sentenced to deportation to Algeria, 239 to Cayenne. Although 5400 peasants were tried, and 40 per cent of detainees in the Vaucluse were peasants, many of the rural rank-and-file escaped arrest. Two thousand café-owners were prosecuted. Radical bourgeois, like J-B Noir in Jura, received tough sentences even if they had played no part in the insurrection. They were loathed as ambitious immoral class-traitors who had threatened bourgeois class-rule by perverting the masses. Mayors and teachers were dragged in chains through village streets, insurgents tracked through the woods like animals. Hundreds of cafés were closed down. All this bequeathed a legacy of bitterness, family legends, a martyrology which made the 'regime of 2 December' an 'insult, not just a description' (V. Wright) in the countryside of the Midi and the centre. It lay at the heart of the revival of the left in these rural areas later in the century.

Analysis of the ferocity of repression must stress the inevitable qualifications. Some PGs retained legalistic scruples. Some prefects expressed tactical doubts that the savage repression of, for example, general Rostelau in Hérault, would prove counterproductive. Some of the *Mixed Commissions* established to sentence the insurgents showed leniency to 'misguided' rustics. Louis Napoleon commuted one-third of Algerian sentences, amnestied forest offenders. With the left smashed and insurgent villages terrorized, the Basse-Alpes tried to avoid further repression by registering a 74 per cent pro-Bonaparte vote in 1852 elections. Prefects like Chapuys in Isère tried to continue the tradition of Bonapartist 'populism'. Some rebels had thought they were rising to defend Bonaparte, as president of the republic, against a royalist coup! Yet the insurrection showed Bonapartism's true colours. For once the populist mask had slipped. The future 'peasant emperor' had come to power by surpressing the largest rural rising in western Europe in the nineteenth century. Parts of rural France were never to forget or forgive.

Part Three

An Authoritarian Interlude (1848–71)

Chapter 5

Bonapartism – a Modernizing Dictatorship?

I The Political Economy of Bonapartism

The image of the Bonapartist regime as a repressive, authoritarian pseudo-democracy was established by decades of subsequent republican and socialist historiography. Since the 1930s, however, historians have reinterpreted the second empire in a more favourable light. A system in which a weak parliament was overshadowed by a firm, economically interventionist executive has been presented in favourable contrast to the political impotence and economic stagnation of the late Third Republic, and as a precursor of technocratic Gaullist modernization.

The business world received the coup with relief, stock market shares rose immediately, confidence revived as the 'red' threat receded. But the new regime's contribution to capitalism moved beyond this. The emperor lent an ear to St Simonian advisers like Michel Chevalier, who became a member of the *Conseil d'État*. Technological modernization and economic growth were advocated as remedies for political instability and class conflict. Dynamic elements among French industrialists would be encouraged by bureaucratic technocrats and state funding to overcome 'Luddite' elements in parliament. State expenditure rose by 50 per cent between 1852 and 1855, before levelling off to 30 per cent above the 1852 rate. The cyclical slump of 1857 was countered by increased state orders to naval shipyards. The regime consulted businessmen, arranged industrial exhibitions. Aided by a world trade boom, fostered by improved communications, the gold boom, and by inflation after decades of price stagnation, the regime presided over rapid economic growth in the 1850s, but slower, more erratic growth thereafter. Between 1851 and 1869, industrial production increased by 50 per cent, exports by 150 per cent.

The 1852 decision to foster rail construction has been praised by L. Girard as a major breakthrough after delays during the previous fifteen years caused by local rivalries, timid financial orthodoxy, entrenched vested interests and political chaos. The 90,000 miles of track completed by 1857 sparked the boom. The state encouraged mergers to produce six large rail companies. A 500 per cent rise in rail investment in 1852–60 bore witness to investor confidence, boosted by ninety-nine-year concessions granted to these companies. Faced with the 1856–7 slump and problems of raising capital for less profitable branch-lines, the state sustained the momentum with financial aid and guarantees of 4 per cent minimum returns on capital. By 1870, 18,000 kilometres of line had been completed, the railways transported 50 per cent of internal trade as against 10 per cent in 1852. The state had given 634 million francs to rail companies, which made 11 per cent profits on the 7000 million francs invested, and rail tycoons like Mires had greased the palms of key members of the imperial entourage, notably Morny.

The rail booms of 1853–6 and 1860–4 were the peaks of economic growth, making demands on engineering, heavy metallurgy and coal sectors, all of which attained annual growth rates above 6 per cent, stimulated by orders for rails, 5000 locomotives, 122,000 wagons and 12,000 carriages. By 1864, 80 per cent of French iron was coke-produced. Engineering and metallurgy began to concentrate around the Loire and Nord coalfields. The regime overrode local protest to encourage mergers. Fifty-three per cent of iron and steel was produced by the eight largest firms by 1860, with the *Comité des Forges* (1864) emerging as the first powerful cartel. Alliances between banks, railways, and metal firms, such as that between the *Société Générale*, the Paris-Lyon-Marseille rail company and Le Creusot, were established. Schneider, head of Le Creusot, was president of the *Corps Législatif*. The development of the Pas-de-Calais coalfield trebled coal production to 15 million tons, though for political reasons the regime discouraged excessive coal mergers.

Deeper pits, rail expansion and coke furnaces – five time costlier than charcoal forges – produced an unprecedented demand for capital, necessitating some easing of the restrictions in the capital market. The pioneers of industrial banking were the Pereires, whose *Crédit Mobilier* tapped the savings of smaller investors to finance the rail and public utilities boom. Via Bonaparte's influential cousin Morny they had access to the emperor, and broke the hold of the more cautious *Haute Banque*. Deposit banks, typified by Henri Germain's *Crédit Lyonnais*, initially helped channel savings towards industry. Mme Caroline, in Zola's *L'Argent* has the 'sudden conviction that money was the manure in which the humanity of the future was growing . . . from this great evil, good was emerging.' Hostile socialists remarked that 183 financiers controlled 20,000 million francs capital, that some bankers were directors of 50 companies.

The Pereires, epitomes of Bonapartism's financial and industrial coup d'état, found triumph short-lived. Their successes angered older financiers. The Talabots blocked their Marseille-Sète rail project, and their scheme for a Paris-Midi line via central France ran short of capital. A strategy of short-term borrowing and long-term loans created a liquidity crisis, and left them over-extended as the economy slowed down. The government blocked their frenzied efforts to raise fresh capital in 1862–3, and the *Crédit Mobilier* collapsed.

Falling interest rates, easier share-marketing, closer bank-industry links accelerated capitalist development. Yet the 'credit revolution' remained incomplete. Railways always received more capital than industry, and between 1866 and 1869, the *Crédit Lyonnais* cut its industrial portfolio by two-thirds, scared by the Pereires' fate. By the late 1860s a 'haemorrhage' of capital, as banks, receiving high commissions, channelled French investors' money into foreign state loans and overseas mining and railways, slowed domestic industrial development, and left some sectors and regions starved of capital. Capital exports increased from 2000 million to 15,000 million francs between 1850 and 1870, with the regime ignoring critics who urged restrictions on this outflow.

Canal and road projects, land-reclamation and, above all, urban renewal, testify to the regime's willingness to risk deficit financing to accelerate economic modernization. Building-sector activity doubled between 1853 and 1869. Paris, which grew to two million inhabitants, provided construction jobs on stations, markets, boulevards, theatres, department stores, as Prefect Haussmann, like the Pereires, gambled on the future, raising loans, and spending in anticipation of long-term revenue. Le Havre, Lyon and Marseille witnessed similar activity. But by 1866 Haussmann was in difficulty: the real-estate profits of Parisian speculators were being denounced as corrupt by opposition politicians, his 'easy credit' policy viewed as unsound by orthodox financiers. Yet, in sacrificing Haussmann, the regime was cutting its links with projects which epitomized its halcyon boom days.

Free trade, inaugurated in 1860 by the Cobden-Chevalier treaty with Britain, proved to be the regime's most controversial strategy. Bonapartism showed its ability to 'stand above' the vested interests of protectionist sectors by pursuing a policy designed to strengthen the competitiveness of French capitalism, and, in addition, to cement friendly relations with Britain. An allocation of 40 million francs was granted to help manufacturers to adapt. Bracing winds of international competition would, it was hoped, accelerate technological modernization, and improve productivity. The effect of free-trade remains difficult to evaluate, for the American Civil War disrupted exports and raw cotton imports, and a disaster-prone foreign policy weakened business and investment confidence. Exports rose 80 per cent in the 1860s, as against 44 per cent in the 1850s, with wine, silk and luxury sectors clearly boosted by free trade. Innovative Alsatian and fashion-conscious Nord cotton and woollen entrepreneurs responded creatively to competition, increased sales to Britain, and introduced self-acting mules. However, the coarser Normandy cloth was badly hit by British competition, the American cotton famine and the rising costs of rural outwork, as a rural exodus began. Older southern centres like Lodève and Castres went into steep decline. Self-financing family-firms remained the basis of the industry, and textile growth was a modest 2 per cent per annum.

The plight of traditional textile and metal sectors in the face of foreign competition provided ammunition for critics, who played on deep-seated Anglophobia to demand protectionism. Liberal and republican politicians won a business audience, with demands for greater parliamentary control of economic policy. East Aquitaine expressed regionalist outrage as its industry succumbed to foreign and northern competition, claiming that banks drained capital from their region, and monopolistic rail tariffs discriminated against them.

By the 1860s, the economic miracle was stumbling, as the regime began to question its pump-priming strategy, and Finance Minister Fould, responsive to 'Orleanist' financial orthodoxy, pushed the emperor into acceptance of cuts in public works expenditure to levels below those of the July Monarchy's last years. A mood of uncertainty, accentuated by foreign policy alarms and poor harvests, hit investment, and unemployment rose.

The balance sheet of Bonapartism's political economy was uneven. In his Rougon-Macquart novels, Zola emphasized a new world of railways, coal mines and department stores. *L'Argent* portrayed a religion whose temple was the stock exchange, where share values trebled in two decades. Dabbling in shares became an obsession, encouraged by share indexes published by the new mass-circulation papers like *Le Petit Journal* which spread the capitalist ethos. Industrial banking, a doubling of foreign trade and growing overseas investment suggested major economic change. The legislation regulating industrial enterprises was made steadily more liberal. *Conseil d'État* approval had been needed to establish joint-stock companies, restricting these to ten per annum in 1825–56. Business had resorted to the *société en commandite par actions*, for which legal formalities were minimal, and in which directors had unlimited liability but total control. Investors' rights were increased in 1856, then joint-stock companies were freed in 1867. Until then 73 per cent of joint-stock capital had been in railways. Though the old system had been more flexible than some accounts suggest, the new legislation was obviously beneficial to capitalist expansion. An affluent bourgeoisie began to frequent fashionable department stores. Profit levels kept well ahead of the 30 per cent price rise. Nevertheless startling advances in key mining, metallurgical and engineering sectors were not matched in other industries, where old structures survived. The overall employer-worker ratio remained under 1:3. Agriculture still contributed half of the gross national product. A growth rate of 3.8 per cent p.a. in 1850–5 had fallen to 1.16 per cent p.a. by 1865–70. Wine and silk remained the major exports, while heavy industry employed only 10 per cent of the work force. The expansion of the Pas-de-Calais and Alsace was offset by deindustrialization of parts of the Midi and the south-west. Population growth fell to 0.27 per cent p.a., half the rate of the 1830s, with periodic visitations of typhoid and cholera accentuating the effects of the falling birth rates. This had potential long-term implications, in terms of inelastic domestic demand, though contemporaries were more worried by the military implications of demographic stagnation.

II The Bonapartist State and the Elites

The enigmatic emperor was viewed with some disdain by French *notables*. Thiers dismissed him as a 'cretin'. His faith in his 'destiny' was ridiculed as absurd pretension. Many scorned him as an upstart parvenu, sadly deficient in the classical culture of the elites. He was criticized for frequent hesitant wavering, and for proceeding by underhand subterfuge. Yet, he retained certain fixed goals which he refused to abandon, and, as Rémusat reluctantly admitted, a disturbing capacity to change the world to fit his fantasies. If his ideas frequently contradicted those of the *notables*, this was what gave Bonapartism its distinct character. He insisted that France's cycle of repression and revolution could only be broken if some mass aspirations were satisfied. In contrast with the Orleanist formulae of protectionism and internal laissez-faire, still espoused by much of French business, he was prepared to experiment with a fresh mixture of free trade and a measure of internal state economic *dirigisme*. In foreign affairs, he abandoned passive acceptance of the 1815 settlement, and hoped to redraw the international map at the expense of the conservative powers, increasing French influence by making France the patron of rising nationalities.

The regime's political system was *sui generis*, without contemporary European parallel. It was a 'blue' regime, claiming to safeguard the legitimate gains of 1789 against 'white' reaction and 'red' revolution. It maintained a democratic-populist façade. Universal suffrage was restored, against the advice of many worried conservatives and prefects. Parliament was elected every six years. The regime consistently won general elections – though between 1852 and 1869 the opposition vote grew inexorably from 0.66 million to 3.3 million. 'Liberal' concessions were steadily made in the 1860s, as political exiles returned, press controls were eased, strikes permitted (1864) and public meetings tolerated (1868). Yet, if Louis Napoleon was baptized with the waters of universal suffrage, he did not intend to live with his feet in a puddle. The electoral system was rigged and gerrymandered. The number of parliamentary seats was cut by nearly two-thirds. Urban seats were appended to large rural constituencies to swamp radical working-class voters. There was adroit manipulation of sticks and carrots. Sète in lower Languedoc was threatened with the loss of the Bordeaux-Midi rail terminus if its opposition voting persisted. Loyalist villages were promised roads and school buildings. Minor state officials including mayors, postal workers, and the purged teaching corps, were mobilized by prefects as official electoral agents, while opposition electoral propaganda was systematically sabotaged. Political clubs remained outlawed; prior permission was needed for publication of all press articles. Parliamentary sessions were reduced to three months per year. The lower house could discuss but not initiate legislation. The press could not report parliamentary debate. Ministers, responsible to the emperor, were not allowed to be deputies. Decisions on foreign and commercial policy were the emperor's prerogative. Louis Napoleon's lack of interest in detail left much of the framing and implementation of policy with the 'disinterested' bureaucrats of the *Conseil d'État* and the prefectoral corps who had helped stage the coup d'état.

Bonapartist internal political strategy comprised three key elements. There was an attempt to end endemic class conflict through economic expansion and prosperity. Efforts were made to defuse intra-elite ideological and cultural conflicts between anticlericals and Catholics, republicans and royalists. Above all, there was an attempt to preserve the regime from a close identification with the interests of the royalist *notables*, by emphasizing the role of the disinterested, impartial state above class interests. In 1852, the regime restored universal suffrage and confiscated Orleanist family estates – gestures designed to win mass sympathy, and which aroused alarm among royalists at Bonapartist demagoguery.

During the 1850s, the strategy appeared to succeed. Yet, it relied excessively on an economic boom, which could not be sustained, and on the reconciling of ultimately irreconcilable class interests. Above all, Bonapartism lacked a party. It claimed indeed, to be 'above parties'. Yet, its directing elite of policy-makers had to be recruited from somewhere. Inevitably, it was forced to 'borrow leaders', as bureaucrats, deputies, ministers. And such men included figures like Morny or Fould, drawn from the old elites, suspicious of Bonapartism's populist-*dirigiste* rhetoric, not sharing Louis Napoleon's own preoccupations. The prefects were political technicians from previous regimes who were, at the local level, forced to reach agreements with existing socio-economic elites. Morny, insisting on the need to win over 'practical men', landowners and industrialists respected by 'their' workers and tenants, dissolved local petty-bourgeois Bonapartist committees lest they alienate the *notables*. In short, Bonapartism's claim to be above parties was undermined by its reliance on old conservative cadres, Orleanists like Fould, dynastic opposition men like Baroche, right-wing republicans like Fortoul. Some were partly converted to Bonapartist policies. Rouher, an ex-Orleanist who had been a repressive justice minister in 1850–1, was such a case for, as R. Schnerb shows, he was won over in the 1850s, as public works minister, to St Simonian *dirigiste* ideas on transport and credit expansion. Yet, in the 1860s, as the regime's strong man, he resisted political liberalization, and criticized the 'rash' public works projects of Haussmann.

Other ministers remained simply conservative bourgeois, seeking law and order. Baroche, president of the *Conseil d'État* in the 1850s, was, as Maurain argues, essentially another Thiers. He defended entrenched *grand bourgeois* interests, was suspicious of universal suffrage, disapproved of public works expenditure, had little sympathy with the emperor's vague social romanticism. The financially 'orthodox' Fould, as finance minister in the 1860s, did much to undermine the Pereires' credit innovations. Morny was a business speculator, a neo-Orleanist, a slightly more flexible Guizot. In the face of the entrenched conservatism of such men, one can understand the feeling of impotence which overcame the liberal education minister Duruy in the 1860s, when he attempted to introduce progressive measures such as free compulsory education. An ex-republican, he had been moved by the emperor's apparent sympathy with the idea of an extended and secularized 'democratic' education system – only to find himself isolated by the lack of real support against conservatives like Rouher.

Such problems existed at all levels of Bonapartist government. The *Conseil d'État* remained dominated by men of legal training from military, bureaucratic and diplomatic families, and of Orleanist sympathies. Parliament was monopolized by the elites – with 24 per cent of deputies from business, 19 per cent landowners, 26 per cent upper bureaucrats, 8 per cent military officers, and 13 per cent lawyers. Persigny, a rare authentic Bonapartist, lamented that 'we, who have our friends only down below, have abandoned parliament to the upper classes.' In 1869, over half the deputies had personal incomes above 30,000 francs per year. The power of these parliamentary *notables* should not be underestimated. As V. Wright has shown, the power of the *Conseil d'État* to frame and implement policy fell in the 1860s, as the regime's ministers were forced to take account of the local power of entrenched socio-economic elites, whose representatives monopolized parliamentary seats.

Bonapartism relied on the state bureaucracy, which included 360,000 troops, 24,000 gendarmes, and a public service which doubled to 265,000. Teachers and postal officials were expected to act as political agents for the regime. Yet, the ideal of a neutral bureaucracy above class interests, a loyal monolithic instrument of Bonapartist authoritarian populism, was always unattainable. Inevitably, many senior bureaucrats and magistrates retained their royalist sympathies, and saw their roles as control of the 'reds'. The powers and salary of the prefects were substantially increased in 1852. They controlled local police, nominated mayors and teachers, implemented laws, licensed cafés. A minority, typified by the prefect of Eure, Janvier de la Motte, were authoritarian populists, not unafraid to offend local elites. Yet, essentially, they were drawn from impeccable aristocratic and upper bourgeois backgrounds, trained in the *École Polytechnique*, reluctant to alienate their fellow *notables*. Though Bonapartism attempted to bolster prefectoral power by channelling public funds to localities via the prefect, in practice, *notables*, with strong Parisian connections, retained their share of local patronage.

In the Nord, as Ménager shows, an entrenched Orleanist elite of businessmen and large landowners, with a strong regionalist pride, was deeply resistant to Bonapartist state intrusion. Attempts to impose an 'outsider' as official candidate, as with Bortelle in 1863, were resented, as were attempts to gerrymander constituencies in Flemish areas. The bourgeois dynasties were too rich, self-confident and technically competent to submit to arbitrary interference in 'their' department. Many Bonapartist prefects, after 1870, made a swift, smooth transition into the business world with which they always had close family ties. Within the department, their powers were, in practice, restricted by the influence of the *Conseil Général*. Over one-third of the membership of the *Conseils Généraux* came from large landowners, many of whom accepted the regime unenthusiastically as a law-and-order necessity. Twenty-seven per cent of CG members were nobles in 1870; 45 per cent, army generals; 34 per cent, *Conseillers d'État*. In many areas Bonapartism was forced to compromise with legitimists whom it could not oust. In short, the state remained too reliant on the elites for any attempt to substitute the bureaucracy for the elites to succeed.

As Marx had predicted, Bonapartism, though reliant for its mass appeal on its illusory independence from the old elites, could not exist suspended in a vacuum. There was no Bonapartist party – and to have formed one would have contradicted the rhetoric of a regime which denounced parties as divisive, and aimed to rally all 'good' Frenchmen. In part, the role of a party was assumed by the bureaucracy, yet, the bureaucratic machine remained colonized by men from the old elites with conservative and royalist sympathies, who accepted Bonapartism for law and order, took what they wanted from the regime, and ignored the populist element in Bonapartist ideology. Attempts to recruit 'new men' were doomed to failure. As Guizot observed, soldiers repressed riots, peasant voters could win elections, but these were 'not sufficient to rule with. One needs support from the upper classes who are natural leaders. Yet, for the most part, these are hostile to the president.' The regime was trapped, needing the elites to govern, yet the masses for support. The class war of 1848–51 could not be swept permanently under the carpet. Irreconcilable interests of workers and capitalists could not be reconciled. Even Louis Napoleon, as the contemporary political observer Prévost-Paradol commented, could not forever be 'simultaneously M. Thiers and M. Proudhon'. Only the economic expansion of the 1850s allowed the balancing act to survive as long as it did.

The difficulties involved in the Bonapartist attempt to conciliate conflicting elements of the elites emerged most clearly in religious and educational policy. The regime enjoyed a short honeymoon in its relations with French Catholics. Fear of socialism made Catholic opinion favourable to the 1851 coup, and amenable to a deal with Bonapartism. The Falloux Law allowed the expansion of Catholic secondary schools, and the employment of religious orders in public primary schools. New western dioceses were created, and clerical salaries raised. The fact that the church retained '1848' liberties which others had now lost, eased the conscience of liberal Catholics like Montalembert at accepting the coup d'état, and reconciled *ultras* like Veuillot to the survival of the state *Université*. The loose rein permitted to the church in the 1850s allowed close contacts with Rome, increased power for the religious orders, and a steady erosion of surviving Gallican elements in the clergy. However, Bonapartism, which had hoped to utilize the church to create a bogus national unity, by weakening the left and undermining the legitimist right, was to find itself after 1859 hoist with its own petard. It tolerated the growth of a buoyant clericalism, whose arrogance inflamed the latent anticlericalism of wide strata of French society. Equally, the regime ran the risk of jeopardizing its own 'blue' image. Already, by 1856, Rouland awoke to the danger, tightening state inspection of Catholic schools, and easing censorship of the liberal anticlerical paper *Le Siècle*.

Then, in 1859, French troops invaded northern Italy as allies of Piedmont against the Habsburgs. The emperor's mixed motives included a certain romantic sympathy with Italian nationalism, Bonapartist dynastic hostility to the Habsburgs and to the 1815 Settlement, a desire to gain influence in Italy, the prospect of territorial gains, and the desire to woo liberal and leftist approval while diverting domestic attention from the post-1857 economic slump. The ensuing threat to the papal states aroused French Catholics to feverish defence of the Temporal Power and criticism of the regime for precipitating the crisis. The attempts of Catholic liberals like Montalembert to argue that the papal states were unessential for papal independence were disowned by Rome and most of the French clergy. As priests preached against the regime, and Catholic deputies like Keller defected to the opposition, internal political conflicts between clericals and anticlericals intensified, and even the Bonapartist cadres were divided. Some Catholic *notables* urged the necessity of reasserting parliamentary control over foreign policy. Feeling betrayed by the clerical viper which it had nourished in its bosom, the regime retorted by suspending *L'Univers*, appointing the anticlerical Duruy to the education ministry and suspending the salaries of outspoken priests. Yet, it also sought to appease Catholic voters by maintaining French troops in Rome to repel Garibaldi.

Local studies emphasize the intensity of intra-elite conflicts. In Poitiers, the legitimist bishop Mgr Pie was an aristocrat, who insisted that the state's prime duty was 'to recognize the fact of

Original Sin'. In 1851, he had, reluctantly, sided with the Bonapartist sabre against the revolutionary dagger, fearing that victorious reds would 'burn churches'. But his vigorous war on liberalism, Gallicanism and the *Université* was soon resumed. He treated the Bonapartist regime as an army of occupation, boycotted the prefecture, and, like fellow legitimists throughout France, manipulated the charity resources of the St Vincent de Paul society as an electoral weapon. The regime's attempts to woo legitimist *notables* with seats on the *Conseil Général* proved abortive in the face of the rival seduction of honorific papal titles. The Bonapartist cause was waged by *Procureur Général* Damay, a liberal deist, who, insisting that Bonapartism implied religious toleration, acceptance of '1789' and economic and scientific progress, attempted to win over the professional middle class. He rejected appeasement of legitimism as futile, prosecuted its leaders for breaches of the public meeting law, and suspended the salaries of *curés* who preached against the regime's Italian policy. His efforts were aided by the growing detachment of the peasantry from puritanical and meddling village clergy, which eroded legitimism's populist support. But the regime's early hopes of achieving reconciliation with the old elite remained unfulfilled, and the appeal of Catholic colleges to bourgeois families perpetuated Damay's fears of legitimist 'seduction' of the middle class.

In Mayenne, too, legitimist rallying to the regime was ephemeral – though facilitated by the fear of socialism, the agricultural boom of the 1850s, the industrial investments of *notables*, like mine owner Le Rochelambert, and the regime's generosity to the church in the 1850s. Yet legitimists viewed Bonapartism as vulgar, excessively wedded to change, prepared to replace local *notables* by the state bureaucratic machine. Michel Denis portrays a world in which, paradoxically, legitimist landowners attempted to utilize the profits of market agriculture to prop up a rural idyll. The rail link with Paris permitted profitable livestock-breeding specialization. Yet local rail links with the Mayenne interior were resisted, to avoid infecting legitimist rural bastions with foul-talking rail navvies. Sharecropping was maintained, eulogized as a form of harmonious paternalism. Agricultural profits were channelled into château-building, slowing the rural exodus by providing construction jobs. Sixty per cent of churches were rebuilt in a Romano-byzantine style. Legitimist counter-society had its own ideology, buttressed by religion, genealogies, parish monographs, praise of the ancien régime. 'Liberty' was defined as defence of Mayenne by landed *notables* against Parisian centralization. Bonapartism was a godless regime, tolerating urbanization, obscene novels, Sunday work. Bonapartist 'order' was 'unnatural', relying on force and prosperity. Plebiscitary populism was fundamentally flawed for, as de la Boise observed, 'to demand of a people *if* they wish to be commanded is, implicitly, to recognize that one has not the *right* to command them.' Yet the focus of anti-Bonapartism was more Pius IX than Chambord; the church as much the master as the servant of legitimism. The Catholic youths who flocked to enlist in the volunteer army (*zouaves*) raised to defend the papal states were more papist than royalist.

The tone of the Catholicism of these years, with its emphasis on miracles, its devotion to a pope whose Syllabus of Errors (1864), denounced rationalism, democracy, progress and dozens of similar heresies, and with its hatred for the 'liberal' state education system deepened conflicts within the elites. Moderate Gallican bishops, like Mgr Thabault in Montpellier, found themselves ostracized by their ultramontane clergy, unable to stem the spread of Roman liturgy. Lower clergy appealed constantly to Rome against episcopal policy, and remained fervent allies of the legitimist aristocracy of the Midi. When a clergyman was found in bed with the wife of a Montpellier diocesan dignitary, the lower clergy spread rumours that their liberal bishop was the culprit! Intensified local educational conflicts pushed the regime into taking sides. In Poitiers Damay became alarmed that the Jesuit college was undermining the 'lycée. Catholic secondary pupils doubled to 36,000 between 1850 and 1865, with one-third of the major colleges Jesuit-run. In much of the west, the central Massif, Lyonnais and Provence, state lycée attendance became limited to sons of state officials, as Catholic colleges tapped the snobbery of bourgeois parents eager to educate their offspring alongside young aristocrats. A combination of muscular Christianity and moral supervision was reassuring to parents who blamed '1848' on the sins of half-educated atheistic *déracinés* from state schools. Only Catholic education, Mgr Dupanloup claimed, could control depraved human nature, thereby guaranteeing social stability.

Yet Catholic education posed an implicit threat to Bonapartism. It rejected '1789', deepened existing ideological divisions within the elites. Vannes college alone produced 100 papal *zouaves*. Catholic colleges disseminated a self-conscious, anti-scientific ethos in the decade of Darwin. One Catholic headmaster insisted that science implied materialism, which engendered socialism. Catholic schools did train pupils for the baccalauréat, key to access to bureaucratic careers. Twenty per cent of *grandes-écoles* entrants in 1868 came from the Catholic sector. But they taught by rote, excluded discussion, got pupils through the philosophy exams without contaminating their minds with thought. They excluded post-1789 history, seen as subversive, and denounced 'pagan' classics, held responsible for renaissance, reformation, enlightenment and, hence, the revolution. Jesuit colleges banned liberal newspapers from their common rooms. Such colleges became 'well-arranged hot-houses, with chinks carefully stopped up to exclude modern draughts' (*Padberg*), producing pupils with priggish disdain for the modern world. They viewed the *Université* as a hotbed of atheistic radicalism, though most lycée teachers remained cautious conformists, anxious only for acceptance by local respectable society.

During the 1850s Education Minister Fortoul made substantial educational concessions to Catholic interests, placing Christian texts on school syllabuses, sacking atheistic teachers, downgrading subversive subjects such as modern history, and replacing classroom discussion by dogmatic assertion. After 1859, as the Catholic educational upsurge undermined hopes for cementing unity of old and new elites via shared cultural values, municipalities were encouraged to support secular schools against Catholic rivals. Duruy, made education minister in 1863, regarded Catholicism as an obstacle to a modern education system. Hoping to train liberal wives as fit companions for bourgeois husbands, he rashly proposed secular secondary schools for girls, provoking a reaction of extraordinary virulence from clergy who regarded their near-monopoly of female education as the key to control of future generations. Mgr Dupanloup, evoking the spectre of legions of atheistic blue stockings, sprang to the defence of French womanhood and chastity. The regime, under increasing pressure from social unrest and fearful of undermining religion as a prop of the social order, was forced into tactical concessions, including the jettisoning of Duruy in 1869.

Indeed the entire field of post-primary education illustrates how

Bonapartism risked becoming trapped by conflicting priorities, principles and interests within the elites. Efforts to 'modernize' structure and curricula to meet the needs of an industrializing economy met fluctuating fortunes. During the 1850s Fortoul established 'bifurcation' in the lycées, founding a scientific stream alongside the traditional classics baccalauréat. Advocates of the reform viewed classics as a hangover from a bygone age and claimed that scientific education would produce apolitical technocrats, trained for economic expansion, thus ending the danger from overproduction of arts graduates who became subversive *déracinés* once they failed to get posts in an overcrowded bureaucracy. St Simonians emphasized the need for technocratic elites and technologically literate intermediate cadres. 'Bifurcation', popular in industrial centres like St Étienne, increased science teachers by 50 per cent, yet was abandoned within a decade, victim of the vested interest of the *Université* classics lobby, alarmed at the declining quality of Latin prose, and of the snobbery of parents, who feared that the science baccalauréat lacked authentic bourgeois status.

The training of intermediate cadres for the industrial hierarchy drew a similarly erratic response from a regime which purported to recognize the industrial implications of education. Despite the existence of three Écoles des Arts et Métiers, a mining school and the *École Turgot*, which taught science and practical subjects to the Parisian petty bourgeoisie, the field was left largely to private initiative, strongest, as Oberlé shows, in industrial centres like Mulhouse where even sons of the middle bourgeoisie attended the 'professional' college. By the 1860s business lobbies were urging state support for technical classes, on the lines of those pioneered in chemistry and textiles in Mulhouse. In 1865 Duruy established an *École Normale Spéciale*, at Cluny, to train technical teachers, together with three experimental colleges. However, technical schooling remained concentrated in the 'special' streams of lycées, frequented by petty-bourgeois pupils who were not to sit for the baccalauréat. Despised by a supercilious *Université* hierarchy, contemptuous of the 'little Americans' which it produced, technical education remained the poor relation of secondary education.

Duruy, aware of the military and economic importance of science, made belated efforts to remedy the shortcomings in pure and applied scientific research in French universities exposed by Renan and Pasteur. The science laboratory of the Sorbonne in the

1860s was in a disused basement kitchen! Increased state funding did promote a distinct upsurge in applied science research, if from a fairly low starting point. Yet Bonapartism, for all its technocratic image, proved, as Anderson stresses, rather better at railways than at education, where its interest proved erratic and spasmodic. It fed in inadequate funds, began reforms but failed to sustain them, left too much to private initiative, remained the prisoner of the classical bias of the *Université* and of the snobbery of bourgeois parents.

To what extent did education establish a meritocratic ladder, open the way to a more fluid, open class system? Harrigan's recent analysis attempts to dispute the standard picture of a rigid two-tier education system, yet remains unconvincing. His survey of 27,000 secondary pupils in 1864–5 suggests that 40 per cent came from peasant or petty-bourgeois families. Low day-fees meant a secondary system less elitist than in Victorian England. Yet non-bourgeois pupils rarely completed full secondary schooling. In Rennes, as Gildea shows, 33 per cent of 'special' pupils in the *lycées* were non-bourgeois, barely 12 per cent of the baccalauréat stream. France had 2.5 million boys in primary education, yet a mere 65,000 in secondary schools, and a mere 6000 baccalauréat pupils. Education, in short, reproduced and consolidated existing class hierarchies. In Brittany access 'upward' into the professional bourgeoisie was limited to sons of commercial and bureaucratic classes. The elites guarded the baccalauréat as a badge of bourgeois status, while that handful of bright scholarship boys who ascended the narrow ladder usually ended as timid lycée teachers, grateful for their individual promotion, loyal to dominant bourgeois values.

III The Nature and Limits of Bonapartist Populism

Bonapartism and the Peasantry
Despite the terror produced in the countryside by mass arrests after the 1851 insurrection, and by subsequent police surveillance of suspect villages, prosperity rather than repression holds the key to explaining the strength of Bonapartism in rural France. Republicans came to describe peasants despairingly as ignorant election fodder, providing blank cheques for authoritarianism. To win a marginal seat in Nantes in 1869, the regime had merely to

append one extra rural canton, Vertou, to the constituency. The 69 per cent to 15 per cent winning margin in the 1870 plebiscite was essentially achieved in rural France. As one Toulouse republican lamented, 'the peasant supports the emperor, and does not wish to hear about a change. If you ask him why, he will say "we are selling our produce. Prices are high. It is not certain that business would be as good under any other government."'

Marx predicted that, for the peasantry, Bonapartism would prove a sad deception, because it would accelerate capitalist development, and thus eradicate small, inefficient rural producers. However, in the short term, the rail network encouraged commercial specialization, and nurtured an agrarian boom in which some peasants flourished. In the red bastion of lower Languedoc, the advent of railways allowed the import of cereals, thus encouraging the concentration on wine monoculture for markets in northern France and Europe. In Hérault, 100,000 hectares were switched to vine growing; in Pyrénées-Orientales, the vine area doubled between 1836 and 1870. High wine prices allowed *vignerons* to pay off debts and to survive on plots with support from wages from part-time day-labour on large estates. In 1852, 18 per cent of the Hérault population were smallowners, by 1872, 26 per cent. Upland peasants migrated to the high-wage coastal vineyards. A similar shift towards wine monoculture occurred in Provence. Prosperity muted initial political hostility to the regime in the rural Midi.

This pattern of specialization and prosperity was repeated elsewhere. In the Limousin, commercial livestock-rearing developed, the quality of cattle improved, and the number of peasant-proprietors swelled by 20 per cent, as sharecroppers profited from high veal prices to purchase land. The Paris building boom increased the real wages of the peasant-masons, dulling the edge of their radicalism despite the continued personal popularity of the exiled Nadaud. In 1857, the opposition polled 49 per cent of votes among Limoges porcelain workers, only 8 per cent in the surrounding countryside. In Loir-et-Cher, high agricultural prices guaranteed Bonapartism the support of middle-peasants, the vagrant bands of 1846–51 disappeared, and rural discontent was narrowed to marginal forest-dwellers and lumbermen. In Brittany, the Léon peasantry prospered on market gardening for Parisian consumers.

Public works projects attracted surplus population from the countryside, easing the demographic pressure which had fuelled the radicalism of forest and upland departments like Basses-Alpes and Ariège. Indeed, in the 1866 agricultural *enquête*, landowners complained that rural exodus was driving up farm wages, and making labour scarce. In the Loir-et-Cher, agricultural wages rose 66 per cent in two decades. The bourgeois landowner in Zola's *La Terre*, remains hostile to rural education for fear that it might accelerate the rural exodus.

Neither the transformation of the rural economy nor the decline in social tensions should be exaggerated. Areas of the central Massif, south-west and west remained locked into subsistence polyculture. In the absence of investment and technical innovation, the spread of maize and the potato failed to produce an 'agricultural revolution' in east Aquitaine. Small *vignerons* remained beset with storage problems, vulnerable to overproduction crises, and excessive rail tariffs and customs dues reduced their urban sales. 300 kilometres of rail-construction in the Limousin were too little to erode a psychology of isolation, a sense that a Paris-based government gave them low priority. Rye and buckwheat remained the main cereals there, phosphate fertilizer was scarce. French grain-yields remained 50 per cent below those of Holland. 3.6 million farms shared 9000 mechanical harvesters in 1862. Regional differentiation was extremely marked – only one of the poorest 23 departments was in northern France, and even in the rich cereal-growing Beauce of *La Terre* middle-peasants lacked fertilizer, spent any surplus capital on more land rather than on machinery, and mistrusted the agricultural innovations of the few large farms.

Change in the countryside was cultural as well as economic. If the regime's interest in mass education was, at best, spasmodic, the number of villages without a school fell from 5000 to a mere 312, and conscript illiteracy from 39 per cent to below 20 per cent. The proportion of those in the five- to fourteen-year age group at school rose from 51 per cent to 68 per cent between 1851 and 1866. Increased market contacts made more peasants aware of the utility of literacy, numeracy and command of French. The Allier sharecroppers in E. Guillaumin's *La Vie d'un Simple* were becoming ashamed of their patois, as their landowner's relatives made mock of it. The railway completed the decline of rural *colportage*, already weakened by the police repression of the

Second Republic. Annual sales fell from 9 million to 2 million items between 1851 and 1869 and the old staple diet of *almanachs* and fairy stories was replaced by cheap *romans feuilletons*. Police repression of carnivals as potential instruments of seditious disorder hastened their decline. The sexually mixed, inward-looking, patois-speaking *'veillée'* retreated in face of the taste for the male-dominated café. Guillaumin's hero, who brawls with village artisans in rare moments of contact in the 1840s, is, by the 1860s, regularly playing billiards with them. The number of rural *cabarets* increased by 60 per year in the Loiret in the 1860s. The village of Rognes in *La Terre* has, plausibly, two cafés for a population of only 300. For many *curés*, the only compensation was that the peasants occasionally had the virtues of their vices – their Sunday work and ferocious meanness meant that they spent less time in cafés! Clergy lamented the spread of wine-drinking, cards and brothels, in the wine bourgs of the Midi. The spread of Sunday work and birth control accentuated peasant-*curé* tensions in commercial farming areas. Oil lamps improved the lighting of cottages. The black jackets and white shirts worn as 'best' by Midi peasants at fêtes began to resemble bourgeois attire – with Provençal bourgeois regionalists adopting the 'folklore' costumes of the peasantry just as the peasants were discarding them!

The regime developed a sophisticated strategy for manipulating the peasant electorate. The emperor's 'reward' for a tour of east Aquitaine, promising a railway network, was a 98 per cent poll in the 1852 plebiscite. Sète was warned that the persistence of radical voting would jeopardize its chances of becoming the lower Languedoc rail terminal. Appointed mayors, village teachers, postmen and tax officials were expected to act as government election agents. Café owners risked losing their licence if they refused this role. The Bonapartist deputy in *La Terre* keeps the villagers loyal by promises of government aid for local road-building. Prefects like Chapuys de Montlaville in the Isère, and Pietri in the Ariège cultivated a populist image with amnesties for forest offenders, and insisted that Bonapartism should keep its distance from the landed elites and convince the peasantry that benefits flowed to them from the government, and not from the *notables*. 'Oligarchy, patronage outside the administration . . . is an evil,' emphasized one prefect, for 'if it might appear to give us strength today, it will certainly be a danger for tomorrow'. Tarn prefect Taillefer was sacked in 1853 for his legitimist associations. In Calvados, as Desert shows, the conservative and still Catholic peasantry remained fearful of a return to the ancien régime. More 'subjects' than 'citizens', they craved for a regime which guaranteed order and prosperity. But the prefect wisely did not choose legitimist de Caumont as official candidate in 1852, when one peasant elector shouted 'Long live Napoleon, but down with the hunting laws and the *curés* who want Henry V!' Bonaparte was the 'candidate of those who do not read', tapping an egalitarian-populist streak in an otherwise 'apolitical' peasantry. The regime maintained 80 per cent of the Calvados rural vote, though its urban support there slipped by 1869 to 46 per cent. In *La Terre*, Zola describes a *veillée* reading of a government pamphlet, 'The Misery and Triumph of Jacques Bonhomme', which evokes the horrors of feudalism from which Bonapartism had rescued the peasantry.

The regime's conflicts with the clergy over Italian policy were often a political bonus in the countryside. In the Limousin the 1863 Bonapartist vote was higher than that of 1857, because of the clergy's virulent attacks on government policy. In the Isère, churches emptied when *curés* preached anti-government sermons, and villagers welcomed the new official severity towards church schools. In the Dordogne in 1867, Bonapartist peasants assaulted churches in which the 'seigneurial' insignia of local legitimists had been restored to pews. As Zeldin shows, Bonapartism's net impact on peasant France was paradoxical, for after suppressing rural radicalism in 1851, it proceeded to encourage a gradual emancipation from landed and clerical elites, which paved the way for subsequent radical conquests of the countryside, notably in the south-west.

Yet there were obvious limits to Bonapartism's rural populism. Landed *notables* dominated departmental *Conseils Généraux*, and required constant wooing by governmental patronage. In flirting with peasant anticlericalism in innumerable village disputes over education, the expenses of church repairs, or mayor-*curé* feuds, the regime ran the risk of permitting the re-emergence of radicals who had kept a low profile since 1851. But when, as in the Isère in 1869, it sought to appease royalist elites by sponsoring legitimists as official candidates, it threw peasant voters into the arms of a resurgent republicanism. Despite the purge of radicals in 1848–52, many village teachers remained violently hostile to a clergy which appeared determined to hand rural education over to the religious orders, and latently hostile to Bonapartism for maintaining the *Loi Falloux*. By 1869, many of the 'red' bastions of 1851 were reappearing on the electoral map. The sub-prefect of Béziers had predicted in 1852 that repression would exacerbate 'personal, family and party' hatreds which would 'bleed for a long time'. In lower Languedoc, villagers cultivated the vines of political detainees, cafés shut to avoid serving passing military units, red belts were worn at the civil funerals of 'men of '48'. News of the emperor's military defeat in 1870 prompted celebration dances near Lunel (Hérault). Two decades of relative prosperity failed to kill Provençal radicalism, for by 1869 Marseille socialists were founding sections in Var villages. Radicalism revived in the Limousin, as the Paris building boom faded. By-passed by the Paris-Lyon railway, alarmed at rumours of conscription, bitter at erosion of their forest rights by nobles like La Rochejacquelain, Morvan hill villages began to vote for ex-teacher Malardier, a *Dem-Soc* from 1849. The plans for wider conscription led to widespread rural unease.

However, while resurgent rural protest was neither isolated nor negligible, it cannot divert attention from the success of the regime in maintaining high levels of peasant acceptance. In 1870, Limoges workers voted 49 per cent 'no' in the plebiscite, the peasantry of the surrounding countryside, 2.9 per cent. Village 'reds' remained, in general, like the drunken poacher Jésu-Christ in *La Terre* or the tiny group in Eugene Le Roy's *Le Moulin de Frau*, isolated and aware of their impotence. The Gers illustrates perfectly the ability of Bonapartism to maintain its rural hold, despite some decline in support. The department had been 'red' in 1849–51, but 57 per cent of those arrested for resisting the coup had been bourg dwellers – in a department where only 11 per cent lived in settlements above 2000 inhabitants. Thereafter, a 10 per cent population decline eased demographic pressure. High grain and wine prices boosted Bonapartism for, as one republican said, the peasantry perceived that empire and prosperity coincided and interpreted this as cause and effect. Armagnac *vignerons* remained isolated peasants lacking the sociability of larger Provençal villages. Bonapartism posed as the defender of the peasants against a feudal-clerical restoration, in an area which was Catholic, but anticlerical. Cassagnac's electoral machine, based on control of public officials, 'delivered' the vote. Republicanism did revive by 1869, shrewdly exploiting a 30 per cent fall in grain prices, and rural hostility to conscription and the wine tax. Yet the combined opposition polled only three-fifths of the government vote and won a majority only in the bourgs among artisans and petty-bourgeois.

Bonapartism and the Workers

Disillusion with the Second Republic, repression of militants and rising real wages go some way to explaining the quiescence of French labour in the 1850s. Many workers saw Louis Napoleon, with his reputation for social concern, as preferable to Falloux and Thiers. The regime made some effort to woo the working class. The emperor made shrewd populist gestures, such as meeting delegations of St Étienne miners in 1852 and agreeing to break up the giant Loire coal combine. In 1859 he, similarly, met Marseille stevedores, threatened by port modernization. Prefects interceded as 'impartial' arbitrators in industrial disputes, so that both the Anzin mine company and Schneider at Le Creusot expressed indignation at the 'pro-worker' stance of local bureaucrats. In 1866, 1000 Loire miners paid a night-time visit to the prefect to thank him for assisting them to establish an independent mutual aid society. As Kulstein has shown, the regime made efforts to beam propaganda at the working class. In Toulouse, it sponsored the pamphlets of a stonemason, Rigault, which reminded workers of their betrayal by the bourgeois republicans in 1848. Prince Jérome's Palais Royal group attracted Parisian artisans with its emphasis on the benevolence of 'social Caesarism', and that 'firm and respectful' petitioning of the emperor could produce concessions such as the 1864 'right to strike' – although strike *organization* and picketing remained virtually illegal – or the 1868 repeal of article 1781 of the Code, which took the employer's word in disputes.

Such benevolent paternalism had obvious limitations. No Saône-et-Loire prefect would resist a call by the powerful Schneider for troops to control Le Creusot strikers. Complaints from the Carmaux coal company about the Tarn prefect's handling of a strike secured his dismissal in 1869. The enthusiasm with which Lyon workers greeted the emperor on his way to 'liberate Italy' in 1859 was soon soured when French troops propped up the papacy.

Economic expansion bought the regime several years of relative industrial peace. Rail building and urban renewal mopped up unemployment. Real wages rose by 20 per cent in the 1850s, as did *per capita* meat and wheat consumption. 'Old style' food crises faded after 1856–7. If conscript records show a working class still physically stunted, the proportion of conscripts unfit for service fell from 16 per cent to 10 per cent.

How successful was the regime in reducing political and industrial militancy? There is no simple answer. Anzin miners and Valencienne metalworkers, who voted for Bonapartists in national elections, continued to vote for 'reds' in municipal polls in the 1850s. Working-class Bonapartist voting was strong in much of northern and eastern France – Alsace, Marne, Aube, Pas-de-Calais. The small Nord textile towns voted in 1863 for a Bonapartist against the Orleanist Thiers. Catholic miners and textile workers in Tarn, and rural weavers in the Cambrésis showed a strong resistance to left-wing or republican seduction.

Pierrard's study of Lille emphasizes that the factory still engendered more fatalistic resignation than revolt. Lille was an ugly, dirty, damp city, in whose filthy canals working women were forced to do their washing. Wells were polluted by factory waste, typhoid took a regular toll. Twenty-six thousand textile workers lived in cellars or jerry-built housing, which drove many parents to café-drinking. Urban renewal produced central boulevards, a new prefecture, but little worker-housing. Forty per cent of children died before the age of five. Still-birth rates rose, as in France as a whole, due to the deformation of mothers by industrial labour. Life expectancy in the city was twenty-four years, barely two-thirds the national average. Rickets, digestive diseases, syphilis, and gastroenteritis were endemic, and the potato-based diet produced phosphate deficiency and bone diseases. The sunken chests and potbellies of children caused horrified liberal observers like Jules Simon to lament the 'bastardization of the race'. Cholera killed 2000 in 1866 – but workers, terrified of hospitals, preferred exotic folk-remedies for diseases, such as drinking urine to prevent the vomiting of blood.

Within the factories unguarded machinery was commonplace, but under 2 per cent of accidents led to prosecution of negligent employers. Mothers working thirteen-hour shifts in hot, humid mills, fed babies opium at night to secure much needed sleep. Reliant on wages from child labour, worker families conspired with the employers to evade desultory efforts by the factory inspectors to enforce the child-labour regulations. Unemployment during slump years of the 1860s reached 30 per cent. Workers spent two-thirds of their income on food, whose adulteration went unchecked by food inspectors. The local garrison swelled the clientele of prostitution, which comprised the 'fifth quarter' of the working days of many mill-girls. Poor relief was controlled by the *bureau de bienfaisance*, which linked food distribution with religious regimentation of the poor. To 'moralize' their brutalized workforce, the Catholic *patronat* subsidized a library of cheap books, portraying a Manichean world, in which honest workers resigned themselves to a life of toil, brave wives struggled against drunken husbands, and the seductions of shifty, crafty, unshaven, atheistic socialists were resisted. Illiteracy remained above 60 per cent as factory children dozed through the hour or two of lunchtime classes.

During the 1850s, only the odd socialist pamphlet smuggled from Belgium disturbed the police. The mass unemployment of the 1860s stimulated unrest, but strikes were largely confined to skilled engineering and dye workers. The employers attempted to channel discontent against free-trade policies, but growing law-and-order fears pushed them back into the arms of the regime. High illiteracy, long hours, slum dwellings, and a largely unskilled workforce made organized protest difficult. The major cultural breakthrough was a growing rejection of the clergy, who charged excessive fees, preached against birth control, and tied poor-relief to Mass attendance – but this opened the way not to socialism, but to the influence of republican lawyers and doctors who campaigned on the issue of secular education, and who captured 80 per cent of the votes in 1869.

How far can the factors which obstructed organized protest in Lille be generalized? In his brilliant, impressionistic survey of popular culture, Duveau portrayed the distaste of older, sober, self-educated artisans for the brutalized proletarian lifestyle. The worker-poet tradition died out. Political songwriters like Pierre Dupont were supplanted by the anodyne ballads of Colmance. Tolain lamented the passing of the reading public for the serious socialist press of 1848, and the taste of workers for cheap *romans feuilletons*. Corbon, who wrote of the need for technical training for workers, deplored the popularity of militaristic dramas on the popular stage. Juvenile delinquency in Paris, essentially petty theft rather than violent crime, was swelled by the decline of the number of apprenticeships available. Between 1848 and 1860, the adolescent population of the city rose by 40 per cent, apprenticeships by 13 per cent. Austere radical artisans were saddened by the popularity of music halls and dance halls, the domination of workers' sociability by gambling and billiards. Lille had one café for every eight inhabitants. Paradoxically, Proudhonists and Catholic paternalists shared a vision of the emerging industrial world as the new Sodom.

Yet such cultural assessment may be too pessimistic. Textile workers continued to send their children to the mills, but metalworkers, in an industry with less child labour, were keen on education. A favourite popular novelist remained Eugène Sue, whose books contained strong elements of populist anticlerical radicalism.

Despite the threat from mechanization, and the division of labour, an 'artisanate' survived to act as a leaven on the rest of the working class. Autodidacts continued to read Hugo, Balzac, Proudhon, and books on science. Artisans had smaller families, attended evening classes, showed an interest in secular education, kept alive the aspirations and memories of 1848. The ascetic Varlin was introduced to socialism by a left-wing teacher. If Proudhon remained a major influence, many came to question his apolitical mutualism, and to urge the necessity of political organization and strikes.

Paris's revolutionary past, and its nucleus of skilled workers, fed aspirations wider than those of factory towns. Developments there gave increasing concern to the regime. The population grew to nearly two million. Haussmann's urban renewal demolished popular quarters of central Paris, evicting workers to the northern and eastern *faubourgs*. Haussmann's construction programme mixed 'barbarism and frivolity' (Marx), and, by concentrating on theatres, boulevards, fashionable stores, bourgeois apartments and barracks, worsened the housing problem. The city's social problems were exported to the outer *faubourgs* of La Chapelle, St Denis, Belleville, out of sight of English tourists. The process hurled together 'artisans' and new factory and railway workers. Many were forced to walk long distances to work, lacked access to the cheaper food of the central market of Les Halles, had inadequate sewerage, water, housing. If money wages rose, at least till the early 1860s, there was a sense of a deteriorating urban environment. The 'psychological real wage' fell. Zola's Nana, wandering through the demolished quarter of her childhood, experiences an acute sense of alienation – though her class-vengeance was to spread VD to her upper-class clients! Abandonment of public works projects in 1868 left thousands of building workers idle.

A fascinating insight into the mentality of Parisian skilled workers comes from Denis Poulot's *Le Sublime*, written in the 1870s by an ex-foreman turned engineering employer, who was a republican, critical of the empire, but keen to resist socialism by gradualist reform and capital-labour co-operation. Poulot subdivided Parisian workers into seven categories. At one extreme was the 'true worker' – sober, loyal to his employer, aspiring to social promotion – the model of Poulot's own career. Sadly, the majority of fellow workers viewed him as a class-traitor. At the opposite pole was the *sublime* – insubordinate, sometimes drunk at the weekends, absent on Mondays, endlessly changing jobs, undeferential. Yet, unlike bourgeois moralists, Poulot's portrait is tinged with reluctant admiration. The *sublime* was, Poulot concluded, symptomatic of a disease which 'penetrated everywhere'. What did it signify? A. Cotterau suggests one answer. Despite the continued predominance of the small workshop, Paris was no longer an artisan centre in the old sense. Barely 3 per cent of its work force were independent craftsmen. Division of labour, dependence on entrepreneurs and department stores, had extended inexorably since the 1840s. The craftsman was suffering, as one militant remarked, 'a loss of his knowledge, which becomes useless to him', becoming 'a day labourer subject to brutalizing production', losing the 'intrinsic value' of his craft. The gold-chain maker in Zola's *L'Assommoir* has been reduced to endless repetitive tasks. Such workers were tied by 'invisible chains' to large capitalism, even if not, as yet, in factories. Poulot's own rivet-making plant, which initially employed 85 per cent skilled *sublimes*, introduced machine tools which de-skilled the workforce, and undercut the 'insubordination' of craftsmen. '*Sublime*-ism' was, thus, a strategy of threatened groups against erosion of their status, an attempt to resist new work-processes, foreman-control, discipline, piecework systems, such as those introduced in the Cail engineering plant, by slowing work-pace, refusing overtime, mocking foremen. To Poulot's despair, such tactics won admiration from the average worker (*ouvrier mixte*) who respected the skill and audacity of the *sublimes*. And this workshop conflict was translated into politics, for *sublimes* took the floor as speakers in the mass meetings of 1868–70, which marked the resurgence of the revolutionary left – and which rank-and-file workers attended in large numbers.

Poulot was further alarmed by another element of worker culture. He was a strong advocate of stable marriage for workers, convinced that the wife – *la bourgeoise* in argot – was a force for sobriety and moderation. Sadly, the wives or mistresses of *sublimes*, themselves often from the sweated sub-proletariat of laundresses and garment outworkers, sided with their menfolk, defended them against employers and police, denied that 'St Monday' drinking implied that their men were lazy.

Radicalism resurfaced gradually in other industrial regions. In Lyon, Prefect Vaisse's public works projects had provided construction jobs to mop up unemployment and calm the agitation of 1848–51. Government orders helped cushion the silk industry in the 1856 and 1867 slump and, as an exporter, the silk sector favoured free trade. Those co-operatives which survived 1851 tended, as elsewhere in France, to abandon socialist perspectives in favour of a pragmatic stance, adopted commercial practices, hired managers, and allowed members to accumulate capital. The regime encouraged these as a harmless diversion from militancy, and provided some financial subsidy.

Despite the slump in American markets, competition from cheap labour in rural mills, foreign competition and raw-silk disease, which raised raw material costs, the small workshops hung on tenaciously in the silk industry. They survived, as Sheridan shows, by shifting production 'down market', by replacing male journeymen with cheaper female labour, often recruited from the countryside. Master artisans worked increasingly long hours themselves. Hence, by 'feminizing' the workshops, and by self-exploitation, they kept a toehold in their industry. Their skills were still required for fancy work, their independent workshops allowed merchants to keep down their capital outlay. They were an ageing craft-group; one third were above fifty years of age by 1866. Yet their old radical spirit was uncrushed. Many retained cooperative socialist dreams, resisted ruralization of the industry, fought to raise rural price-rates, and were active in organizing semi-clandestine unions.

Lyonnais workers remained, as the *procureur général* lamented, 'profoundly alienated', forced into submission, rather than rallied to the empire. 132 arrests followed strikes in 1855. Mechanized mills were hated. If the emperor briefly became a hero in 1859 for his Italian policy, it was only 'alongside Garibaldi, I regret to add', as the prefect lamented. Mutual aid societies evaded government supervision, and ran illicit unions. The regime received no electoral pay-off for its 'indulgence'. By 1869–70, Lyon militants, affiliated to the First International, were coordinating a regional strike wave involving Stéphenois miners and ribbon weavers, building workers, Vienne textile workers, Roanne cotton and shoe workers, Grenoble and Annonay leather workers and Bas-Dauphiné silk weavers – an interesting combination of 'artisan' and 'proletarian' trades.

Similar radicalization infected Toulouse, where the *procureur général* voiced amazement at the absence of 'gratitude' for government public works projects. Master tailors, who fell from 45 per cent to 30 per cent of their trade, resisted proletarianization, the American war disrupted furniture exports, 18,000 workers in mutual aid societies escaped government controls. Geographic class-segregation was accentuated, and the proportion of the population dying propertyless had risen from 46 per cent to 58 per cent since the Restoration. By 1869, with police raiding cafés and smashing protest demonstrations, 80 per cent of the electorate were voting for radical-republicans, whose paper *L'Emancipation* espoused semi-Proudhonist ideas and campaigned for basic amenities in working-class suburbs.

The Toulouse example illustrates, however, that rejection of Bonapartism did not necessarily imply that workers would espouse socialism. The Toulouse bourgeoisie were hit by free trade, and by exposure to northern textile and metallurgy competition. Public works contracts went to Parisian firms, and local canal and transport networks were controlled by the Pereire monopoly, charging high freight rates. Bourgeois republicanism could exploit regionalist economic grievances to cement an alliance with a workforce which still spoke occitan patois. As the regime moved into crisis, it remained unclear whether worker protest, a key factor in that crisis, would remain autonomous, or be channelled by the 'progressive' wing of the republican bourgeoisie.

IV Decline and Fall (1868–70)

Bonapartism's collapse in 1870, in part the consequence of domestic political and social unrest, was accelerated by defeat in an unnecessary war with Prussia, the culmination of a decade of foreign policy blunders. Pragmatic conservatives argued that, with relative demographic decline eroding France's status as the major European power, the realistic response to the challenge of emerging nationalist powers on her eastern and south-eastern frontiers should be to bolster the *status quo* by making an alliance with tsarism and the Habsburgs to check the rise of united Germany and Italy. Instead French policy was ill-conceived, incoherent, producing the worst of all possible worlds by alienating Britain and the Holy Alliance without winning tangible gratitude from Bismarck or from Italy. Despite employing conservative-Catholic foreign ministers like Walewski, the emperor, taking a personal involvement in policy-making, made the priority the ending of the 1815 settlement, the disruption of the Holy Alliance, the rekindling of the St Helena myth of Bonapartist sympathy for emerging nationalisms. Louis Napoleon, retaining personal empathy for the Italian cause, hoped, perhaps, to make France the protector of new nations and, as with Gaullism in the 1960s, to confuse the domestic left-wing opposition by pursuing a 'progressive' foreign policy.

The Crimean expedition appeared a promising start, for it gave the regime an alliance with Britain directed against Russia's Mediterranean expansion. However the Italian policy launched in 1859 proved to be a protracted embarrassment. The motives behind the policy were many and varied, ranging from a desire to disrupt '1815' and take over Habsburg influence in North Italy, the hope of territorial annexation of Nice and Savoy and the dream of winning gratitude from Italians, to the need to divert domestic attention from the 1857–8 economic recession and the expectation of winning liberal applause in France. The net result was to alienate Italian nationalists by demanding Nice and Savoy. Italian 'gratitude' waned as French troops withdrew after early battles in North Italy and then returned to garrison Rome to prop up the tottering Temporal Power of the papacy. The British entente, carefully cultivated by the free trade treaty, was sabotaged because of London's suspicions of Bonapartist expansionist ambition. French Catholics were outraged by the danger to the papacy, the left outraged by the garrisoning of Rome.

This proved the prelude to a succession of miscalculations. When the Poles revolted in 1863 France alienated the tsar by pro-Polish rhetoric, while offering no practical aid to the rebels. The bid for a Mexican empire proved an embarrassing fiasco. A French mercantile colony of some 6000 in Mexico, stressing the potential of the region as an outlet for French textiles and wine, urged the need for intervention to end internal civil war which was producing forced loans on French traders and the cancellation of debts to French investors. Financiers with claims on the Mexican government bribed Morny, while the US civil war created a brief power vacuum. Though French exports to Mexico rose 400 per cent between 1861 and 1865, the French-backed pretender was defeated and killed. This disaster was soon compounded by inept handling of the 1866 Prusso-Austrian crisis. Underestimating Prussian military strength and anticipating a protracted war, Bonaparte stood on the sidelines while Austria was crushed and a new Germany emerged. Then, belatedly, Louis Napoleon attempted to 'cash' the informal agreement made in earlier talks with Bismarck, only to have his claim for 'compensation' in Luxembourg published by Bismarck. The result was humiliation and further worsening of relations with London, whose fears of French expansionism appeared confirmed.

Humiliated, diplomatically isolated and faced by powerful new neighbours, the regime now yearned for some foreign policy triumph to divert attention from domestic problems. Attempts to bolster military strength by the Niel army reforms, designed to move from a small full-time army to wider conscription, foundered on internal liberal opposition and the reluctance to alienate a peasant electorate endemically hostile to conscription. Bonaparte then fell into Bismarck's trap, turning the attempt of the Prussians to achieve a dynastic marriage with Spain into a *casus belli*. In this crisis France stood alone. The Habsburgs, abandoned to defeat in 1866, resisted attempts to cement an anti-Bismarck alliance. Italy resented the Roman garrison, London had been outraged by Bonapartism's territorial ambitions, Russia alienated by the Polish issue. The decaying regime blundered into a fatal 'prestige' war with barely 235,000 men mobilized against an enemy with huge trained reserves. The ageing and sick emperor compounded his errors by taking personal command of the army, and bearing personal blame for the military defeats which, by 4 September 1870, had brought his regime down.

The war, which began in mid-July, proved an unmitigated disaster both for the regime and for the French army. The Germans had the advantage of a huge trained reserve and of a powerful officer corps with very recent experience of modern warfare. With key units in Rome and in Algeria, and the railway network hopelessly clogged up by men and equipment, it took the French a fortnight to assemble 200,000 troops. Despite the recent re-equipment of some French units with new weapons such as the *chassepot* and the *mitrailleuse*, the Germans had a crucial superiority in field artillery. Within days Alsace was lost, and Lorraine invaded. When a large force under Marshal Bazaine was cut off at the border fortress of Metz, the emperor launched an ill-conceived counterattack, ignoring contingency plans for a slow strategic retreat towards Paris. On 1 September the emperor, with 84,000 troops, was surrounded at Sedan and forced to surrender. This disaster undermined the empire's already shaken prestige. When the news reached Paris a republic was proclaimed.

Zola's novel *Nana*, which culminates with overconfident chauvinistic crowds chanting 'To Berlin!', portrays the debacle of 1870 as a fitting finale to a corrupt, decaying regime. Bonapartism's apologists would deny this, arguing that the military disaster grew out of diplomatic blunders, which cut short a promising phase of political renewal. The opposition polled 40 per cent of the votes in 1869, yet remained hopelessly divided between socialists, republicans, liberals and legitimists. Rural prosperity kept the peasant vote loyal. Industrial militancy remained largely economistic, while any revival of the 'red peril' would drive the propertied elites back to support the regime. Above all, the empire could be seen as evolving in the 'liberal' direction always desired by the emperor. Morny had always urged concessions in order to avoid being swept away by the democratic tide. By 1869, after relaxing press controls and permitting the partial erosion of the 'official candidate' system, the regime had recruited ex-republican Emile Ollivier, who claimed to see the emperor as a benevolent ruler capable of reconciling liberty, democracy, order and gradual reform. In 1870, 7.1 million electors voted 'yes' in approval of reforms already underway. Some historians, thus, view the war as a brutal, accidental end to a creative experiment.

Such an assessment is too optimistic. Reforms had been piecemeal, halting, half-hearted. Indeed, the 'liberal empire', far from representing a shift to the 'left', signified the recapture of the regime by Orleanist and Catholic *notables*. Many industrialists resented free trade, Catholics deplored the Italian policy, the *Haute Banque* had always mistrusted public works projects. In the Nord, as Ménager shows, industrialists, alarmed by labour unrest, resented the regime's concessions of strike rights. The supporters of the 'liberal empire' in the Nord were, thus, Conservative, Catholic 'Orleanist' with business interests. All agreed on the necessity of tighter parliamentary controls on the executive. Duruy's education reforms were sabotaged. Foreign policy fell under the influence of the Catholic empress.

Ollivier's ministry attempted to square the circle, to provide a liberal façade to this rightward shift. A constitutional hybrid emerged, in which parliament could initiate legislation and question ministers – who remained, however, ultimately responsible to an emperor who controlled policy, and could appeal to the populace via plebiscites. The peaceable Ollivier was impotent in the war crisis. The belligerent court party demanded guarantees from the Kaiser that Prussia would never revive her Spanish marriage plans, and concealed the failure to secure a Habsburg alliance. Pushed into belligerent rhetoric to avoid appearing a feeble liberal, Ollivier succeeded only in fuelling Prussian obstinacy and mindless French chauvinism. Ollivier's prefects assured him that the public wanted war.

Like his hero Lamartine, Ollivier was an overoptimistic, confused, posturing egocentric – who sought subsequently to justify himself in a seventeen-volume history of the liberal empire. He was persuaded by his own rhetoric of the possibility of healing class divisions. His anodyne reform package included such cosmetic proposals as parliamentary control of public works and arbitration to settle industrial conflict. His actual policy involved smashing strikes and prosecuting labour leaders. Timid half-measures on tariffs appeased neither free traders nor protectionists.

The regime's successes in the 1850s rested on police repression, economic expansion, and a 'populist' ability to appear to stand aloof from the elites. After 1860, as the economic boom faded, the regime's attempts to appease the liberals and the left merely permitted a resurgence of the republican and labour movements, viewed with alarm both by the regime and conservatives in the propertied elite. One response to this danger was a revived Party of Order, masquerading as 'liberalization'. The threat to social and political stability finally tempted the regime into risking a short war. Already on 6 October 1868, the *procureur général* of Toulouse, alarmed by growing opposition successes, stressed the desirability of a war to divert opinion from 'these . . . irritating questions of internal politics'.

The labour unrest of 1869–70 was political, not merely economistic. The wave of public meetings in Paris illustrates the appeal of revolutionary ideas to a sizeable minority of the city's workers. In 1868, the regime had attempted to appease worker opposition by legalizing public meetings. Over 1300 were held in two years. Six thousand regularly packed the *Folies Belleville* and other dance halls in the northern and eastern *faubourgs*. Most were dominated by Blanquist and internationalist speakers, future communard leaders – casting doubt on the cliché that Blanquism was a sectarian movement without popular support, and that the Commune was simply an accidental by-product of the war. The liberal Molinari lamented that the meetings showed that 90 per cent of thinking workers were either socialist or in the process of becoming so. Rejecting Proudhonist, apolitical, mutualist ideas, most speakers emphasized the need for revolutionary overthrow of a capitalist, Bonapartist state which used troops against strikers, manipulated the law, and used clerical schooling to keep workers in ignorance. The betrayals of 1830 and 1848 were invoked as warnings against middle-class republicanism. By mid-1869 rioting became endemic in Paris, with 900 arrests in Belleville, on 11 June alone, and the regime began to reimpose meeting controls and prosecute militant speakers.

Nor was such militancy confined to Paris. By 1869, the First International group in the Lyonnais, a small sect in 1867, were coordinating a regional strike wave. In 1869, Lyon gave 75 per cent of its votes to Raspail, and the local prefect saw worker-capitalist conflict becoming 'general and permament'. Albert Richard addressed mass meetings in 1870 declaring 'war on capital, the bourgeoisie and power in all its forms', and insisting that a republic was necessary but not sufficient for social reforms. Lyon financier Aynard expressed a growing pessimism as Bonapartism lost its grip.

Yet workers' leaders like Richard, or Bastelica in Marseille, shared a central dilemma. Did the desire to destroy the Bonapartist regime imply an alliance with republicanism? Personal inclination warned them against this. Richard feared a trap, and urged workers to abstain rather than vote republican. Yet most came to accept the need for tactical cooperation. They shared a common interest in anticlericalism, secular education, and in overthrowing the regime. Bastelica joined the education pressure group *Ligue de l'Enseignement*. In Toulouse, workers rallied behind the radical paper *L'Emancipation*. In Paris, as Wolfe shows, most workers rallied to radical-republican candidates in the 1869 election. Socialists were drawn, reluctantly, into a broad anti-Bonapartist front, aware of the dangers, but convinced that they could not overthrow the regime unaided.

Republicanism had made a strong resurgence after the impotence of the 1850s, when its leaders had been exiled, their contacts with France monitored by the political police. Bonapartism's manipulation of universal suffrage stole their clothes, reducing them to tracts like Hugo's *Napoleon the Little* which portrayed the emperor as a scheming nonentity, but failed to analyse the Bonapartist phenomenon. Their one, limited, outlet was the anticlerical *Le Siècle*, tolerated by a regime which was always slightly wary of its Catholic 'allies'. The 'liberalization' which followed the Italian war and free trade persuaded some to rally to the regime, in the hope of reforming it, and many admired Duruy's education policies, while moderates like J. Simon, who rejected hard-line Voltairean or positivist anticlericalism, flirted with liberal Catholics in the 1863 Liberal Union and the 1865 Nancy Programme, which purported to see decentralization as the key to France's problems. Yet few Bonapartists had any illusions about their ability to seduce the republican movement as a whole. By 1862, prefects were alarmed at increasing evidence that the 'factious' republican middle class was reorganizing itself.

Historians agree that republicanism was dominated by the middling strata of French society – lawyers, doctors, journalists, provincial businessmen – who played down the 'extremism' and 'socialism' of 1848, and hoped to attract broad peasant and worker support through educational reform and anticlericalism. At this point, historical consensus breaks down. Elwitt has portrayed republicans as cynical manipulators, utilizing a 'progressive' rhetoric to sell bourgeois values to rural and urban masses, in order to defend essential capitalist economic interests more effectively. Auspitz sees them as genuine progressives, liberating France from authoritarianism and clericalism. Republican militants, as even their enemies confessed, were sober, industrious men. Denis Gros, editor of the ferociously anticlerical Lyon paper *L'Excommunié*, was of 'irreproachable conduct, regular habits'. Although only a minority were Protestant many shared a quasi-puritan work ethic.

Their anticlericalism was not a mere tactical device to woo the workers, but deep-seated, and deeply felt. They remembered the church bells and obsequious sermons, which had greeted the 1851 coup, and the clergy's unique freedom to organize in the 1850s, a freedom denied to all other groups. Republicans saw themselves the custodians of the authentic moral values of modern society, denouncing Catholicism for its failure to instil personal, internalized values necessary for citizens in a democracy, for encouraging sloth and vice by condoning it in the confessional. The republican leader in Voiron (Isère), a bicycle manufacturer, campaigned ferociously against wasting local resources on a Madonna overlooking the town, emphasizing the poverty and illiteracy which accompanied clericalism in Italy and Spain. The clergy were unproductive, contributing nothing useful to society. As intellectuals espoused Littré's positivism, and medical students like Clemenceau read Darwin, the Syllabus of Errors and the ultramontane obsessions with miracles appeared both absurd and pernicious. In *Clericals and Bonapartists*, published in the early 1870s, P. Joigneaux stressed that clericalism had gained an increasing hold over the empire. The consequences in education would be that teachers would have to condemn Galileo as an imposter; doctors would have to abandon drugs and use Lourdes water; peasants would have to abandon chemicals and return to prayers and processions to fight crop diseases!

One central obsession was the clergy's control over women, the door to control of children, and, thus, of future generations. The republic would never be safe while 'our wives and our daughters are brought up by our enemies', asserted Michelet, who bore the psychological scars of having his mistress turn to a priest in her dying days. Religious practice was increasingly 'feminized'. Hard-working republican husbands lamented losing influence over their wives to feline priests, who had mastered the art of flattering small talk. Zola's novel *A Priest in the House* was to attribute the decline of republicanism in a small Provençal town to the secret sexual influence of a priest over the wives of the bourgeoisie. Republicans shared Flaubert's conviction, in *Madame Bovary*, that convent schooling made middle-class girls idle, ill-educated, and sexually obsessed by the erotic mysticism of religious imagery. Republicans were patriarchal rather than authentic feminists. They shared Duruy's concern to heal the 'intellectual divorce' between husbands and wives by encouraging secular secondary schooling for bourgeois girls – in order to produce suitable wives for liberal husbands not, of course, to encourage female access to professional careers. The success of Mgr Dupanloup's crusade against Duruy's modest proposals convinced them that only a republic could implement such reforms.

Republicans also emphasized that only compulsory, laic primary schooling could liberate workers from the rote-learning and catechism of Catholic schools, which kept them in brutalized ignorance. Many workers, increasingly preoccupied with educational issues, were potentially responsive to republican propaganda in this area, offering the prospect of wider career prospects for the educated working-class child. More cynically, one could argue that republican industrialists felt that economic efficiency demanded a literate workforce, that schools should disseminate laissez-faire values, and that education was a more appropriate device for establishing bourgeois cultural hegemony than was a Catholicism tied to the old elites, and increasingly anathema to an anticlerical proletariat. Jean Macé's *Ligue de l'Enseignement* (*LE*) regarded education as the weapon for inculcating republican values. It grew out of a number of existing local, liberal, educational pressure groups involved in running adult classes. Although some Bonapartist education officials welcomed the *LE* as an ally against clericalism, most treated it with suspicion and obstructed it as potentially subversive. Despite Auspitz's emphasis on the all-class character of the *LE*, with eight of its first fifteen members in Lyon silk weavers, there is little doubt about its essentially capitalist nature. It was backed by Protestant Alsace industrialists like Koechlin and St Simonian tycoons like Arlès-Dufour in Lyon. In the Yonne, where it was active in establishing popular libraries and holding lectures, it built upon the deep-seated anticlerical radicalism of artisans and wine growers, but was to be dominated by men like timber-merchant's son Paul Bert. Macé saw it as a 'League of Internal Peace', designed to bridge the unfortunate gulf between bourgeoisie and workers, and praised a lycée teacher, who held workers' classes in his home, for showing to the workers 'the propriety and courtesy of well-bred people'. Jules Ferry, a republican lawyer and future architect of the Third Republic's education reforms, claimed that Frenchmen of all classes would now mingle on the school bench – the prelude to a society where employer-worker relations would be based no longer on deference, but on mutually agreed contracts between equals! Republicans stressed that they believed in 'solidarity', but not in absolute equality. Bourgeoisie and proletariat were both needed in society, just as the body needed head and hands, but capitalist division of labour created both diversity and interdependence.

During the 1860s, a vigorous network of clubs, masonic lodges and agronomy groups emerged to give concrete form to republican counterculture. The defeat of 1851 was viewed as due to a failure to create organizations which could inculcate republican values.

Auspitz's portrait of the progressive idealism of the 'radical bourgeoisie' is suggestive, but one-sided and rose-tinted. For, as Elwitt clearly shows, central to the republican revival were hard-headed but disaffected businessmen such as Derègnaucourt of Roubaix, who desired a regime of property and order, which they felt that the empire was now unable to deliver. Authoritarian coercion could not guarantee social peace, for stability required a modicum of concensus. Fearing worker revolt, they wished to pre-empt it, organize it, and set its limits. They represented newer provincial industrial capitalists, critical of a regime excessively tied to mercantile and financial interests, hit by high freight rates charged by monopolistic rail companies, angry, as in Toulouse, that lucrative public works contracts went to Parisian firms. In Rheims, republican woollen manufacturers and textile-machine makers like Jules Warner and Villeminot-Huard resented the influence of older mercantile and wine interests over the local prefect. In St Étienne, medium-scale metallurgical employers like Dorian were republican, while big engineering magnates like Arbel were still conservative. Dorian hoped to head off the militancy of local workers by constructing a 'progressive' but non-socialist alternative to Bonapartism. He denounced the 'feudal' threat from aristocracy and clergy. Republicanism was, in that sense, an ideology permitting capitalists to appear 'progressive with regard to the Middle Ages'.

Men like Allain-Targé were, thus, advocating a republic on the American model, 'democratic' but capitalist. Anticlericalism was both a deeply held conviction and an ideal diversionary strategy to turn worker militancy away from attacks on capitalism. Gambetta, a southern lawyer from a humble petty-bourgeois background who became the republicans' rising star by winning an election in Belleville on a radical platform, insisted that the clergy had become 'the cadres of an outdated spiritual authority, too weak to secure order, but well-equipped to trouble it'. The republican historian Quinet argued that religious wars were much preferable to civil or class wars, for in the former rich and poor could be found on the same side!

The republican package offered in 1869–70 proposed secular schooling, church-state separation, tax reform, and cheaper credit. Businessmen were promised cheaper freight-rates, and protectionist tariffs. In Roanne, a textile town near St Étienne, local resentment at the influx of British textile imports was channelled into a joint employer-worker crusade against free trade. Dorian – a Protestant, St Simonian, an 'enlightened' employer – wooed workers with abuse of the empire and the clergy, while smashing strikes.

The success of this strategy was not inevitable. Roanne textile workers threatened to escape Dorian's control. Bastelica denounced Gambetta's 'liberal double talk', which promised to emancipate workers 'without conflict, and without compromising the position of those favoured by wealth'. A. Richard warned of a 'dupe's alliance'. And yet, such militants saw the workers as needing allies to confront Bonapartism. They were susceptible to the lure of secular education – indeed, Bastelica was in the *LE*. When military disasters overthrew the empire on 4 September provincial businessmen like Dorian crowned years of patient planning by seizing local control.

V The Paris Commune – a Socialist Revolution?

A government of national defence was established, which attempted to use republican patriotism to achieve social cohesion, while secretly working for a rapid ceasefire with the Prussians, and national elections to free itself from dangerous dependence on radical Paris, whose petty bourgeoisie and workers responded to the Prussian siege with neo-Jacobin patriotic defiance. News of further army capitulation at Metz triggered an abortive revolution in the capital in October.

The task of rekindling the national spirit of 1792 to resist the Prussians fell to the interior minister of the government of national defence, Gambetta. Having purged the bureaucracy of Bonapartist officials, he attempted to recruit fresh armies. Despite his efforts the Germans pushed steadily westwards in the autumn towards the central Loire, leaving Paris besieged in the wake of their advance. In October Bazaine's army of 173,000 surrendered at Metz, possibly because their Bonapartist commander had done a deal with Bismarck to keep his forces intact for future use against Parisian socialists. Prussian forces were thereby released from the frontier region to throw back Gambetta's attempts to relieve Paris from the Loire valley and compel the French government itself to retreat to Bordeaux.

Paris remained under siege across the winter, with Bismarck choosing to starve it into submission. Within the capital resistance was increasingly organized by the left in a mood of neo-Jacobin defiance. For many 'moderates' the essential priority became not the winning of the war but 'to repel the forces of anarchy and prevent a shameful revolt in Paris' (Favre). By January 1871, with Gambetta's counterattacks increasingly ineffectual and with the Prussians bombarding Paris, Thiers was able to implement his strategy of negotiating an armistice with the Prussians in order to permit national elections, form a new government and sign a peace treaty.

Already within Paris news of the Metz capitulation had triggered an abortive socialist rising in late October. As the siege was prolonged across the winter months of 1870–1, material hardships and food shortages accentuated popular militancy. There were calls for the election of a Commune to run the city. Worker-clubs mushroomed in the popular *quartiers*, dominated by Blanquists in the twentieth *arrondissement*, and Internationalists on the Left Bank. Local vigilance committees established a *Central Committee of the Twenty Arrondissements*, which urged the government to link the continued war-effort with a social-democratic programme, including trade-union rights, and the abolition of the Paris police prefecture. In January 1871, 140 signatories from the vigilance committees tried to spark a popular rising by appeals for an elected commune. With the siege at its height, this evoked sympathy, but little active response, and an attempted coup in late January proved abortive.

The national elections of 6 February witnessed a majority vote for peace, expressed by large royalist gains in much of rural France, with Prussian troops occupying northern and eastern regions. Yet in Paris a revolutionary socialist party won fifty thousand votes, and the capital gave a huge majority for radicals urging a continuation of the war. Most alarming for the new government, determined to make a rapid peace in order to avoid turning the war into an armed popular struggle, was the attitude of the Parisian National Guard. Swollen to over 300,000 during the siege, providing the only income for thousands made redundant by economic disruption, this militia had been outraged by the mixture of military inactivity and suicidal sorties of the winter. It feared that the new government would re-establish the monarchy and surrender to Prussia. A *Central Committee of the National Guard*, fiercely patriotic and republican, if ill-organized and lacking clear political strategy, resisted such threats – and by 13 March 215 of 270 guards units had rallied to it.

Four provocative measures served to widen the gulf between Paris and the new administration. Thiers denied Parisians the right to elect their own municipality, abolished the 1.50 franc daily National Guard allowance, and ended the moratorium on debts and rents declared during the siege, outraging wide sections of the Parisian petty bourgeoisie, who had hitherto voted republican. Thiers, determined to seize his opportunity to smash the Parisian left, insisted that only a reassertion of governmental control over the capital could rebuild business confidence to raise loans to pay indemnities to the victorious Prussians. But an attempt by regular troops to seize cannon in northern Paris in March provoked a violent popular revolt. With bourgeois radicals like Clemenceau unwilling to challenge Thiers by force, leadership passed to socialists like Varlin. Fresh elections within the National Guard battalions gave many officer posts to artisans, and in an election for a commune the left's share of the poll rose to 80 per cent from its previous peak of 25 per cent – though the numbers voting had dropped by one-third on the February level.

From March until May the Commune held out against Thiers's troops, reinforced by prisoners released by Bismarck, for, as Marx noted, in the war against socialism, French and Prussian reactionaries eagerly made common cause. But was the Commune 'socialist'? This issue has been central to subsequent historiographical debate, and been confused by conflicting ideological traditions, themselves full of paradoxes. Modern liberal scepticism about communard 'socialism' was, at times, expressed by Marx himself, while subsequent left-wing mythology and hagiography, which idolizes the Commune as the first embryonic proletarian government, coincides with contemporary rightist opinion, which was convinced that 'communard' meant 'communist'.

Recent liberal historiography has been concerned to debunk the Commune's 'socialist' credentials. The revolt is portrayed as a patriotic and municipalist upsurge of a city which bore the brunt of the siege, felt betrayed by the capitulation of a 'royalist' government, and injured in its municipal pride by its failure to secure rights of electing its own local administration. Greenberg has claimed that the municipalist autonomy platform was echoed in Lyon, Marseille, and elsewhere, and was part of a broad reaction against Bonapartist centralization, shared by many provincial republican moderates. The 19 April appeal of the Parisians to provincial towns was couched in language of decentralist federalism. It is argued that, until March 1871, the revolutionary-socialist left had polled only 25 per cent of the city vote, and that the 'leftward' shift of the petty bourgeoisie came only because of economic grievances, accentuated by the debt and rent issue. Wolfe's study of the eighteenth *arrondissement* emphasizes that the sizeable, but strictly minority, appeal of its revolutionary club from 1869 onwards was converted to local political supremacy only because of disgust with the failure of radical-republicans to resist Thiers's seizure of the cannon.

Once in power, it is argued, the communards' policies were populist rather than socialist. Leaders like Delescluze were neo-

Jacobins, interested in political rather than social revolution. The obsession with anticlericalism, church-state separation and laicization of schools emerged because this was an issue which could unite workers and petty bourgeoisie. Despite the demands of local clubs for confiscation of the resources of major financial institutions, the Commune's approach to financial matters was timid. The socialist novelist Vallès described the 'terror of the poor' in face of piles of banknotes in the Bank of France. Jourde and Beslay tried to solicit the sympathy of bank officials, in a futile effort to appease provincial opinion – and the latter was 'rewarded' with safe conduct to Switzerland to escape the May bloodbath. Many of the Commune's reforms were piecemeal and pragmatic. Rents were cancelled, a three-year delay on debt repayment was decreed, artisans were permitted to reclaim pawned tools, bakery nightwork was ended. There was no attempt at systematic national-ization.

Marx is often credited with the creation of a 'myth' which ignores such realities. Yet Marx had warned against a bid for power, which he felt to be doomed to end in military repression, was overtly critical of valiant neo-Jacobins who 'knew history too well', drew their poetry from past revolutions, dreamed that a coup in Paris would trigger European revolution, and wasted energy on peripheral targets like the clergy. Only two communard leaders were 'Marxist'. The future French Marxist leader, Guesde, later insisted that 'it was not a question of communism, but of the Commune, a very different thing.' A decade later, Marx himself summed it up as the rising of a city under exceptional war conditions. Its majority, he added, were not socialist, nor could they have been. The term 'Commune' was suitably resonant but imprecise – evoking '1793', municipal autonomy, patriotism or socialism to different groups. In part, Marx's emphasis on the Commune as the 'glorious harbinger of a new society', a model for a future socialist worker's state, stemmed from conscious myth-making, an attempt to salvage a martyrology from the wreckage.

Yet the right's own paranoia fostered this socialist legend. The ferocious repression, leaving 100,000 Parisians dead, jailed, or exiled, which followed the capture of the city by Thiers's troops in late May, was concentrated on the workers. One English journalist reported an officer shooting a prisoner in the face after asking him his occupation, with the phrase 'Ah, so it's the stonemasons who would rule now!' The normally unsqueamish *Times* noted, of the mass shooting and bayonetting of women and children: 'So far as we can recollect, there has been nothing like it in history.' The First International, a loose amorphous body, was elevated by the right's plot theory into the satanic organizing force, and banned across Europe. Right-wing literature created a nightmare beast of socialist hordes of criminals, drunks, *déclassés*, prostitutes and feminists which haunted the 'crowd theory' of Taine and Le Bon in subsequent years. The savagery of bourgeois revenge was fuelled by those conservatives who stayed on in the city during the Commune. Apart from some protests from mayors of wealthy *arrondissements* like Tirard, their internal resistance had been insignificant, limited to spreading defeatist rumours. They then sought psychological compensation for their impotence by braying for blood. One elderly bourgeois, Leon Colin, wrote to Thiers calling for mass extermination and volunteering for the honour of participating in the firing squads.

Yet, the contemporary right grasped essential truths apparently lost in the nuanced qualifications of sceptical modern liberal historians, who denature the Commune by reducing it to sober quantification (only *x* per cent of Parisians voted socialist etc.), thereby robbing it of its specific characteristics. Marx rightly claimed that its achievement lay in its working existence as a government, however ephemeral, run by and for groups outside the capitalist elites. Thirty-five of the 80 Commune members were workers, largely artisans rather than *faubourg* proletarians. The grass-roots worker clubs had genuine insights into the need to destroy the existing state machine, rather than attempting to use it. They stressed the need for direct democracy, popular control of the militia, the creation of new alternative popular governing cadres to replace the army, police and bureaucracy. They envisaged popular control over a state elected to achieve an egalitarian social order.

As Schulkind emphasizes, the authentic commune lies as much in local popular club activity as in the decrees of the central Commune which, inevitably, was preoccupied with military survival. As we have seen, the extraordinary upsurge of revolutionary demands voiced in the Parisian mass meetings of 1868–70 undermines the cliché that it was simply the war which radicalized the city. The establishment of 43 producer cooperatives, and proposals that commune orders should go to these, provides a clear link with the 'associationist' socialism of 1848. The confiscation of the factories of capitalists who had deserted the city was a measure which was carried with little or no opposition on the commune executive. 'Neo-Jacobins' like Vermorel were not simply reliving '1793', their emphasis on continuity with the revolutionary tradition was fused with a new emphasis on the social emancipation of the proletariat.

Worker anticlericalism, too, was more than a mere atavistic diversion, for it expressed a deep hostility to the 'black crows' who overcharged for weddings and funerals, to nuns who supervised convent workshops whose laundry and embroidery prices undercut those of working-class women. Workers retained bitter memories of the clergy's Bonapartism, resented the 'obscuranist' education of church schools, and the humiliation of the paupers' bench where many had been educated. Vaillant's education committee, which advocated free, secular schooling which should include elements of technical training, was responding to expressed working-class aspirations. It also urged equality for girl pupils, for, despite the residual male chauvinism of Proudhonist artisans, women's issues played an important role in the social debate of the communards. Though subsequent rightist myths of squads of female petrol-bombers (*pétroleuses*) were exaggerated, the subproletariat of laundresses and seamstresses was mobilized. A female clothing cooperative was established in the eighteenth *arrondissement* to provide National Guard uniforms. There were demands for crèches and postnatal rest for working-class mothers. The Commune took responsibility for widows and orphans, and sanctified common-law marriages (*unions libres*) by ending discrimination against illegitimate children.

If the commune began with overtones of a municipalist-patriotic movement, these faded as the weeks passed, and the initial lower-middle class republican support waned. The vote in the 16 April by-elections was below that of March, as support narrowed along class lines. If the Commune executive was preoccupied with military defence, local clubs and associations were involved in a widespread social experiment. As H. Lefebvre claims, the Commune was a 'festival of the oppressed', whose fervour escapes the quantification of liberal-positivist historiography. It was an attempt of working-class people to change their lives, live differently, to try to achieve goals hitherto thought impossible. Class-consciousness moves in leaps, not with steady, measured tread. The *faubourg* workers were, symbolically, reoccupying *their* city, from which Haussmann's urban renewal had expelled them. The spring sunshine stimulated street theatre, songs; a mood of carnival. The revitalized Courbet headed an artists' association. Cartoons and newspapers proliferated. The Paris working class rediscovered and recognized itself.

None of this can disguise the Commune's many weaknesses. It was short-lived, left no tangible legacy. Its defeat persuaded Engels that, in the face of modern military technology, the urban armed insurrection had become obsolete. Its leaders exhibited a superfluity of ideas. Their official documents reveal pomposity, lunatic fantasies and tired propagandist slogans alongside incisive insights and imaginative proposals. It was torn by internal feuding. Proudhonists rejected the creation of a Committee of Public Safety as a return to pernicious 'Jacobin' dictatorship. The Commune executive clashed with National Guard commanders. Marxists later commented on the fatal absence of a revolutionary party. Blanqui, who *might* have provided a unifying presence, was in jail. Catholics in the government refused to exchange him for Mgr Darboy, and happily watched the communards shoot the archbishop in the last days of the conflict, for Darboy was a liberal Catholic who had opposed papal infallibility! The strong *esprit de quartier*, which had been a source of strength when the women of Montmartre refused to allow General Thomas's troops to seize 'their' cannon, with the name of the *quartier* engraved on its bronze, proved, as Vallès noted, a weakness in the last days of the fighting when each *quartier* seemed preoccupied with its own defence.

And yet, these myriad divisions were drowned in the ocean of blood which followed the defeat. The right resurrected old legends about the criminal and dangerous classes. Bonapartist judicial records were scoured to prove the criminal past of insurgents. *Le Figaro* called the communards 'thieves' and exhorted 'honest men' to 'exterminate' the 'democratic vermin'. Thiers informed his prefects that the 'horrible sight' of piles of massacred corpses would produce a 'useful lesson' to keep workers in their place. In fact, as Rougerie has shown, the unskilled floating poor, prominent in 1869 police records, were relatively scarce among the Commune's defenders. The 'NCOs' of the insurgents came from skilled printing and wood trades. The rank and file mixed 'sweated' artisans, though fewer than in 1848, with metal and building workers, who comprised 18 per cent of the Parisian population, but 30 per cent of the deportees. Some of the metalworkers were employed in the enormous Cail and Gouin engineering plants, although as skilled men with recent experience of artisan workshops, they had not been reconciled to the tight disciplines of the factory. It was, in short, an 'intermediate' working class, poised between 'proletarians' and 'artisans', leaning still towards its past. For the right, however, the fact that workers had succeeded in running the city made discrediting them that much more urgent. Legends of communard pillage and rape were manufactured. When, later in the decade, Zola wrote *L'Assommoir* to show how the misery of social deprivation drove workers to drink, bourgeois readers interpreted the novel as proving that alcoholic workers brought misery on their own heads. The massacre of captured communards by the triumphant forces of order in the days after the fall of the city was on a much larger scale than in 1848, more open, less furtive. There were no gestures of pardoning 'misled' rank and file. Unable, for once, to hide behind any patriotic mask, the right's class vengeance was naked.

Yet, the repression was an error as well as a crime. It gave the Commune, which could perhaps have faded into oblivion, a final heroic, tragic grandeur. Throughout the Third Republic, the left made its annual pilgrimage, often under police harassment, to the Père Lachaise cemetery. Left-wing politicians like Raspail were jailed in the 1870s for daring to advocate amnesty for the survivors. A century later, with '1968' fresh in its mind, the Gaullist Fifth Republic was too apprehensive to permit official centenary commemorations.

Marx hoped that a decisive lead from Paris might inspire a broad populist alliance of provincial workers, peasants and petty bourgeoisie, although under working-class control not, as in 1848–51, dominated by the radical bourgeoisie. Such hopes remained unrealized. Yet the usual contrast made between Paris and the conservative provinces in 1870–1 is misleading. In the south, a radical regionalist third force emerged which, while reluctant to give full support to the Commune, genuinely loathed Thiers. Labour unrest and mass political meetings had involved Lyon, Marseille and Toulouse in 1869–70. Southern cities and surrounding peasant areas had often voted 'no' in the plebisicite, with worker leaders like Bastelica making the overthrow of Bonapartism the priority. The early weeks of the war had seen demonstrations against Bonapartism's military incompetence. If an anarchist coup in September in Lyon was abortive, a radical municipality proceeded to secularize schools, abolish the *octroi* tax, and provide public works jobs. A *Ligue du Midi* emerged to coordinate the defence of the south, but calling also for separation, secular education, taxes on the rich, a bureaucratic purge, and municipal autonomy.

The commune revolt triggered sister communes, in late March in Lyon, Marseille, Toulouse, St Étienne, Narbonne and Le Creusot, although radical bourgeois leaders retained a control which they had lost in the capital, and even in proletarian La Guillotière, near Lyon, priority was given simply to education and tax reforms. They welcomed the Commune's manifesto of 19 April with its stress on municipal rights – a tactical device by the Parisians to woo provincial support by suggesting that each municipality should have the freedom to proceed with reforms in line with local opinions and priorities. On 14 May a congress of radical municipal councillors in Lyon urged a compromise between Paris and Thiers – though rejecting a motion that war against the latter should be waged if he remained intransigent.

The existence of this broad-based movement dispels the standard picture of monolithic provincial conservatism. It echoed the *Dem-Soc* peasant mobilization of 1849–51 although two decades of rural prosperity or rural exodus had muted the radicalism of some 'red' departments – and foreshadowed the 'municipal socialism' of the 1890s. It fed on Midi regionalist hostility to the 'northern' state and on fears of royalist restoration. Anti-army and anti-conscription feelings were strong, there were mass desertions from the 52nd Regiment in Narbonne, and calls for a citizens' militia. If they failed to aid Paris in its agony, they were appalled by the repression, rejected both royalist moral order and the conservative republic. In the early 1870s Lyon clung grimly, in face of prefectoral hostility, to its laicized schools.

Part Four

The Bourgeois Republic (1871–1914)

Chapter 6

Republican France

I The Making of the Conservative Republic (1871–98)

In 1879 Gambetta claimed that the 'period of dangers' for the republic was over, though a 'period of difficulties' had still to be faced. The republic's triumph was, essentially, that of the more 'progressive', flexible and strategically perceptive sections of the capitalist class, which outmanoeuvred their royalist and radical rivals by attracting a broad cross-class alliance of petty producers into a national consensus which they defined and controlled.

Yet, as Gambetta suggested, the 1870s were marked by acute dangers for the republicans. Until 1876 the republic existed by default. The empire had perished in military disaster and the royalist parliamentary majority, produced by the February 1871 elections, failed to restore the monarchy only through the royalists' inability to negotiate a compromise between the rival dynasties. The legitimist pretender, Chambord, became, as Thiers noted laconically, the republic's 'George Washington', its true founder, with his refusal to accept the tricolour as a symbol of compromise with Orleanism. Despite his own Orleanist past, Thiers came to favour a republic as the regime which would divide Frenchmen the least, which alone could avoid civil war, and, as cynics suggested, which alone could make M. Thiers himself the first citizen, 'King Adolphe I'. His role in smashing the Commune, the culmination of his own pet strategy, conceived in 1848, of evacuating Paris in order to return to annihilate the left, won his version of the republic the sympathy of conservatives, including opportunistic Orleanists, more concerned with order than with the name of the regime.

Barral has outlined the close relationship between the moderate republican Casimir-Périer and his Orleanist brother-in-law, the duc D'Audiffret Pasquier. Family and business interests pushed both men into joint effort to secure a conservative republic. H. Germain, head of the *Crédit Lyonnais*, alarmed by Bonapartist foreign policy adventurism, and fearing that a monarchy would provoke 'anti-feudal' popular revolt, admired Thiers as the destroyer of the commune for, as his son noted, 'there is in each *grand-bourgeois* some obstinacy and some ferocity. It was because of his bourgeois prejudice that he exalted Thiers, the intransigent apologist of property and supreme incarnation of the bourgeois.' Germain helped Thiers raise the loan to pay the indemnity to the Germans and was prevented from becoming finance minister only through the veto of rival financier Rothschild. As J. Bouvier emphasizes, many bankers shared Germain's fear that monarchy might produce chaos and confusion.

Thiers attempted to woo European sympathy for the new regime by promoting a crusade against the First International. The large indemnity was paid to the Germans with great alacrity and without any dangerous breach of financial orthodoxy. Loans were negotiated by Rothschild, who took a sizeable cut. Indirect consumer taxes were raised. Hundreds of thousands of provincial bourgeois investors were tempted to contribute to the loans. Suggestions of financing the indemnity through progressive income tax were indignantly rejected. As R. Schnerb argued, such policy represented 'economic reaction under the guise of financial necessity'. When conscription was introduced in 1872, Thiers, as in 1848, rejected the principle of the equal liability of bourgeois offspring.

The influence of the German government on the young republic should not be overlooked. Bismarck had released French prisoners to defeat the Commune, and the presence of German troops on French soil till 1873 gave him considerable 'leverage'. Unlike the Reich's ambassador, Arnim, Bismarck viewed a moderate republic as ideal for German purposes. A radical regime would pose a 'Jacobin' threat of social revolution, while a Catholic monarchy might secure an anti-German alliance with the Habsburgs and provide support for south German Catholics, Bismarck's domestic political opponents. A conservative republic would appear too radical for European monarchies, yet would pose no social threat to European conservatives. Thiers, thus, posed as *the* statesman capable of securing a deal with Bismarck for rapid German troop evacuation. The heavy indemnity which ensured this withdrawal, financed by indirect taxation, may have been a factor weakening French economic performance in the 1870s, as indeed the loss of industrially advanced Alsace-Lorraine to Germany certainly was.

The royalist parliamentary majority tolerated Thiers until the German issue was settled in 1873, but with increasing anger at his apparent leniency towards Gambetta's propaganda which was resulting in republican by-election gains, culminating in the success of Barodet in Lyon, who supported amnesty for communard exiles. Such developments, they feared, were leading to 'anarchy'. Yet, German influence outlasted Thiers's fall. Bismarck expressed calculated disapproval of his successor, the Orleanist Broglie, using the public prayers of the bishop of Nancy for the recovery of Alsace as a pretext for fomenting a war scare. Fearful of the consequences of another war, pragmatic conservatives turned to Décazes, whose cabinet was essentially Thiers-ist. One major element in republican electoral gains in 1876–7 was that Gambetta portrayed himself as a guarantor of peace, implying that Catholic-royalists planned war against Italy to restore papal temporal power which would involve confrontation with the anti-Catholic Reich. Once the republicans dominated government after 1877 Bismarck expressed approval of the regime, permitting German painters to send works to the 1878 Paris Exhibition. Gambetta, who had quietly shelved demands for *revanche*, gave Bismarck the government he desired.

Royalists made determined efforts to salvage their declining cause between 1873 and 1877.* They used their parliamentary majority to establish a senate and a powerful seven-year presidency, both seen as preludes to a constitutional monarchy. They placed their hopes in President McMahon, an officer of royalist sympathies. When the republicans won the 1876 elections, by 360 seats to 150, McMahon refused to offer the task of forming a government to Gambetta, choosing instead J. Simon. He accepted the post in an effort to show that a conservative republic could exist, free of radicalism and excessive anticlericalism, and hoped to create a broad coalition from Broglie to Ferry, using his control of governmental patronage to win over Gambettists. However, Simon's liberalism was trapped in the crossfire between Catholic-royalists, agitating for support for the papacy, and Gambettists who demanded a tough line against ultramontane clergy. Caught between a republican parliament and a royalist president and senate, Simon's position was hopeless. Prompted by

* See chapter 7.

his royalist backers, McMahon dissolved parliament and called new elections in 1877. He used his powers to harass republicans. Two-thirds of the prefectoral corps were purged, 1743 mayors dismissed, republican officials and teachers sacked, cafés closed and newspapers prosecuted. Yet such pressure failed to ensure republican electoral defeat, for they secured 54 per cent of the vote and lost only 40 seats.

This triumph owed much to Gambetta's political evolution. In 1869 he had appeared a radical firebrand, a quasi-socialist who alarmed conservatives. After 1871 he changed his spots, happily accepting the label 'opportunist' from radicals who viewed him as a traitor. He abandoned calls for *revanche* and sought a *modus vivendi* with Thiers, who viewed his radical rhetoric as harmless. He accepted the senate. He preserved a studious neutrality over the Commune issue, his hand stained with the blood of neither Versaillais or communards, and refused to agitate for an amnesty. Portraying the royalists as the new warmongers, he posed as the true conservative. His republic meant order, prosperity, peace and national unity. Republicanism was the 'conservative party which assures the legal and peaceful working-out of the French Revolution'. His oratory gave life to stale clichés, while phrases like 'Clericalism! There is the enemy!' caught the imagination of the crowds who came to hear the republic's leading travelling salesman. Unlike Simon, who sought an alliance with clergy and old *notables*, Gambetta was prepared to preach a pseudo-class war against the clerical-feudal elites. Beyond this he rejected class-analysis, using the term *couches* (strata) 'not classes, a distasteful word which I never employ'. The republic was portrayed as the natural alliance of healthy, productive, useful capitalists with rising *nouvelles couches* – lawyers, doctors, teachers, peasants. Only the republic could reconcile 'sacred property rights' with the legitimate aspirations of the masses. With universal suffrage and political democracy the social question ceased to exist. If Midi peasants continued to utilize busts of *Marianne* complete with the red phrygian bonnet, the iconography of republicanism shifted rapidly to mirror this new respectability. The official *Mariannes* who adorned town halls by 1880 wore a halo of flowers and the motto *Concorde*, moving towards that anodyne statue which France sent to her fellow capitalist republic as the Statue of Liberty.

Gambetta's biographer, J. Bury, sees his hero as subjectively sincere in his insistence that the republic *per se* had solved the social question. Elwitt's analysis, however, allows one to get beneath seductive democratic-progressive rhetoric to the real interests and strategy of the capitalist groups whom he defended. In the Pas-de-Calais Alex Ribot, lawyer son of a Calais tulle manufacturer, had feared Gambetta in 1869 as an extremist. His personal tastes were for Tocquevillian moderation. He admired Montalembert, respected the USA and Britain, feared the masses and became a lecturer in the new *École Libre de Sciences Politiques*, for he felt the need for a trained elite to run a democracy. In 1876–7 he defended victims of McMahon's bureacratic purge. Backed by Calais shipowners, he stood as a republican candidate in 1877, seeing a republic as essential for internal stability, but a conservative republic which alone could win over conservative Pas-de-Calais peasant voters. In Le Havre republicanism was typified by J. Siegfried, a Protestant anticlerical businessman, described by his son as governmental by temperament, 'inflexibly moderate', 'almost physically hostile to disorder, demagogy, radicalism, extremism, revolution', who 'had not, properly speaking, any political principles'. Such incarnations of integral pragmatism made perfect opportunists. They did not speak for the entire capitalist class. If A. Motte, the Roubaix textile manufacturer, admired the republic, fellow industrialists in the Motte dynasty remained Catholic-royalist paternalists, as did many Nord *patrons*, Grenoble glovemakers like Perrin, mineowners like de Solages and, as Cayez shows, many Lyonnais silk manufacturers.

The alliance of provincial capitalists with peasants and petty bourgeois in the republican cause raised obvious problems. The need to woo petty producers precluded over-rapid capitalist concentration. If Gambettist rhetoric eulogized productive capitalism, it retained a populist tone, critical not merely of the 'feudal-clerical' elites but of the unacceptable face of French capitalism – big monopolies, high rail-freight charges. Internal tensions within the republican alliance made the rail issue a key element in the republican programme. By emphasizing this, the Gambettists and their provincial capitalist backers could simultaneously further their own economic interests, woo the peasants with promises of cheaper transport for their marketable surpluses, and direct grievances against large financial and railway monopolies, still partly tied to royalist politics. J. Siegfried claimed that Le Havre was losing Atlantic trade to Hamburg because of high rail-freight rates and H. Germain, in his capacity as Aix deputy, argued that an inadequate rail system prevented the broadening of the provincial base of French capitalism, since more and cheaper railways could integrate local producers to the market economy. With the economy already sluggish with the advent of the Great Depression, the republicans' 1876 electoral promise of railway prosperity was a vote-winner. During the 1877 election, during which a local Charente rail firm was bought up by the Paris-Orléans company, republicans argued that royalist politicians like Broglie were pawns of big rail monopolies, involved in an unholy coup d'état plot with the clergy against honest republican producers.

As the recession deepened some Gambettists, like their republican predecessors in 1848, urged state involvement in railways which should be viewed as public utilities, not assessed by narrow profit- and-loss accounting. Encouragement of local lines would stimulate overall economic growth. L. Say, a colleague of Rothschild and a director of the Nord railway, precipitated a stock-exchange decline by refusing the post of finance minister in disapproval of such creeping collectivism. As disciples of a parvenu Midi lawyer, a grocer's son, the Gambettists remained suspect to many *grand-bourgeois* as a crowd of bohemian *déracinés*. Leading Gambettist journalist Spuller was the orphaned child of small-peasants. To that extent Gambettism embodied the populism of the *nouvelles couches* whose entry into politics their leader proclaimed. Yet, for all their verbiage about the 'little man', they had no real desire to pick a quarrel with major capitalist interests. The Freycinet Plan, aimed at extending the rail network and named after a technocratic engineer and pragmatic politician from impeccable Protestant *grand-bourgeois* stock, proved the ideal compromise. Peasant and local business interests applauded the 16,000 kilometres of railway to be constructed. There was an element of pump-priming to assist metallurgical and engineering firms in the recession. Bureaucrats like A. Picard conceived a positive role for the state in 'improving' the market economy. Yet leftist critics saw the final package as excessively favourable to the rail companies, who acquired seats on the *Conseil Supérieur* established to plan transport. The conservative economist Leroy-Beaulieu praised the plan for signalling a welcome entente between high finance and the republicans. Plans for state purchase were shelved, dividends for private investors guaranteed and L. Say's acceptance of the finance ministry reassured private capital. Though the Plan appeased, for a while, Gambetta's petty-producer electors, the rail companies, aided by a venal press, had essentially 'milked' it.

J. Lhomme concluded his analysis of the 'upper bourgeoisie in power' in 1880. Certainly the 'democratization' of politics in the 1870s, marked by the advent of lower social groups to municipal control in some areas, meant that the economic elites no longer enjoyed the monopoly of political control which they had once had. Yet they retained ample levers of power, not merely through control of the commanding heights of the economy, but through domination of access to the *grandes écoles*, their contacts with the bureaucracy, their organization of cartels and pressure groups, and their bribery of a notoriously venal press. In the absence of a truly secret ballot workers in company towns, such as employees of the engineering magnate Schneider at Le Creusot, still felt obliged to vote for their employer's candidate. Individual economic titans played a more direct political role. A Casimir-Périer was, briefly, president in the 1890s, while the absence of a truly secret ballot until 1913 meant that Le Creusot remained the electoral fief of the Schneiders, for only the rashest workers dared vote for the left in such company towns.

The tensions between Gambettist 'populism' and large capitalism proved, in the short term, capable of resolution. If a minority of Gambettists became Radicals after Gambetta's death, most happily allied with the more respectable *gauche republicaine* parliamentary group, led by Ferry, with its solid core of established provincial industrialists. Most had been attracted by Gambetta's charisma rather than by any alternative Radical policy. They found Ferry's mixture of moderate anticlericalism, colonial expansion and firm government to their taste.

Not all economic issues proved as easily resolved as the railway issue. In the 1870s many republicans equated free trade with royalism and Bonapartism, posing as a protectionist defenders of French businesses and jobs. The tariff issue proved too complex for such partisan over-simplification, for while the depression swelled the protectionist lobby among textile, mining and metal interests, key export sectors remained free traders. All this confused Gambetta who, as one critic observed, found 'making speeches on the economy considerably more difficult than making speeches against "enemies of the republic"'. Trapped in the crossfire between sectional business interests, he was reduced to uncharacteristic hesitancy. For once hollow anticlerical phrasemongering was inadequate to resolve a major issue which required resolution if the republican elites, faced with recession, unemployment and social unrest, were not to subside into suicidal intra-class squabbling.*

Education was the other major plank of the republican platform. Between 1879 and 1886 the Falloux Law was repealed, clergy were ousted from university councils and Catholic faculties lost the right, conceded only in 1875, to award degrees. Free, compulsory, secular primary schooling was introduced in 1881 and, after a delay to permit the training of laic schoolmistresses in 67 new *Écoles Normales*, the teaching personnel of public primary schools was secularized. Civic morality textbooks replaced religious indoctrination. The school building became the authentic monument of the Third Republic.

The exact blend of cynical manipulation and democratic idealism in these reforms remains a matter of historiographical dispute. Auspitz regards them as authentically progressive measures by a 'radical' bourgeoisie which gave the French masses a degree of equality, self-respect and dignity unparalleled in Europe. They commanded genuine popular support. Workers were among the members of the *Ligue de l'Enseignement* (*LE*), which ran adult education courses in Rheims, lectures and libraries for Yonne artisans and peasant wine growers. In Lyon there had been worker involvement in the stubborn defence of secular schools established in 1870–1. Socialist dye- and metalworkers were involved in laic defence committees, demanding that their children be taught by 'equals' not by celibate clergy 'strangers to our customs'. When fifteen Lyon teachers were prosecuted in 1872 for failure to provide religious teaching for their pupils, one replied in court, with exemplary humanism: 'I made [the children] understand that they must act with respect for themselves and utility for their fellows.' Some secular schools banned corporal punishment, encouraged collective rewards rather than individual prizes. Rightist prefects made determined efforts until 1877 to crush this movement,

* For the resolution of this dilemma see pages 229–30.

banning laic texts, closing libraries, provoking popular resistance both in the cities and the Burgundy and Midi countryside.

Auspitz concludes that the *LE*, which coordinated this laic crusade, was part of a broader 'radical' programme which involved commitment to progressive taxation and extensive social-democratic reform. However, in the 1870s radicals were a small minority in the republican movement, forced to subordinate social concerns to the priority of founding the republic. Moreover Ferry, the key figure in the laic legislation, was a conservative, passionately uninterested in social reform. Such republicans regarded educational reform as an *alternative* to social reform. Certainly the *LE* played a key role in the 1870s in linking republican deputies with grass-roots republican militants. Yet local *LE* stalwarts were rarely 'radicals', more often socially conservative businessmen like J. Siegfried or J. Steeg of Bordeaux. The *LE* leader in Beaune was an 'advanced' banker. One *LE notable*, who distributed rewards for successful laic propaganda, the deputy Menier, was a chocolate manufacturer with Nicaraguan plantation interests.

In short, Ferry was a revamped Guizot, manipulating education in the interests of capitalist elites, yet aware that 1880 was not 1833, that egalitarian rhetoric was required to give the policy the necessary conviction. Political socialization would wean the masses from the pernicious influence of clergy and socialists, 'black' and 'red' internationalists, alike. Republican businessmen, who saw themselves incarnating progress and economic development, regarded clerical 'truths' as outmoded, suitable for agrarian feudalism, not for capitalist society. The fervour of Paul Bert, Ferry's assistant in the laic programme, stemmed both from being the offspring of a dynasty of Yonne wood merchants who had acquired church lands, and from his scientific training which made him loathe the intellectual obscurantism of Syllabus Catholicism. Ferry's positivist intellectual mentor, Littré, saw education as the key to social harmony through the inculcation of common values. Primary schools could deepen patriotism. With the physical training instructor standing by the teacher's side, pupils could be prepared for military training. Lavisse's textbook informed schoolboys *You Will Be a Soldier*, while Bruno's famous *Tour of France by Two Children* emphasized both the fertility of French regions and the hexagon's essential unity.

Illiteracy, still 17 per cent among adult males, was detrimental both to France's economic and, as 1870 showed, her military efficiency. The laic schools made a cult of '1789', in order to stress that future revolution was unnecessary. For under a republic 'everybody rules'. 'The entire nation speaks with the voice of universal suffrage. Against whom should one revolt? Against France? That would be treason!' Education was claimed as the key to social mobility, class barriers were anachronistic in the new meritocracy. The ethos of the laic textbooks, with their stress on moral rules derived from conscience, emerged from a mixture of Kantianism and liberal Protestantism. To this was added a stiff dose of petty-bourgeois moralizing, emphasizing thrift, sobriety, punctuality, hard work, order and property.

Behind the democratic façade of these reforms, made plausible by the ferocious Catholic denunciation they encountered, lay hard-headed bourgeois realism. Primary education was social reform on the cheap, offending no vested interest except the church. Macé wanted a France of intellectual and moral unity, not of social equality. Despite the fig leaf of a few scholarships for bright primary pupils, many of whom became grey, sober, lycée teachers, and the strengthening of technical and commercial training for the petty bourgeoisie, French education remained a rigid two-tier system, perpetuating and stengthening existing class-divisions. Lycée education cost around 1000 francs per year, approximately the annual wage of an industrial worker. The percentage of children who received secondary schooling failed to increase, remaining below 5 per cent. Institutions like the *École Libre des Sciences Politiques* were established to train upper-middle class students for the bureaucratic elites. The 'radical' Clemenceau insisted that democracy was 'essentially a regime in which the people are governed by elites. To find the best method of forming those elites is the primary problem which confronts democracy.' The perennial republican nightmare about clerical influence over their womenfolk prompted the establishment, by Sée law in 1880, of girls' lycées. Republican politicians remained patriarchal 'feminists'. They desired suitable liberal wives for bourgeois husbands, mothers for future republican children. As Mayeur stresses, there was no intention of opening professional career prospects for middle-class girls. Girls' lycées had a restricted syllabus, did not prepare pupils for the baccalauréat. The emergence of a thin stream of women entering universities and, thence, infiltrating the professions, occurred *despite* the intentions of the framers of the law.

Republicans like Léon Richer patronized decorous feminist movements, of a controlled and restricted variety. Reluctant to breach male domination, and terrified of endangering the republic by enfranchising clergy-dominated women who might vote royalist, 'official' republican feminism limited itself essentially to demands for greater legal and property rights for married women, playing down suffragette demands.

Opportunist education reform was, thus, designed to weaken the clergy, to appease genuine worker and peasant demands, yet also to preserve the substance of an elitist education structure which perpetuated bourgeois class domination. Workers who had received some primary schooling would, it was hoped, develop respect for education and, consequently, greater veneration for those talented, educated experts who were their 'natural' leaders. The republican bourgeoisie thus utilized its monopoly of the baccalauréat to legitimate its status as the ruling elite. In education it remained true that to him that had, much more was given. Nevertheless the mythology of social mobility via educational opportunity proved seductive to broad strata of the petty bourgeoisie and peasantry and a key factor in legitimating bourgeois republican hegemony.*

The anticlericalism of post-1877 opportunist governments was real but controlled. At least in theory, Ferry differentiated between Catholicism and clericalism. It was the latter, held to be responsible for the Falloux Law, Bonapartism and McMahon's 'coup', which was the enemy. It was incarnated by the Jesuits, with their pernicious hold on key sectors of secondary education. Hence, in 1879, Ferry attempted to ban religious orders which had not, under the terms of the Organic Articles, obtained authorization to practise in France. Only a minority of conservative republicans shared J. Simon's interpretation of this measure as illiberal 'persecution' which would make the necessary *modus vivendi* with Catholicism impossible. Numerous other minor anticlerical measures were introduced. Divorce was legalized, state subsidies withdrawn from Catholic workers' circles, municipal authorities'

---

* For the impact of primary schooling on the working-class and the peasantry, see chapters 8 and 9.

controls over religious processions strengthened. Yet Ferry's anticlericalism remained pragmatic and limited. His positivist creed saw Catholic ethics as 'servile and inadequate', and he hoped to see Humanity live without God or King.

Yet, against Radical demands for separation of church and state, he clung to the Concordat, regarding state control of episcopal nominations and clerical salaries as an essential republican weapon without which the clerical beast would be uncontrollable. Like Ribot in the Pas-de-Calais, Ferry was constantly aware that his own Vosges peasant constituents voted republican to secure stability and from fear of 'feudalism'. Yet they remained practising Catholics, devoted to their processions, capable of revolt against 'atheistic' policies. Opportunists like Waldeck-Rousseau, lawyer son of a Nantes Catholic family, were austere Gallicans rather than atheistic militants. Despite the furore over the laic laws, Ferry's republic was, as Pope Leo XIII appreciated, *less* anticlerical than contemporary Italian or German regimes. In time a common antisocialism and a shared interest in colonial expansion would bring Paris and the Vatican closer together.

Opportunism introduced a variety of liberal measures. Controls on the press and public meetings were abolished. There was a modest purge of the 'royalist' bureaucracy. Republican lawyers like Gambetta and Waldeck-Rousseau, with bitter personal experiences in the hands of royalist judges not shared by Ferry's big business associates, insisted on a minor purge of the judiciary, precipitated by magistrates' resistance to implementation of antireligious legislation of the early 1880s. Yet Radical proposals for an elected judiciary were ignored. Similar decorous half-measures occurred in local government, where municipal councils secured the right to elect their own mayors, but decentralist proposals from the 1860s were abandoned and Paris remained under the government-appointed prefects and was denied its own mayor.

Beyond this the Opportunists offered little positive domestic policy in the 1880s.* Orthodox laissez-faire financiers like L. Say dominated treasury policy. Republicanism meant 'order' in the budget as in the streets. Several features of the political system can be invoked to explain governmental inertia. The senate, established as a sop to royalist landed *notables* in 1875, survived.

---

* For protectionist and colonial policy see pages 234–5.

Elected indirectly, via municipal councils, it greatly exaggerated the weight of rural France. 370 villages with less than 100 inhabitants each shared 370 voters, while eleven cities with 2.5 million inhabitants had 264. Though life senators were abolished in 1884, the senate faithfully fulfilled the reactionary role for which it had been conceived, its collection of geriatric politicians and bureaucrats carried from its benches to their graves after passing their declining years obstructing progressive legislation on income tax, old-age pensions, factory conditions *et al.* By 1893 there were 50 socialist deputies, yet the first socialist senator appeared in 1906! The constituency boundaries discriminated against fair representation for growing proletarian suburbs in the lower house, which was very slow to reflect those 'new social strata' of which Gambetta boasted. In 1848 there had been 30 working-class deputies, in 1881 there was one. Eighty-five per cent of deputies in 1893 were from the upper and middle bourgeoisie, two-thirds of all deputies between 1871 and 1898 had received some higher education. Even in 1900 barely 30 deputies came from peasantry or working class.

The republic's critics denounced it for producing ephemeral, feeble, unstable coalition governments, averaging three for every two years of the republic's existence, incapable of coherent policy or action. With historic and religious allegiances cutting across socio-economic class ties, a stable two-party system proved unattainable. A bourgeoisie polarized between Catholics and anticlericals failed to generate a conservative party. A multi-party system, compounded by extremely weak party discipline until the 1900s, made all governments coalitions. The 'best' prime ministers were nonentities who offended as few politicians as possible. The charismatic Gambetta was kept from this office until the last months of his life. Cabinets which attempted to push through legislation saw their majorities evaporate. Pragmatic centrist careerists, assured of a place in any cabinet, were encouraged. Many bills reached the stage of parliamentary committee discussion only for their sponsoring cabinet to fall. Alarmed by Bonapartist precedents, republicans insisted that the president should remain a figurehead – although as with President Grévy's reluctance to offer Gambetta the premiership, one capable of negative obstruction. Presidential elections, by the two houses of parliament, consistently favoured anodyne nondescripts over strong candidates like Ferry.

Except for a brief interlude in the 1880s, the electoral system was one of single-member local constituencies, with the leading candidates from the first ballot contesting a second ballet run-off. The system, critics claimed, fostered parochialism, made constituencies 'little, stagnant, stinking pools'. Deputies became ambassadors to Paris; their role, to pester ministers for governmental patronage for their electors in the form of civil service jobs, school funds, tobacco licences, conscription exemptions. The Bonapartist 'democratization' of state patronage at the expense of traditional *notables* was, thus, completed. Ligou's biography of the Gard deputy, Desmons, estimates that he received 3000 requests per year for favours. The absence of secret ballots until 1913 encouraged electoral corruption. Electoral funding increased rapidly. Lebaudy, a sugar manufacturer, safeguarded his Seine-et-Oise constituency by paying mayors to make coal and bread deliveries to electors.

Criticism of weak, ephemeral government can be exaggerated. A certain 'stability of ministers' counteracted ministerial instability, 40 of the 94 cabinets between 1879 and 1940 contained more than half of the ministers from the previous government. Ferry was education minister in five of the eight governments between 1879 and 1885, Freycinet prime minister nine times after 1885. Over 50 per cent of the Third Republic's deputies sat for two terms or more. Changes of government often resembled cabinet reshuffles. And the solidity of the permanent bureaucracy, in which key figures like Dumay (religion) or F. Buisson (education) held post for decades, assured a degree of policy continuity. Internal army autonomy reduced the impact of ephemeral war ministers. *Quai d'Orsay* bureaucrats moulded foreign policy strategies. Masonic lodges helped compensate for the weak party structure, and key educational, business and colonial lobbies guaranteed continuity despite changes of ministry.

The policy inertia of the 1880s owes more to dominant laissez-faire prejudice than to the weakness of the political system. There was no tax reform, no separation, no counter-depression economic policy. Men like Ribot had a conservative-juridical approach towards social reform. Ferry was 'progressive' only in educational issues. The son of a wealthy legal family, he had married into an eastern textile dynasty. Opportunists used the peasant base of their electorate to excuse their conservatism, though not all peasants were conservatives. Their response to rising unemployment and labour unrest was minimal. Gambettists like Barbaret had flirted with moderate labour leaders in the 1870s. Waldeck-Rousseau, as Sorlin shows, expressed interest in profit-sharing schemes and in the legalization of unionism to create a pragmatic British-style labour movement. Yet mention of trade unions alarmed Ferry, and once Waldeck-Rousseau became Ferry's interior minister he became a law-and-order man, smashing unemployed demonstrations, treating reformist miners' leader Basly as an 'anarchist', seeing the solution to the recession as a mixture of strong government and wage restraint. If he outstripped his cabinet colleagues with his vague interest in social issues, his actual ideas were anodyne and cosmetic.

The possibility of a stable conservative majority which could be achieved through a deal with Catholic moderates tempted the Rouvier government of 1885, but was to be achieved only in the 1890s. Before this the Opportunist republic underwent a new period of peril. The 1885 election saw the Opportunist parliamentary representation cut from 69 per cent to 44 per cent of seats, as Radicals and the right exploited the recession-induced economic grievances of workers, peasants and petty bourgeois, Catholic hostility to the laic laws, leftist resentment at the lack of social reform and widespread anger at the cost of colonial expansion. P. Cambon, a friend of Ferry, returning to Paris from Tunis, claimed 'there is no government in France' and feared that the republic was near the end of its brief existence. The disclosure of the involvement of President Grévy's son-in-law, Wilson, in the sale of honours, accentuated growing criticism of the corruption of the political elite. Faced with an explosive mixture of neo-Jacobin and right-wing populist assault, the opportunists survived the 1888–9 Boulangist crisis* only through tough, if belated, action against paramilitary leagues, through rallying radicals to defend the 'republic in danger', and through courting the peasant vote. Thousand of village mayors attended the 1889 banquet in Paris to celebrate the revolution's centenary; 'a gastronomic and republican feast offered to the provinces who were about to save the regime'. The Opportunist parliamentary strength was stabilized at 45 per cent.

* See chapter 7.

The apogee of the conservative republic came in the 1890s. The collapse of Boulangism convinced many Catholics and royalists that overthrow of the regime was improbable. Fear of the growing socialist movement led to appeals for an alliance of all 'good citizens'. A deal with Catholics was, claimed opportunist Pas-de-Calais deputy Jonnart, son-in-law of a Catholic Lyonnais financier, *the* key to 'social peace'. As Opportunists talked of a 'new spirit' of toleration in state-church relations, the religious orders were allowed to return, and the pace of laicization of primary schools slowed. A shared interest in colonial expansion united opportunists and the clergy. Republicans like Méline took a tough anticollectivist stance, outlawing anarchists, resisting income tax viewed as inquisitional and 'un-French'. Protectionist tariffs united the interests of heavy industry and large ex-royalist landowners. With Catholic support, the Opportunists captured 54 per cent of seats in the 1893 election. Waldeck-Rousseau, grown steadily more conservative as his barrister's practice flourished, sponsored the *Grand Cercle Républicain* which attracted Catholic industrialists like E. Motte into an antisocialist front which helped unseat the Marxist Guesde in Roubaix in 1898.

Yet this attempt to consolidate a conservative party proved ultimately abortive. At the local level many opportunists preserved their gut feeling of anticlericalism. Catholics still resented the laic laws, were tempted to use financial scandals like Panama to discredit republican politicians, perceived Ribot's modest proposals for a tax on religious orders' wealth as evidence of renewed persecution. When the Dreyfus Affair surfaced in 1898 and appeared to threaten the republic with a clerical-military coup, atavistic loyalties resurfaced. While a minority of Opportunists under Méline stayed with their Catholic allies, the majority, including Poincaré and Waldeck-Rousseau, were driven into an incongruous centre-left alliance with Radicals and reformist socialists, since the problems of regime and religion appeared, as in 1877, to take priority over socio-economic issues.*

* See also chapter 7.

II Capitalist Development and the French Bourgeoisie (1870–1914)

Anglo-American historians have been critical about the economic performance of French capitalism, entrepreneurs and governments in the late nineteenth century. France is seen as lagging ever further behind vigorous newcomers such as the USA, Germany and Japan. A recent comparative international survey by Trebilcock, discounting more optimistic assessments, concludes: 'Palace revolutions in historiography may come and go, but the Industrial Revolution in France remains timid and spasmodic.' Critics allege that the republic abandoned the dynamic *dirigisme* of the 1850–60s, replacing it with a spineless subservience to vested interest pressure groups. 'Excessive' tariff protection is seen as cushioning small inefficient business and peasant farms. Cautious, undynamic 'Malthusian' entrepreneurs are said to have avoided risk and innovation.

There are, undeniably, elements of truth in this portrait. Yet such arguments have been exaggerated, creating a misleading stereotype of a sluggish economy and society. It will be argued that the French economy, though marked by 'uneven' development, was less static than its critics suggest, and that many, though not all, of the charges against governmental policy and entrepreneurial attitudes have been unbalanced. Too many critics have adopted an unhistorical, 'economic' approach, which ignores the socio-political context within which the French elites operated and took decisions. The republic was founded, as we have seen, on a political alliance of the capitalist bourgeoisie with urban and rural petty producers. The capitalist elites wanted economic development, but also, with the Commune fresh in their minds, they wanted balance and stability. Needing the peasantry and petty bourgeoisie as electoral allies, they were obliged, politically, to shelter them from harsh economic winds. Nor was France unique in this. The Bismarckean Reich, too, made efforts to prop up its 'Mittelstand'.

Undoubtedly French economic performance until 1896 was distinctly unimpressive. Lévy-Leboyer calculates that the overall growth rate for the 1865–96 period was as low as 0.6 per cent per annum. Unemployment exceeded 10 per cent in the 1880s. Bouvier and Gillet have charted a sharp fall in metallurgical and mining profits from the mid-1870s. Prices fell by 20 per cent in 1880–6, while the steady decline in share values till 1896 forced some rentiers into the indignity of seeking paid employment! European and American tariff barriers disrupted French exports, already weak in cheap mass-produced sectors. If all industrial nations suffered the Great Depression, its severity in France was particularly great. In the Lyonnais, as Y. Lequin emphasizes, the crisis hit both the old staple silk industry and iron and coal, the leading sectors of the 1860s.

Agricultural growth rates as low as 0.26 per cent per annum in the 1865–1900 period may have had serious implications for the overall economy. Despite undoubted progress, both in rural transport and monoculture specialization,* poor credit facilities, undercapitalization, poor marketing techniques and excessive subdivision of land persisted. Yet peasants clung to the land. The rural exodus, at 143,000 per year in 1880–1914, was lower than in the previous decades. The rural population declined only very gradually, from 75 per cent to 59 per cent of the overall population between 1846 and 1901. By 1901 France had 15 cities above 100,000, Britain 50 and Germany 42. Birth control, a rational peasant response to fear of subdivision of small farms, accentuated demographic stagnation, which restricted the internal consumer market. By 1914 Germany had a population of 67 million, France of only 38 million. As the population aged, the number of 'inactives' rose from 12 to 14 million. Some regions, such as Lorraine, were forced to recruit industrial labour from abroad.

Critics of the republic's economic elites have argued that such factors were not 'given', were not natural and unavoidable obstacles to industrialization. Trebilcock claims that 'release of existing resources could have raised the level of economic activity, and swelled the tide of consumer demand.' It is argued that governments could, and should, have reformed the inheritance laws, abandon protectionism which cushioned inefficient peasant farmers, and accelerated rail-building to speed up the rural exodus. Undeniably governmental agriculture policy had deficiencies, not least the paucity of technical education resources. Yet much of this criticism is unbalanced. Germany, too, resorted to tariffs to safeguard her peasantry. One major agricultural disaster – the phylloxera vine-disease – was 'natural', or, perhaps, sent by God

---

* See Chapter 9.

to punish an atheist republic as one Midi *curé* claimed. With Italian, Belgian and Spanish cheap immigrant labour readily available, and difficult for the labour movement to unionize, it is misleading to argue that French industry suffered from labour shortages.

Correlations between peasant birth control, demographic stagnation and economic sluggishness are plausible. Yet the economy boomed after 1896 at a time when population growth had virtually ceased. Arguments that the elites 'should have' got rid of the peasantry are politically naive. The republican system relied on peasant support to offset the dangers from working-class socialism and from the Catholic right. In 1885 the Opportunist republicans suffered heavy electoral losses, to left and right, because the agrarian crisis weakened its peasant foothold. Attempts to eliminate the peasantry through denial of tariff-protection would have courted social chaos and political catastrophe.

French secondary and higher education has been attacked for its alleged failure to adapt to the requirements of an industrial society. Critics point to the failure of Fortoul's efforts to create a scientific baccalauréat syllabus, and to the continued higher prestige of the classical and philosophy streams in the lycées. Observers like Renan cited the poor quality of university science and the absence of both financing and research as a major factor in the war defeat of 1870. The continued expansion of Catholic secondary schooling, which came to control 50 per cent of pupils, was, obviously, not the fault of republican anticlerical politicians. Yet the antipositivist, antirationalist ethos of these colleges, and their tendency to 'cram' pupils for baccalauréat exams as an entry to military and bureaucratic careers, could be viewed as diverting sections of the elites away from industry and science. Although Duruy's technical schools had 900 pupils by 1871, and had been designed to supply industry with its qualified 'NCOs', their success was limited. They lacked prestige, and failed to expand. One 1913 survey claimed that only 7 per cent of entrants to commerce and industry had adequate technical training. As Terry Shin concludes, the dominance of the *École Polytechnique* was healthy neither for French higher education nor for industry. Its essential role was to legitimize and perpetuate a narrow oligarchy, which controlled the state bureaucracy. Its education was expensive. Entry required a classical baccalauréat. Sixty-one per cent of its pupils between 1840 and 1880 came from the upper bourgeoisie. Its ethos favoured bureaucratic and military careers. Of 14,000 pupils before 1880, barely 8 per cent had entered careers in pure or applied science. The self-esteem of *Polytechnique* graduates was too great to permit them to work for small family firms. Their training was largely abstract, with little experimental work. They tended to despise 'practical' engineers, and to use their influence to obstruct alternative higher education institutions and reform proposals.

The net outcome has sometimes been portrayed in pessimistic terms. Camille Cavillier, head of the Pont-à-Mousson engineering works, claimed to be driven 'mad with rage to see that in our country, where education is pursued to a high level, it is so impractical . . . the young are all studying to be scholars, none to do anything practically useful'. Yet the professed gloom of such technocratic philistines was a little exaggerated by 1900. The republic set up the *École Libre des Sciences Politiques* to establish a solid grounding in economics and other practical modern subjects for its conservative elites. By 1905 there were thirteen *Écoles Supérieures* for commerce. V. Karady has emphasized the impressive quality of laboratories and research in Paris and other university faculties after 1870. There is evidence of an emerging symbiotic relationship between government, industry and regional universities. Chemistry faculties flourished at Nancy and Paris, hydroelectricity courses emerged at Grenoble. Regional industry began to rely on the applied science of its local university. The supposed massive German supremacy in applied science may be a myth. Parisian graduates proved as skilful in exploring Lorraine iron-ore resources as their counterparts across the frontier trained in the *'technische Hochschule'*. C. Day has emphasized the significant role played by the *École Centrale des Arts et Métiers* in attracting pupils from the middle bourgeoisie and training graduates in applied science for the engineering, chemical and electrical sectors. Many such engineers resented the prestige and power of less 'practical' *École Polytechnique* graduates.

After decades of inferiority, professional engineers developed a strong *esprit de corps* and a growing confidence, based on their key role in expanding sectors such as automobiles, rubber and chemicals. Between 1897 and 1909 five major provincial universities established engineering degrees. The society of professional engineers quadrupled its membership to 6000 between 1882 and 1914. Engineering graduates from the Paris faculties rose

50 per cent to 300 per annum between 1904 and 1914. Industrial tycoons like Cail, the Parisian engineering magnate, sent their sons to study for scientific degrees. Renault and Citroën were products of technological courses. Eventually, as the prestige and salary of army officers fell, even *École Polytechnique* graduates began to gravitate towards careers in new, large, joint-stock companies. In 1882 20 per cent of such graduates were in the private sector, by 1918 78 per cent. The age of *pantouflage* had arrived.

Recent analysis of the development of French tariff policy has questioned the cliché that it was damagingly ultra-protectionist. It was a deal, worked out over a decade, between free-trade and protectionist lobbies. This compromise was essential for the coherence and unity of the French elites, for serious intra-class friction could have generated suicidal conflict which might have 'unmade' the republican synthesis. Protectionism must be viewed in the context of bourgeois political stability in the troubled 1880s, marked by economic depression, unemployment, strikes and widespread anti-republican sentiment. The free-trade lobby, given intellectual support by Leroy-Beaulieu, editor of *L'Économiste Français*, found its strength among shipping and mercantile port interests. In Marseille, oil, sugar, and flour refiners relied on imported produce. In Paris, hub of the rail network and centre of luxury exports, import-export magnates like d'Eichthal were free traders, as were Lyonnais silk exporters and Bordelais wine merchants, for Bordeaux's wine exports to Britain rose 800 per cent between 1859 and 1876. Large bankers, key figures in 1870s reparations payments to Germany, favoured international trade. In 1877, 41 of 53 leading chambers of commerce still supported free trade.

The growing protectionist lobby was less cosmopolitan, more industrial. Textile sectors were its hub, although tulle and worsted manufacturers in Rheims relied on imported yarns. 'Dumping' by Dundee manufacturers was undermining the Somme jute industry. The carded-wool of Sedan was under intense pressure from Bradford. Twenty-five per cent of the Nord's linen-mills collapsed in the decade after 1867. Manufactured cotton imports rose 400 per cent between 1873 and 1877. Leading Opportunist politicians like Ferry, Waddington and Méline had close ties with Vosges and Rouen textile interests. Protectionism won support among heavy metallurgy and engineering threatened by oversupply in world markets, technological change and the end of the brief 1879–82 rail boom. Le Creusot exports fell 60 per cent in 1874–7, as did exports of locomotives from Batignolles. Pig-iron prices fell 40 per cent in 1872–6. There was some friction between engineering companies, who favoured some cheap imports of pig iron and heavy-metallurgy producers who wanted complete protectionism. However these two groups worked out a compromise by 1880.

The years 1879–82 witnessed intense lobbying as the free trade treaties of the 1860s came up for renegotiation. Protectionists attempted to establish an alliance with agricultural groups, alarmed at the flood of cheap food imports, despite much mistrust on both sides. Free traders won apparent success, for treaties were renegotiated with Switzerland and Belgium, and eleven bilateral trade treaties were signed in 1881–3. However this proved a Pyrrhic victory. Steel prices fell 45 per cent between 1880 and 1888, profits declined sharply. Falls in agricultural prices led to substantial rural electoral protest in 1885. Led by Méline, 'provincial' protectionists steadily ousted 'cosmopolitan' free traders in the Opportunist leadership. The 'Méline tariff' of 1892 was, however, a hybrid compromise. Flexible minimum tariffs were permitted. Duties on raw silk, raw wool, textile machines and low-gauge yarn for the worsted industry were low. Despite a tariff increase in 1910 and surtaxes against foreign 'dumping', France was *less* monolithically protectionist than USA, Germany, Italy, Spain or Russia. Thirty-four countries, by 1914, were paying minimum tariff rates.

In short, tariff policy was not myopic, but a rational and nuanced compromise, designed to conciliate divergent interests within French capitalism. Protection permitted a degree of cartellization among firms, in iron and steel, cotton, northern coal, which survived the depression. It was part of a wider consolidation of the business community, designed to minimize intra-class friction. A National Association of Chambers of Commerce (1898) was formed, which attempted to maintain dialogue between large and small firms. Employers' associations multiplied, links between business and the state bureaucracy were increased, lobbying techniques perfected.

The post-1896 economic boom provides interesting evidence with which to assess criticism of government policy and entrepreneurial attitudes. The growth rate of 1.6 per cent per annum in 1896–1928 nearly trebled that of the previous three decades. Industrial production rose at 2.4 per cent per annum.

Growth was particularly rapid in the decade after 1905. The size of the industrial workforce increased suddenly after decades of stagnation. Industrial investment doubled in 1890–1914, after falling in the 1880s, contributing to a 57 per cent rise *per capita* in industrial productivity between 1901 and 1911. Prices rose 36 per cent in 1896–1913, after falling 17 per cent in 1880–96. Average dividends rose 60 per cent between 1894–8 and 1909–13. Bouvier estimates that mining and metallurgy profits in 1913 were treble those of the 1870s.

How can one reconcile this performance with the stereotype of an economy dominated by cautious, 'Malthusian' entrepreneurs? Criticism of French economic elites clearly has *some* foundation. A. Detoeuf's novel, *Les Propos de M. Barenton* (1938) caricatures the archetypal Third Republic entrepreneur in the figure of an ice-cream manufacturer who avoids risks, rejects outside finance, works hard, tries to do the jobs of his ill-paid subordinates whom he mistrusts, and consequently has no time for his own. J. Vial's studies of French ironmasters emphasize their fear of outside capital. The de Wendels, a Lorraine metallurgical dynasty, married its daughters to army officers and avoided the financial markets till 1908. D. Landes's study of the Nord textile dynasty, the Mottes, argues that their austere, paternalistic, self-financing ethos, though effective earlier in the century, became anachronistic in the new age of falling profits, labour unrest and high-cost technology.

Entrepreneurial sluggishness exacerbated, it is claimed, France's problem of modest and poorly located coal deposits. The effects of such 'natural' obstacles could have been minimized by a more rational economic strategy. Coal production remained only 15 per cent of British levels, and 30 per cent of French coal in the 1870–1914 period had to be imported. Faster rail construction could have reduced internal fuel-transport costs earlier. Protectionist tariffs benefited the selfish coal lobby at the expense of the national economy. Coal companies, in part as a result of governmental policy, remained too small and undercapitalized. More enterprising planning could have channelled resources, as in Switzerland, into alternative energy sources such as hydroelectricity.

The distant relationship between finance and industry had also been used as evidence of the backwardness of French capitalism. Even Schneider preferred auto-finance, and Cavillier expressed a typical industrialist's suspicion of financiers in his claim that 'bankers support a client like a rope a hanged man!' Banks appeared reluctant to lend to industry. The *Crédit Mobilier* found no immediate successor. The *Crédit Lyonnais*, having burned its fingers investing in chemicals in the 1860s, shied away from industrial involvement, and concentrated on foreign loans. 'Be you Greek, Chinese or Brazilian, the *Crédit Lyonnais* will make you an advance, but if you are French you will get nothing,' noted one commentator. British capital financed Normandy railways. Critics alleged that French industry was starved of capital as French banks, encouraged by governments and by foreign bribing of a venal Parisian press, directed 50 per cent of all French savings by 1914 into overseas loans, much of it to Russia to bolster France's new tsarist ally.

The validity of such criticism is questionable. Returns on domestic capital in the 1880s were so low that foreign investment appeared rational. R. Girault emphasizes that profits on Russian investment were high, if uneven.* There are indications that the banking oligarchy gradually led their passive, security-conscious small investors towards industrial investments. Bar-le-Duc banker Varin-Bernier financed eastern industry, Nancy banks financed local metallurgy. Small-investor savings were tapped as the banking system spread. The *Société Générale* and *Crédit Lyonnais* had 907 branches by 1910, while funds of the four main deposit banks increased by 2500 per cent in 1870–1913. The agricultural depression shifted bourgeois investment patterns away from land, although often, initially, into urban real estate.

There is clear evidence of the emergence of dynamic, new industrial sectors, and of the reorganization of older key industries. Chemicals, rubber, hydroelectrics and automobiles suggested that French capitalism was far from moribund. Despite weaknesses in basic production, chemicals, spearheaded by Poulenc in Lyon, achieved growth rates of 5.9 per cent after 1896. Hydroelectricity boosted the economy of the Lyonnaise-Dauphiné, devastated by the crises of the silk and metallurgical sectors, spawning a new engineering technology of pylons and turbines. Rubber achieved a spectacular 8.5 per cent per annum expansion rate. In automobiles France ranked second behind the USA in 1914, despite the multiplicity of small firms and the lack of

---

* For further consideration of the role of overseas investment see pages 240–5.

standardization. French cars were of high quality, aimed at bourgeois markets, yet their export value exceeded that of American cars by 1911–12, and annual production, at 45,000, was double the British level. At Billancourt, Renault employed 4000 workers and was introducing scientific management, time-and-motion study and similar technocratic innovations from Detroit. Such practices found an audience among the business elite, in the Arbel works at Douai, the Penhoët shipyard, and the Cail engineering works, run by the Taylor-ist Lechatelier. The technocratic and theoretical grounding of *grandes écoles* graduates suited them better for 'scientific management' of high-technology industry than it had for family textile firms of the first industrial revolution.

One could regard such dynamic sectors as atypical in an economy still dominated by archaic small firms. In 1906 only 12 per cent of the industrial workforce was employed in plants of 1000 or more workers. Yet such criticism requires careful qualification. As Lévy-Leboyer emphasizes, there is no *necessary* correlation between small size and inefficiency. In the garment sector small firms adjusted rapidly to market and stylistic trends. In eastern France the Peugot firm acted with exemplary flexibility in moving from textiles to bicycles and then into automobiles. In some regions dual structures emerged, with big firms subcontracting to small accessory and supplier satellites, in precision-toolmaking for example.

Nevertheless a degree of concentration *was* occurring in key sectors. Cartelization and price-fixing accelerated in the textile sector in the 1890s. Protectionism permitted a breathing space which allowed the Vosges to adopt modern technology, to fill the role vacated by Alsace. Inefficient firms lost ground. The number of cotton-spinning mills in Lille fell from 43 to 20 between 1860 and 1900. Roubaix-Tourcoing came to dominate the woollen sector, at the expense of Sedan and Rheims, while Lille's linen industry undermined that of the Mayenne. The silk industry recovered from its 1880s trough, and the threat of Swiss and German competition, by rapid mechanization of looms, concentrated in the big Dauphiné mills, and by concentration on cheap, light products. Patterns of regional specialization emerged, with Nord concentrating on fine yarns, the Vosges on medium.

The coal industry remained dominated by medium-large firms,

rather than by giants. Yet its degree of concentration, if below that of the Ruhr, was higher than that of Britain. Limited cartelization occurred. Gillet shows that nine firms controlled 80 per cent of the production of the northern coalfield. Prices and profits rose in the 1900s, and the tie-up between Commentry-Fourchambault metallurgy and the Lens coal company foreshadowed a degree of vertical integration. The iron and steel sector began to cluster round the Nord coalfields and, above all, round the newly worked Briey iron-ore deposits. Moselle steel production grew from 2000 tons per annum in 1880 to 271,000 tons in 1900, and Longwy came to employ 6000 workers. The engineering sector was prominent in moves towards cartelization. Legal decisions of 1901 and 1912 relaxed restrictions on company mergers, which were occurring at 200 per annum by 1910, double the 1900 level. The proportion of French firms which were joint-stock companies rose from 20 per cent to 25 per cent between the 1890s and the 1900s. Investment in high-technology processes was too heavy for family firms to accomplish. The leading ten metallurgical companies controlled 70 per cent of the industry's capital. The leading cartel was, undoubtedly, the *Comité des Forges*, whose master lobbyer, Pinot, was highly influential with politicians like Poincaré. Tariff protection permitted such cartelization, which raised domestic prices, allowing steel and engineering giants to finance export subsidies. Leading industrialists had access to key bureaucrats, often classmates from school or from the *École Polytechnique*. The *Comité des Forges* pressured governments into linking French financial loans to exports. The arms race increased the power of firms like Schneider Creusot. The aluminium consortium, established in 1912, gave France an advantage in world markets over American competition.

III Economics and Empire?

Despite opposition from left and right, Ferry's governments of 1881–5 extended the existing Algerian colony into Tunisia and enlarged the French foothold in Indo-China by fighting China for control of Tonkin. Attempts were made to implement grandiose plans to link west African trading stations with the Sudan via the southern Sahara. Madagascar was annexed in the 1890s, Morocco steadily penetrated in the 1900s, and France also carved out a stake in the Congo.

Between 1880 and 1895 the French colonial empire grew from one million to 9.5 million square kilometres. Much recent historiography has been concerned to refute an 'economic' or Marxist interpretation of this phenomenon. By 1914, it is emphasized, French colonies took under 10 per cent of French foreign investment. In contrast Britain had 45 per cent of her investment in her empire. Only 12 per cent of French trade was with her colonies. Cautious investment banks channelled savings into 'safe' state bonds. In 1898 the colonial enthusiast, Chailley-Bert, confessed that his dreams of an economic empire had been 'premature'. Quality-obsessed French industry was ill-suited to provide cheap mass exports. Poverty-stricken colonial populations made poor consumer markets. French businessmen, he argued, lacked the energy and initiative to exploit colonial markets. Bankers proved reluctant to invest in colonies and provoked the wrath of colonial lobbyists, who envisaged French monopoly control of colonial economies, by their apparent willingness, as in Morocco, to cooperate with German financiers.

A demographically stagnant France had produced a mere 885,000 colonists by 1914, three-quarters of them in Algeria. The kith-and-kin ties which made Victorian Britain passionately imperialist were thus very weak. The rhetoric of Ferry in the 1880s justifying colonies as necessary for markets, raw materials and investment has, thus, been portrayed as a collection of platitudes plagiarized from colonial ideologues like P. Leroy-Beaulieu, which disguised different motives. Colonies, in reality, were millstones round the neck of French taxpayers, whose bill for military and administrative expenditure had risen to 116 million francs by 1912. Profits on colonial investment were little higher than those in the metropolis. Only 0.1 per cent of French raw cotton imports were from the colonies. Imports of food and wine from the empire frequently competed with domestic produce. The bulk of European exports to French colonies were from France's competitors, and carried in foreign ships, for the French merchant marine remained small.

In place of an economic analysis of imperialism, historians have offered a mélange of military, diplomatic, cultural, religious and patriotic explanations. Above all it has been interpreted less as the 'highest stage of capitalism' than as the 'highest stage of nationalism'. The military humiliation of 1870 appeared to confirm Prévost-Paradol's assertion in 1868 that only colonial expansion could save France from decline. Any number of statements by leading politicians can be offered to support their thesis. Ferry justified his Indo-China expansionism by insisting that France 'cannot simply be a free country; she should also be a great country'. Gambetta, congratulating Ferry on the annexation of Tunisia, exulted that 'France is reassuming its rank as a Great Power'. The leading colonial lobbyist, Étienne, later claimed that 'we had to prove to Europe that we were not finished'. West African annexations of the 1880s are viewed as a reaction to the insult of British gains in Egypt. Colonialism was, thus, a psychological necessity to dispel post-1870 despair, at a time when direct confrontation with Bismarck was not feasible. If Étienne claimed that the future of France in the 1900s depended on seizing Morocco before the Germans, the future of French business was clearly *not* so dependent, for Morocco accounted for only 0.5 per cent of foreign trade by 1914. French public opinion was slow to respond to colonialist propaganda. In 1889 Ferry claimed that the only aspect of the colonies which aroused Frenchmen's passion was the belly dance. As late as 1913 colonial lobbyists lamented that, outside a few ports, the 'colonial education' of the French remained 'unstarted'. Yet such public enthusiasm as colonialism did arouse, over Morocco or over Fashoda in 1898, derived from nationalist rivalry with Germany or Britain.

The quasi-independent role of the military has also been emphasized. Cambodia in the 1860s was run by admirals. In West Africa officers carved out territorial fiefs, ignoring orders from Paris. The empire provided outdoor relief for an officer corps many of whose Catholic-royalist members found in the colonies an opportunity to serve 'France' while keeping their distance from the hated republic. In the absence of European war they relied on colonial conflict for action, promotion, decorations and relief from the boredom of garrison life. Possibly this military independence declined in the late 1890s, as Foreign Minister Delcassé vetoed suggestions for annexing China for fear of alienating the European powers.

Military strategists also showed a fascination with the prospect of utilizing native troops to offset German military-demographic superiority. This dream, expressed in Colonel Maugin's 1910 *La force noire*, was echoed in Melchior de Vogüé's novel *Les Morts qui parlent*, which discounted the economic benefits of sub-Saharan Africa, but fantasized about the potential of savage yet obedient black and yellow soldiers. If Britain ruled the world with her sepoys, why not the French with their Senegalese? Actual recruitment, in tens not hundreds of thousands, fell below such hopes.

The colonial idea was 'militarized' by the carefully constructed mythology of the great military proconsuls like Galliéni and Lyautey. Their 'pacification' of Madagascar had, allegedly, been followed by altruistic reconstruction programmes, road and irrigation building, provision of disinterested justice in the fulfilment of a bucolic idyll of peace and rural progress. Kanya-Forstner has emphasized that the wild schemes for linking West Africa with the Sudan were the brainchild of military adventurers, innocent of economic motives, motivated by patriotism, careerism and boredom. The upper Nile and Chad attracted predictably little business interest. The French Congo received much less investment than its Belgian counterpart. The 10,000 francs contributed by industry to the *Comité de l'Afrique* was 'an unremarkable figure even by the standards of cathedral restoration funds' (C. Andrew).

Expansion was also, allegedly, fuelled by a burning faith in France's 'civilizing mission'. Paul d'Ivoi's *Le sergent Simple à travers les colonies* (1895), highlights the latent Anglophobia in this tradition. Whereas the British exploited their colonies, produced tea and cotton in India while natives starved, the French genius was to spread culture and to be rewarded by native gratitude. This myth had the useful advantage of reconciling Catholics and laic republicans, the former peddling redemption and salvation and the latter science and progress. As early as 1873 the clergy had helped disseminate the idea that the Tonkinois masses desired liberation from their Annamite rulers by French troops – a myth fostered by the Gambettist press. Opportunist politicians quickly realized that the clergy were key allies in imperial expansion in the 1880s, when anticolonialism was still strong. Anticlericalism was not for export. Mgr Lavigerie of Algiers combined his dream of a Latin-Catholic Africa with appeals to Alsace refugees to colonize Algeria. Significantly he was to be the chosen spokesman for papal efforts to bury the church-state feud and cement an antisocialist front in the 1890s.* A high percentage of extra-European missionaries

* See chapter 7.

were French. But the 'civilizing mission' had its neo-Jacobin façade. Gambettists portrayed it as the continuation of the 1790s crusades of French revolutionary armies against despotism, oppression and poverty. Paul Bert, the apostle of the laic school, became governor-general of Indo-China and emphasized his mission of spreading secular schooling to the colonies, as to Brittany.

In 1883 the conquest of Tonkin was presented not as revenge for the deaths of French commanders Garnie and Rivière, nor as a bid for mineral deposits, but as a blow against Red River pirates and the liberation of the masses from the Annamite oligarchy. A decade later the Madagascar annexation was described as the emancipation of the inhabitants from bloodthirsty Hovas rule. It was the duty, Ferry claimed, of 'superior races' to raise up the 'inferior'. On his trip to North Africa in 1887 he saw colonists making the desert bloom. Such rhetoric contained a residual appeal to the neo-Jacobin left. Utopian socialism had viewed the earth as a huge garden awaiting cultivation for humanity by western technology. Socialists like Jaurès mixed distaste for colonialist 'excesses' with a belief in the progressive nature of French rule.

For all its arrogant assumptions about the unquestioned superiority of western civilization, such rhetoric, at least in theory, maintained that natives could be 'educated', 'civilized', even, in time 'assimilated'. Yet it was frequently combined with concepts, not easily reconcilable with this, of the biological inferiority of non-European races and of imperialism as a necessary stage in a racial-biological struggle for survival. In 1863 Charles Lavollée talked of colonies as guarantees of virility in the inevitable racial battles with Slavs and Anglo-Saxons. In 1874 Leroy-Beaulieu saw the race struggle as global. 'Stifled' within her frontiers, France would find her 'warlike instincts' introverted, producing civil war and social revolution. Already demographic stagnation foreshadowed 'racial decay'. Liberals like Gambetta prophesied race war against 600 million Chinese, warning that 'France must keep its role as the soldier of civilization'. The positivist intellectual Renan claimed that Europeans were soldiers and masters, 'negroes' fit only to till the soil, the Chinese a manually dextrous 'worker race', devoid of a sense of honour, suitable only to be dominated.

Such social-Darwinism was popularized by an abundant sub-Kiplingesque literature, widely read in the 1890s and a major disseminator of imperialist attitudes. From the 1870s there existed a vogue for travel books, in which the reality of colonial exploitation was veiled behind picturesque exotica, fascination with native customs, the heroism of colonial troops – 'colonialism in slippers' for metropolitan readers. Jules Verne's Captain Nemo was the archetypal colonial adventurer, a tough, resourceful leader whose European technology dominates alien environments. The *Librairie des Grands Aventures* filled young minds with virgin jungles, cannibals and ape-like savages, for, as Fanon later remarked, Europeans' imagery for natives was consistently zoological. Such literature popularized 'scientific' anthropology. Darwin's translator, Clemence Royer, established complex racial hierarchies. In colonial literature Europeanized native interpreters were sly, odious, pathetic, suggesting that hopes of 'assimilation' were absurd, for race would win out. Natives were lazy, irrational, fatalistic, spoke a ludicrous pidgin French (*petit nègre*). Psichari, whose *Voyage du Centurion* stressed a common theme of the French as the new Romans, insisted that colonial combat made him a 'man', not just a bourgeois. North Africa belonged to crusading Latin heroes, not to Arab 'shepherds and camel traders'. For Psichari, as for Melchior de Vogüé, the virile vitality of colonial life would regenerate a degenerate metropolis, weakened by flabby intellectualism and humanitarianism. Colonies, insisted L. Bertrand, were a French Wild West, a school of national energy, oxygen for a stifled metropolis. From here would emerge the leaders to combat Germany. The settlers in Randau's *Les Colons* were virile, ruthless, brutal, practical, a new breed of Nietzschean supermen, rejecting anaemic European sentimentality.

Such social-Darwinist writing does much to strip the veil from the official 'civilizing mission' platitudes. Melchior de Vogüé admired military proconsuls like Galliéni who 'attempted everything, showed his superiority in everything. He made Frenchmen obeyed. He made the niggers work.' Such novels were poor literature, their ideas odious and simplistic. Yet they had a wide audience, helped erode initial public indifference to colonialism, imposed a certain vision of the world. They nakedly exposed the proto-fascism lurking behind the republicans' colonial rhetoric.

Yet if imperialism clearly contained this central nationalist element, it is a *non sequitur* to suggest, as does Brunschwig, that this provides an *alternative* to economic or social interpretations of the phenomenon. In 1885, Ferry's colleague and future biographer, A. Rambaud, introducing a translation of Seeley's *Expansion of England*, emphasized the value of colonies for raw materials and markets, linking this explicitly with national revival and national strength. France's grandeur relied on an economic neo-mercantilism. A balanced assessment of French imperialism must take account of three further factors – social imperialism; the vital importance of colonies for key sectors and regions in the French economy; the fact that 'colonialism' is *not* synonymous with 'imperialism'.

It is naive to assume that slow demographic growth made colonialism appear irrelevant. Interest in colonies as a safety valve for 'excessive' urban population was a perennial theme in bourgeois thought from 1830 onwards. Ten thousand workers were deported to Algeria after the June days. Africa was the means to the end of 'Parisian tranquillity', one deputy claimed. After the Commune the Gambettist press saw the 'criminals' as reformable via colonial careers. Gambetta saw the alternative to Tunisian annexation as 'internal conflict . . . anarchy and disorder'. Victor Hugo exhorted, 'Go peoples! Spill out your excessive numbers into Africa and, at the same time, resolve your social questions. Change your proletarians into landowners.' 'Empire or socialism' was a constant theme of alarmed bourgeois writers during the 1880s depression. M. Wahl emphasized the perils of an alliance of over-educated petty-bourgeois *déracinés* with victims of technological or cyclical unemployment. Empire was a 'virile hygiene' for such social diseases. The Lyon chamber of commerce showed a constant interest in working-class emigration. Ferry, who saw industrialization as necessary, felt that only empire could sublimate or export its attendant social tensions. Imperialism had the advantage of easing the tensions between petty producers and capitalists in the republican alliance. Radical politicians, like Bordeaux shipowner Menier, could exhibit their populism by arguing that Algerian farms be provided for peasant and working-class settlers. French capitalists' political alliance with the peasantry involved the economic disadvantage of limiting the consumer power of the metropolitan market, a 'contradiction' which, it was hoped, colonial markets could resolve.

Overall trading and investment statistics, arbitrarily curtailed at

1914, are a misleading index for assessing the importance of economic imperialism. On the eve of the Great War colonies took 'only' 9 per cent of French foreign investment, and 12 per cent of her trade. Yet colonial investment rose 300 per cent in 1904–14. Certain sectors of the economy were heavily reliant on colonies. Sugar refiners used colonial cane sugar, and sent two-thirds of their exports to the empire. Fifty-five per cent of French phosphates, 14 per cent of rubber, were imported from the colonies, while 65 per cent of soap exports, 41 per cent of metallurgical exports and 33 per cent of cotton exports went to the colonies. Several major ports owed their nineteenth-century revival to colonial expansion. Marseille merchants and industrialists were involved in Algerian lead mines and railways, Tunisian banking, Far East raw silk imports. Key raw materials for the city's oil and soap industries came from West Africa. Eugene Étienne, powerhouse of the parliamentary colonial lobby, began his career in the Marseille import-export business. Charles-Roux, organizer of the 1906 Colonial Exposition, vice-president of the parliamentary colonial group and vice-president of the Suez Company, was a Marseille soap-manufacturer. Senegal was a key Bordeaux trade colony. The port had supported Faidherbe's mission there during the Second Empire, and been rewarded with a trebling of its trade. Trade rivalry between France and Britain in West Africa was intense in the 1870s, *pre-dating* Britain's Egyptian takeover which, allegedly, awoke French nationalist interest in that region. French textile protectionism in West Africa provoked the colonial agitation of Lancashire textile interests in the 1880s. The mercantile elites of such ports dominated the navy, commerce and colonial ministries of post-1877 Opportunist governments.

As Laffey has shown the classic case of 'municipal imperialism' was that of Lyon. The silk disease pebrine had driven the city to support French expansion into Syria, then Indo-China, in the search for alternative raw silk supply. By the last quarter of the century the bulk of Lyonnais raw silk came from the Indo-China colonies. Such expansionist interest pre-dated 1870, making it difficult to explain in terms of humiliation by Prussia. Lyon businessmen maintained close ties with Catholic missions, employing clergy as commercial scouts. But one Lyon businessman was frank enough to admit that France's civilizing mission was a 'hypocritical' formula which deceived no one. Hard-headed Lyon, the Birmingham of France, knew that the balance sheet of empire was not calculated in saved souls. In 1901 the chamber of commerce insisted that 'to civilize people, in the sense which moderns give to the word, is to teach them to work, to acquire, to spend, to exchange'.

With many politicians indifferent to colonial issues, the 200-strong parliamentary colonial lobby was extremely influential over precarious and ephemeral ministries, controlling key posts on major parliamentary commissions. The *Parti-Colonial*, ten-thousand strong, was the major pressure group, sponsoring projects to map mineral resources, organizing lectures and publications to win popular support. Andrew and Kanya-Forstner have suggested that its members were essentially writers, academics, explorers – men united by psychology, patriotic faith in a greater France, but an atypical minority, representative of no class. Such an analysis ignores the strong business dominance of the leadership. Twenty-four of the 34 officers on the key committees of the *Parti-Colonial* held directorships, as did 132 of 271 members. The president of the *Comité de Maroc*, F. Guillain, was head of the metal cartel, the *Comité des Forges*. As Miller and Abrams claim, they were 'a group of the most powerful industrialists and bankers in France', capitalists adept at manipulating the machinery of government to secure overseas economic gains. The Asia, Madagascar and Moroccan committees were all reliant on business funds. Delcassé and subsequent foreign ministers were sympathetic, the *Quai d'Orsay* was reorganized in 1908 to set up a commercial section. The *Parti-Colonial* had considerable influence on both the quality and the popular press, helped spread the cult of the colonial army and erode the public indifference to colonies exhibited in the 1880s. Inevitably it did not always get its own way. Governments had wider perspectives, they had to take note of agricultural pressure groups who feared colonial competition. In Morocco Delcassé felt obliged to restrain Schneider, fearing that French economic domination might alienate the other powers. Embarrassing scandals made governments wary of giving colonial lobbies *carte blanche*. In the Congo, companies paid the state a fixed sum in return for full control, producing the scandal of high profits achieved through ruthless labour exploitation in a pillage economy.

The colonial expansion of the 1880s occurred because

Opportunist governments were genuinely alarmed about the impact of the Depression on economic, and hence socio-political, stability. It was the German tariffs of 1879 which cut French exports by 25 per cent within a year, not simply the German military triumph of 1870, that prompted Ferry's policy. On occasions, as with Tunis in 1881, fantastic El Dorado-style mineral bonanzas were invented to persuade parliament to support annexations. Yet Tonkin *did* have coal and mineral resources. Politicians and businessmen were staking claims for the future, not simply interested in short-term returns. By the 1900s the empire was beginning to move from the expansion phase into that of economic exploitation. Colonial trade increased 67 per cent in 1901–13. French Guinea may be taken as exhibiting a 'typical' pattern. It was acquired to prevent pillage of coast-bound caravans by the tribes of the interior and out of rivalry with Manchester-based traders in Sierra Leone. For decades it proved highly costly, as native rebellions were suppressed, roads built, an administrative infrastructure created. But the imposition of a poll tax forced natives into tapping raw rubber for French companies, in order to acquire cash. Only after 1918 was a plantation economy, using forced labour and diversifying into fruit and mining, fully developed. By the 1930s 27 per cent of French trade, 45 per cent of her foreign investment, was in the colonies. Some historians have attempted to minimize the economic value of the empire by emphasizing both that administrative costs were high, and that the average profits of colonial enterprises were little higher than returns on metropolitan investment. One should remember, however, that the costs were borne by taxpayers, while the profits went to private companies. Also, had surplus capital stayed in France, rates of profit would have fallen.

As Lenin knew, and his critics frequently forget, 'colonialism' and 'imperialism' are not synonyms. The latter characterized by the close ties of industry and banking, marks a stage in capitalist development to which colonial expansion may only be a prelude. How far can pre-1914 France be seen as fitting the Leninist model of 'finance capital' and capital export? Jean Bouvier has emphasized that major qualifications need to be made. The interconnection of industry and banking was less than in Germany. Gillet has emphasized that the northern coal companies still relied on auto-finance. Industrial banks, such as the *Crédit du Nord*, tended to service industry rather than to control it. Cartelization was limited. Connections between capital investment and exports often, as in the Near East, southern Europe and Russia, appeared weak. France supplied 33 per cent of Russian foreign investment, only 4 per cent of her imports. The *Comité des Forges* expressed frequent anger at the failure of French banks to tie their foreign loans to French engineering and arms exports.

Yet certain trends are of significance. French finance capital found its real métier in capital exports. France's overseas portfolio quadrupled between 1870 and 1914, rose from 25 per cent to 33 per cent of non-landed investment 1892–1913. By 1914, with the equivalent of £1500 million invested abroad, France was the world's second largest financier. Moreover loans to Greece, Turkey, Latin America were, after 1905, increasingly tied to demands to purchase French equipment. Major new banks such as *Parisbas* (1892) and the *Banque de l'Union Parisienne* (1904) had heavy industrial portfolios. Capital export became crucial to the balance of payments, a key area of French economic and political pressure necessitating major state involvement. During the 1880s Depression, as Michalet shows, bankers had been alarmed at falling profits. The *Crédit Lyonnais* complained, 'We are buckling under the weight of excessive capital. We do not know what to do with it.'

Thobie's analysis of French penetration of the Ottoman empire reveals a classic model of 'non-colonial' economic imperialism. Such a system provided high profits without the costs of colonial administration. France controlled 60 per cent of the Ottoman state debt and supplied two-thirds of the cadres of the *Banque Ottomane*. French capital controlled half the Turkish ports, 37 per cent of railways, with guaranteed profits. Urban transport, gas, water and mining were all dominated by French capital. Loans raised on the Paris Bourse had, increasingly, political and economic 'strings'. Attempts by the Germans to raise loans in Paris for the Berlin-Baghdad railway were blocked. The Ottoman government was pressured into purchasing arms from Schneider. Nine per cent of imports by 1913 were from France. As 1914 approached Cambon and Poincaré, sensing the imminent disintegration of the Ottoman regime, were preparing for a French carve-up of Syria and Anatolia. Initially a measure of cooperation between French and German financiers had suggested that Kautsky's thesis that European capital might ally in joint exploitation of the underdeveloped world was plausible. But bitter rivalry with Germany in Turkey by the 1900s made the region a classic example of Lenin's thesis that 'imperialist' economic conflicts were pushing Europe to war.

Tsarist Russia became, as Girault comments, in economic terms, a French 'Far West'. The director of BUP bank, Hughes Darcay, became involved in a major Russian metal cartel. The *Société Générale* bank had major holdings in petrol, chemicals, coal, iron and tobacco. Whereas in 1892 only one-quarter of French foreign investment had been in industry, this rose to one-half by 1910–13. French capitalists were learning to set up subsidiaries in foreign countries to avoid tariff barriers and exploit cheap labour. There is, thus, evidence for a belated, partial, but nevertheless expanding 'finance capitalism'.

IV The Radical Republic? (1898–1914)

Until the 1890s Radicalism constituted the major 'left' opposition in parliament to opportunism. Despite increasing bitterness towards Gambetta, the 30 Radical deputies were prepared to ally with fellow republicans in 1876–7 against the threat of a royalist coup. Despite regarding Ferry as too lenient to the clergy, radicals helped pass the laic laws. Some Radicals flirted with populist extra-parliamentary opposition to the conservative republic in the 1880s, yet most rallied to the opportunists to thwart Boulanger in 1889.

However, when the regime itself appeared in less peril, Radicals voiced populist resentment against an Opportunist elite which they denounced as a tool of big business. Their leadership was, it is true, difficult to distinguish in socio-economic terms from that of their Opportunist rivals. Ten of their 34 deputies in 1876 were lawyers, a handful were businessmen. Ten were doctors – among them Raspail and Naquet, who had been sacked from the Paris University faculty in the 1860s. Clemenceau, the party's most powerful parliamentary orator, was, likewise, a doctor by training, though his practice was limited to a few clinics in the slums of Montmartre where he was mayor. He had inherited his neo-Jacobinism from his father, a violently anticlerical Vendée doctor-landower who exerted a powerful influence over his son.

The Radical electorate came, essentially, from a petty

bourgeoisie of schoolteachers, vets, minor officials, small traders and artistans, together with peasants in central and southern regions and, initially, from industrial workers. Peasants, artisans and workers comprised 60 per cent of the large radical *Société Républicaine* in the Isère in 1890. Radical electors were tied disproportionately to the 'traditional' economy, and petty producers looked to Radicalism to provide some state protection against the chill winds of competition from big business and from abroad.

Radicalism's 'heroic' phase was in opposition in the republic's early years. Although it held a few cabinet posts in the hung parliament of 1885 and, briefly, under Léon Bourgeois, headed a government in 1895–6, it became the centrist party of government only after 1898. By then the qualities and principles displayed in opposition had, largely, been jettisoned. Historians such as Loubère and Ellis have insisted, however, that the conservative complacency of twentieth-century Radicalism must not be permitted to obscure the crusading zeal of early Radicalism. Loubère views the Radicals of the 1870s and 1880s as authentic social-democrats, heirs to the legacy of 1848–51, attempting to establish a mixed economy and an embryonic welfare state. They espoused the 1869 Belleville programme, abandoned by Gambetta's apostasy to complete the social reforms implicit in '1789' but abandoned by the conservative bourgeoisie. They denounced Opportunism for 'calling stagnation progress, and sterility wisdom', and viewed Gambetta as a traitor for accepting the senate and for distancing himself from calls for an amnesty for the communards. Like the *Réforme* Radicals during the June days they had felt trapped by the Commune, loathing Thiers yet unable to support working-class insurrection. Indeed, with Nadaud, Joigneaux and Blanc as ageing Radical luminaries, the links with the Second Republic were strong. They still favoured a quasi-'socialism' of cooperatives and state economic intervention. As mayor of Montmartre, Clemenceau expressed a concern for social problems, urged the need for improved health provision, foster homes, increased school budgets and crèches for working mothers.

By 1881, Radicalism had captured 14 per cent of parliamentary seats, and Clemenceau became Ferry's most ferocious oratorical opponent in the 1881–5 chamber. This confrontation was based on both political and social issues. Radicals insisted that the senate should be abolished, not merely reformed. Viewing the magistracy as crypto-royalist, they pressed for direct election of judges. They viewed the implementation of the laic laws as too gradual, and other aspects of Ferry's religious policy as inadequate. 'Removing the Capuchins' furniture' was a 'useless and ineffectual' substitute for separation of church and state. Opportunist socio-economic policy aroused their wrath. Agrarian protectionism coddled large landowners, at the expense of workers forced to purchase dearer bread. Radical bills for income and inheritance taxes and for old-age pensions were blocked by the senate. Aware of popular sympathy in working-class *quartiers* of Paris for the exiled communards, Clemenceau had argued that they were mistreated and misled victims, not the criminal scum of conservative mythology. Radicals were active in proposing legalization of trade unions. Nadaud, now a building contractor but once a stonemason, had spent his years in exile after 1851 in England, and admired pragmatic British unionism. When the 1884 Trade Union Act appended police controls of union membership lists, the Radicals denounced these as illiberal. Blanc insisted that union freedom should be genuine and concrete, nor merely theoretical, and Radicals introduced three abortive bills for fining of employers who sacked union officials. They opposed the *livret* and denounced governments for using troops against strikers, as in the Grand Combes' mine strike of 1882. They pushed their hostility to the big railway and mining companies to the point of demanding that the state should revoke its concessions to these 'financial feudalisms'. Clemenceau denounced the mining companies for their labour-control policies and use of company-stores.

Clemenceau also proved the most eloquent critic of imperialist expansion, although Ferry's fall on the Tonkin issue occurred only because patriotic deputies saw colonialism as a diversion from the German issue, because Catholics were seeking any excuse to overthrow the laic laws' architect and because fellow-opportunists like Rouvier viewed Ferry's colonial policy as rash. His Jacobin patriotism was outraged by the thought that colonialism would play into Bismarck's hands by creating needless tensions between France and Britain. He claimed that Ferry's policies were underhand, carried out without parliamentary approval. They ran the risk of involving France in war with China. French taxpayers and troops were paying in money and blood to safeguard the profits of a few financiers and businessmen. True prosperity flowed from international trade not from military expansionism. The hypocritical rhetoric of the 'civilizing mission' obscured exploitation of colonial peoples, while Ferry's invocation of the rights of 'superior' races was founded on a pernicious racism which ignored the great historic cultures of the non-European world. Above all, colonialism diverted energy and resources from domestic reforms.

Radicalism's admirers view these policies as evidence of a commitment to progressive social reforms so genuine that Marx himself was, briefly, persuaded that Clemenceau might be an ally of socialism. Many French socialists were more sceptical. Guesdists viewed Clemenceau as a 'parliamentary athlete', compelled to voice progressive rhetoric to maintain his working-class vote in Montmartre. Radical social reform proposals were mere tokenism, an attempt to prevent further alienation of workers from the republic and to prevent the growth of authentic socialism. Some critics of Clemenceau have argued that the violence of his parliamentary assaults on Ferry were a major cause of that ministerial instability which made the passing of any serious legislation impossible. This charge is implausible, for the Radical deputies were too few in number before 1885 to be held responsible for cabinet instability. Ellis has, however, claimed that there *were* serious flaws in Clemenceau's political judgement, stemming from deep-seated psychological causes. Clemenceau is portrayed as ceaselessly attempting to live up to the expectations of his dominant neo-Jacobin father. He viewed himself as a sufferer for the cause of the oppressed and disinherited, yet experienced pervasive doubts about his own capacities and exhibited a disturbing tendency to manufacture 'failure situations' to avoid 'corruption' by success.

Ellis argues that Clemenceau could, and should, have sought an alliance with the left-Gambettists to create a larger progressive bloc in parliament for piecemeal reform. Instead Clemenceau's brutal, sarcastic oratory and his denunciation of Gambetta, still a hero to many republicans, made such an alliance impossible. Tactical compromises were precluded by his intransigent all-or-nothing approach. Political impotence proved the price of clinging to unsullied ideals. In addition lack of concern for fellow-Radical deputies made him a poor party leader. Vehement, temperamental, constantly interrupting parliamentary speeches and fighting duels, he became a quasi-dandy, rode in the Bois de

Boulogne, slept with actresses, sabotaged his marriage, flirted with dubious financiers like C. Herz and rashly promoted the career of General Boulanger which almost wrecked the republic. Whether such interesting psychological speculation bears the weight which Ellis places on it is doubtful. It is by no means clear that a progressive majority could be achieved in the parliament of the 1880s.

Radicals won 19 per cent of seats in the parliament of 1885, 20 per cent in 1893. With Clemenceau in eclipse after the Boulanger affair, leadership passed to Leon Bourgeois, who headed a brief cabinet in 1895–6, which fell when the senate blocked its plan for income tax. Bourgeois was the promoter of a new doctrine of 'solidarism', an attempt to cobble together a plausible amalgam of individualism and collectivism. Unbridled laissez-faire was condemned as a 'deceitful liberty' which permitted the strong to exploit the weak. Individuals were born with debts to past society. The state had the duty to give to the creditors and to make the debtors pay. Such ideas underlay industrial accident legislation in 1898 and proposals for aid to the aged poor. Solidarism may be interpreted either as a genuine, if naive, belief in a welfare state or as an attempt to hold back the growth of socialism in the 1890s by integrating workers into the capitalist republic. For radical leaders became, simultaneously, more hostile to collectivism. Clemenceau denounced Marxists as 'red Jesuits', socialism as a threat to 'integral liberties', offering only a world of regimented slaves. He claimed, from experience in his native Vendée, that socialism was impossible in France, since peasants would tear to pieces anyone peddling collectivist ideas. Such claims were, however, less plausible in the Var, where he was now a senator, for the Provençal peasantry were already voting for Marxist deputies.

Radicalism was outflanked on its left by the growing socialist movement. Its support for cooperatives and emphasis on the access of workers to small property appeared increasingly irrelevant to a more collectivist and proletarianized labour movement. Radical Jacobin-patriotism became divorced from socialist internationalism and antimilitarism. The geography and sociology of Radicalism changed. In 1875 33 per cent of radical deputies sat for Midi constituencies, 25 per cent for Paris. The party appealed to workers and to 'red' peasants. Gradually it lost ground in Paris and industrial areas to the socialists or to the new populist radical right, while making gains in ex-Bonapartist fiefs in the south-west. In the Isère it declined in Grenoble and industrial centres like Vienne and Voiron, but compensated by winning votes in rural cantons. Clemenceau sat as senator for the Var, where radicalism increasingly appeared a centrist party as socialists won seats in the lower house thanks to votes from small wine-growers.

In 1898 Radicals won 25 per cent of parliamentary seats, and came to form the backbone of the *Bloc des Gauches*, formed to defend the republic against the threat from the far right. Radicalism had matured into *the* republican party. Its strength was based on a network of interlocking groups and committees which provided the framework for a national organization even before the development of a party machine. Most notorious of these were the masonic lodges, denounced by papal encyclicals and Catholic exposés as the headquarters of the devil's army. Freemasonry was essentially one expression of a deep-seated bourgeois anticlericalism, and, as ever, Catholics mistook sympton for cause. Yet it did act as a 'cement' to hold together the Radical republic. Republicans had utilized the lodges as a cover for their political activities in the 1860s, and in 1874 Broglie had ordered his prefects to keep a close watch on masonic activity. The initiation of the philosopher Littré in 1875 had symbolized masonry's espousal of positivist values, the stress on evolutionary progress, rational non-dogmatic morality and the concern with the 'scientific' education of the masses.

McMahon closed several lodges during the *Seize Mai* crisis. Although many opportunist politicians had been freemasons, masonry became 'radicalized' in the last years of the century. In Tarn-et-Garonne the Montauban lodge, dominated by merchants, remained moderate, but the Caussade and Moissac lodges, with many petty-bourgeois members, moved to the left. Masonic membership quadrupled to above 40,000, with lodges multiplying in the Midi, and south-west. If membership remained predominantly bourgeois, nevertheless Midi artisans, many primary schoolteachers and even some Nord workers joined, while G. Martin even recruited a few women. Radical notables like pastor Desmons in the Gard were masons, as was F. Buisson, viewed by the Catholic historian Capéran as the evil genius of the laic laws. Combes's Radical cabinet of 1902 contained ten masons, and his anticlerical policies had been widely debated in the lodges over the previous decade. When Radical cabinets clashed with the army after the Dreyfus crisis they looked to the lodges to help spy on Catholic officers in provincial garrison towns.

Radicalism relied, too, on the *Ligue des Droits de l'Homme*, whose 40,000 members included some trades unionists alongside intellectuals and professionals. *Libre Pensée* groups, key organizations in ritualized local conflicts with the clergy, presided over civil funerals and baptisms and Good Friday carnivorous banquets – attracting teachers, café owners, railway workers and Burgundy vignerons. *Universités Populaires*, run by academics, attempted to give substance to solidarist rhetoric by teaching courses to skilled workers. The *Ligue de l'Enseignement* remained a powerful pressure group, and a network of provincial newspapers, including the influential *Dépêche de Toulouse*, was established. All these helped hold together a broad populist alliance, viewed with some suspicion by more conservative republicans.

However the nature of Radicalism changed rapidly after 1900. Its hold on its working-class clientele became precarious. The *Université Populaire* experiment collapsed. *Libre Pensée* groups splintered on class lines, as workers attempted to apply rational free thought to issues like property and *Patrie* as well as to religion. In Burgundy, Dauphiné and the Nord some *Libre Pensée* societies drifted towards socialism. As the Radicals, alarmed by the growing threat of socialism and the far right, began to develop their loose coalition of groupings into an organized party, the unions were notable absentees.

In the aftermath of the Dreyfus case the Radicals, the dominant group in the centre-left coalition government, focused their policies against the church, and to a lesser degree the army. This use of anticlericalism to hold together a populist coalition made radicals the new Opportunists. The 'real' issue in French politics in the 1900s was the relationship between the capitalist state and a growing and militant labour movement. Radicalism hoped to obscure this by reviving old religious feuds in order to rebuild a laic front which would enable the progressive wing of the bourgeoisie to reassert its leadership over the popular classes. Anticlericalism was, thus, an attractive solution to the potential state crisis and was proclaimed as the quasi-official state ideology in the hope of channelling popular grievances against the clerical-feudal enemy. In Laval

(Mayenne) employers and workers rubbed shoulders as members of the local radical group – while a left-wing shoemaker in the town was expelled from the small local branch of the socialist party for marrying in church. Combes, the prime minister from 1902 till 1905, was a small-town Charente doctor-politician, who had trained for the priesthood, but had come to see the uselessness of religious life. His government concentrated its energies on expelling unauthorized religious orders and ending the Concordat.* Attempts by Jaurès to use reformist socialist support for the Combes government to achieve social reforms proved abortive. Education Minister Leygues rejected demands for free secondary schooling and radical ministers showed little interest in Millerand's efforts to introduce conciliation and arbitration procedures into industrial relations. Combes himself argued for 'prudence' on the income-tax issue in order not to alarm important 'interests'.

Once the separation of church and state had been achieved (1905) the bloc's reforming potential was exhausted. Already in 1904 Paul Doumer, Radical chairman of the influential parliamentary budget committee and an ex-colonial administrator, was urging his party to distance itself from Jaurès and to cultivate relations with pro-business Opportunists like Poincaré. A *Comité Républicaine du Commerce et de l'Industrie* facilitated contacts between Radical deputies and the business world. Rouvier, who succeeded Combes as prime minister, was a staunch opponent of income tax. Despite its populist image in parts of the south, Radicalism was degenerating into a party of the 'satisfied' political centre, its leading deputies increasingly more hostile to socialism than to the right. The influence of old-style neo-Jacobins like Pelletan – who as navy minister in 1903 ended 'christening' of warships and socialized with dockers and shipyard workers on his official visits to ports – was steadily eroded. In 1906, as Réberioux observes, Radicals won a seat in the Côte-d'Or against a socialist challenge. The Radical candidate, significantly, was a large brewer, president of the Dijon chamber of commerce, who attracted conservative votes. Between 1906 and 1914 Radicalism came to control over 40 per cent of parliamentary seats. It was becoming a 'responsible' governing party. As Radical education expert Buisson observed: 'By the very fact of its victory the party occupies a central position in the republic. Whoever flatters himself that he can

* See chapter 7.

continue the old Radicalism of yesteryear is blind.'

With anticlericalism running out of steam, radicals were faced with a choice between social reform and immobilism, and plumped for the latter. Despite uttering a few tired anti-monopoly clichés, the 1907 party congress affirmed that the solution of the social question must lie in the access of workers to private property. Clemenceau posed as a 'realist' against the 'utopian' Jaurès. As prime minister from 1906–9 Clemenceau, who had once defended the right to strike and denounced the police as authoritarian, utilized an unreformed police system to infiltrate the unions, plant *agents provocateurs*, arrest labour leaders and defeat strikes, taking pride in his new role as 'emperor of the stool-pigeons'. Radical governments refused to question the alliance with the tsar who was busily engaged in smashing the 1905 Russian revolution. Radical anticolonialism was discreetly abandoned. The symbiotic ties between Radical deputies and colonial bureaucratic and business interests became stronger. Doumer had extensive Indo-China metal interests. Combes's agriculture minister, Mougeot, who had opposed the Madagascar expedition in the 1890s, became chairman of a Madagascar company and owner of sizeable Tunisian estates. In one of many major colonial scandals Paul Bourdes, agricultural director of Tunisia, was shown to have given huge Tunisian estates to 30 men, including nine deputies and eight senators. Perchot, owner of the daily *Le Radical*, had extensive Moroccan interests. Radicalism began to claim itself to be the party of 'patriotic' Frenchmen, and Radical governments jailed leftist militants for antimilitarist and anticolonial propaganda.

In 1906 the Radicals' election manifesto outlined seventeen major reforms; Clemenceau's three-year ministry managed to pass just one. Pelletan confessed that the party's theoretical support for fiscal reform was undermined by the fact that radical voters belonged, precisely, to 'those middle classes who will pay the additional taxes when our reforms have been voted'. Increasingly the party's local base moved away from 'ideological' groups such as *Libre Pensée* societies, its deputies became politically colourless technicians of pork-barrel politics. Efforts by socialists to raise issues such as proportional representation foundered on this localism. The balance sheet of Radical social reform was unimpressive. The 1910 pension law, providing financial aid for those over 65 years of age in a population where life expectancy was still under 50, granted 'pensions for the dead' as socialists ironically noted. 'Briandism' was symptomatic of the degeneration of radicalism. Briand headed four cabinets between 1910 and 1914. A renegade from syndicalism, Briand was a flexible, suave, ambitious lawyer, keen to build a centre right coalition through an alliance of radicals, Opportunists and moderate Catholics, to whom he offered the olive branch of a conciliatory interpretation of the 1905 separation law. He broke the 1910 rail strike, secured Poincaré's election as president, ended the feud between the regime and the army, and sought to achieve a coalition based on antisocialism and resistance to income tax. Not all Radical deputies followed him. Traditional Radicals were made uneasy by strike-breaking, peasant radical voters disliked increased conscription. Heavy armaments expenditure emphasized the injustices in the taxation system. In 1911–12 Caillaux, a maverick financier who feared that war would destroy the European economies, became prime minister. Although he angered the left by refusing to reinstate sacked railmen, he claimed that there was a need to end immobilism, hinting at state-control of railways, income tax and measures against land-speculators. His fall, precipitated by the second Moroccan crisis, was greeted with relief by business interests. However the conscription and tax reform issues maintained a 'leftist' mood among sections of the Radical electorate which produced gains for left-Radicals and socialists in the 1914 election and a centre-left coalition ministry under Viviani. Whether this suggests that Radicalism was about to enter a new phase remains uncertain, for the war crisis intervened.

Chapter 7

An Intransigent Right (1871–1914)

I The Decline of Royalism

The royalist election triumph of February 1871 was a freak result. With half of France occupied by German troops, the peasantry, desperate for peace, had sheltered behind local landowners and rejected bellicose republicanism. Yet royalism had been resurrected as a political possibility. Suddenly, as the Radical propagandist P. Joigneaux observed, 'We have princes of all ages and colours. It is raining pretenders.' Only dynastic squabbles prevented a restoration, for three royal backsides could not fit on one throne.

The reappearance in parliament of names like Casimir Périer and Dufaure among some 200 Orleanist deputies suggested that constitutional monarchism had been reborn. Leaders like Broglie accepted parliamentary government but expressed deep Tocquevillean fears that democracy involved mass mediocrity and the erosion of true liberty. They portrayed the 1870 defeat at the hands of disciplined monarchist Prussia as the logical consequence of the weakening of organic French development by revolutionary excesses. The products of the recent Catholic education revival, they sensed a deep moral crisis in France and saw priests as necessary allies. Yet their Catholicism remained liberal-Gallican. Observing the excess of ultramontane piety, 'the word superstition came to their lips, but they refrained from pronouncing it' (Remond). They felt trapped in the crossfire between anticlericals and ultramontane theocrats. They hoped that the legitimist pretender, the childless Chambord, might accept the tricolour, take the throne, and then bequeath it to their pretender. Yet they remained political pragmatists. Twenty-five per cent of their deputies in 1871 were businessmen, who shared economic interests with conservative republicans. In time many rallied to Thiers's law-and-order republic, sharing Flaubert's fear that the probable consequence of an attempted restoration would be a violent popular anticlerical revolt. By the 1880s many accepted the Opportunist republic as preferable to the uncertainties of the violent populism of the radical right. In 1887, when many royalists flirted with the Boulangist assault on the republic, the Orleanist duc d'Aumale, with substantial business investments in companies headed by republicans, felt very queasy.

Bonapartism recovered from the 1870 disaster to win 100 seats in the 1876 election. Its synthesis of authoritarianism and populism retained its appeal to conservatives unhappy with either republican democracy or legitimist clericalism. Yet internal disagreements over strategy meant that Bonapartism was in crisis even before the Prince Imperial's death in 1879. Essentially the party's *notables* failed to lay sufficient emphasis on Bonapartism's populist strand. While Jules d'Amigues gained election in Cambrai by winning workers' votes against a republican business candidate, the party's bigwigs viewed his preoccupation with social reform and proletarian grievances as 'expertise in an occult science' (Rothney). South-western 'bosses' like Baron d'Eschassarieu maintained effective political machines which delivered the peasant vote in a region where the empire appeared a golden age of high wine prices. Yet the survival of such electoral manipulation required control of the state machinery, and by 1876 barely ten prefects were Bonapartists. Gradually the republicans stole the Bonapartists' clothes, offering their own middle path between 'feudalism' and socialism. The tone of national leadership was set, fatally, by the violent Cassagnac, dreaming of military coups, and by conservatives whose flirtations with clericalism alarmed peasant voters. Captured by conservatives, Bonapartism betrayed its populist heritage. Lacking a charismatic hero it became just another party, lost its specific identity. Even its south-western bastions finally crumbled.

Legitimism's failure to capitalize on its 200 seats of 1871 owed much to tactical incompetence. Chambord's stubborn rejection of the tricolour sabotaged the possibility of a deal with the Orleanists. Despite a smattering of St Germain sophisticates, legitimism was dominated by provincial diehards with little political acumen. One observer noted acidly of Mgr Dreux-Brézé, bishop of Moulins, 'he thinks the Assembly must limit itself to proclaiming Chambord King. When one speaks to him of finding a majority, he understands nothing.' As Locke has emphasized, not all legitimists were backwoods gentry. Fifteen per cent of their deputies were businessmen. Men like northern textile-owner Kolb-Bernard of Lille attempted to reconcile capitalism with legitimist ideology by emphasizing paternalism, running their businesses as enclosed, patriarchal industrial villages. The coal and iron magnate Benoit d'Azy expressed pained incredulity on hearing that 'his' Alais forge-workers had begun to vote for the left. Yet over half legitimist deputies were landowners, 55 per cent of them were nobles. In Dordogne in 1871, 19 of the 22 legitimist mayors were aristocrats.

Until 1876 legitimist 'moral order' rhetoric dominated parliamentary debate. They opposed divorce, defended parental rights to reject state education, put priests on to welfare committees, urged *livrets* for farm workers. Cushioned by the deferential tenantry of their western bastions, they had no understanding of the rising peasant yearning for democratic independence, which they diagnosed as a disease carried by migrants and *déracinés*.

The roots of their political decline can be found in their attitude towards the social question, the state and the papacy. Albert de Mun, an aristocratic officer appalled by the Commune, sought to woo back a proletariat, alienated by capitalist laissez-faire, through workers' circles, social reform legislation, and the promise of a counter-revolutionary return to the guild system of the ancien régime. Sadly his social Catholicism was paternalistic social tinkering, his circles attracted more clerks than proletarians, his proposed factory legislation was sabotaged by legitimist businessmen who saw 'life's duty' as calling 'the worker's child in the factory, the bourgeois child to the lycée'. Legitimists praised decentralization, advocated moving the capital to Tours, criticized the prefectoral bureaucracy – yet fought in the army against the Commune, retained state appointment of mayors to prevent radical municipalities appointing 'reds'. Their devotion to the papacy allowed a suicidal crusade in favour of French aid to restore the Temporal Power, permitting republicans to brand them as foolhardy warmongers willing to risk conflict with Italy.

Even after Chambord's death in 1883, legitimists remained tempted to exploit any crisis to smash the republic. Yet the power of the aristocracy waned. In 1871 nobles, elected in 72 departments, made up one-third of the deputies. By 1910 the aristocracy provided

9.4 per cent of deputies, elected in 33 departments. In a few Breton fiefs they still continued to stand for election unopposed; in villages like Chanzeau in Anjou peasants were still marched to the château after Mass for interrogation on the sermon. They retained 90 per cent of their lands in Loir-et-Cher and the Pas-de-Calais, still controlled 17 per cent of the area of Calvados. Yet in Normandy peasant voters now had to be wooed by electioneering styles which nobles had once condemned as vulgar when practised by Bonapartists. In the Dordogne, where nobles could still be found among the leading landowners in 44 of 125 villages, the proportion of nobles on the *Conseil Général* fell from 12 per cent to 4 per cent between 1870 and 1900, and they provided no deputies in the 1880s – a consequence less of the decline in their landed power than of the skilful republican campaign against the threat of the return of 'feudalism' and the tithe.

Yet undoubtedly the decline of landed incomes during the Great Depression did weaken their power. In Mayenne local industry was dominated by the republican bourgeoisie. Ideologically dubious about speculative overseas investment, the *notables* relied on land. Yet wheat prices fell to 60 per cent of 1860s levels; labour costs rose. Economic rationality suggested a switch from arable to pasture, yet this would have accelerated the rural exodus which they deplored. A new breed of bourgeois middle-landowners emerged, often livestock dealers, who became republican mayors, controlled their tenants, established *syndicats agricoles* to challenge aristocratic rural control. Aristocratic absenteeism, in spa towns or on the Riviera, reflected and accelerated their declining influence. Careful contraceptive practices, designed to avoid subdividing estates, backfired when old families failed to produce heirs. Local scholars twisted the knife by proving that the proud legend of Mayenne aristocrats' heroism in medieval crusades was a seventeenth-century forgery. Unable to stomach the new France of railways, laic teachers and republican nouveaux riches, one local aristocrat died fighting for the Boers. Legitimism became proud but marginal, the despairing creed of a declining elite.

Religion became the real focus of the politics of the traditional right. Republicans experienced the Moral Order years, 1871–6, as a crusade to restore medieval theocracy. The Sacré Coeur was built to expiate the sins of the nation. The Virgin Mary appeared in the Hérault; her statue in Nancy wept. Mayenne pilgrims sang that the

Virgin who had appeared at Pontmain had prevented the Teuton hordes penetrating the Catholic west, while Satan ruled over the alcoholic criminal scum of Paris, the modern Babylon. The Virgin of La Salette vowed to her peasant shepherd children that she would cease weeping only when the Bourbons were restored! With 51,000 secular clergy, 157,000 regulars and control of 40 per cent of school pupils, the church had reached the apogee of its nineteenth-century power. An extraordinary politicized mysticism pervaded French Catholicism. The loss of Alsace was explained as punishment for the sins of a godless nation. When Third Republic anticlericals voted, the image they had of 'religion' – obscurantist, credulous, reactionary – was, as McManners observes, based on stereotypes derived from the 1870s, not on the threadbare *curé* who called when auntie died.

How involved were the clergy in right-wing politics? Barely 12 per cent of bishops were nobles, and Sulpicien-training taught many moderation in dealings with the state. A few, like Mgr Ginoulhiac, were learned men, capable of intelligent debate with scientific unbelief and biblical criticism. A handful of Gallican liberals urged compromise with the republic. Yet they were a minority, swept along by the ultramontane tide which had produced papal infallibility. Pius IX viewed liberal Catholics as a greater evil than communards. Half the episcopate, it is true, followed Mgr Dupanloup, a 'liberal' because of his reservations about the Syllabus of Errors. Yet Dupanloup was a royalist, frequented châteaux, wanted atheistic papers banned. The losing battle which he fought to stem rural anticlericalism in his Orleans diocese inclined him towards authoritarian solutions to France's problems. He encouraged the *Seize Mai* coup in which the royalist President McMahon dissolved the republican-dominated parliament and used administrative pressure to attempt to elect a royalist majority. Dupanloup was 'moderate' only in comparison with those 68 prelates of the 1870–83 period who, like Mgr Pie or Mgr de Cabrières, favoured indirect or direct clerical control of government. Veuillot encouraged ultramontane clergy to hound and spy on their 'liberal' bishops. Mgr Guilbert found his own theological writings banned from his diocesan seminary in Amiens! Ultramontane vicars-general made life intolerable for liberal prelates in Arras; Vannes was an 'ungovernable' diocesan chaos.

Clerical pressure established Catholic university faculties in

1875. The church budget was increased by 8 per cent. Clergy openly yearned for a monarchy 'sheltered from the surprises of universal suffrage', safe from Gambettist tavern-orators. Yet clerical electoral meddling merely fuelled the anticlerical backlash which swept the republicans to power after 1876. Only belatedly did Mgr Guilbert's emphasis on the need for some *modus vivendi* with the republic receive support from the diplomatic flexibility of Leo X after 1878.

Yet ongoing conflict over the Ferry laws precluded any easy compromise. In the Nord, a 'Catholic' department despite the anticlericalism of Lille workers and the Avesnois petty bourgeoisie, cautious prefects slowed the pace of school secularization, republication municipalities turned a blind eye to crucifixes on school walls, the proportion of Catholic-educated pupils fell only marginally, violence was minimal and the clergy did not, as in the Midi, burn laic textbooks in public. Yet, as Ménager shows, politics was poisoned for two decades. The virulent Catholic newspaper, *Croix du Nord*, blamed the laic school for higher taxes and juvenile delinquency. Laic teachers were boycotted in Flemish villages, their pupils denied First Communion. The Nord bourgeoisie polarized between Opportunists and Catholic-royalists. Denunciation of the 'immorality' of laic teachers provoked counter-assaults on the 'sexual perversions' of unmarried Catholic teachers. 168 were arrested in Lille rioting against a *frère* accused of child molestation.

II From Nationalism to Proto-fascism?

If Catholic hostility to the godless republic was one strand of rightist politics, it became intertwined in the 1880s with the discontent of other groups, fuelled by different grievances. The defeat of 1870 was, initially, exploited by Gambettists who claimed that it proved the necessity for education reform to mould a united nation. The patriotic textbooks of the laic school won approval from nationalists. Yet such patriotism, once unleashed, had its own momentum. Super-patriots like Déroulède came to insist that Frenchmen had been too altruistic, wasting their energies on crusades for European liberty. Faced with the demographic, military and economic threat from Germany, it was now time to put

France first. Envy, xenophobia, obsession with revenge elbowed aside the internationalist façade of Jacobin nationalism.

Parliamentary democracy appeared feeble, as republican cabinets came and went, obsessed with party squabbles, tainted by financial corruption, flunking the German challenge, dividing national unity with sectarian anticlericalism. Liberal values were luxuries which France could no longer afford. Even imperialism was a needless diversion of national energy, encouraged by Bismarck to involve France in conflict with Britain. Déroulède claimed that in Alsace-Lorraine he had lost two sisters – while Ferry was offering him only twenty black servants. Initially an admirer of the laic school for its 'rites, symbols, apostles and martyrs', he came to criticize it for peddling humanitarian nonsense and ignoring military training. Significantly, Déroulède announced his rejection of the republic at a speech to gymnastic and rifle clubs. In 1869 France had had a mere 40 gymnastic societies, Germany 2183. Déroulède exhibited a mixture of fear and admiration for Germany. He saw physical training as a key step towards a healthy, fit military race. Déroulède was obsessed with the idea that sedentary modern life would produce racial degeneration. By 1910 France had 200,000 gym-club members, 200,000 in rifle clubs, 70,000 in military training clubs. A thriving sports press emerged, dominated by racist, social Darwinist and nationalist values, articles on 'thick-skulled' black boxers, and on sport as a way of 'showing the Boche'.

For Déroulède 1870 was proof of the superiority of virile authoritarian Prussia over a France grown flabby through an excess of democracy. His *Ligue des Patriotes* grew into a noisy, vulgar, violent pressure-group, 30,000-strong, worshipping the army, flirting with street violence and acquiring paramilitary overtones. Its populist rhetoric accused oligarchic Opportunism of neglect of the 'little man'.

Though this *mélange* of authoritarianism, nationalism and populism recalled Bonapartism, it lacked Bonapartism's peasant audience, relied essentially on the petty bourgeoisie of Paris, the major cities and eastern frontier towns. The mood of small businessmen and shopkeepers was of extreme volatility. Prices and profits fell as the depression cut sales. In St Denis in northern Paris only 15 of 203 small firms established between 1850 and 1874 collapsed; between 1875 and 1890 106 were set up, 73 went under.

Competition from large stores alarmed small traders. The twelve largest Parisian department stores employed 1700 in 1881, 11,000 three decades later. Small retailers controlled 17 per cent of Parisian wealth in 1820, 3 per cent by 1911. Tax returns suggest extremely slim profit margins for most of France's 1.5 million shopkeepers. Small manufacturers were ardent protectionists, and the trade wars of the 1880s fuelled xenophobia. The old revolutionary alliance, forged in the *sans-culotte* movement of 1793, between small business and skilled craftsmen collapsed, with the former alienated by an increasingly strike-prone proletarianized labour movement. Squeezed between large capitalism and labour, vulnerable to foreign competition and bankruptcy, the sometime-republican petty bourgeoisie thrashed around for explanations, panaceas – and scapegoats. Its mentality is captured by Céline's *Mort à Credit*, a novel charting the decline of one thrifty, industrious Parisian family. The mother runs a lace shop: and Parisian textiles were to lose over 100,000 employers, retailers and workers in the decades after 1880. The father, a clerk, finds promotion in an insurance firm blocked by bright young men with diplomas. A visit to the Paris Exhibition machine room awakes a dim awareness of their fate as individuals, as a family, as a class. Fleeing in terror the father voices impotent fury at intriguers, *nouveux riches*, destiny – and at freemasons and the Jews.

The atavistic hatred of the small man for big business, once expressed through Jacobin populism, found a new outlet. As Jacobin patriotism degenerated into xenophobia, so hostility to speculation and finance acquired strongly anti-semitic overtones. This transition from 'left' to 'right' was accelerated by developments within French socialism. If some socialists urged tax cuts to protect the small trader, Marxists came to argue that the petty bourgeoisie was inexorably doomed by capitalist concentration. Shopkeepers resented the growing threat from socialist consumer cooperatives. A *Ligue Syndicale*, foreshadowing the Poujadist movement of the 1950s, claimed 180,000 shopkeeper members by 1894, urging tax penalties against chain stores, idealizing the small retailer as the 'cornerstone of sociability' in urban *quartiers*. L. Christophe, its president, began as a Gambettist freemason, yet by 1888 the *LS* was flirting with anti-republican movements and, by 1892, it had strange Catholic and anti-semitic bedfellows.

The social basis for a new right was thus emerging among an urban petty bourgeoisie whose wounded nationalism was aggravated by foreign economic competition in a decade of imperialism and tariff wars, and whose socio-economic position was threatened by depression, labour militancy and capitalist concentration. Yet a genuine mass movement against the 'liberal' republic needed, also, the support of alienated Catholics, and of workers disillusioned by unemployment and the absence of social reform. Only an ideology utilizing common hatreds could unify any such alliance of disparate groups and traditions. Anti-semitism alone offered the possibility of achieving this, because the multifaceted stereotypes of 'the Jew' were sufficiently elastic to provide a target for all the disaffected and, thus, to paper over the new right's internal contradictions. As Maurras observed: 'All seems impossible without this providential anti-semitism. With it all falls into place and becomes simplified.' Had the Jew not existed, the new right would have needed to invent him.

The Jewish community, the target of this politics of paranoia, was 80,000-strong, under 0.25 per cent of the French population, and essentially urban. It ranged from the thousands of poor proletarians in the Paris Marais, via small businessmen through the liberal professions to a small elite of financiers. Most were republicans, though Rothschild was a royalist and some workers were socialist. Most were 'assimilationist', fervently loyal to France as their second Promised Land, which had emancipated them in 1789. Religious ties were weak, with Jews apeing republican secularism, sending children to laic schools. Instinctively they responded to anti-semitism by keeping a low profile, professing faith in French justice and hoping that the nightmare would pass. Many redoubled their patriotism, ignoring Russian official pogroms by praying for the republic's new ally, the tsar.

Anti-semites could exploit several features of Jewish socio-economic activity. Rothschild epitomized high finance; Jews were involved in 'usury' in the eastern countryside; Jewish refugees from Alsace set themselves up in trade in Lille, where Drumont's father was a struggling small businessman. Drumont was to be the gutter-king of anti-semitic propaganda, his monstrous sprawling *La France Juive* (1886) going through 200 editions in fifteen years. Family pride in the high success rate of Jewish students in competitive examinations for the *grandes écoles* or the medical and legal professions was interpreted as 'proof' of an 'incorrigible' Jewish passion for domination. Several thousand orthodox Jewish refugees from eastern pogroms provided anti-semites with an easy target – and many assimilated Jews gave a lukewarm reception to newcomers whose odd dress and religious customs were an embarrassing reminder of their own ghetto past. Yet anti-semitism flourished equally, like anti-migrant xenophobia in the 1930s, in the Catholic west where Jews were rare.

One major source of anti-semitism lay among the militant Catholics of *La Croix*, for whom the Jew served to explain the decline of Catholic influence. The paper's founder was the Assumptionist Père d'Alzon, from the Catholic elite of the Gard, weaned on generations of bloody conflict with local Protestantism. D'Alzon abhorred compromise, despised liberal Catholics. He had organized mass pilgrimages to woo the masses back to the church, but Ferry's laic laws accentuated his Manichean vision. 'In place of the rule of Christ [the Republicans] wish the rule of Satan.' *La Croix* became a lively paper, less austere than *L'Univers*, with a circulation of 170,000. Its mediocre intellectual level and vehemence suited the average *curé*. It received funds from Nord industrialists, boosted its sale through local supplements. It viewed daily events as manifestations of divine will. The death by fire of English Protestant children was providential, for it might bring a heretic nation back to God. Initially, *La Croix* merely flirted with traditional Christian anti-semitism – Jews loved money and crucified Christ. Then the laic laws became 'a real Jewish trick played on the French people', and the collapse of the Catholic *Union Générale* bank in 1881 opened the floodgates. This crash was due to rash investment in European railways, but Catholic investors were persuaded by Bontoux, its director, that 'Jewish money power' aided by 'governmental freemasonry', had sabotaged their Christian rival. Aided by a stream of cheap novels about Jewish bankers, with titles like *Baron Vampire*, *La Croix* disseminated this conspiracy theory. Jewish deputy Naquet was blamed for the legalization of divorce, aimed at undermining the Christian family. Lists of Jewish civil servants were published to underline Jewish control of the republic. The Talmud was said to teach Jews to cheat, steal, commit ritual murder. The fantasies of Leo Taxel were published, detailing the 'confessions' of 'Diana Vaughan', a girl allegedly kept prisoner in the rock of Gibraltar, where Jews and

Protestants plotted world domination. When Taxel confessed that this was a hoax, leading bishops took this as proof that he, too, had been corrupted by the Jews. Eugen Weber emphasizes the extraordinary fascination of the radical right, both Catholic and agnostic, with palmistry, superstition, sorcery, devils and satanic plot theories.

La Croix's 'religious' anti-semitism merged, gradually, with Drumont's racial variety. Front-page cartoons portrayed hooknosed Jews gloating at Christ's crucifixion, snakes with 'Jewish' heads biting French soldiers. The Dreyfus affair was a 'race war', 1889 was 'the Yids' Centenary', for 'Jews were slaves 100 years ago, and the churches full'. Parish priests facing empty churches and lamenting the decline of peasant deference found plot theories less upsetting than sociological analysis of the causes of their plight. The Virgin appeared at Lourdes, because God still ran the countryside. Satan and the Jews ran the cities and their 'sodomite factories'. No bishop ever reprimanded *La Croix* for its racialism. As Sorlin observes, the Assumptionists were medieval crusaders, refusing to turn the other cheek. Their prejudices were widely shared by Catholic novelists and intellectuals whose writings in the 1880–1914 period display an extraordinary mixture of deliberate credulousness, satanic plot theories, the cult of miracles, idealization of simple peasants as against corrupted rationalist intellectuals, anti-semitism, xenophobia, hatred of opponents and praise of violence.

Anti-semitism was the meeting ground for Catholic and petty bourgeois hostility to the republican system. *La Croix* had many readers among shopkeepers in towns such as Armentières, where 2500 stores served 27,000 inhabitants, profits were low, bankruptcies frequent. It helped establish shopkeeper associations which argued that 'big shops established in all provincial towns are ruining local commerce. One sees some Levy or other . . . establish himself in an area and, by means only the Jew knows, soon force local commerce to collapse before unbearable pressure.' The *Union Nationale* cultivated such economic anti-semitism as part of a strategy of 're-Christianizing' urban France via Catholic crèches, cooperatives, and job agencies. Its founder, Abbé Garnier, an ex-*Croix* employee, was a powerful, populist figure. 'Large, fat, with all the vulgarity of a country priest . . . he imposes himself by the simple device of . . . acting like a market porter. He never speaks, he yells,' commented one police report on a man who would clearly have been at home in Ulster politics. The UN congresses declared war on Jewish financiers who controlled ministries, ran industry, forced peasants off the land, dominated education and treated the French like 'a herd of cows to be milked'.

Nationalist and racist anti-semites expressed occasional contempt for anachronistic 'religious' anti-semitism, just as Catholics expressed some unease at the biological racism of Drumont. Yet such nuances were not major obstacles to an alliance based on economic anti-semitism. This alliance between Catholics and petty bourgeoisie made the new right a growing presence in Paris. Guérin's *Ligue Antisemitique* recruited heavily among small businessmen in the 11th and 18th *arrondissements*. However to achieve a truly broad-based populist alliance there was a need to divert workers from class-based socialist politics. An embryonic 'national-socialist' ideology was framed, in which solutions to working-class problems were shown to lie in protectionism, repatriation of immigrant labour, control of 'parasitic' Jewish capital. M. Perrot has emphasized the susceptibility of French workers in the 1880s to xenophobic violence, their rhetoric of abuse was frequently tinged with a racism fed by imperialist assumptions – immigrant blacklegs were denounced as 'Hottentots', 'Kaffirs'. Bordeaux, hit by the shipbuilding slump, boasted a *League for National Labour*, headed by merchant-marine officer Ch. Dupon, which preached import controls, a ban on capital export, expulsion of Spanish workers and war on 'cosmopolitan' Jewish capital. It got support from Jourde, the local 'Marxist' leader, who was in the *Ligue des Patriotes*! The latent anti-semitic streak in French socialism accentuated the danger of such trends. Socialists like Mâlon and Chirac continued the tradition of Proudhon and Blanqui in linking usury and finance-capital with Jews. Even Jaurès was sometimes guilty of the linguistic shorthand which equated 'Jew' and 'capitalist'. Until the Dreyfus crisis of 1898 Socialists were linguistically slipshod, too blasé about the perils of anti-semitism. Socialist anticlericalism made them view Judaism as superstitious and retrograde. Essentially the target remained, for such socialists, capitalism rather than Jews, whereas the new right was seeking to divert workers' anger against Jews to protect French capitalism. Even Chirac, who habitually used 'Jewing' as a synonym for 'parasitic usury' insisted that its main practitioners were Christians, and that Drumont's 'race war' was 'medieval savagery'. Jewish workers had little love for the Rothschilds. 'It is they who turn us into pariahs,' one insisted. 'If there were no big Jewish financiers then ... perhaps, there would be no hatred against the Jewish race.' And the charity they dispense? 'Their poor cost them less than they spend on their horses.' Yet, whatever reservations one makes about socialist anti-semitism, and however clearly most of the left subsequently rejected anti-semitism, the verbal equation of 'Jew' and 'capitalist' in much leftist rhetoric undoubtedly aided the new right in its effort to attract a working-class audience.*

The first major threat from the resurgent right emerged in the Boulangist movement, an ephemeral but briefly formidable alliance of ultimately incompatible 'outsider' groups alienated from the Opportunists' republic. In 1881 the Opportunists had swept to a convincing electoral victory, leaving a dispirited rump of 100 rightist deputies deeply divided over issues such as imperialism, royalist loyalties and social reform. By 1885 Opportunism, reduced to 200 deputies, was caught in the crossfire from 200 Radicals and a resurgent right with 180 seats. Workers were hit by unemployment after the end of the rail boom, peasants threatened by price collapse, Radicals angered by the failure to end the Concordat, abolish the senate and initiate social reform. The right, playing down its atavistic royalism, mobilized on economic and religious issues, denounced the laic laws, argued that Ferry's imperial ventures were a costly diversion from *revanche*.

One concession made by opportunists to the radicals, in order to patch together a shaky coalition, was a post as war minister for Clemenceau's protégé, General Boulanger, a young officer who gave the appearance of being one of the rare republicans in the officer corps, and who soon won populist acclaim by urging his troops to share their rations with strikers and by his bellicose defiance of Bismarck in a minor frontier incident. When the government, alarmed at the prospect of war, sacked Boulanger he was adopted as a figurehead by a range of disparate anti-Opportunist groups. Radicals fantasized about a plebiscitary Boulangist regime implementing social reforms. Blanquists like

---

* Such remarks apply, equally, to the liberal-radical establishment. It would be easy to pick out racist comments on Jewish characteristics in the writings of pro-Dreyfus crusaders like Zola and Clemenceau.

Grainger responded to the apparent blend of patriotism and social protest represented by the General. Even the Marxist Lafargue welcomed the phenomenon as an expression of deep-seated anti-Opportunist dissatisfaction. Catholic royalists denounced the corruption of a parliament embarrassed by disclosures of sale of official honours by President Grevy's family, while plying Boulanger with secret funds. Déroulède viewed Boulanger as the plebiscitary dictator needed to save France from the debilitating feebleness produced by party politics, and the *Ligue des Patriotes* expelled Deloncle, a founder member who had remained a loyal republican.

In 1888 Boulanger staged a mini-plebiscite, winning seven by-elections in turn. In the Nord, votes from Catholics and workers helped him defeat an opportunist business candidate. With the Radical Naquet running Boulanger's Paris organization and royalists contributing millions of francs to party funds, Boulanger kept shrewdly silent on policy issues, beyond stressing the need for strong government to break the mould of French politics. The momentum slowed, briefly, when the bellicose Déroulède, standing as a Boulangist candidate in the south-west, proved unpalatable to Charentais peasant voters and when Boulanger's charismatic machismo was dented by an incongruous wound in a duel with a civilian politician. Yet votes from *faubourg* workers gave him a spectacular January 1889 victory in a Paris by-election. The regime was alarmed into vigorous counter-measures, backed by Clemenceau, now terrified by the monster he had helped create. A return to single-member constituencies robbed Boulanger of the opportunity of standing on every departmental list and of turning the 1889 general election into a virtual plebiscite. Prosecution of the *Ligue des Patriotes*, the key organizational force in local Boulangist politics, precipitated Boulanger's flight into exile. Deprived of its leader, Boulangism won a modest 38 of the right's 167 seats. Some Boulangists allied with the left, some moved to anti-semitism, some Catholics arranged an antisocialist alliance with the Opportunists.

Boulangism brought to political prominence the writer Maurice Barrès, elected in Nancy, who came to epitomize the values and perceptions of the new right. His early novels had emphasized an egotistic quest for self-fulfillment. Their hero, Philippe, made anaemic by rationalist laic education, is revitalized by the 'real' world of passions, animal instincts and mass politics. To appeal to the herd-like instincts of the masses required emphasis on 'those qualities which a crowd shares in common, and which are always the lowest – hatred, fear or stupidity'. For instinctive hatreds, not rationalist tolerance, would regenerate France. Barrès admired the mystical sadism of the Spain of the Inquisition and the bullfight, 'where man becomes man again, has the desire to see blood, to bite, to claw'. During the 1890s the right campaigned to defend Midi bullfighting against liberal humanitarian abolitionists. Then, increasingly, Barrès stressed 'rootedness'. Truth came not through intellect but through race and milieu – for 'our dead give us orders which we must obey'. The 'Rights of Man' were meaningless abstractions: 'What man, where does he live?' Barrès enquired. French schools should teach French truth not universal truths.

Barrès's ideas reflected wider trends in contemporary intellectual life. The fear, expressed in his novel *Les Déracinés*, that students were becoming alienated and confused by laic rationalism, echoed the obsession of Catholic writers like Paul Bourget, whose *Le Disciple* portrayed the pernicious effects of the bloodless doctrines of the teacher Adolphe Sixte on his young pupils. Yet if Catholics denounced 'positivism', 'science' itself made its own contribution towards undermining the republic's liberal-rationalist ideology. Taine's stress on race and milieu as determining factors in history, Bergson's anti-rationalist philosophy, social Darwinism, the elitist political science of Pareto, social anthropology, scientific criminology and work on the social psychology of crowds combined to expose the naive liberal hope of a humane democratic society based on the Rights of Man as absurd delusions. Human society, like Darwin's nature, was based on violence, force, the survival of the fittest. Man, insisted Montpellier University teacher Vacher de Lagouge, was an animal who killed to survive. 'Fraternity' was pious nonsense. Sorbonne professor Jules Soury defined liberty as the understanding of racial determinism. Anthropologists 'proved' the inferiority of colonial peoples by measuring brain-size; criminologists argued that 'criminals' were born with distinctive skull shapes. 'Science' made prejudice respectable.

Gustave Le Bon, whose *Psychology of Crowds* (1895) went through 25 editions in 34 years, became the major popularizer of right-wing social 'science'. He viewed history as biological evolution determined by natural selection, 'peoples' as racial organisms, each with their own mental constitutions. Since 'superior' races had a larger brain-size, one could 'award a negro a doctorate; one cannot make him civilized'. Like Taine and Gabriel Tarde, Le Bon was haunted by defeat in 1870, by the spectacle of a divided France with corrupt rulers and impotent elites. Mobs of communards, strikers and May Day demonstrators were brutal, drunken baboons. Terrified by fears of castration by militant feminists, Le Bon insisted that women shared the genetic inferiority of blacks. Crowds, essentially 'female' in mentality, acted impulsively on subconscious instincts which reason was powerless to analyse or control. However, Boulangism elated and reassured him. A charismatic hero could hypnotize and manipulate crowds to act as tools not enemies of the elites. By perfecting the arts of manipulating the crowd's imagination, by creating images and scapegoats for their frustrations and hatreds, the new Caesar could subvert democracy, prevent the growth of socialism. In his last years, predictably, Le Bon became an admirer of Mussolini, while remaining a bitter enemy of the republic which denied him a seat on the *Académie Française*.

It was the dubious achievement of Barrès and the new right to disseminate this poison. As a native of Lorraine, who cultivated the myth of France's lost provinces, Barrès became fascinated by the patriotic charisma of Boulanger. His Nancy electorate included a sizeable proletariat of textile and iron-ore workers – non unionized, sensitive to *revanche* in a frontier region, made xenophobic by the presence of 30,000 immigrant workers. Workers comprised three-quarters of local Boulangist militants. In his violent campaign Barrès mixed denunciation of Orleanist 'plutocracy' with attacks on 'Jewish' finance and calls for repatriation of immigrants. Once in parliament Barrès, together with half the Boulangists, often voted with the tiny socialist group on social issues. Should Boulangism thus he located on the 'left', as Sternhell argues, as a sad testimony to the chauvinism and ideological bankruptcy of French socialism?

Such a thesis is not, ultimately, convincing. Certainly Barrès voted alongside socialists for old age pensions, protested with them when troops shot unarmed workers at Fourmies (1891), shared the columns of *La Cocarde* with syndicalists. Yet this 'alliance' was ephemeral. Boulangism was disintegrating. Naquet, a Jew, quit in disgust at the growing anti-semitism of F. Laur. Déroulède refused to criticize the army over the Fourmies shootings. Disclosure of royalist funding of Boulangism was embarrassing. Barrès began to praise the army, support colonialism, urge an alliance with Catholics to achieve 'national unity'. His 'socialist' phraseology of 1889–91 was exposed as a dilettante pose. He denounced class conflict and socialist internationalism, and broke with his Blanquist electoral ally in Nancy, A. Gabriel, who was demanding equal pay for immigrant workers. His anti-semitism, initially a tactical electoral device, became more insidious and biological, just as socialists began to shy away from it. No socialists were present when Barrès gave his funeral oration for the anti-semitic gang-leader Morès. Barrès came to argue that failure of Boulangism could be explained by the refusal of its leaders to play the anti-semitic trump-card, while the guilt of Dreyfus could be deduced from his racial origins.

Catholic politicians like de Mun and Mackau had flirted with Boulangism. But its failure convinced Leo XIII of the futility of tying the church to anti-republican vendettas. Over half the bishops, republicans or pragmatic royalists, agreed. The papacy thus envisaged a realignment involving a compromise, based on shared antisocialism, in which opportunists would relax the laic laws in return for a *de facto* Catholic acceptance of the republic. 'Wise and sensible' conservatives, believers or non-believers, should forget old squabbles in order to defend order and property. The church could coexist with any form of government – although in private, Leo XIII assured Mgr de Cabrières that he retained royalist sympathies and hoped that royalism could win a majority for a peaceful restoration. Orleanist alarm at Boulangism's populist demagoguery, and growing cooperation between French colonialism and Catholic missions, facilitated the new course. Significantly it was the toast to the republic in November 1890, proposed by Mgr Lavigerie of Algiers seeking support for his African mission work, which launched the new Catholic strategy.

This *Ralliement*, after a slow start, won cautious approval from opportunists Méline and Spuller, who invoked a 'new spirit' and promised flexibility on the schools issue. A variety of heterogeneous Catholic groups responded positively. Catholic industrialists welcomed a broad antisocialist coalition in face of leftist gains in the Nord. In the Mayenne it accelerated the long process in which clergy and new *notables* wrested domination of the right from royalist aristocrats. Royalism retreated to isolated cantons like Quatrebarbe's Bierné fief; monarchist families like the

Villebois-Maveuils retired from politics in disgust; Senator Le Breton decided, regretfully, not to follow his instinct to boycott President Faure's reception in Laval – for the republic was conservative and defended agriculture. In Finistère, de Mun, allowing his royalism to be overruled by his loyalty to the papacy, won as a *rallié* candidate with clergy and peasant support, despite the hostility of local nobles. The encyclical *Rerum Novarum* (1893), by recognizing the evils of laissez-faire, increased the enthusiasm of young *abbés democrates*, keen to rescue religion from the politics of moribund elites.

Yet the *Ralliement*'s success was limited and ephemeral, undermined by atavistic loyalties and internal contradictions. Royalist nobles in the west and the Midi, still major providers of church funds, rediscovered a long-forgotten Gallicanism to condemn Leo's interference in French politics. Only three of 37 *ralliés* elected in 1893 were nobles, but 32 of 64 royalists. Convents allegedly prayed for Pope Leo's conversion, Catholic intellectuals denounced the pope for sacrificing the sheep to reconcile the wolves with the dogs! The social problem fragmented the *rallié* group, for de Mun's concern with factory legislation was anathema to Catholic industrialists who had allied with opportunists precisely to fight such 'creeping socialism'. In Hazebrouck there was an election conflict between the social-Catholic *abbé démocrate* Lemire and such a laissez-faire *rallié*. Directives from Rome or Paris failed to prevent the continuation of local conflicts, particularly on the schools issue. The Ribot ministry provoked Catholic wrath in 1895, when it tossed anticlericals the bone of a small tax on the wealth of the congregations. *Rallié* deputies split three ways in parliament on this bill. Despite the new conciliatory policy from Rome, the assumptionists of *La Croix* continued to extract anti-semitic and anti-republican lessons from the involvement of Jewish financiers and republican politicians in the financial scandal over the Panama canal project. Even congresses of the *abbés démocrates* flirted with anti-semitism. Thirty-eight bishops were still described by the government as 'violent'.

Despite the tactless demands of *rallié* leader Lamy for immediate repeal of the laic laws, which revived latent opportunist anticlericalism, the *Ralliement* was still alive in 1898. Piou urged royalists to think less of their ancestors, more about their children's future, and *ralliés* mustered 74 seats at the expense of royalists, who declined to 32, though 200 Radicals and 64 socialist successes signified an Opportunist slump to 215. However the Dreyfus affair proved the *Ralliement*'s death-blow. Dreyfus, a Jewish general staff officer, was convicted of espionage in 1894 on the strength of a memo, allegedly in his handwriting, found in a basket in the German embassy. Private doubts among his family and a few friends became public when Zola, in an open letter to the republic's president published in Clemenceau's *L'Aurore* in January 1898 accused the High Command of an anti-semitic conspiracy to pervert justice. Old doubts about the role of the army in a democratic republic were revived. Republicans had neither forgotten nor forgiven military participation in the Bonapartist coup of 1851. A mini-purge of senior officers had followed the flirtation of General Ducrot in the 1877 *Seize Mai* affair. In 1878 it was estimated that 75 per cent of army officers had royalist sympathies, and the officer corps continued to provide a career refuge for sons of royalist families, remaining 'half aristocrat, half bourgeois, with developed clerical prejudices' (Bédarida). 29 per cent of major-generals were nobles in 1899, and a high, if declining, proportion of St Cyr cadets came from Jesuit colleges. Yet relations between republic and army had been remarkably smooth. Gambettists had wooed the military's professional interests, offering increases in army budgets, improved equipment, conscription and a maximum of autonomy with a minimum of parliamentary control. St Cyr doubled its annual intake. Royalist officers showed little Boulangist sympathy, for the general was despised as a vulgar careerist. Aristocratic officers appeared to accept the republic as a patriotic regime, concerned with France's military strength. After 1889 Freycinet, as war minister, sponsored the emergence of new command structures while colonial expansion gave officers the chance of action and promotion. By 1890 it appeared that an expanded, modernized army had been integrated into the republican system.

It is possible that latent anti-semitism was a factor in the indictment of Dreyfus. Evidence from the handwriting on which Dreyfus was convicted was inconclusive. Documents – later discovered to be forgeries – produced by Colonel Henry to bolster the evidence, were withheld from Dreyfus's lawyers. By 1895, as rumours of irregularities grew, War Minister Mercier refused to reconsider the evidence and General Boisdeffre moved an officer named Picquart, who was collating evidence of the forgeries, to safeguard the army's reputation. Two other factors were, probably, of comparable importance. The case began in an atmosphere of spy-mania and xenophobia, fed by rumours of a German preventive war to smash France's new Russian alliance. There were fears that tsarist pogroms might alienate liberal French opinion. Colonel Sandherr was already compiling lists of foreigners and subversives, destined for internment camps in the event of war. Mercier was closely involved with counter-espionage in the *deuxième bureau* which uncovered the anti-Dreyfus evidence. Porch argues that the case arose more from the efforts of an incestuous, technocratic general staff elite to cover up a classic bureaucratic error, in order to safeguard its *esprit de corps*, than from the anti-semitism of Catholic officers.

Nevertheless it was *La Croix*, which had inaugurated the press crusade against Jewish officers, and which now orchestrated the howl of outrage that greeted Zola's accusations. Eighty per cent of the press were hostile to Dreyfus, including 'apolitical' mass circulation dailies like *Le Petit Journal*. Méline's republican government was reluctant to open a can of worms which threatened to wreck the *Ralliement* and to poison relations with the army in a year of industrial unrest and colonial conflict with Britain. As evidence of a miscarriage of justice grew, the opportunists split, with a majority of them, including conservatives like Poincaré, pushed by fears of a clerico-militarist plot into an uneasy alliance with the left to 'defend the republic'. The *Ralliement* alliance, for which the socialist menace had been the essential political issue, was crumbling.

The issue soon transcended the personal fate of one unfortunate prisoner. Idealistic students like Péguy joined a Dreyfusard crusade for 'justice' and 'individual rights' against militarism and clericalism. For 'democracy' appeared to be threatened by an alliance of Sword and Holy-Water Sprinkler. In turn, the right mobilized a formidable array of intellectuals to denounce the interference of unpatriotic, rootless, radical intellectuals in politics. The term 'intellectuals' was an 1890s neologism, with marked pejorative overtones. Academics were no more competent to tell politicians how to do their job than they were to instruct bricklayers how to lay bricks! Dreyfus's guilt could be assumed from his race, yet, Maurras insisted, his guilt or innocence were irrelevant. Since France needed a strong army, and Dreyfus's acquittal would undermine the army, then it was necessary for him to remain 'guilty', whatever the evidence. French society itself depended on this. While there could be society without justice, there was never any justice without society.

The *affaire*, which polarized educated opinion and realigned party politics till 1905, revealed the susceptibility of the public to the prejudiced distortions of the mass press. However it coincided with no major socio-economic crisis, which limited its mobilizing effects. Urban dwellers, students, nationalist leagues were all involved. Yet one study of the Isère suggests that agitation there was largely confined to Grenoble, with the peasantry much more concerned with crop prices than with abstract arguments over justice. However Zola's article sparked off anti-semitic rioting, which continued sporadically for eighteen months, in 60 towns. The *Ligue Antisemitique Française*, which coordinated most of the rioting, had stagnated in the early 1890s, despite Drumont's journalistic exploitation of the Panama scandal. The Marquis de Morès, eccentric aristocrat, one-time North Dakota rancher, self-styled champion of the 'little man', whose La Villette market-porters terrorized Jewish traders in Paris, possessed the charisma to hold the anti-semitic movement together, but was killed in Africa. Guérin tried to assume Morès's mantle. Having burned down his Aubervilliers business to collect on the insurance, he then portayed himself as a small industrialist, ruined by Jewish finance! The *LAF* claimed 270 branches, dominated a belt of northern and eastern Paris including Belleville, Pigalle and Batignolles, had 2800 members in Nancy alone. Attracting petty bourgeois and artisans, Guerin posed as a tough street politician, criticizing Drumont for being too 'clerical', assumed a populist stance despite accepting funds from royalists. He established a newspaper, *L'Antijuif*, an employment office to provide jobs for French workers and a fortified headquarters. The 1898–9 riots involved crowds of up to 4000 and lasted up to five days. Synagogues and Jewish business bore the brunt of the violence, though only in Algiers were Jews killed. In parliament a bill to exclude Jews from public service was defeated, but secured 158 right-wing votes.

Déroulède, still a powerful street orator, mobilized a revitalized *Ligue des Patriotes*. Less 'populist' than the *LAF*, its 30,000 members included professional and businessmen, its financial backers included at least one millionaire. However, an abortive coup, in which nationalist league leaders vainly tried to involve leading army generals, in the autumn of 1899 gave the government an excuse to jail Guérin and exile Déroulède. Nationalists continued to dominate the Paris municipal council after 1900, but they differed in crucial ways from the Boulangists of 1889. Boulangism had been an anti-centrist alliance, linking the far right with maverick leftists and attracting working-class support. Subsequently mainstream socialism, alarmed at nationalist domination of the city streets, had largely jettisoned anti-semitism. Paris workers voted socialist in increasing numbers. Nationalism now placed greater emphasis on antisocialism, reflected small business hostility to strikes and to income tax. Its strongholds shifted to respectable bourgeois areas like the 10th *arrondissement*. It flirted with clericalism. It had, in short, drifted from 'radical-Right' national socialism towards orthodox conservatism. With the economy more buoyant than in the 1880s the edge of petty bourgeois extremism had temporarily been dulled.

Yet the violence of 1898–9 fed republican fears that the regime was in danger. Army and church were to bear the brunt of subsequent reprisals, justifiably or otherwise. The army's role in the crisis was ambivalent. Déroulède's attempts to involve generals in his coup were abortive. The republican's myth of a Jesuit-inspired army plot, centring on General Boisdeffre's confessor, père du Lac, was a conspiracy theory which mirrored Maurras's fantasies about the judeo-masonic republic. Yet senior officers *had* framed Dreyfus, obstructed his retrial, openly attacked civilian 'meddling', championed army 'honour' and its blinkered vision of national security, against 'justice'. Many *were* Catholic, with latent royalist sympathies. This nurtured middle-class republican antimilitarism, already increasing because of the reluctance of bourgeois youths to fulfil their post-1889 conscription obligations. Novels such as L. Descaves's *Sous-Offs* or G. Darrien's *Biribi* popularized an image of aloof officers allowing brutal NCOs to impose savage discipline in filthy barracks, of a life of greasy soup and VD. The eager liberal audience for Zola's revelations was, as Porch stresses, based on an 'antimilitarism' rationalizing the reluctance of bourgeois youths to leave home.

General Gallifet, chosen for the delicate task of revising the Dreyfus verdict without alienating the army, believed in Dreyfus's guilt, refrained from punishing Mercier or Boisdeffre, refused to 'pressure' the second court martial, held in late-1899, into delivering a non-guilty verdict, then resigned when its absurd verdict of 'guilty with extenuating circumstances' provoked calls for an army purge from left-wingers whom he despised. Civil-military relations remained strained for a decade. War Minister André outraged the right by using freemasons and regimental cobblers to spy on the religious views of garrison officers. Promotion became linked to political acceptability, St Cyr candidatures fell by 50 per cent. Officers, who accepted their task as strikebreakers without protest, resigned in protest when asked to 'break down church doors and chase nuns' to control Catholic demonstrations against radical anticlerical legislation. They resented being forced to inculcate republican civic values into conscripts, were outraged when Clemenceau made Picquart, whose revelations had exposed the Dreyfus scandal, war minister. Discipline and morale slumped as government slashed 'useless expenditure' on officers' batmen and tennis courts, ranked generals below sub-prefects at official cermonies, weakened the autonomy of the High Command. On the eve of 1914 the army was demoralized and ill-led.

There were many genuine reasons why republicans should mount an anticlerical counterattack after 1898. A rare Catholic Dreyfusard reported that fellow Catholics treated him as the perpetrator of the eighth deadly sin. Hundreds of *curés* accompanied their donations to the fund established for the widow of Colonel Henry, who had committed suicide in jail when his forgeries were disclosed, with messages expressing their desire to possess 'Yidskin bedmats' so they could walk over the Jews morning and night. *La Croix* had outdone Drumont in its anti-semitic virulence. The bishop of Nancy had urged Christians to boycott Jewish shops. Yet Republican policy was also determined by sordid tactical considerations. Priest-baiting and the flogging of ancient clerical horses were, as ever, cheap substitutes for social reform. Anticlericalism by winning worker support at minimal cost, served the function that anti-semitism performed for the right. Until 1902 Waldeck-Rousseau's policy was measured and Gallican. He disciplined the Assumptionists and insisted that 'unauthorized' religious orders register. Combes, a small-town doctor weaned on provincial anticlericalism, had fewer inhibitions. He closed 30 per cent of Catholic schools and exiled many of the orders.

Resistance to this 'persecution' was mobilized by de Mun. His

Action Libérale Populaire (*ALP*), financed by funds from the orders laundered through London banks, allied with Méline's conservative republicans, the 'respectable' nationalists of the *Ligue de la Patrie Française* and Catholic youth organizations. Though it won 78 seats, mainly in western and northern areas, in 1902, its legalistic approach angered neo-royalists like Cochin, and de Mun had to intervene to prevent Breton peasants resorting to shotguns.

While demands for immediate separation of church and state came from socialists, eager to settle the religious question in order to turn to social issues, Combes flirted with separation rhetoric as a bluff to force the Vatican to appoint republican bishops, a strategy based on Leo XIII's known desire for viable relations with France. However Pius X, woefully ignorant of French realities, was convinced that the *Ralliement* had proved to be a futile appeasement of the satanic republic. He called Combes's bluff by sacking two pro-republican bishops for sexual immorality. The suave Briand then framed a separation bill designed to be conciliatory, offering pensions to older clergy and control of church buildings to parish *associations cultuelles*.

To resist this threat Mun attempted to broaden the *ALP*'s appeal by reviving emphasis on social reform issues, but his strategy failed to achieve a consensus on the right. Catholic employers, who funded the *ALP*, were little keener on Mun's factory legislation and pension schemes than were the *ALP*'s allies among Méline's conservative-republicans. Neo-royalists continued to urge violent resistance. From the other flank Marc Sangnier's lay-Catholic and reformist *Sillon* movement regarded the *ALP* as too hierarchical, insufficiently democratic. When the *ALP*, pressured by an outraged Vatican, condemned an official visit of President Loubet to Rome, this caused a quarrel with Mun's sympathizers among French nationalists who saw the state visit as a justifiable attempt to woo the Italian government away from its German alliance.

The right's response to separation proved agitated but incoherent. The *ALP*'s violent rhetoric obscured its pragmatic realization that a compromise was the most the church could win. Two-thirds of the bishops urged compromise, 30,000 clergy applied for pensions, some Catholics welcomed the church's potential new freedom. Yet such voices were drowned by hysteria from domino-theorists in the Vatican who predicted similar disasters in Spain and elsewhere. The *associations cultuelles* were denounced as giving power to parishioners which belonged to the hierarchy. Neo-royalists and the radical-right hoped that violent resistance to proposed inventories of church property would produce martyrs. In early 1906 major clashes occurred in 20 departments. Western gentry mobilized their tenants in 'folklore' protests, in an atmosphere of holy war. Localist rural sentiment was outraged by the 'sacrilege' involved in inventory 'desecration' of shrines. Bears were chained to Pyrenean church porches, aristocratic Breton ladies emptied chamberpots over gendarmes, Nord police shot one protester. Nationalist extremists coordinated urban protests. However Clemenceau, by shrewdly portraying his radicals as a governing law-and-order party standing between France and anarchic violence from syndicalist strikers and Catholic-nationalist extremists, wooed the 'Orleanist' wing of the Catholic elite, alarmed by social disorder and assaults on the police. Pragmatic Normandy, strongly Catholic, voted republican in 1906, many of Méline's conservative republicans shrank from supporting a clerical crusade. In Besançon, royalist aristocrats denounced the 'cowardice' of bourgeois Catholics who shied away from violent direct action. The right lost 60 seats in the 1906 elections. Electoral disaster persuaded many Catholics that open resistance was futile. A *modus vivendi* emerged whereby local priests were left to run churches. Funds were collected to pay clerical salaries – though the end of guaranteed state finance cut applications for the priesthood by 50 per cent. A growing Catholic youth movement, and embryonic white-collar trade unions, showed the potential vitality of the church in some regions. By 1914 Catholic sports clubs with 180,000 members alarmed republicans with the spectre of muscular Christianity and paramilitary gymnastic societies. Inevitably there were Clochemerle-style clashes as republican municipalities tried to deny Catholic football teams access to pitches and rival republican and Catholic sports groups fought, as in Roanne in 1911. In 1914 France had two national football teams, one laic, one Catholic!

Encouraged by the extreme right, the Vatican continued its intransigent stance. Episcopal appointments went to anti-republican hardliners. Theological 'modernism' was condemned. The *Sillon* was condemned for using a 'disfigured and degraded Christ' to pursue its 'social dreams', for allegedly subordinating religion to politics by supporting popular sovereignty. Yet, paradoxically, while condemning the Catholic Sangnier, the

Vatican allied itself with Maurras, leader of the *Action Française* (*AF*), a positivist agnostic who, waving the sword of *raison d'état*, emphasized the supremacy of national interest over morality. Dreyfus was guilty because French security required him to be so. Henry's forgeries were moral because expedient Maurras seduced the Vatican by claiming that, historically, there was a correlation between a strong France and a strong church. The church created 'order' without which there was no civilization. France was the product of her medieval bishops. *Metaphysically AF* members could be whatever they chose; *politically* they must be Catholic. Young *AF* militants were prominent in resistance to the inventories. Piux X thus found Maurras's positivist writings 'condemnable, but not to be condemned', refraining from placing the books of such a gallant author on the index. The intellectual idol of so many pre-1914 Catholic students, of novelists like Bernanos, of bishops like Mgr de Cabrières, of Catholic officers like Psichari, was, thus, an agnostic who did 'too much good' defending authority to be criticized.

Despite the drift of post-1900 nationalism towards anti-socialist conservatism, and the high visibility of the religious issue, the extreme right did not abandon attempts to establish a working-class following. Two contrasting strategies were pursued. The first, the 'yellow' trade union movement, declined after 1908. It began as a classic company-union movement after the strike failures of 1900–1. Lanoir, its first leader, was a railman, expelled from the Paris trade-union movement, who accepted funds from Méline, nationalist politicians and employers like Japy, before retiring to the Riviera on the proceeds. His successor, Biétry, adopted a 'national-socialist' stance, criticized Lanoir as a bosses' man, and claimed 100,000 members among dockers, Nord textile workers, eastern railmen and Montceau miners. The rhetoric of his successful election campaign in Brest in 1906 recalled the Barrès of 1889. The world was a jungle, internationalism a fraud, Marxism judeo-German. The future lay with a 'latin socialism' of class solidarity and profit-sharing. Laws against immigrants and Jewish finance would safeguard the true patriotic French working-class family, which loathed 'reds' as German agents.

Although 'yellows' did participate in some strikes, Biétry, too, by accepting business and royalist funding, was gradually weaned from proto-fascism back towards the mainstream right. His efforts to form a party failed as his credibility as a proletarian leader crumbled, and he emigrated to Indo-China. The way was clear for an alternative strategy, espoused by Valois of the *AF*, which sought tactical allies among the militants of the syndicalist left. Syndicalist rhetoric, with its hostility to parliamentary electoralism, its praise of virile militant 'warrior' proletarian elites, its anti-intellectualism, voluntarist activism and contempt for the materialist conformism of the 'average' workers, shared certain apparent common features with radical-right irrationalism. G. Sorel, the 'theorist' of syndicalism, an intellectual playboy with a random series of attractions, was influenced by Bergsonian stress on *élan vital* and by Le Bon's emphasis on the irrational in politics. He saw Dreyfusism as a sordid, bankrupt triumph for careerist politicians, who duped workers with anticlerical gestures. Valois saw in a possible alliance with syndicalism a bold rejection of the bourgeois-conservative nationalism of the *Ligue de la Patrie Française*. He encouraged *AF* militants to cooperate with unionists, fight alongside strikers against Clemenceau's police. Janvion's *Terre Libre* insisted that the 'Jewish' republic, capitalist, masonic and triggerhappy, was exploiting the workers. Meeting in the *Cercle Proudhon* Sorel and Valois agreed that Proudhon was the authentic French socialist – anti-Marxist, anti-semitic, anti-parliamentary.

The significance of this fascinating syndicalist-fascist flirtation has, however, been exaggerated by historians such as Sternhell and Mazgaj, eager to brand proto-fascism as left-wing. A few *AF* thugs found syndicalist street-violence a useful arena. The odd syndicalist was seduced by anti-semitism. But Janvion was a minor figure. Syndicalists and the *AF* opposed the republic on different grounds and with different aims. The basic incompatibilities were exposed in 1912–13 as syndicalists mobilized against the three-year conscription law, which the *AF* supported. Maurras did not share Valois's preoccupation with workers, and came to fear that 'radicalism' was alienating potential allies from the *AF*. The average *AF* student was more at home assaulting his Jewish professor than attending trade-union meetings. Sorel, living quietly in his Paris suburb on his *rentier*-income from Tsarist bonds, had little real influence on the syndicalist movement. The antimilitarist-socialist Hervé, who did flirt briefly with the *AF*, was shocked into a change of course when *AF* thugs intimidated the Jewish playwright Henri Bernstein from staging his play featuring an army deserter. *AF* historians like Bainville hated 'democracy', but their views were closer to Burke than to Lenin. The populism of the elitists of radical-right was largely fraudulent.

The radical-right had, thus, clearly declined after 1900. Its street demonstrations and anti-semitic riots fell away. In 1906 the nationalists lost one-third of their 55 seats. Déroulède returned to literature, and the *LP* became 'respectable'. Yet, paradoxically, the right's values had infiltrated mainstream politics. Barrès, now a pillar of the literary establishment, confessed that 'Boulangism, then nationalism failed', yet added, 'their content survives them. Our terminology can be rejected, our doctrines are being realized. We find them in the speeches of Poincaré.* What does it matter . . . that the nationalist party fades away, if we see the opposing parties being nationalized?'

A complex sea-change was under way. Much of the radical right played down its extremism in favour of a more 'conservative' nationalism. Simultaneously Radicalism became the law-and-order governing party, espousing imperialism, smashing strikes, beginning to conciliate the army, needed for internal order and to meet the German threat to Morocco. Barrès, with the growing clericalism of middle-age, praised Briand's conciliatory Separation, his provision of funds for crumbling historic churches and his rejection of protests of anticlerical insomniacs against bellringing. Areas such as Normandy, where Catholicism was the key element of the right, were thereby appeased and de Mun led the *ALP* back towards a new *Ralliement*. The Moroccan crises, antimilitarism and strikes put his world in peril. Obsessed with the danger to France, he came to see Clemenceau the priest-baiter as a patriot, Briand as the new Méline. His criticism of laissez-faire disappeared. International perils no longer allowed 'the leisure of internal discords'. A Republic which smashed Arabs in Morocco, proclaimed Joan of Arc as a national heroine, sacked antimilitarist teachers and increased conscription was one where de Mun could happily live. Even the lifelong anticlerical Poincaré submitted to the fate of a Catholic marriage ceremony with his mistress! Barrès, the sometime 'national socialist', mellowed with age, sat for a well-heeled Parisian constituency, praised Briand's strike-breaking and advocated a 'Republic of honest men', with Poincaré as the new Boulanger

---

* Elected president of the republic in 1913.

Shopkeeper politics underwent a similar evolution away from populist crusades against 'Jewish' department stores towards hostility to strikes and income tax. Control of shopkeeper organizations passed to G. Maur, of the *Phares de la Bastille* store, a friend of Poincaré and an opponent of shop-assistant unionism. M. Colrat's *Association pour la défence des classes moyennes* promoted an alliance of large and small employers against collectivism. Hostility to income tax and support for rearmament made them allies of conservative republicans. The centre of gravity of shopkeeper politics shifted to provincial towns, as the antisocialist, patriotic front superseded attacks on big stores.

Domestic and external factors moulded a complex nationalist revival. German designs on Morocco united colonial and revanchist groups whose priorities had hitherto differed. Strikes and the German threat necessitated a republican rapprochement with the army. Despite left-wing hostility, three-year conscription was introduced, political files on army officers were abandoned, the High Command structure was strengthened by a revived *Conseil Supérieur de Guerre* – although as Porch stresses, the scars of the previous decade had not fully healed, officer morale remained low and there remained serious weaknesses in heavy artillery.

Chauvinist euphoria built up as 1914 approached. Déroulède's funeral attracted crowds of over 100,000. The patriotic novels of Barrès and R. Bazin were typical of a wider genre. Catholics from the youthful Psichari to the venerable Mun wrote enthusiastically of war as a poem of blood and violence, necessary to provide spiritual regeneration to expiate decades of laic sins and the stench of parliamentary politics. Péguy evolved from socialist Dreyfusard into bellicose Catholic-nationalist, who welcomed the assassination of Jaurès in 1914 as that of a traitor who was trying to prevent war. R. Martin du Gard, appalled by these repulsive views, recognized their prevalence. The eponymous hero of his *Jean Barois* spends his best years as an idealistic Dreyfusard, a champion of science and laic 'progress'. His life turns sour. Dreyfusism degenerates into party politics. His daughter becomes a Catholic. The young students, Tilet and Grenneville, reject progressive values to espouse discipline, heroism and the national spirit. An anti-intellectual cult of activism, speed, sport, patriotism, rejection of humanitarian pacifism, a craving for order and hierarchy represented the ethos of university students interviewed in one 1912 enquiry. The ageing Barois succumbs, in weakness, to his disillusionment and, as a final symbol of the wreckage of his life's meaning, returns to the bosom of the church.

Despite the recent denials by the German historian Krumeich, this 'National Revival' must be appreciated in the context of internal politics, as an attempt to build a coalition of nationalists, Catholics, ex-Opportunists and Radical 'moderates' against an 'unpatriotic' left. All could share an enthusiasm for the new cycle race, the *Tour de France*, established by the nationalist entrepreneur Desgranges as a symbol of the unity of the Hexagon. Maurras, Péguy and Poincaré could share a common veneration for Joan of Arc. The energy of this coalition was largely directed against strikers, supporters of income tax, pacifist teachers. Its press was more preoccupied with these internal traitors than with Morocco or the Balkans. Before the July 1914 crisis the success of the strategy remained in doubt. The left, critical of the military build-up, won the 1914 election. Poincaré, convinced after 1911 that war was inevitable, envisaging under Joffre's *Plan XVI* an offensive war and fearful of the 1913 German army build-up, welcomed the 1914 crisis on the basis that war was better sooner than later, through fear that the left would repeal the three-year conscription law and introduce income tax and social reform that might threaten the French elites.

Chapter 8

Integrating the Workers?

I The Workers and the Republic: Alienation or Integration?

The attitude of workers towards the Third Republic was consistently ambivalent. Many recognized it as a capitalist regime in which, behind a façade of parliamentary democracy and progressive rhetoric, a narrow bourgeois elite remained dominant. And yet the myth of 1793 or 1848 persisted. *Marianne* retained her egalitarian aura. The persistence of clerical and authoritarian rightist movements could persuade workers that the republic deserved to be defended. However inadequate in its existing form, was not the republic a step in the right direction, offering secular education and electoral and civil rights? The oscillations produced by such ambivalent perceptions persisted until 1914 because there remained strong pressures both for 'integration' and for alienation of workers from the republican system.

Republican propaganda emphasized the alliance of the 'people' – productive bourgeoisie, peasantry and workers – against 'parasitic' clergy and aristocrats. The strike wave of 1878–9 was triggered by worker expectation that new republican prefects would support them against authoritarian employers. Y. Guin has emphasized the loyalty of the Nantes workers to their mayor, the 'Good Doctor' Guépin. Guépin had acquiesced to the repression of the Commune – but, as an anticlerical, attracted worker support in a region where Catholic-royalism ran the countryside, Catholic charity was mobilized to pressure workers' wives, and where attacks on Catholic missions and schools remained central to local popular militancy. *Libre Pensée* groups in Burgundy, lower Languedoc and the Tarn had working-class members, alongside middle and petty bougeoisie, celebrating a range of anticlerical ceremonies – civil funerals, secular marriages, Good Friday banquets. In Roubaix, dominated by its Catholic *patronat,* worker-militants were early converts to the laic school and Macé's *Ligue de l'Enseignement.* In

Carmaux, where employment and promotion in the mines depended on church attendance, the miner's battle for the laic school became the first step towards emancipation. In the 1880s, strikers still sang the *Marseillaise* as a protest song.

Conciliatory politicians strove to present the republic as something other than the guard-dog of the employers. Workers were encouraged to view the prefect as an ally against intransigent mining companies. The 1884 legalization of trade unions was a conscious attempt to foster 'moderate' pragmatic, 'British' unionism. A law of 1892 established strike arbitration procedures involving JPs. Some workers utilized this as a weapon against employers, and the 'success rate' in arbitrated strikes was above average. In 1898 employer legal liability for industrial accidents was established. Many employers viewed the labour ministry, inaugurated by Millerand after 1900, as excessively pro-worker. During the strike wave of 1900–2 Waldeck-Rousseau issued veiled threats to employers that troop protection might be withdrawn if they refused concessions – and the use of troops against strikers did decline, if gradually. All this gave some plausibility to the image of the republic as a regime willing to defend worker interests.

Rising real-wages and improved living standards may have reduced worker alienation. Rougerie has suggested that nominal wages rose by some 50 per cent between 1871 and 1913. Unemployment remained a permanent threat, but declined after the 1880s. Diets became more diverse and balanced. Workers consumed more meat, fruit, vegetables, butter and wine. In the 1830s workers often spent 30 per cent of their budget on bread. By 1900 this had fallen to around 11 per cent. Food prices fell in the Great Depression – though they soared again on the eve of 1914. Declining clothes prices allowed workers to dress 'en bourgeoise' at weekends. In the Lyonnais, the work day fell from 14 hours in the 1870s to 11 hours by 1900. Child-labour laws and compulsory schooling reduced the proportions of under-twelves in the workforce from 6.5 per cent to 1 per cent 1876–86, and the loss of child earning power accelerated trends towards smaller working-class families, made feasible by the rapid spread of abortion. Thus the seductiveness of the republican myth, education and social reform, and rising living standards may have defused class tensions.

Wide strata of the labour force remained difficult to organize, and relatively free from industrial or political militancy. The growth of large-scale mechanized industry produced a stratum of semi-skilled machine-minders (*ouvriers specialisés – OS*) who comprised one-third of industrial workers by 1900. Simple repetitive jobs were often despised by artisans, but represented relative promotion and stability for rural migrants, apparently willing to acquiesce to fast work-pace and foreman control in return for higher wages. Hanagan has emphasized the industrial passivity of the *OS* workforce of the giant St Chamond arms factory in the Loire. Renault defeated its 1913 car strike by making wage-concessions to its *OS* workers and sacking skilled militants. One syndicalist leader denounced the *OS* workers as 'unconscious instruments of the bosses, authors of their own grief . . . accomplices in capitalist crimes'.

With birth rates falling, and the demand for industrial labour rising, the sub-proletariat was increasingly recruited from rural migrants, immigrants and women. All three groups proved difficult to recruit to the labour movement. The Breton migrants who came to work in the northern Paris *banlieue* at Bezons from the 1870s onwards maintained their old cultural patterns for three decades. They worked as semi-skilled labour in the mechanized cable and rubber plants. The poor transport of the *banlieue* kept them culturally isolated from the older skilled Parisian working-class *quartiers*. Religiosity and birth rate remained high. Poor wages and conditions were accepted as improvements on the misery of the Breton countryside. Only in the decade before 1914 was the local political control of conservative republican farmers challenged. Second generation workers began to challenge their elders, church practice slipped from 90 per cent to below 50 per cent, illegitimacy rates grew and contact with Parisian militants gradually produced pragmatic union demands and socialist voting. Brunet's analysis of worker politics in St Denis suggests that this pattern was common to much of the Parisian *banlieue*.

By 1911 there were 1.16 million immigrants in France, comprising some 10 per cent of the industrial workforce. Their presence during the Great Depression helped nurture the wave of working-class xenophobia which accompanied the Boulangist agitation. Trade wars with Italy fuelled anti-Italian feelings in the south east, just as revanchist aspirations coloured the anti-German feeling in eastern France. Employer use of Italian blacklegs in the 1890s strikes in the Rive-de-Gier glass industry produced xenophobic reactions among leftist militants in the Loire. Foreign workers feared deportation if they became involved in trade-union activities. Café fights and verbal abuse of immigrants were a perennial feature of working-class life in the 1880–90s. One of Jaurès's last articles in *Humanité* in June 1914 was a plea for greater sympathy for foreign workers.

The labour movement proved equally slow in assimilating female workers, who came to comprise 38 per cent of the industrial workforce. Falling birth rates allowed women greater opportunity to enter paid industrial employment. However, the attitude of male trade unionists did little to raise levels of organization among women. Skilled workers, fearing 'dilution', refused females entry to unions. Over 20 per cent of printers were female, but the use of women blacklegs to break a printing strike at Nancy in 1901 accentuated stereotypes of women as cheap docile workers which culminated in the 1913 Couriau affair, in which the printers' union expelled a member who had secured his wife a job at equal pay, and its leader Keufer instructed husbands to control their wives and keep them out of the labour market. Artisans feared a deliberate employer strategy of female dilution of skilled trades. In the fine-metal industry, where mechanization reduced the workforce by nearly 50 per cent, the proportion of woman workers rose from 20 per cent to nearly 40 per cent.

Protective legislation, such as the 1892 law banning female nightwork, proved a mixed blessing because Lille male spinners invoked it to persuade employers to sack women workers. Male workers made redundant at an Ivry electric-bulb works petitioned against employment of females there because chemicals used could harm pregnant women! Many militants shared Proudhon's patronizing paternalism which assumed that women should be protected from the toil and promiscuity of factory labour. H. Vivienne's typical ideal was 'a good housewife, whom I could keep by my labour and who would have time free to bring up my children'. The iconography of French trade-union propaganda juxtaposed the brawny male breadwinner with his staunch wife and children at home. Female wage-labour was one of capitalism's most impious and sordid crimes. In consequences male militants spent more energy excluding women from the labour market than aiding their embryonic unionization – oblivious to the feminist arguments which stressed that lack of female job opportunity led either to prostitution or that persistence of female religiosity of which socialists complained.

The nature of female employment accentuated difficulties involved in recruiting women to the unions. Most female jobs were unskilled factory tasks, sweated outwork, or in the tertiary sector. Thousands of Parisian women in the sweated clothing industry were subject to alternating pressures of a long 'dead season' followed by frantic '*veillées*' in which they worked round the clock to meet the demands of society ladies. Many were widowed or divorced, worked for department stores, had small children to keep and competed with convent or prison labour. Jeanne Bouvier tells of walking miles home at 2 p.m. after 21-hour shifts and of a neighbour, a fellow worker, who lived on bread and milk and was driven to suicide. The 25,000 artificial flower girls in Paris earned 1 franc per day in 1913 and suffered from chemical poisoning. Fourteen per cent of women workers were employed in the textile sector, working an eleven-hour day in the Nord in 1914 despite the 1904 Ten Hour Act. In the 1880s Lyonnais silk girls, exposed to dusty mills, airless dormitories and nun supervision, were working a fifteen-hour day. They were unskilled, bullied by foremen, easily replaced. Forty per cent of textile women were under twenty years of age, their jobs an interlude before marriage and family, their wage a supplement to their parental budget. If, later, they worked while mothers of families, they suffered the double burden of wage-labour and household duties, which left little time or energy for militancy. Excluded from the franchise and from the sociability of male-dominated cafés, they were distanced from 'politics'.

Women thus contributed under 10 per cent of strike disputes despite comprising over one-third of the labour force. Their higher religiosity exposed them to Catholic paternalism – the only 'unions' in Paris outwork were clerical class-collaborationist bodies which tried to provide cheap restaurants and 'kind' employers.

The tertiary sector, where female workers increased by 400 per cent between 1866 and 1906, presented different problems. Typists, bank workers, cashiers and school teachers (*institutrices*) comprised a new white-collar proletariat, often recruited from educated daughters of the declining petty bourgeoisie. Their concerns with female education, training and job opportunity were often nurtured by a desire for individual promotion which coincided more with reformist feminism than with industrial militancy. *Institutrices* achieved equal pay with male colleagues in 1908. Such 'Queens of the Proletariat' had no desire to be considered '*ouvrières*'. Shopgirls in department stores such as *Bon Marché* were often ill-paid, lodged in cramped dormitories, subject to curfews and customer arrogance. Yet employee solidarity was undermined by ferocious sales rivalry. The class status of these girls, who dressed well and frequented city cafés in the evenings, was ambiguous. Women made up over 80 per cent of the one million domestic servants. Assessment of domestic service varies widely. T. McBride has portrayed it as a ladder of upward mobility for peasant girls who learned useful skills and saved for dowries which permitted marriage into the petty bourgeoisie. Others, more plausibly, emphasize daily humiliation, employer arrogance, cramped quarters, poor food and the cycle of seduction by masters, pregnancy, dismissal and prostitution. All agree that the environment of domestic service produced a mixture of isolated personal resentment and petty-bourgeois aspiration, not class solidarity. The only active protest lay in sporadic attacks on exploitative job agencies.

However, as C. Sowerine suggests, the strained relationship between socialism and feminism, may, paradoxically, indicate the underlying strength of class antagonism in France. Sponsored by republican moderates like L. Richer, cautiously reformist and legalistic, avoiding mass agitation and suffrage demands, mainstream French feminism, epitomized by Marguerite Durand, was essentially bourgeois. Militant suffragettes like Hubertine Auclert were expelled. The tone of Durand's approach to working women was patronizing. Benevolent tinkering marked the policy of feminism in labour affairs. Society ladies were urged to stagger their clothing orders so as to avoid tiring '*veillées*' among seamstresses. Mistresses were urged to 'be fair' to servants by ensuring a weekly rest day. 'So I will cook the lunch for my maid?' demanded one incredulous bourgeois feminist in response to this suggestion. They did champion crèches and maternity pay for women workers, but much of their preoccupation was with job opportunity for middle-class careerists. Working women, hopefully, would fight battles for their bourgeois sisters who would supply brains and organizations. French socialism responded by accepting the need for female emancipation, while emphasizing that feminism was a bourgeois movement which disguised the class war by preaching a sex war.

Only socialism could emancipate women. Feminism was offering diversionary palliatives. Women comprised a mere 3 per cent of socialist membership in the 1900s. Among these a minority, led by the Poitiers seamstress, Louise Saumoneau, accepted the party's official priority, giving precedence to the class war, despite underlying unease that the party was a 'male-club'. They kept a low profile during the Couriau affair. Saumoneau insisted that frictions between male and female workers were minor in comparison to fundamental capital-labour conflict.

By 1914 there were hopeful signs that the unionists' attitude to women's problems was changing. Aware of its failure to organize female workers, the *CGT* began a programme of enquiries and propaganda. Union leaders like Monatte denounced the 'antediluvian' male chauvinism of the printers. Female wage labour was accepted as a permanent, if brutal, reality. Efforts were made to unionize women rather than exclude them from the labour market. The percentage of women in trade unions rose from 6.8 per cent to 9.8 per cent in 1900–13. The *CGT*'s campaign for the 'English week' emphasized the 'joy' which working mothers would find in having Saturday afternoon free to clean the house! The role of women in labour militancy grew. Strikes spread to Marseille tobacco girls and, belatedly, to the Lyonnais silk sector. Women played a vital role in anti-landlord leagues and in organizing '*soupes communistes*' during strikes. In the Valenciennes coalfield, married women tended to stay at home, but their role in running household budgets and children's education, made them respected matriarchs. They were the focus of the sociability of mining villages. When they could no longer 'make ends meet', it was they who influenced the timing of strikes and 1911 food demonstrations.

Faced with the socialist challenge, bourgeois ideology abandoned the paternalism advocated by the disciples of the Catholic sociologist, Le Play, which aimed to use charity, religion and the family to control a passive workforce, and evolved a rhetoric of social reform, and social solidarity. Strike militancy, troop-worker clashes and Paris street riots in the early 1890s aroused a miniature '*Grande Peur*' among the bourgeoisie, and provoked Gustave Le Bon's crude denunciation of workers as primitive savages swayed by drink and demagogues and Gabriel Tarde's revived clichés about the correlation of socialism with rising crime statistics. A more sophisticated response came from the sociologist Durkheim who argued that unrest reflected the 'anomalie' of workers seeking values in a rapidly changing society. Socialist utopianism would, however, recede. Social reform could persuade workers of the benevolence of elites. '*Solidarism*', the doctrine of 'consensual integration' espoused by radicals like Leon Bourgeois, should be disseminated via the schools. '*Solidarism*' modified laissez-faire by emphasizing the interdependence of social groups and the debt of individuals to past achievements. The republican elites of doctors, engineers, professors were portrayed as friends of the workers, disinterested experts framing reforming policies, superior to the declining, parasitic clerical-aristocratic elites. Critics like the Marxist Lafargue denounced such rhetoric as the self-interested propaganda of a new technocracy. 'It is no longer religion which condemns the workers to misery, it is science.' Durkheim denied the existence of a capitalist ruling class, claiming that the republic was led by an open, circulating meritocracy, fired by zeal for public welfare. 'Class' analysis was outmoded – indeed the Radical congress of 1908 demanded the abolition of 'unscientific' class terminology. The 'bourgeoisie' was definable by lifestyle, taste, culture – not by economic power and wealth. Social protest was ephemeral and 'pathological'. Society was cohesive, the state the expression of social integration, not of class oppression. Durkheim's reward for 'proving' that socialism was the primitive cry of protest of workers on the verge of integration was a Sorbonne professorship. The dissemination of such ideas was to be the task of laic education.

Republicans sought to utilize the laic school to consolidate hegemonic bourgeois control over the working class, to dispense pre-packaged bourgeois values. The republic was portrayed as incarnating the democratic gains of 1789, making further revolution unnecessary. Universal primary schooling nurtured the myth of social mobility, open to talent. The schools, with their cadet corps and textbooks praising imperialism, were intended to inculcate aceptance of conscription and the cult of '*La Patrie*'. The system was designed to achieve minimum literacy for an efficient workforce, to train lower cadres for industrial society without swamping the elites, and to syphon off a tiny percentage of gifted boys from the working class via scholarships. The absence of any 'ladder' between primary and secondary schooling kept costs down and reduced the risks of overproducing troublesome *déracinés*.

'Useful' primary schooling for the future workforce was separate from the real culture of the elites – and strengthened a sense of inferiority and deference towards those with a higher education. A genuine popular desire for education was thus controlled and manipulated. The laic syllabus emphasized biological social metaphors – society was a living organism and all members of the body were necessary to its functioning. Traditional Catholic schooling was too wedded to a dying rural-hierarchal society to inculcate bourgeois norms. Laic education thus played a role as a new, more sophisticated opium of the masses. The aim of an increasingly conservative pro-establishment *Ligue de l'Enseignement*, run by businessmen and lawyers, was to produce republican but antisocialist 'conscious majorities'. It emphasized gymnastics and military training, held conferences on local industry and on the colonies, distributed books and prizes, cooperated with chambers of commerce to foster technical training.

A network of 6000 '*petites amicales*' developed after 1894 to provide moral uplift, social control and petty-bourgeois values for working-class adolescents, in the dangerous years when the workshops or the teenage streetgang threatened to erode the school's indoctrination. 'Whatever the cost', it was insisted, 'the adolescent must not be left alone. He must be surrounded by leaders.' These clubs provided elocution lessons, visits to museums, sport, and paramilitary activity. Bourgeois cultural hegemony was extended by development of mass sport and the popular press. Whereas socialist newspapers struggled to sell 60,000 copies, the *Petit Parisien* had a circulation of over one million. Lequin emphasizes the absence of any real left-wing press in the industrial region of St Étienne. Pelloutier, who failed in his attempt to sustain a trade union daily paper in the 1890s, lamented that there was 'little taste for serious reading in France'.

Working-class children could however, learn of recent history from parents who remembered the Commune as well as from schools which preached that the Republic incarnated social justice. The sources of continual worker alienation were many and varied. Unions remained illegal till 1884. Police infiltration of workers' organizations persisted unchecked. In 1893 alone, 33 unions were dissolved for refusal to register members' names with the police under the 1884 act. The state persisted in its paranoid hostility to 'public-sector' unionism among railmen, postal workers and teachers. There were 313 arrests per year between 1884–95 for picketing offences, double the level of the previous two decades. The army remained unpopular among many workers as a strike-breaking force. French employers proved unsuitable partners for the republican strategy of constructing 'modern' industrial relations procedures. Many viewed unions as illegitimate, strikes as mutinies. Employer-union negotiations settled only 1 per cent of strikes between 1898 and 1914. In one strike in eight, two-thirds or more strikers were sacked. In 1884 the Anzin Company astounded the local prefect by dismissing 140 miners for 'blasphemous indiscipline' on the eve of a strike settlement. Employer authoritarianism provoked frequent revolts – as at Cholet where a *patron* attempted to ban an employee's civil funeral. Roubaix textile owners installed steam vents in factory toilets to discourage lengthy visits! At Carmaux, the miners' leader Calvignac was sacked in 1892 when he was elected mayor. Lockouts, company unions, organized blacklegs and armed strike-breakers were everyday instruments of employer strategy. Even modern factories with higher safety and hygiene standards were the product of 'scientific management's' concern with higher productivity and provoked worker hostility to piecework, tight supervision and increased work-pace. Worker rhetoric called the factory a '*bagne*' (prison).

Evidence suggesting a prosperous working class seduced by republican values is at best inconclusive. Anticlericalism frequently escaped republican control. At Carmaux, strike militancy pushed the Catholic *patronat* and sometime anticlerical bourgeois republicans into an alliance against the miners, who became the custodians of the *Libre Pensée* society and of civic funerals, at which God was denounced as a tool of capitalism. Meagre social legislation delayed by the senate, was poorly implemented. Overzealous factory inspectors risked employer anger and dismissal, as at Nantes in 1896. Measuring worker integration by rising living standards is hazardous, for militancy can be fuelled by rising expectations. The fall in food prices in the Great Depression made subsequent increases the more resented. The peasant-miners of Carmaux were forced by company pressure to abandon their small holdings and become full-time workers. Obliged to purchase their food they had the impression of soaring living costs. Rougerie has charted the fall in Paris meat consumption after 1900 and there were deaths in food riots in 1911 in northern and western France. Real wages stagnated before 1914. Paris prices rose 10 per cent in 1911 alone. Interminable working weeks – 72 hours at Renault in 1914 – fuelled the union campaign for the eight-hour day. Housing remained appalling. Fifty-six per cent of Paris worker homes had one or two rooms in 1906. Rents rose 22 per cent in areas of Paris 1910–12. Anti-landlord leagues and resistance to eviction were endemic features of popular protest in workers' *quartiers*. Industrial accidents in 1909 left 2395 dead and 434,000 injured. Doctors frequently obstructed worker claims, under the 1898 act, for industrial compensation. 'What professional harm can the loss of a foot make to a worker who works seated?' asked one company doctor in court. Class gulfs remained wide. Ninety per cent of the population of Lille controlled only 7 per cent of the wealth, 87 per cent of the city's population died propertyless in 1908. Only 1.5 per cent of the pupils of the Douai teacher college, in the heart of the industrial Nord, were miners' sons. Working-class parents began to have fewer children, and to dream of using the education system to secure white collar jobs for their offspring. Yet 'escape' from the proletariat remained rare. Ninety per cent of Lille workers' sons were workers. Sixty per cent of small shopkeepers were, it is true, recruited from the working class, but bankruptcy was frequent.

Can one speak of a class-conscious proletariat? Conflicts within the workforce between French and immigrants, men and women, skilled and OS persisted. In the Lyonnais, Lequin emphasizes the difficulty of achieving unified action among a workforce divided between 'archaic' skilled silk weavers and heavy industry workers in mining and metallurgy. Yet, worker's *quartiers* had a strong sense of communal identity, a solidarity cemented by a social life of the bistro, the corner shop and the '*bal*'. There was a sturdy sense of doing hard physical labour, of being exploited by visible employers, landlords and police. Henri Leyrat, a journalist who ran a Paris café, chronicled the ambiguities of workers' attitudes. Military service imbued a sense of patriotism, and a chauvinistic distaste for immigrants. Many responded to individual gestures from paternalistic employers. Yet, the arrest of 'anarchist' suspects in 1893 sparked deep-seated hostility to the police and the dignity of the anarchist bomber Ravachol was admired. Workers despised social climbers as class-traitors. A revolutionary class-consciousness, though latent, still survived.

II The Search for Socialist Unity (1879–1905)

There was a relative lull in socialist politics after the Commune. Martial law persisted in Paris till 1876, surviving communards were jailed or exiled, unions remained illegal. A Nantes police report of 1874 rejoiced that 'the worker is resigned to his lot'. Cautious pragmatic *'Chambres Syndicales'* among artisans were tolerated, patronized by Gambettist republicans like Barbaret who preached peaceful solutions to the social problem via producer cooperatives. The re-emergence of socialist organization after 1879 produced years of sectarian squabbling. Some degree of unity and electoral success was achieved during the 1890s, though the various socialist groups attracted only 750,000 votes in 1898. It is beyond our scope to detail the endless conflict of 'Broussists', 'Allemanists', neo-Blanquists and independents on such issues as reform and revolution, centralized or federal organization, the primacy of political or industrial action. One useful, if over-schematic model, however, explains these party divisions in terms of the sociological heterogeneity of the working class. The 'Guesdist' Marxists achieved their major implantation in the textile towns of the Nord, among a hitherto passive workforce. An unskilled militant in a textile mill could easily be sacked and replaced. Union membership in individual plants remained modest. However, Jules Guesde's party succeeded in creating political organization outside the mills, and in coordinating strike organization across numerous plants. By winning municipal control in towns like Roubaix, Guesdism could offer local political aid to textile workers. This was the prototype of centralized bureaucratic unionism, led from 'outside', which was to characterize the post-1918 *Confédération Général du Travail* (CGT). Marxism found virgin soil in the Nord, a region untouched by earlier socialist traditions, and offered messianic hope, to a previously cowed and impotent proletariat, of its inevitable imminent triumph. Fifty per cent of Guesdist membership in the Nord comprised textile workers. By 1898 Guesdism had 16,000 members and 40 per cent of socialist voters.

Yet Guesde remained a 'vulgar Marxist' who failed to use Marxism as a tool of analysis of the peculiarities of a French society marked by uneven economic development. Emphasis on the factory proletariat weakened his appeal to the surviving artisanal element on the French left. Subordination of unions to party irritated workers and the espousal of 'iron law of wages' dogmas left the party lukewarm towards strike movements. Guesde's insistence that socialists should remain neutral in the battle between the clerical and anticlerical wings of the bourgeoisie contained a perceptive awareness of the way in which republicanism manipulated anticlericalism to divert workers from social issues. Yet the Catholic *patronat*'s use of religion for social control in the Nord forced grass-roots Guesdists into *Libre Pensée* groups and active resistance to factory chapels.

Coalminers were one bulwark of reformist state socialism. Hitherto miners had oscillated between passivity and brief violent explosions. Coal companies, such as Carmaux, Decazeville or Monceau-les-Mines, maintained notorious 'paternalistic' controls via company housing, pensions and stores. Churchgoing was, frequently, a prerequisite of employment or promotion. The 1880s witnessed a series of revolts against such tyranny. At Decazeville in 1886, company engineer Watrin was thrown from a window by miners outraged at imposition of piecework systems, wage-cuts, company stores aimed at undermining local small traders and foreman-supervision of voting to ensure right-wing success. Decazeville miners, recruited from the Catholic Aveyron peasantry, became secularized and militant, supporting cooperative stores, laic schools, civil funerals, and a radical municipality. However they came to accept that defence of their gains involved wider national union activity. No group of workers made better use of the 1884 act. Fifty per cent unionization was achieved among French miners, and geographical concentration allowed precocious election of pro-miner deputies including Jaurès at Carmaux. Napoleonic legislation allowed state regulation of mines, and miners' deputies used their parliamentary position to ensure the appointment of union safety delegates, for pit disasters were a focal point of concern.

Loire miners' leaders Rondet and Coste haunted ministers' offices in the 1890s. The Arras Convention (1891) witnessed the first employer recognition of union bargaining rights. Pensions were won in 1894. The archetypal miners' leader was Basly, 'The tsar of Lens', tough, pragmatic, a deputy and a labour boss, whose bureaucratic machine had little regard for branch autonomy. He use selective strikes to exact legislative concessions. The parliamentary path to socialism appeared feasible, though Basly's reformism was subject to periodic leftist revolts. To head off militants Basly was forced to press for the eight-hour day in 1900, while in 1906, anger at the 1100 deaths in the Courrières mine disaster produced a surge of support for Broutchoux's syndicalist 'Jeune Syndicat'. The railmen came to adopt a similar strategy. Since the rail companies needed state concessions, rail leader Guérard emphasized the state's duty to regard railways as public utilities, and to oversee wages and conditions.

Alongside the Guesdism of the textile towns and the reformism of the miners, persisted the 'trade socialism' of skilled workers. Sixty per cent of French workers in 1900 worked in units of under ten employees. Despite the second industrial revolution, engineering, building and furniture-making still required skilled men. Half of the 17,000 Paris furniture-makers were employed by the 1890s in mechanized factories. Yet 20 per cent remained in the 'traditional' sector. Many resented the declining quality of their products, the loss of the 'artistic' element in their trade, the erosion of skills and apprenticeships, and concentration on repetitive tasks. Despite some hostility to cheap foreign competition and some sympathy for the employer-sponsored École Boule, which taught traditional skills, cabinet-makers remained open to leftist ideas, active in strikes in the 1880s.

Such workers had little empathy with bureaucratic unions or state socialism. They were heirs to a participatory cooperative tradition, which could oscillate between reformism and revolution. The 1870s had witnessed the dying flickering of optimism about the viability of producer cooperatives. The tactical patronage of these by Opportunist politicians, eager to undermine revolutionary militancy, helped to discredit them. By 1900 the 20,000 members of 300 cooperatives were largely luxury workers, the anachronistic defenders of the vested interest of a small labour aristocracy, though the cooperative dream lingered in the minds of Lyonnais silk and glass workers. During the 1880s Parisian craftsmen flirted with the 'possibilist' socialism of Paul Brousse, their taste for independence attracted by his emphasis on a decentralized party. Yet many felt increasingly ill-at-ease in a bourgeois-led reformist party which stressed collaboration with republican politicians. By

1890–1 the carpenters, joiners and shoemakers who comprised the backbone of Brousse's Parisian strength were turning, instead, to the ex-communard, leather worker Jean Allemane, who urged that all deputies must be under permanent local rank-and-file control. 'Allemanism' with its mistrust of a bourgeois parliament and all politicians, and its sympathy for industrial activism, was significant less as an ephemeral party than as a stepping stone to the syndicalism of the 1900s.

Though the sociological diversity of the workforce thus provides one key to the complexity of French socialism, historical traditions and individual leadership cannot be neglected. In Paris and Lyon the tradition of small revolutionary cells persisted among a few thousand 'neo-Blanquist' artisans of the *Comité Révolutionnaire Centrale*. A minority were tempted to develop Blanqui's nationalism and anti-semitism into proto-fascism. Vaillant epitomized the main tendency of the *CRC* by abandoning hope of a vanguard coup and assimilating elements of Marxism. He empathized with the atavistic anticlericalism of French workers, and, like Allemane, was sympathetic to trade-union autonomy and strike militancy.

A particular 'brand' of socialism could be spread by individual missionary work, as was the case of Vaillant in the Cher. As Lequin argues, historians' generalizations about the sociological basis of different socialist groups can distort grass-roots reality, for many militants were little interested in theory. Lyon workers who voted for reformist mayor Girodet thrilled to the oratory of anarchist Louise Michel. Allemanists and Guesdists cooperated in establishing the Nantes *Bourse de Travail*. Herrier, deputy mayor of Bourges, was an anarcho-syndicalist who professed to despise electoral politics.

The cyclical economic upswing of the 1890s eroded expectations about the imminent collapse of capitalism. Simultaneously, socialists began to achieve major victories in national and municipal elections. Socialist deputies and municipalities felt the need to 'do something' for their voters who faced acute urban social problems. 1893–8 saw greater socialist unity around a programme of pragmatic reformism. The Guesdists became involved, even to the point of accepting the Russian alliance on the grounds that that 'historic mission' of the French proletariat required a 'strong France'! Millerand's *Petite République* newspaper provided an eclectic forum for diverse socialist groups, and the 1896 St Mandé programme urged an end to 'scholastic disputes' and electoral discipline to achieve gradualist reform.

The consequence was to test the Broussists' pet strategy of 'municipal socialism'. Brousse had argued that the Commune marked the end of insurrectionary hopes, but urban dwellers would come to see public control of civic amenities as essential in an industrial France. A decentralist strategy would allow individual socialist municipalities to achieve piecemeal gains at their own pace. The communal question was more than half of the social question, Mâlon claimed. Guesdists initially sneered at 'minuscule versions of the New Jerusalem', yet by 1896 were the dominant force on many of the 150 socialist-run councils in northern, central and south-eastern France. Vaillant, active on the Paris municipality, claimed that 'the commune can become an excellent laboratory of decentralized economic life', and simultaneously, 'a formidable political fortress . . . against bourgeois domination of central power'. Inevitably the bourgeois state mobilized its powers to abort such 'creeping collectivism'. The senate blocked attempts to raise loans for municipal projects and to introduce progressive local taxes. By 1912 there were only eight municipal gas works, no public tramways.

Yet the balance sheet was not totally negative. Socialist municipalities supported strikers, funded crèches, and subsidized school meals, provided legal aid schemes in Roubaix, homes for industrial accident victims in Lyon. Conditions for council workers were improved, public baths and parks constructed – though little council housing. The experience, as J. Scott argues, was not one which integrated workers into bourgeois society. Militant mayors like Dormoy at Montluçon contested prefectoral control of strikebreaking troops and personified popular hatred of police. They presided over civic baptisms, in which parents swore to raise children in collectivist values. Dismissal of popular mayors like Calvignac at Carmaux fuelled local resentments. The municipality acted as the focus of the anti-capitalist sentiments. A Roubaix campaign song of 1896 insisted that the capitalist, king in his factory, was a nobody in the *Hôtel de Ville*. The Guesdists were not totally mistaken, when, after 1898, they reverted to claims that socialist municipalities were prisoners of the capitalist state. Yet these helped deepen and sustain worker hostility to that state.

The Guesdists quit the reformist alliance in 1898 when Guesde himself became disillusioned with moderate electoralist tactics after losing his Roubaix seat to a campaign of employer intimidation of textile worker-voters orchestrated by textile magnate Motte. The Dreyfus explosion found Jaurès supporting the 'threatened' republic, while Guesde and Vaillant stood aloof from the intra-class squabbling of laic and clerical wings of the elites. Millerand joined the cabinet in 1899. Jaurès supported Waldeck-Rousseau, arguing on humanist grounds that Dreyfus deserved socialist support as a victim of injustice, despite being an army officer. He hoped that the affair would radicalize French politics by exposing establishment corruption. Socialist backing for republican defence might accelerate social reform. Jaurès's role in the crisis won many student and intellectuals to socialism. Worker response to Millerand's cabinet appointment was not initially unfavourable. The 1899–1900 strike wave was fuelled by worker hopes of sympathy from their new governmental ally. Disillusionment arrived swiftly. The shooting of strikers by troops at Châlon-sur-Saône, and proposals for compulsory strike arbitration, undermined Millerand's reputation, and his blatant careerism revived deep 'ouvrièriste' suspicion of bourgeois politicians. Initial hope that Jaurès's support for the republican cabinet would produce social reform faded as the victorious Dreyfusards directed their energies against army and church. By 1904, the Seine Socialist Federation had expelled Millerand. Guesdists, who had initially lost ground owing to their sectarian stance, made gains among workers because they had stressed throughout that a republican state remained the tool of capitalist interests. The *Parti Socialiste de France* formed from the alliance between Guesde and Valliant, built up strongholds in the Nord textile towns, among central metallurgy workers, in Paris and in the Midi.

III Strikers and Syndicalists

Many militants were alienated from socialist politics by endless sectarian divisions, by the apparently ineffectual electoralist reformism of the 1890s, by suspicion of careerist politicians. Many workers resented Guesde's autocratic attitude towards the unions. A strong case exists for locating the focus of working-class militancy in union activism and strikes. From 1900 till 1910 the *CGT* was ostensibly controlled by 'revolutionary syndicalists', exponents of the most revolutionary doctrine ever developed in an advanced industrial society, which called for the overthrow of capitalism via the general strike, and its replacement by a decentralized society based on workers' control. P. Stearns has argued that syndicalism was a 'cause without rebels', attracting a vocal but atypical minority. 'Real' workers were as pragmatically reformist as their British counterparts. Syndicalism captured a narrow elite of leaders. Only the absence of proportional representation in the *CGT* constitution allowed this minority to capture the leadership, for larger reformist unions, such as the miners, railmen and printers, were either not affiliated or underrepresented. In 1910 the funds of the printers trade union were ten time larger than those of all the *CGT*-affiliated unions combined. Syndicalist leaders imbibed revolutionary ideas from the national political culture, but the silent majority of workers lacked political interests, adjusted to capitalism, grumbled at mechanization or factory discipline, seeking compensation in wage rises. Barely one million workers were unionized by 1914, and only half of these affiliated to the *CGT*. The syndicalist pioneer Pelloutier, in a despairing moment, appeared to echo Stearns's assessment. 'Compared to foreign labour . . . which endows its membership with . . . the advantage of organization, French unions practice only the strike, badly discourage their members, repel the indifferent and include . . . an infinitesimal part of the proletariat, which industrial barons scorn.' Yvetot confessed that many workers played boules on May Day. Solidarity strikes were poorly supported. Stearns claims, too, that French strikes were no more violent than those in Britain. At most, workers accepted syndicalist aid to organize strikes, mouthed a few 'revolutionary' slogans. However real strike aims were pragmatic, essentially about wages, as inflation threatened living standards after 1900. Despite a panic during the 1906 general strike, bourgeois politicians saw syndicalist threats as hot air. In time, syndicalists bowed to the reformism of their constituency and adjusted to the world of industrial arbitration and wage bargaining. That silent sensible majority who accepted the capitalist *status quo* stifled the protest of activist minorities.

   This interpretation had become the new orthodoxy. However, it is misleading to argue from syndicalism's undoubted failure that it had no basis in the French working class. Syndicalism had its intellectual origins in Proudhonism, its industrial roots in the post-1880s strike explosion. If it retreated before state and employer repression after 1908, it enjoyed a brief but genuine apogee in the preceding years.

From an average of around 100 strikes per year in the 1880s, the norm rose to over 1000 per year in the 1900s. In 1906 there were nine million days lost in 1309 strikes. Union leaders initially viewed strikes as a costly last resort. However, there developed an extraordinary rank-and-file mythology about their potential which extended beyond the ranks of *CGT* members. Strikes expressed worker values. The non-striker was a '*fainéant*' (idler). May Day was a worker festival. The idea of a general strike was not a monopoly of syndicalist leaders, but exerted a messianic general appeal. The nature and extent of strike activity changed. Strikes spread to hitherto quiescent regions such as Britanny, company towns such as Le Creusot in 1899, or to Catholic wool workers in Mazamet (Tarn), whose atavistic anti-Protestantism had hitherto kept them royalist in politics. By the 1900s, organization by trade union or socialist municipality was an increasing feature which helped to treble the average number of plants involved in strikes. Despite the efforts of republican politicians to treat them as a disease, rather than a crime, they continued to provoke vigorous repression. Inevitably, industries with a high proportion of unskilled and female workers, easily intimidated or replaced, maintained a lower strike propensity. Only 6 per cent of strikers were 'female', 12 per cent 'mixed'. Women strikers faced police and press insults. One female striker was dragged back to work by an irate husband and publicly whipped. Female strikes were often short and 'defensive'. Yet there were encouraging signs, such as the Voiron and Vizille 1906 strikes against the nun-controlled barrack discipline of the Lyonnais silk industry led by Lucie Baud. Textile strikes made up 1 per cent of Lyonnais disputes in 1869, 30 per cent by 1890. The Guesdist conquest of the Nord was accompanied by a textile explosion in the 1880s. The songs, drums, dances and banners of female strike demonstrations gave the atmosphere of a village fête, mixing huge joy at temporary escape from discipline with quasi-messianic expectations.

Strikes became 'legal'. They were more peaceful than riots. Yet they resembled class warfare. Their length increased to an average of 21 days by 1901. Strikers lacked funds, faced arrest, blacklisting and dismissal. Their leaders tended to be unmarried, skilled workers, admired for their foolhardy courage in confronting management, yet destined for short 'careers', for militancy was dangerous, exhausting, often dispiriting. Many blacklisted from industrial employment ended as café owners or '*colporteurs*'.

Can the characteristics of French strikes be linked with 'syndicalism'? Stearns claims that the presence of wage demands in two thirds of disputes proves their economistic nature. Yet wage demands frequently disguise other fundamental grievances. Shorter hours, espoused by the *CGT* in a crusade for improved family life for the 'worker machine', involved 9 per cent of demands before 1890, more thereafter. Factory discipline disputes involved 5 per cent of strikes before 1890 as employers sought to impose new work rhythms, piecework systems, fines for timekeeping and to ban singing and limit the fundamental '*droit de pisser*'. Foremen and supervisors were detested as petty parvenus who bullied and molested women workers. The most significant feature of the labour militancy in these years was the overlap between the rearguard resistance of threatened craft-groups, the mainstay of nineteenth-century activism, with the new assertiveness of certain proletarian sectors such as dockers and navvies. Only the massive mechanization of 1914–18 was to kill off the former. 'Syndicalism' was their heroic last stand, during which they attempted to recruit allies by organizing the unskilled. In the Loire, the semi-skilled (*OS*) workforce of the massive St Chamond arms plant were largely quiescent after the sackings in 1883 of the last skilled puddlers ousted by the new technology, who had previously exerted job control and worked in teams.

The new *OS* workers were isolated in the deafening noise of the new mechanized plant, tightly controlled by supervisors. They pleaded for a wage rise in 1911, expressed deferential gratitude to local deputy Briand for securing arms orders for their firm. Yet in nearby Chambon-Feugerolles, whose file-making plants mechanized more gradually, skilled file cutters were still needed in order to fashion uneven quality steel. They provided the nucleus of militancy in the 1900s strikes, resisting 'dilution' of their trade by unionizing local *OS* boltworkers who were their neighbours, relatives and café companions. In Rive-de-Giers, as in Carmaux, skilled glass-blowers had hitherto enjoyed status, security, job contol. Via work in semi-independent teams, they had passed on their skills to apprentices, who were often their sons. The 1890s saw bitter strikes against the advent of the Siemens continuous oven process, which meant that jobs could be learned in days instead of years. The Lyonnais glass industry saw six strikes 1848–85, 43 between 1886–95, as employers imported unskilled Italian blacklegs. At Carmaux 33 per cent of glass-workers were sons of glass-workers in 1870, a mere 12 per cent by 1900. Sacked Carmaux strikers founded a cooperative glass-works at Albi. Such conflicts became endemic in French industry. Whereas in 1885–9 12 per cent of strikes involved job-control issues, this rose to 25 per cent in 1910–14. Milling and grinding machines, specialized lathes, mechanized borers 'deskilled' many engineering processes. Six skilled men were sacked, one by one, for refusing to operate a turret lathe at Hotchkiss.

French cars were initially built by teams of skilled craftsmen. Renault, however, visited the Ford assembly line in Detroit, his engineers devoured Taylor's *Principles of Scientific Management'*, *École Polytechnique*-trained technocrats pioneered new work systems, which involved the growth of tight managerial and supervisory control of work, and semi-skilled workers on piece rates working to produce production norms. The know-how of skilled craftsmen was systematically 'stolen' and made obsolete. Skilled Parisian metalworkers were undeferential, proud. Their singing, drinking, talking and freedom to stroll out for fresh air in work hours amazed American observers. The mere threat of Ford-style rationalization provided the notorious 1913 Renault strike, which ended in the sacking of 436 craftsmen. Division of labour killed craft-pride, skill, job satisfaction. Shoemakers, the core of nineteenth-century craft militancy, found their job subdivided into 92 separate tasks. An industrial dictionary of 1896 listed 858 trades, one of 1909 listed 15,000. By the 1900s skilled workers were reduced to under 20 per cent of the workforce in large industry.

Syndicalism's visionary and martyr was F. Pelloutier, who died in 1900 after a brief life of constant illness. Dismissal from his Catholic college for reading anticlerical novels deprived this son of a post office official of the baccalauréat and of the chance to enter a profession. As a young journalist he was appalled by the hostility of the opportunist press in St Nazaire to the aspirations of local shipyard workers. Moving to Paris, he mixed in anarchist circles and was converted to the idea of a peaceful general strike which would paralyse capitalism by strangling its fuel supplies. His achievement in the 1890s was to build up a National Federation of *Bourses de Travail* (*BT*). He conceived the *BT* as a focus of proletarian culture – simultaneously job-agency, library, centre of leisure activity, strike coordinator and provider of industrial-skill training and adult education. By 1907, 157 had been established. He was keen to throw off the republican patronage under which many had been founded. Pelloutier was a model organizer, keeping scrupulous records for the Paris *BT*, in contrast to his predecessor whose records were tossed into the dustbin by his landlord when he was evicted from his apartment! He aimed to fuse his revolutionary vision with British pragmatism, and was impatient with the Limoges *BT* which resisted regular dues payment.

Pelloutier insisted that worker self-emancipation was essential. 'Laws are useless because the industrial oligarchy controls the state. How can it be hoped that a regime founded on wealth will attack wealth?' Laic education was bourgeois indoctrination. The *BT* should train militants who could help the worker to educate himself. The worker needed 'knowledge of the cause of his servitude, the ability to discern where his blows should be directed'. Libraries, sadly a feature of only 15 per cent of *BT*'s, were vital for the workers' control of their own cultural heritage. Pelloutier championed Zola, social art, popular theatre, female emancipation, and was deeply suspicious of reactionary trends in elite culture such as symbolism and Catholic literary revival. He championed strikes, but warned workers to use the strike weapon sparingly and carefully.

Syndicalism contained an anarchist strand personified by E. Pouget, another *déraciné* son of a republican petty bourgeois who left school before his baccalauréat. After a brief phase as a union organizer in a Paris department store, Pouget drifted into the semi-clandestine anarchist movement of the 1880s. Some 6000 activists, mainly petty bourgeois and artisanal, tended to seek psychological compensation for their impotence by the flamboyance of group names such as 'Panthers of Batignolles.' Their practical activism centred on organizing unemployment demonstrations and tenant anti-landlord protests. They attracted a fringe following of artists, like Pisarro, alienated by the regime's grey positivism, and among 'social bandits' like jewel-thief Clement Duval. The heavy police repression and legal backlash provoked by the brief phase of bombings and assassinations of the early 1890s forced activists like Pouget into stratigic reassessment. From 1889 Pouget edited a fascinating newspaper, *Père Peinard*, whose eponymous hero, an old cobbler, appeared on the title page emerging from his workshop brandishing a leather strap to chastise the bourgeoisie. Written in argot, witty, scabrous and untheoretical, it portrayed a Manichean world of exploited poor and corrupt rich. It despised politicians who flattered the 'sovereign people' while oppressing them. Daily tragedies of worker suicides were evoked. Pouget was outraged that '*Marianne*', once the workers' heroine, had proved a faithless whore:

> 'The Republic she promised, but she lied,
> she just pushes the little guy aside,
> with the big shots she plays,
> with the tyrants she lays,
> while in the streets our brothers have died.'

Cartoons juxtaposed ragged peasants alongside châteaux, with ragged proletarians facing republican monuments. What, Pouget demanded, had really changed? Such polemics touched deep popular chords.

In exile in London, Pouget advocated a new strategy. Anarchists should infiltrate the unions to prevent any drift towards bureaucratic reformism, and act as a yeast to speed the revolutionary fermentation. Strikes could teach workers the daily reality of class oppression, whereas socialist sectarian squabbling divided the left. By 1900 Pouget was assistant-secretary of the *CGT*, editor of its journal *Voix Du Peuple!* Syndicalism ousted reformism among the *CGT* leadership after 1900, although the famous 1906 '*Charter of Amiens*', with its rejection of political affiliations, was supported by reformists like Keufer of the printers as well as by syndicalists. The decade 1900–10 witnessed strike waves, the jailing of *CGT* leaders after the May 1906 general strike, shooting of strikers and military call-up of rail strikers in 1910. Anger in the coalfields at the Courrières mine disaster temporarily shook the hold of the reformist, Basly, on the miners' union. The Belgian and Russian examples proved that a general strike could be reality, not mere 'myth'.

The rise and fall of syndicalism is best illustrated by particular industries and regions. Parisian building trade militancy shows the vitality of the movement. Here small contractors were retreating in the face of a large-scale *patronat* which monopolized public works contracts. The workforce was highly stratified, ranging from 'aristocratic' masons via carpenters to navvies. Chances of rising into the *patronat* were receding. New 'anonymous' firms were disliked. Company stores trapped many workers in permanent debt. Carpenters and joiners were threatened by power-saws, and the increasing use of concrete and metal. Significantly, the 'inventor' of the general strike strategy, Tortellier, was a joiner. Craftsmen had to carry their tools across Paris to the building sites. Eleven per cent of the workforce building the *métro* suffered injury between 1906 and 1911, and lack of decompression equipment led to deaths from divers' 'bends'. Lead paint, easy to spread and hence permitting hiring of unskilled men, produced lung diseases exempt from the 1898 industrial compensation act. Real wages stagnated and firms flouted the wage rates established by the Paris Council for public works contracts.

Weary of socialist in-fighting, and sceptical of republican social reform promises, builders resorted to strikes. The Paris *BT* helped unionize the navvies and reduce intercraft friction which weakened the 1898 strikes. The 1906 eight-hour strike alarmed the Parisian bourgeoisie, union membership soared, and Clemenceau flooded the city with troops. An eleven-month *métro* strike was the most spectacular of 47 conflicts in 1907. However, crisis was at hand. In 1908 the builders' union – *Fédération du Bâtiment* (*FB*) – sent flying pickets to aid a quarrymen's strike at Draveil. When police fired indiscriminately into the local union branch headquarters, killing two and wounding ten, Clemenceau rejected the eye-witness account of one of his radical backbenchers that the killing was 'premeditated', and backed the police. The machismo of the *CGT* and the *FB* was challenged, but their protest rally at Villeneuve-St-George produced a cavalry charge which left four dead, 69 wounded. The 'anarchist' who fired the shot which 'provoked' this charge was a police *agent-provocateur*. A call for a general protest strike was pre-empted by arrest of *CGT* leaders. A building employers' federation counteroffensive began under Villemin, who insisted that 'it is true democracy when each man remains in his place and workers are not caused to believe that they can hope for a better situation.' Lockouts, company unions and intimidation by armed company thugs exacerbated latent tensions between craftsmen and navvies. Despite a nine-month *métro* strike in 1912–13, the *FB* was in crisis. Its buoyancy had relied on the bravado of militants who had talked of an imminent 'great day' to keep harsh reality at bay. Now, activists like Pericat were being isolated.

A parallel trajectory of militancy, quasi-messianic expectations and collapse can be charted in many industrial regions. In Nantes-St-Nazaire, syndicalist dockers and shipyard workers set the tone after the *BT* had helped coordinate wide local solidarity behind a female rope-workers' strike in 1894. The strike committee took over the town hall, resisted troop intimidation and sackings and inspired fifteen new unions in the city. It achieved unionization of 31 per cent of the labour-force, a salutary warning against correlating syndicalism with weak unions. The apogee of years of local militancy came in 1907 with a prolonged dock strike for the eight-hour day and the closed shop. A cavalry charge left one dead and 21 wounded, the strike was smashed and eighteen leaders arrested – including Yvetot the *CGT* leader who had addressed mass rallies preaching antimilitarism and female emancipation. The élan was punctured, leadership passed to reformists, the local labour movement faced the war crisis of 1914, 'numb' and demoralized (Y. Guin).

In the Lyonnais, rising prices produced resentments, while declining unemployment eroded fatalism. Mechanization and increased work-pace produced a widespread sense of loss of dignity and job control among glove-makers, engineers and shoemakers. Time and motion study, as at the Berliet Works in 1912, produced conflicts. Lequin portrays a deep class-consciousness poised between day-to-day reformism and latent revolutionary hopes. Activist minorities were a catalyst for mass action, the general strike less a 'myth' than an immediate hope, a tactic to be tried. Socialist schisms permitted syndicalist control of major *BT*s such as Lyon and Grenoble. Metal strikes were anarchist-led, and strikes spread to 'new' transport and electrical sectors. Reformists almost lost control of the St Étienne miners' federation. After an employer's son shot pickets during a clockmakers' strike at Cluses, a *CGT* organizer was greeted as a messiah. The May 1906 general strike provoked bourgeois alarm. But the momentum slackened, recent union gains were lost, reformists captured the *BT*s, workers failed to find effective weapons against new management strategies. Unity between old craft trades, heavy industry proletarians and the 'new' tertiary sector and chemical and electricity workers proved impossible to sustain.

Evidence of deep hostility to the established order thus exists. Briefly, reformists in the labour movement felt 'like fresh water fish . . . suddenly in an ocean' (Sorel). Syndicalism's failure does not make it trivial or invalid. Syndicalists were a 'representative minority' who tapped a mood of independence, pride and anger. Many workers recognized their aspiration in syndicalist rhetoric. We must not assume that the 90 per cent of French workers outside unions were necessarily integrated and happy. Later strike waves of 1918–20 and 1936 were to tap the latent revolutionary consciousness of unorganized workers. A vanguard of skilled workers helped organize unskilled dockers, navvies. Syndicalists recognized themselves to be a conscious minority – and rejected parliamentary elections and union secret ballots as devices which isolated the individual workers and nullified the dynamism engendered by collective industrial action. Sadly, the future big battalions – miners, railmen, textile workers and the growing army of the semi-skilled, were relatively immune to the syndicalist appeal, more amenable to bureaucratic centralized unions than to job-control preoccupations.

After 1908 syndicalism retreated in face of ubiquitous employer counteroffensives. Company unions multiplied. Over half of post-1910 strikes were confronted by employers' associations. Lockouts, such as that in the Fougères shoe strike, became commonplace. Strike success rates fell. The 'Radical republic' made full use of a police system bequeathed by earlier authoritarian regimes. Reactionary police chiefs and radical politicians found common ground in tough law-and-order strategies. Syndicalists were viewed as public enemy number one. Some radical back-benchers were squeamish at outright repression. A few judges raised legalistic objections. A dozen brigades of *police mobile* were created for strike duty, while the *Sécurité Générale*'s 400-strong trade-union unit compiled the notorious *Carnet B* list of militants to be arrested on the eve of a war. The Paris *préfecture* of police maintained its proud tradition of planting *agents-provocateurs* and 'anarchist bombers' in the labour movement, and had a regular slush fund to pay union informers. Its notorious chief, Louis Lépine, ex-governor of Algiers, and a future Suez Canal director, was an eccentric showman, capable of ordering his officers to beat up pickets as a prelude to jumping into the fray shouting, 'Stop! I forbid you to attack these honest men!' Behind the populist façade was an authoritarian paternalist, a condescending friend of those 'good little people' who did not 'envy their bosses'.

The state's surgical precision in wielding its repressive apparatus was revealed during the 1898 rail and building strikes, seen as posing a security threat during the Dreyfus crisis. There were mass picket arrests, raids on union offices. Army engineers were mobilized to run the trains. Hundreds were sacked. It is possible that *CGT* secretary Legailse was a police agent. Despite conciliatory meetings with union leaders, Waldeck-Rousseau mobilized 95,000 troops to undermine the 1900–2 strike wave. In 1906 Clemenceau began with a conciliatory offer of progressive income tax – yet within months had arrested 700 union leaders, sacked militant teachers. Army electricians ended the 1907 Paris blackout. The years 1906–8 saw 20 workers shot dead, 667 wounded, thousands arrested. In 1910 Briand treated the rail strike as virtual treason. Hitherto he had favoured a sophisticated strategy, aiming to split the *CGT*, woo reformist union bosses, like Latapie of the metalworkers, by offers of pensions and collective bargaining machinery, and thus achieve a centrist consensus. The public sector strike explosion of 1909–10, with 1502 strikes in 1910 alone, jeopardized this plan. Guérard, the reformist rail-union boss, accepted the 1909 pension offer, but syndicalist elements in his union gained backing for minimum wage demands and achieved some unity between footplatemen and others in a traditionally hierarchic and divided workforce. Invoking 'the enormous mass of citizens who want public peace', and fearing that rail chaos would lose votes, Briand mobilized troops and treated wildcats in the north-Paris rail depôts as evidence of a revolutionary plot. Railmen were conscripted – so that strikers became 'mutineers'. The eastern frontier region was barely touched by the strike which had its bastion on the northern lines, but national security was allegedly threatened. Isolated sabotage was magnified by the tabloid gutter press. Two hundred leaders were arrested, 3300 activists sacked and troops smashed sympathy strikes by dockers and electricians.

The *CGT* leadership began its retreat from syndicalist goals to pragmatism after 1910, with new secretary Jouhaux rejecting rash strikes and favouring a bureaucratic model of unionism. The metalworkers' leader, Merrheim, was saddened by the 'crisis of working-class morality' as craft virtues declined. The growing semi-skilled proletariat, with its taste for mass sport and preoccupation with wages above job control, was proof of capitalism's fatal capacity to pervert even the working class. Merrheim saw the process as irreversible. Capitalism was not yet in crisis, unions would have to learn to live with the new systems of scientific management. The 'pessimism of intelligence' was killing the 'optimism of action'. Labour leaders should form industrial, not craft unions, make careful analysis of capitalist cartels and state-industry links. Strike defeats and the growing war threat pushed *CGT* leaders to a reluctant acceptance of the need to cooperate with socialist politicians.

IV From Socialist Unity to the *Union Sacrée* (1905–14)

In 1905 French socialism achieved a belated and precarious unity with the formation of the *SFIO*. Both 'reformist' and 'revolutionary' groups had stagnated in terms of membership and votes since 1899. The reforming possibilities of the Dreyfusard bloc appeared exhausted. Above all, Jaurès, worried about rising international tensions, was sensitive to pressure from the Second International to end suicidal socialist fragmentation.

The ideology of the *SFIO* leaned to the left, for class struggle was accepted, and cooperation with bourgeois parties rejected, despite recognition of the utility of social reforms. The party made tangible gains over the next decade, trebling its membership to 90,000, increasing its vote to 1.5 million and its parliamentary seats above 100. Inevitably, many problems remained unresolved. By breaking with the Radicals, the *SFIO* lost seats in areas where it relied on second ballot deals, while 'autonomous' socialist reformists maintained their personal fiefs and idiosyncratic behaviour. One Lyon deputy, Augagneur, became governor general of Madagascar! The working-class vote remained fragmented, with militant syndicalists refusing to participate in elections, and many areas remaining loyal to republican politicians – or, as with Catholic communities like the Mazamet wool-workers, voting royalist.

Jaurès remained the figurehead of the *SFIO* centre, the focus for attempts to achieve a loose, eclectic unity. A target for the assaults of the clergy in the Tarn, he had no hesitation in supporting republican anticlericalism – while permitting his wife to send their daughter to a Catholic school. As an *ENS* graduate and a philosophy professor he refused to share the scepticism of Marxists and syndicalists about republican education. Aware that a minority working class needed political allies, he adopted a loose definition of 'worker', which encompassed peasants, 'administrative proletarians' and teachers. He attracted intellectuals to the party during the Dreyfus crisis, though some like Halévy and Péguy subsequently quit in disgust at the 'sordid' parliamentary compromises which 'betrayed' the Dreyfusard crusade. His charisma attracted many *instituteurs* to local *SFIO* organizations. A native of the rural Midi, he empathized with the problems of the peasantry and framed policies to attract their vote. He reached a wide audience as editor of the party newspaper *Humanité* which had a circulation of 88,000 by 1914.

Jaurès was no mere Radical *manqué*. He accepted Marxist surplus value theory and saw the proletariat as a class united by its relation to the means of production, a 'class of humanity' which carried all hopes for a more just society. Involvement in the mining and glass strikes at Carmaux in the 1890s transformed him into a genuine workers' tribune. He was charged by cavalry, danced the *carmagnole* on café tables – a far cry from the philosophy professor of the 1880s. His awareness of the repressive role of the army fed his interest in a citizen's militia. With Vaillant he remained the leading voice in the *SFIO* urging dialogue with the *CGT* and rejecting the Guesdists' subordination of the unions to the party. He opened *Humanité*'s columns to syndicalist articles critical of himself, campaigned for public sector unionization rights. Socialist deputies should offer support to strikes, which had an educational role in exposing the true face of capitalism. He refused to condemn the general strike outright, and supported the *CGT*'s campaign against price inflation.

Nevertheless real disagreements divided him from syndicalists. He had flirted with Millerand's plans to introduce strike-balloting in order to force unions to become mass organizations and to institutionalize industrial relations. Pelloutier, who liked Jaurès personally, claimed that 'despite appearances, Jaurès is as sectarian as Guesde, since in the interests of a narrow and futile reformism he disrupts every energetic union action.' Jaurès wanted larger, more organized unions, an end to rash minority strikes which split the working class.

Jaurès had the weakness of his strengths. He was open-minded, his sensibility steadily broadened. He incarnated the left's humanitarian generosity – yet epitomized and possibly accentuated its confusions and myopia. For many workers clearly shared his ambivalent assessment of the republican state, simultaneously tool of an oppressive capitalism and yet carrier of the ideals and mystique of the Jacobin heritage, able to transcend its class-base. After 1906 Jaurès frequently denounced Clemenceau and Briand, but not the regime itself. He also failed to build up a coherent faction within the *SFIO*. He disliked sectarian infighting, and was blinded by his oratory into the illusion that words squared circles. His *SFIO* was a pantheistic broad church, evolving with the proletariat. It aimed to encompass and reconcile revolutionaries and reformists, proletarians, peasants, intellectuals and 'progressive' bourgeoisie. The qualities which made him a statesman made him, perhaps, a poor party organizer.

Guesdism was strong where Jaurès was weak. It had a firm regional industrial base and many militants, maintained a solid 40 per cent of congress votes, dominated the *SFIO* book-club. Yet it suffered some intellectual and organizational ossification. Like a miniature *SPD*, Guesdism was partially transformed by the society in which it was implanted. Marxism grew stale with repetition. As Guesdism expanded its 'alternative society' of cooperatives, cafés, bakeries, youth clubs, Baker suggests that its proletarian subculture may have provided a cocoon for northern workers' lives which acted as a form of 'negative integration'. Its antistrike dogmatism alienated industrial militants, so that revolt against Basly in the northern coalfields benefited syndicalism not Guesdism. It retained its 1890s bastions without making further conquests.

The vitality of minority groups saved the *SFIO* from a drift to reformism. Lagardelle's stimulating *Mouvement Socialiste* review questioned the parliamentary path to socialism, and admired the *CGT* for preserving collectivist values threatened by individualist bourgeois electoralism. Of wider appeal was Hervé's *Guerre Sociale*, which also flirted with syndicalism during the 1906 Limoges general strike. Its emphasis was, however, on the dangers of militarism and war. The *Guerre Sociale*, reaching a circulation of

60,000, tapped popular anticonscription feeling, notably in central regions, and portrayed the army as a strikebreaking force. Hervé won 12 per cent of *SFIO* congress votes and flirted with the idea of a general strike to prevent war. In the Lyonnais *SFIO* militants collaborated with syndicalists in the post-1911 antimilitarist crusade and 700,000 signatures were raised on a petition against the three-year conscription bill.

These issues played an increasing role in party debate. Hervé's approach had three main rivals. The *SFIO* right denied the link between capitalism and war, arguing that the self-interest of financiers and exporters would hold in check the bellicosity of arms dealers. French and German capitalists invested in each other's countries. Guesdists remained passive, arguing that, since capitalism led to war, antiwar crusades were utopian illusions. A unilateral French general strike against war would hand victory to Germany and alienate French workers from socialism. The Guesdists' Nord bastion remained relatively untouched by antiwar propaganda. Jaurès attempted his habitual synthesis of incompatible positions. He felt France should defend her 'progressive' republic against authoritarian Germany if attacked. In 1914, as Becker notes, he never doubted the peaceful intent of the French government. Yet the role of the officer corps in the Dreyfus crisis caused him to favour a citizens' militia. Haunted by the nightmare of coming holocaust, he championed the Second International's peace efforts, trusting the *SPD* leadership to secure multilateral rejection of war mobilization. In July 1914 he attempted an alliance with the *CGT* on the basis of a peaceful general strike against mobilization in conjunction with a similar effort in Germany. His stance was impregnated with bourgeois humanitarianism. Despite Paul Louis's writings on capitalism's imperialist profits, the *SFIO*'s theoretical analysis of imperialism remained on a low level. Jaurès criticized colonialism's 'excesses', but still retained the illusion of a 'good' colonialism, spreading progress. The *SFIO* was eurocentrist, its membership confined to white '*colons*'. Workers in ports like Marseille were dependent on colonial trade while the *Revue Socialiste* group on the *SFIO* right was tinged with social-Darwinist racism.

The *CGT* bore the brunt of antimilitarist propaganda effort. Yvetot denounced the 'idiotic religion' of '*La Patrie*'. Barrack life was portrayed as a source of VD, alcoholism, a 'school of crime and vice, hypocrisy and cowardice'. A *Sou du Soldat* fund permitted *BT*s to keep conscripts in touch with the union movement. Draft evasion doubled between 1890s and 1911, and the retention of conscripts after the passage of the three-year conscription act provoked near mutinies. In 1911 police reported 59 *BT*s active in propaganda activities. A December 1912 one-day antiwar strike aroused some support. Yet state repression called the antimilitarists' bluff. A law of March 1912 established African penal battalions for antimilitarist propagandists. Yvetot, Hervé and countless obscure militants were jailed. Immigrant worker militants were deported, leaders of the 6000-strong teachers' syndicalist organization sacked. A Russian bribe accelerated Interior Minister Klotz's decision to ban anticonscription demonstrations. *Carnet B* was extended to cover union militants, and cavalry charges smashed pacifist demonstrations in Nantes. Jouhaux, powerless to halt the military juggernaut, tried to focus *CGT* activity on wage and price issues.

Nevertheless, there remained signs of vitality on the left. Fears of *SFIO* schism proved exaggerated, Hervé modified his extreme antimilitarism and *CGT-SFIO* collaboration on the war issue strengthened. The left-Radicals, with their peasant and petty-bourgeois base, became alarmed by the right's vehement bellicosity, and suggested a renewed alliance with the *SFIO*, emphasizing that heavy military expenditure hit the poor and made long-overdue tax-reform essential. The 1914 election, by increasing *SFIO* seats from 72 to 103, made a centre-left government possible.

The left's efforts to mobilize against war in July-August 1914 proved abortive. However, it may be unwise to deduce from the response of the workers to a specific crisis broader generalizations about the 'integration' of the French proletariat into the republican system. The militancy of 1906–10 reappeared in 1919–20. Becker's analysis of 1914 needs careful attention. The widespread assumption that Germany was the aggressor triggered a 'republic in danger' response. Only 2 per cent of conscripts failed to answer the mobilization call. The speed of the outcome took labour leaders by surprise, for they envisaged a prolonged crisis, not one which took Europe to war within weeks. 27–29 July saw large *CGT* demonstrations, with 500 arrests in Paris. However, Jaurès persuaded the *CGT* of the need for united action with the *SFIO* and independent union activity was called off. The *CGT* leaders feared mass arrests, even syndicalist stalwart Péricat later confessed that he had feared death from military firing squad or chauvinist mobs. Against police advice, the interior minister Malvy shrewdly delayed implementation of *Carnet B* arrests and maintained the mood of national unity by reinstating sacked rail strikers. The response to the martyrdom of Jaurès was numb and muted. At his funeral Jouhaux claimed that the fallen hero would have chosen to defend the republican *patrie*. When war came Vaillant shook hands with de Mun, Guesde became a minister and reformists urged *CGT* collaboration in the war economy.

Was '1914' thus the vivid exemplification of the success of the regime in wooing the working class? The schools, press and barracks had accomplished their task. Workers were clearly not immune to patriotism. Working-class consciousness was weakened by frictions within the labour force between skilled and unskilled, men and women, French and immigrant workers, anticlericals and Catholics. The heroic resistance of craft groups to technological change was being crushed, the consciousness of the 'new' *OS* proletariat was in its infancy. Yet the war mobilization showed more resignation than enthusiasm, the *union sacrée* was specific and ephemeral. The post-war labour unrest and birth of the communist party showed the very imperfect integration of workers into the republic – though the nucleus of the revived militancy of 1918–20 had shifted to the 'new' working class of the Parisian *banlieue*.

Chapter 9

Peasants into Frenchmen?

I The 'Modernization' of Rural France?

In a brilliant, evocative book, making extensive use of anthropological and 'folklore' evidence, Eugen Weber characterized the decades after 1870 as the period in which the French peasantry was 'modernized'. The rapid decline of 'traditional' rural society was, he argued, due to the combined impact of railways, schools and conscription. The expansion of the rail network from 18,000 to 65,000 kilometres, supported by a comparable improvement in local roads, extended the possibility of commercial farming to regions of subsistence polyculture. Peasants then experienced the need for literacy to keep accounts. Père Tiénnon in Guillaumin's *Vie d'un Simple* sends his children to school when confronted with balance sheets in a household 'where no one knew how to write a figure'. The status and importance of schoolteachers, their pride and independence boosted by the Ferry laws, swelled as they became the village *notables*, prophets of republican progress. National unity was cemented as the laic school eroded patois, still spoken by half the population in the 1860s, and disseminated the cult of *La Patrie*. Universal military service, introduced in 1872, accustomed young peasants to urban values and tastes. Conscripts spoke French in the barracks, ate meat for the first time. Anticonscription feelings, hitherto endemic in the countryside, declined as the army ceased to appear as an occupation force in a foreign land. Peasant families learned the value of literacy from the need to communicate with conscripts. Already in 1870, when the family in Guillaumin's novel have to ask the grocer's daughter to read letters from the front, 'ignorance appeared hard, because we were more disadvantaged by it than usual.' By 1914 the peasantry, mobilized to fight in the Great War, responded with dutiful resignation which contrasted with the indifference to the 'national cause' shown in 1870.

The transport revolution accelerated rural-urban migration, often via an intermediary stage in the local bourg. In 1861 11 per cent of Frenchmen lived outside their native department; by 1918, 25 per cent. The lure of bright lights, high wages and easy women drew Bretons to Paris like moths to a flame. The village school played a key cultural role in facilitating this transition to city life.

A variety of cultural changes transformed village life. Cheaper fuel meant less need to huddle together in collective *veillées* on winter evenings, and bicycles allowed young men to go to the nearby village or bourg to spend their evenings in cafés. Violent sports such as shooting of live chickens, pig-baiting and cock-fighting were gradually ousted by more decorous pastimes such as cycling, rugby in the south-west, and organized municipal shooting clubs. Midi bullfighting became commercialized and professionalized. Intervillage bloodbaths, masquerading as games of *choules* between rival neighbouring communes, declined – although one Breton priest in the 1880s was bound and gagged for attempting to prevent a traditional contest. The collective folk dances of the past, often functional, used in Brittany for flattening land for house-building, were replaced by privatized dancing by couples of waltzes and polkas, brought back by conscripts from the towns. Weekend dances in the large villages became the norm. Harvest chants, protest songs against cheating millers, 'crude' patois songs gave way to the choral group singing from official songbooks such as those distributed by Jules Simon in 1872. By the 1900s folklorists were collecting the traditional songs like extinct butterflies. Disorderly and chaotic local fêtes, discouraged by the authorities after their manipulation by the 'reds' in 1848–51 were transformed into the greater decorum of 14 July – an awkward fête in that it fell at harvest time. In Franche-Comté, teachers cultivated a fête on 15 December, the anniversary of the annexation of the region by France. *Charivaris*, similarly suspect because of their politicization, retreated to peripheral mountain regions and to their original function of punishing remarried widows. Tight forest controls checked midsummer bonfires, threshing machines killed off practices of gleaning, the replacement of thatch by tiles eroded a village craft, reduced the danger of village fires, and pleased the insurance companies. *Colportage* finally collapsed, killed by the railway and the diffusion of mass, anodyne, apolitical newspapers like *Le Petit Journal*. Grocers, shops, selling spaghetti, chocolate, coffee, made rural diets more varied; cheap cotton clothes made dress more comfortable. New value-systems emerged. Time became money – and the assumption that the old words were the wise words died as 'progress' made the wisdom of the older generation appear obsolete.

For the first time, Weber claims, politics became relevant to the peasantry. Hitherto national political labels had simply been used to legitimize local feuds. What passed for political divisions had, essentially, been the defence of community traditions, atavistic squabbles, as in the southern Massif, between bourg Protestants and rural Catholics, or the conflicts between the clans and clienteles of rival local *notables* competing for the spoils of state patronage. Now, however, widening economic and cultural horizons made issues such as agricultural protectionism the focus of authentic political concerns.

On balance, Weber believes, these changes represented genuine progress. Quinine defeated malaria in the swampy Sologne, as prayers to saints had never done. The fatalistic passivity of the old was replaced by a new optimism. The introversion of the *petits pays* was ended. Education encouraged independence from the *notables*, wider career prospects, a sense of pride and hope, liberation from the superstitious fears spread by the old *veillée* stories. Nadaud, who had walked thousands of miles to and from Paris in his childhood, could not but welcome the railway as a relief for the sore feet of his fellow Limousin migrants. Those who lamented change, one could argue, were 'sociological romantics' like René Bazin, rural bourgeois weeping for a dying culture, nostalgic for the 'good old days' which the peasantry abandoned without any backward glance. Mistral's Provençal regionalists, eccentric folklore enthusiastics, *curés* saddened by their declining influence – such were the atypical, essentially non-peasant, opponents of 'progress'.

Weber accepts that an argument could be made that these changes constitute 'internal colonialism'. A northern urban, bureaucratic state was imposing its values on the west and the Midi. Peasant traditions, customs, beliefs and language were treated with contempt as savage, proof of imbecility. Agrarian entrepreneurs like Jules Rieffel opened up internal Brittany just as they were doing in North Africa. Local memory and history was suppressed or distorted. City dwellers expressed a quasi-racial contempt for

Limousins and Bretons – today Arab workers at Renault are dubbed 'brown Bretons'. Yet, with typical liberal optimism, Weber concludes that the colonial analogy is inexact. Bretons and Provençals could *become* French, and most wished to do so. The gulf in ·literacy, diet, health between 'developed' and 'underdeveloped' France narrowed, just as the gap between elite and popular culture was bridged by the development of a common national culture.

Yet, for all its Chaucerian style and breadth of example, Weber's plausible thesis must not go unchallenged. Even if one were to accept the dubious modernization model on which his argument is based, major objections to his chronology can be suggested. By concentrating his examples in regions such as inland Brittany, the central Massif and the Pyrénées, he seriously underestimates the market orientation of much peasant agriculture before 1870. Nor was the countryside really in a unlinear progression from isolated subsistence polyculture to commercial farming. The peasants of Marlhes, a hill village near St Étienne, did move towards an economy which relied on market dairy farming, supported by the wages sent back by daughters from the urban textile mills. Yet earlier in the century Marlhes had augmented its farming with outwork for the ribbon industry – just as tens of thousands of peasants had worked in woollen weaving, clog-making or charcoal iron-forges in the 'traditional' economy. Indeed it could be argued that the nineteenth-century developments made the countryside *more* rural and 'peasantized', less 'modern' if one wishes to use that terminology. For not only did rural outworkers succumb to factory competition, but many of those literate, radical culture-brokers who had provided the contacts between the peasantry and the urban world in 1848–51 – wood floaters on the Yonne, carters, bargees, blacksmiths, village shoemakers, Provençal cork and barrel-makers – were precisely the groups hit by urban competition, or by changes in transport, who quit the villages first, along with agricultural labourers, who declined from 4.5 to 3 million between 1860 and the 1900s.

Weber's political arguments are even less convincing. To reduce pre-1870 rural politics to feuds between *notable*-dominated clans and atavistic communal loyalties, family feuds and religious divisions is a serious distortion of reality. As we have argued* the

* See chapter 4.

Second Republic witnessed a genuine radicalization of certain regions. It is a strange purist definition of 'politics' which denies the political consciousness to a Midi peasant because his republican preferences are based on atavistic communal solidarities and the desire to defend his village community. If the conflicts between 'whites' and 'blues' in western villages, or between Protestants and Catholics in lower Languedoc, are denied political status one wonders how many conflicts in 'modern' western states deserve the accolade. It is surely patronizing to deny peasants political consciousness on the grounds that, inevitably and unsurprisingly, their behaviour reflected local economic grievances or because they projected local problems or village conflicts on to national political parties.

Wine taxes and forest laws had aroused as much interest in the 1840s as protectionism in the 1880s. Conflicts with local clergy in the nineteenth century were constantly accompanied by an underlying peasant fear of the return of the tithe. A real, if exaggerated, fear of 'feudalism' was a powerful political sentiment in the countryside throughout the century. Again, many of Weber's examples are drawn from departments like the Haute-Alpes or Haute-Loire, little touched by the Second Republic, where 'politics' *did* revolve round a few *notables* clans. But it is misleading to generalize so widely from such isolated areas. Inevitably many sharecroppers, tenants and day-labourers continued to comply with the political preferences of their landowners for fear of eviction. Yet such pressures existed, in the absence of a secret ballot until 1914, and were as strong in the 1900s as in the 1860s.

Weber's thesis thus requires careful qualification. It suggests a relatively smooth transition from 'traditional' to 'modern'. It underplays the real cultural shocks experienced in much of the west and the south, the highly ambivalent responses to cultural change. By emphasizing the progress of commercial agriculture it plays down the vulnerability of peasant farming to wider market forces which the Great Depression was to emphasize. By emphasizing the economic, political and cultural integration of the peasantry it obscures real class-conflict in the countryside. Wine growers in the Midi 'revolt' of 1905–7 were able to mobilize surviving elements of their regional culture in their songs and banners. The frequent use of *charivaris* against unpopular *curés* suggests that Weber may have killed them off prematurely, and, as he admits, priests were still ringing bells to ward off thunderstorms in the 1940s! Village youths still, today, use the 14 July fête as an excuse and occasion for a punch-up, much as their 'traditional' ancestors used the village fête of yesteryear. Readers of A. Sylvère's *Toinou: le cri d'un enfant auvergnat* may find in its savage autobiographical portrayal of sharecropper poverty in a world of potato soup, violence towards children, exploitation and overwork, a salutory reminder that, after decades of 'modernization', the notion that the 1900s were the *Belle Époque* would have appeared to many peasants as a sick joke.

II Agricultural Development and the Great Depression

The network of local rail-lines constructed by the republic accelerated the diffusion of market agriculture and regional specialization. Land under the plough declined in all but thirteen departments, and by 9 per cent in all between 1882 and 1912, as regions were freed from the necessity of growing their own grain. A fourfold increase in chemical fertilizer after 1890, and the advent of hybrid grains, increased grain yields by over 30 per cent. Wheat advanced at the expense of other grains. The mixing of local stock with British cattle breeds, Ayrshires and Durhams, signalled a new scientific stockbreeding in north-western France. Urban meat consumption, which rose by 50 per cent after 1890, stimulated beef production in lower Normandy and the Charolais. Refrigerated rail wagons permitted a 'milk revolution' in the Charentes, where 73,000 farmers joined cooperatives, and modern dairies emerged. Exports to northern Europe and growing urban markets fostered market-gardening in Brittany, Provence and the lower Loire, with early fruit and vegetables the speciality. Nord sugar-beet yields improved steadily while the decline in the numbers of agricultural labourers tended to boost agricultural wages and provide an incentive for mechanization. The number of reapers doubled in the 1890s.

Yet commercial farming brought difficulties and dangers as well as opportunities. Cereal monoculture was vulnerable to foreign imports. The wine sector entered long years of crisis as phylloxera devastated the Midi in the 1870s, Burgundy and the Loire in the 1880s, Champagne in the 1890s. Vineyard area fell by 25 per cent between 1879 and 1899. Attempts to combat the disease by planting in sandy soil, use of sulphuric products or submerging vines in water proved costly and met only limited success. The effective remedy, the planting of tough-rooted American vines, completed on 1 million hectares in 64 departments by 1899, was extremely expensive during a period when the value of the wine crop fell by 40 per cent in twenty years. Economists argued that the weeding-out of smaller, inefficient producers was beneficial, but such capitalist rationalization was viewed rather differently by thousands of small *vignerons,* who lived through years of agony as their precious vines were uprooted and burned and whose dreams of independence, nurtured by the post-1851 boom, were cruelly shattered. By the 1890s a new threat emerged as reviving domestic production, swelled by Algerian imports, led to a market glut and a price collapse.

The *vignerons* were not alone in their distress. Raw silk producers, already struck by pebrine in the 1850s, were swamped by Far East imports which caused a 40 per cent fall in domestic prices between 1867 and 1882. The number of silk producers fell from 170,000 to 95,000 between 1880 and 1895. Foreign competition destroyed the Midi olive oil sector, artificial dyes wrecked the market for 'garance', gas lamps caused a 90 per cent decline of the area under rape seed. Yet the Midi had no monopoly on such disasters. Rapid sea transport made France vulnerable to transatlantic grain and meat imports. Between 1870 and 1895 cereal prices fell by 27 per cent and meat prices by 20 per cent.

The socio-economic consequences of the coincidence of expanding commercial farming with agricultural depression were diverse and complex. Cheaper transport acccelerated the exodus of tens of thousands from areas such as the central Massif and Brittany, central France and the south-west to the towns, often with an intermediate stop in the local bourg. However the majority of migrants were not peasants but rural artisans, outworkers or agricultural labourers, their trades destroyed by urban and factory competition or rural mechanization. Over 60 departments showed a population decline in the decade after 1901.

The depression accentuated friction between tenants and landowners, as the former agitated for rent reductions to compensate for price decline. When the rural exodus eased demographic pressures landowners were, briefly, in a weak bargaining position. Rents fell 44 per cent in Loir-et-Cher, perhaps

30 per cent was the norm elsewhere. When crop prices recovered after 1900 tenants enjoyed a brief boom period of low rents and incomes which rose by 71 per cent in Loir-et-Cher between 1900 and 1914. With land prices falling by one-third after 1879, up to two-thirds in parts of the Midi, some large *rentiers* began to move to non-agricultural investment, or sell land to larger peasants.

The impact of the depression was selective. Mixed farming regions such as the Paris basin, involved in cereals, livestock, sugar beet and market gardening, suffered less than monoculture areas. Quality wine regions like the Bordelais suffered less from the wine-price collapse than did the *vin ordinaire* regions of the Midi. As some marginal peasants were expropriated, and some *rentiers* quit the land, the beneficiaries included larger peasants in some areas, big estates in others. Village monographs show the great diversity of adaptation by local communities. In Pont-de-Montvert and Lourmarin in the south the emphasis was on rural exodus and demographic decline. In the hills near St Étienne the village of Marlhes adapted to the collapse of rural outwork for the ribbon industry by sending sons and daughters to work in urban mills, from which they sent home part of their wages, while larger peasants changed to commercial dairy farming. Yet even so the population fell by 25 per cent between 1861 and 1911. Ackerman's study of Bonnières-sur-Seine, to the north of Paris, shows a community which actually expanded under the shrewd control of the Michaux family, which acquired the estates of the Duchesse de Berry, turned them over to commercial dairy farming and established a small distillery and glue factory in the village, which attracted docile Breton migrants.

The instinctive response to the decline of cereal prices was the demand for tariff protection, orchestrated by a powerful alliance of northern capitalist landowners, western aristocrats and large peasant farmers. They emphasized France's inability to cope with falling Atlantic freight rates, competition from cheap labour economies such as Russia or with growing foreign protectionism. The results of the 1892 tariff were, at best, ambivalent. Imports fell 13 per cent in the 1886–96 decade, but exports fell 27 per cent, while exporters like Champagne wine growers and market gardeners lamented the demise of free trade. However the cereal lobby was too powerful to be swayed by economists who urged the remedy of cheaper French production costs, or by urban consumers who resented higher bread prices.

Republican governments offered peasant agriculture little real aid beyond tariff protection and agricultural merit awards. Applied science and agricultural training received low priority. A belated *Service des Améliorations* (1903), designed to assist technological change, boasted a mere 50 engineers in 1914. *Syndicats Agricoles*, presided over by republican *notables*, did offer bulk purchase of grain and fertilizer, though their role was partly political – an effort to match attempts by Catholic-royalist elites to revive their influence by organizing peasant agriculture. After 1898 there was some tentative state aid for rural credit and, as Y. Renauldo shows for the Var, *Crédit Agricole* institutions were beginning to supersede the ubiquitous 'usurer' as the providers of rural credit by the 1900s, as the rural bourgeoisie switched its investment into stocks and shares and away from money-lending.

The balance sheet of French agriculture after 1870 is, thus, rather ambivalent. Optimists could emphasize higher labour unit productivity, selective breeding, use of fertilizer and machinery. Hubschner calculates a 40 per cent rise in grain yield in the Pas-de-Calais between 1860 and 1914, due to the capital investment and fertilizer. Labour-intensive toil increased peasant yields in overpopulated Brittany. Critics argued that the pre-1875 boom years induced a sense of false security as prices rose and social and demographic tensions and pressures eased. World competition then exposed underlying structural weaknesses. Forty-eight per cent of farms in 1906 had no hired labour. Small peasants lacked capital and used any profits to buy more land. Yet large owners must share the responsibility for sluggish performance. 2.5 per cent of owners in the 1880s held 46 per cent of the land; 16 per cent of French farms covered two-thirds of the area. But landowners invested too much in state bonds or conspicuous consumption, too little in agriculture. Even the Nord sugar-beet sector had yields one-third below its German counterpart.

III Education in the Countryside: 'Progress' or Cultural Genocide?

The classic account of the impact of the school on a village community remains R. Thabault's *Mon Village* (1944). Here the school, founded after the 1833 Guizot act, remained poorly attended until the advent of the railway in the 1860s permitted the shift from subsistence polyculture to commercial dairy farming and, needing to keep accounts, peasant parents came to value literacy. The emergence of white collar jobs as rail-clerks, postmen or minor bureaucrats raised hopes of social promotion into the tertiary sector for literate peasant sons. Fatalism and routine were broken. Teachers, once marginal figures subordinate to the *curé*, assumed a new prestige. Adults attended evening classes, and newly literate peasants entered the municipal council, eroding the hold of the royalist *notables* on village politics. The advent of grocers' and butchers' shops symbolized a new prosperity. Republicans established a milk cooperative and resisted 'useless' expenditure on the church as religious practice declined.

An optimistic interpretation of the Third Republic might see this as a microcosm of 'progress' in the late nineteenth-century countryside. The 120,000 laic teachers of 1914 were the black hussars, the secular apostles, of a regime epitomizing prosperity, educational opportunity, upward mobility. The republic, by consolidating the promise of 1789, made further change unnecessary. A republican version of French history was disseminated in textbooks, songs, statues and essay competitions. The fertility of the soil was ascribed to France's happy geography and her industrious people, not to God. Teaching was in French, not patois. 14 July became *the* village fête.

Yet these stereotypes need careful qualification. Teachers were less respected in the alpine hills than in the valley, in the Vendéen *bocage* than in the plains, in the Breton interior than on the coast. In Catholic areas they were often boycotted and harassed. The novel *Jean Coste* (1905) presents an image of stark poverty. A teacher with fourteen years' experience earned barely four francs per day, half the rate of a Paris printer. Many lived in a social no-man's-land, too educated to mix with the peasantry, too poor to mix with the republican elite of doctors and lawyers. Many lived solitary lives. Yet they had state support. The Ferry laws meant less *curé* interference, improved buildings, the right to teach civic morality not catechism, evolution not creation. Pupils no longer quit the school *en masse* in the summer. Teachers' training colleges imbued a sense of mission. By 1884, 25,000 of them were town clerks, a post which provided additional income and the chance to dispense legal or taxation advice, to act as intermediaries between peasants and the state. Fewer were quitting the profession.

The press image of bitter feuds with the clergy was no mere fabrication. Many teachers, it is true, remained Catholic or, if freethinkers, compromised by undergoing Catholic marriage ceremonies to appease parents-in-law or local opinion. Few acted as militant agents of atheism in Catholic areas. Yet many were offspring of republican peasants and village artisans, entered the *École Normale* rather than the seminary precisely because their parents resisted *curé* pressure. There was a deep professional recollection of the arrogant domineering behaviour of the clergy towards them in the 1860s. Social life in many villages was polarized between rival Catholic and republican cafés, sports groups, mutual aid societies. In Poitou, it was said that only the unity of the fire brigade prevented there being Catholic and laic fires. Many were pilloried by local clerical newspapers for teaching evolution or suggesting that Joan of Arc may have imagined her voices. Many became freemasons, some merely to placate republican *notables* whose patronage facilitated successful careers.

If the far left accused the teachers of being agents of mindless patriotic mass conformism, conservatives expressed alarm that such *déraciné* socialists should be spreading pacifism and birth control. Some rural teachers were in the *SFIO*, and their union did flirt with antimilitarism. Yet many teachers rejected even the idea of a trade union. One old left-wing teacher, interviewed in the 1960s, confessed that till 1914 he had accepted the textbook myth of a progressive humanitarian French colonialism. 'Perhaps I was naive,' he added, sadly. In 1914–18 one-quarter of the 35,000 mobilized teachers died 'for the *patrie*'; their letters from the front breathe an idealistic patriotism. The link between the teachers and socialist pacifism was largely an interwar phenomenon.

The gains and cultural losses of educational 'modernization' are most graphically illustrated by the Breton example. Here the power of old aristocracy and clergy had survived virtually unchallenged till 1870, with the region's bourgeoisie frequently aping the old elites. The influence of the rural clergy was buttressed by their role as defenders of local superstititions. Berger portrays a Finistère countryside of stony soil, hills, wind and rain. Hedges and ditches impeded internal communication, roads served the few ports. The department was remote from the main trade routes, the habitat scattered, birth rates were high, the supply of doctors 60 per cent below the national average.

The transport revolution saw surplus population migrate to work in Paris, St Nazaire and Brest. Real, if limited, agricultural changes included more fertilizer, less fallow land, increased yields and market-livestock rearing. Family farms were consolidated as younger sons migrated to the cities.

Laic teachers proceeded with discretion in a hostile environment, avoided explicit republican propaganda, yet gradually came to guide local opinion, to play a key role as 'universal secretary, disinterested arbiter, economic expert, obligatory, free and laic counsellor, the walking repertory of all knowledge' (Singer). They acted as mayors' secretaries, wrote letters, interpreted mortgages, gave tax advice, surveyed land, introduced fertilizers. They established cooperatives to purchase seed, utilized solidarist rhetoric. They became impresarios, organized lantern slide shows and rail trips, ran shooting and cycling clubs. They wooed Breton peasants less by abstract republican ideology than by practical expertise, through actions not words. Their pupils' exam diplomas and speech-day prizes became a source of parental pride – even to many reluctant 'whites'. Manipulating a carefully cultivated image – black suit, cropped hair, polished shoes – they became uncrowned village kings.

In consequence illiteracy had receded to below 10 per cent among adolescents in all western departments by 1900, although still 29 per cent among adults in Morbihan. The notorious St Malo-Geneva line, below which literacy had traditionally been weak, faded. The hitherto enormous gulf between east Breton and Normandy literacy was closed, as Désert shows. Illiteracy had, it is true, already fallen from 67 per cent to 38 per cent in Finistère between 1840 and 1870, but the attempts of recent *Annaliste* historians to deny all connection between bourgeois-republican political control, education policy and growing school attendance remain unconvincing. An 'army of Breton mothers' were seduced by the vision of prestigious white-collar jobs for their sons. Catholic *notables* found their political influence restricted, as Siegfried found in Finistère, to their own tenants. Education eased the problems of rural-urban migration and calmed the endemic violence of village populations, though in *The Horse of Pride* Hélias notes that his parents' wedding, on the eve of the Great War, was accompanied by the traditional intervillage brawl.

As ever, progress had its price. Though Hélias's family were staunch republicans who welcomed the advent of education, his book is a lament for a dying world – and the success of the book in the 1970s an illustration of the powerful atavistic appeal of that message to thousands of ex-peasants condemned to live in the featureless suburbs of modern French cities. The poverty and superstitious credulity of the old culture are not denied. Peasants wore the same hemp shirt for months on end, lived eight to a room, their lives a constant struggle against the 'World Bitch'. The bulk of the land was owned by an absentee bourgeois in Quimper. The *curé*, the 'lord priest', was feared as a sorcerer with magic books, capable of casting spells. He still collected tithes, tried to forbid dances. Disease was combated by pilgrimage to holy fountains and by folk medicine, doctors only called to certify death. There was a neo-pagan cult of death, portrayed as a skeleton with a scythe, an obsession with cemeteries, a fear of bogeymen. Youth culture was marked by intervillage violence.

'Progress' came. Linen shirts replaced stiff hemp, super-phosphates raised crop yields. Parents and grandparents viewed the children's education prowess with pride, as the key to 'bread and meat every day'. With the French language one could 'go anywhere', while Breton tied you 'on a short rope, like a cow to its post. You have to go round your tether – and the meadow grass is never plentiful.' The laic school was the 'real seat' of the republic, and only the tenants of royalist landowners, with their tied cottages, continued to frequent the church school. The daughters of republican peasants, with the advantage of secular schooling, began to aspire to jobs with the post office or as schoolteachers. Hélias's father was almost provoked to physical assault on the priest who tried to pressure his wife to remove children from the laic school. The older generation welcomed the children's command of the French language as a symbol of emancipation, evidence that local urban traders could no longer scorn them as 'dung-covered nitwits'.

Yet Hélias persuasively argues that much was lost in this process. He portrays with warm affection his grandfather who, like the old man in Olmi's classic film *Tree of Wooden Clogs* set in the Italian countryside of the 1890s, brings up the small children and passes on the accumulated capsules of wisdom of the old culture, tells stories, gives moral lessons and practical ones: 'pee with the wind and shit with your face into it.' The grandfather told him, 'listen to your schoolmasters, who are much more learned than I am.' Of that Hélias remained unconvinced. He evokes the mutual aid of the villagers, the way poor peasants cooperated to clear land, the collective grief at death as church bells tolled and messengers were sent to inform those working in the fields. The grandfather fainted with grief when his wife died – a striking refutation of those modernization theorists who inform us that there was no affection in 'traditional' pre-capitalist families.

Within the schools the Breton language was condemned as 'vicious', pupils humiliated and punished for daring to use Breton phrases. Breton conscripts were treated as *plouks* (country hicks) by NCOs. Military service may have integrated Bretons into national life, as with the Sardinian peasant in the Italian film *Padre Padrone*, yet its brutality could provoke the first stirrings of protest, though Breton nationalism remained, till 1914, the preserve of threatened local elites clinging to their hierarchic rural society and fragmented between Francophobes and Breton-speakers. The linguistic revolution was a cultural shock for a generation which lost control of its native language while failing to master French accurately. French was rational, gave access to a sense of chronology, abstract and general concepts. Yet it was cold, lacked the evocative colour of Breton. Peasants were conditioned to accept prepackaged urban bourgeois values with little scope for criticism. To suggest that such peasants were experiencing a certain cultural deprivation, as old songs, dances, poems, proverbs and fêtes died away, is not necessarily to be guilty of selective romantic nostalgia. Breton peasants were very imperfectly integrated into a political system which showed little concern with their problems.

In 1901 Daniel Halévy voiced a lament for the old ways. 'In other ages there was a popular culture. The humblest serfs knew the myths of this faith. Traditions initiated him to the beauty of nature. The sun reminded the peasant of a thousand stories. But to our contemporaries it means nothing. The symbolic spirit declines steadily. The last rural storytellers are dying out. Stripped of religion, of poetry, what does the man of the people have left to him?' At worst there appeared a cultural void in villages, which school and newspapers could not fill. The dynamic young left, communal life collapsed, families turned in on themselves. Through school and army, peasants were being 'standardized', taught French and a particular version of French history, programmed to pay taxes and accept conscription and, as 1914 showed, to march obediently to war. Yet the recent resurgence of peripheral regionalist protest in southern and western France suggests that, if few really wished to return to the old peasant world, many felt deeply a sense of a lost culture and community. Sadly the two departed together. Such sentiments were dismissed by the Third Republic spokesmen as 'reactionary', and obviously they were voiced by local *curés* and rightist literacy figures like René Bazin. Yet they could be shared by Eugène le Roy, the Périgord regionalist writer, a 'Jacobin', a man of the 'left', whose novels reflect both the deep-seated populist hatred of 'feudalism' and oppression of the Dordogne countryside, yet a sadness at the decline of the old folkways and patois, an acute sense of loss as the cultural colonialism of the bourgeois republic triumphed. It is no accident that Thabault conceived the idea of his book after working for the French education service attempting to spread French schooling among the reluctant Arabs of the north African deserts.

IV Rural Anticlericalism

Across the nineteenth century conflicts between villagers and their priests undoubtedly played a key role in establishing the link between local issues and national politics in peasant consciousness. This did not, as Weber claims, begin mysteriously in the 1860–70s. After 1876 anticlerical republicans consistently won electoral victories in a still predominantly rural France. The classic battle between *curé* and the mayor-teacher duo, immortalized in *Clochemerle*, lay at the heart of village politics. The map of religious practice remained enormously diverse. Catholicism retained its traditional bastions on the west and the central Massif and Flanders, yet even Breton practice suffered from the impact of the opening of its economy through urban migration and the patronage power of the republican state. A growing stain of de-Christanization spread out from the Paris basin, the Limousin and Languedoc-Provence, although great contrasts persisted, or emerged, within individual dioceses. In the Tarn the wine growers of Gaillac and the Gresigne woodcutters were anticlerical, whereas the villages of the Castres mountains and the sharecroppers of the large southern estates remained staunchly practising. In lower

Languedoc the coastal wine plains contrasted sharply with the high practice of the uplands, marked by high vocation rates, short baptismal delays and the prevalence of processions to pray for rain. Religiosity was actually stronger in towns like Montpellier or Narbonne than in the surrounding countryside.

It should be emphasized that political anticlericalism became more widespread than 'de-Christianization'. In Normandy, the Vosges, the Tarn high overall religious practice coexisted with republican voting. Faury argues that the Tarn peasantry showed little sympathy with the bourgeois or working-class militant atheism of *Libre Pensée* societies, which flourished in Albi and Carmaux. Yet by 1881 republicans won parliamentary seats with peasant votes from the Vaurois, where religious practice remained high, a symptom of the rejection of clerical control of communal life, personal morality, and education by a still 'Catholic' peasantry.

Local conflicts frequently stemmed from clerical interference in municipal administration. Such anticlericalism reflected grass-roots desire for local autonomy rather than 'modernization' or diffusion of ideas from urban culture-brokers. Republicanism grew out of the resistance of village democracy to *notables*, prefects and clergy. After the 1851 coup, buoyant priests assumed the right to dominate villages and control welfare provision. The 1860s saw an epidemic of clashes over expenditure priorities within villages, with peasants rallying to their elected municipalities, against clerical meddling. During the Second Empire this was the one form of politics tolerated by the regime. Between 1852 and 1875 one-third of villages in Vendômois (Loir-et-Cher) witnessed such clashes, one-sixth had municipal resignations in protest at clerical or prefectoral interference. Municipal councillors came to feel that laic teachers were better qualified than religious orders, laic education more 'useful' – but also that *they* could control the laic school whereas a Catholic school was dominated by the *curé*. Feeling inadequate in the face of ceaseless taunting from rural petty-bourgeois rivals such as vets, chemists, teachers, clergy lashed out at their tormentors. Marcilhacy emphasizes that seminary education left most village priests ill-equipped to counter the scepticism of their local critics. One Vendômois *curé* complained that the mayor served the interests of hell, spoke of the Virgin Mary as a whore and claimed the sun as his father, the earth as his mother. The imposition of mayors on reluctant villages during the Moral Order years intensified bitterness. After 1876 municipalities took their ritual revenge, asserted their right to ring church bells to signify republican victories or, as in one Isère village, ceremoniously removed crucifixes from school walls and hurled them down the school lavatory!

The clergy's royalism fuelled peasant hostility. Gambetta's electoral trump card was the threat that a triumphant clericalism would restore the ancien régime and the tithes. Indeed the persistence of tithe collection, under a variety of pseudonyms, in a number of regions gave plausibility to such fears and accentuated peasant distaste for 'excessive' clerical fees for the rites of passage and for masses. Around Saintes the church bells were said to toll *'Donne! Donne! Donne!'* ('Give! Give! Give!')

Many bishops encouraged prolonged resistance to the Ferry laws. In 1881 26 priests from the Montpellier diocese alone were accused of royalist electoral 'excesses' – and Mgr de Cabriènes actually promoted a *curé* jailed for election violence to a cathedral chapter post. One-third of his diocesan Catholic committee were nobles, who attempted to manipulate charity to exert royalist electoral pressure. 'Should we help our opponents?' one asked. 'Our peasants would not understand. Our fund receives money only from the supporters of Order and Religion. Let us not invoke the great word Charity. The Scriptural maxim of giving back a good deed for an insult is not applicable in these present times.' In the Tarn there were 86 village conflicts over laic textbooks, with 50 priests suspended for publicly burning books or denying first communion to laic pupils. In Orleans Mgr Dupanloup's royalist activities, and his rejection of peasant aspirations for political, social or economic emancipation as 'hedonism', meant that his three decades of hard work, which included meticulous diocesan enquiries into religious attitudes, came to nothing. Religious practice obstinately failed to rise, his diocese became a 'terrifying burden' to him as the peasantry of the Loire valley, the Beauce and Montargis voted anticlerical vets and café owners on to muncipal councils. In the Limousin, deeply shocked by the deaths of hundreds of migrant building-workers in the commune, the rhetoric of Moral Order was distasteful and caused a major slump in already mediocre church attendance. Many Midi clergymen became defenders of local patois against French, 'the language of Voltaire'. The benefits gained from this were doubtful – for many peasants now viewed French as the language of emancipation, patois the symbol of their old inferiority.

Clerical puritanism, and a more scrupulous Catholic orthodoxy, continued to inspire further conflicts. Rural religion had always been bound up with the peasantry's sense of powerlessness before natural disasters. The spread of science undermined the priest's traditional role. Chemicals not crosses drove rats from the barn, quinine not St Viatre cured the malaria of the Sologne swamps, artificial fertilizer boosted crop yields. However an odd mixture of latent anticlericalism with ignorance and superstition frequently survived. Cholera in lower Languedoc boosted veneration of St Roch. Phylloxera was a 'great missionary' (d'Alzon), producing an ephemeral religious revival in the Midi, causing the Virgin Mary to quit her usual mountain bastions in the Pyrénées to appear to a Hérault coastal wine grower in the 1870s! Southern radicals were not immune to religious atavisms. One of Hugo's characters was 'of that race who wear a red bonnet . . . make complicated 'Spanish' signs of the cross, kneel down to blaspheme and call on their patron saint with threats: "Great Saint, give me what I want or I'll throw a stone at your head!"'* Yet by cutting themselves off from 'pagan superstitions', ceasing to ring church bells against thunderstorms, expressing unease when Bourbonnais peasant girls rubbed themselves against the private parts of St Grélichon to guarantee fertility, or expressing doubt on the efficacy of holy fountains, the clergy failed to appease village Voltaireans while abandoning traditional functions which alone made them appear useful even to anticlerical peasants. In Weber's metaphor, while pruning the tree of religion, they sawed off the branch on which they were sitting!

Nineteenth century seminary training appears to have produced a more puritanical clergy. By denouncing the drunken revelry of *pénitent* groups and attempting to replace riotous traditional religious celebrations with the decorous cult of the Virgin Mary, austere northern bishops in Midi dioceses unwittingly 'feminized' religion. In Condes (Tarn), where the *curé* boycotted the procession to the Holy Crucifix in disapproval of the unruliness of the ensuing fête, the republican municipality organized the procession without him, complete with 'republican liturgy'!

---

* An old peasant woman in *La Terre* greets a storm by shaking her fist at the sky and shouting, 'Sacred Pig up there in Heaven! Can't you bloody well leave us in peace!'

'Suggestive' new dances like the waltz intensified the crusade against dancing. Over 10 per cent of *curés* in the Albi diocesan enquiry of 1901 denounced 'pagan' wedding dances, mixed-sex dancing in *veillées* and the spread of weekend *bals* in the rural bourgs. Polkas were 'truly satanic', waltzes 'excited the passions', so sacraments were denied to dancers and musicians alike. Père Marie-Antoine's widely used *Textbook of Piety* insisted that women's role was to 'pray, work, keep quiet and suffer', not to dance in low-cut dresses. Peasants viewed dancing as the natural prelude to courtship – and certainly more 'moral' than the dubious discussions on birth control which priests had with young women in the confessional. Anticlericalism involved a good deal of male chauvinist machismo, jealousy at the access of priests to women's confidences, derision at the sexual oddities of celibate clergy. The suggestion in Zola's *Fault of the Abbé Mouret*, that clerical celibacy produced unnatural repression and sexual hallucination was widely believed by republicans. Yet, at least, anticlericals were not puritanical killjoys. It was the *curés'* role as 'resident and interfering Mrs Grundies' (Weber) which pushed Catholic areas of the Tarn into the arms of the republic.

Such conflicts grew into a dialogue of the deaf. Anticlericals portrayed the clergy as puritanical yet salacious authoritarians attempting to dominate villages, uncharitable in refusing burial to suicides, royalists trying to restore the ancien régime, obscurantists blocking the spread of education, traitors subordinating France to Rome. Behind this was the emphasis that they should stick to their job, narrowly defined as saying Mass. Yet the most liberal of clergy could not accept such marginalization, insisted on the right to play a role in education and social life.

In the lower Languedoc wine plains, with their market bourgs, cafés, brothels, Sunday work on the capitalist estates, and boom-slump cash economy, militant anticlerical 'practice' appeared in the countryside. The clergy were tied closely to a declining legitimist aristocracy, weakened by Gallican-ultramontane feuds and practice often fell below 10 per cent. In Caisses-et-Veyrac no man attended Mass afer 1845. Vocation rates in the Biterrois fell by nearly 90 per cent after 1846. Victorious republican municipalities took revenge, after 1877, for the 1851 repression by banning church processions, de-baptizing streets. Secular education petitions received signatures, vets presided at republican civil funerals, meat was eaten at ostentatious Good Friday banquets. In contrast to the Tarn, laic funerals spread to the peasantry. One child was 'baptized' Lucifer Blanqui Vercingetorix! The birth rate fell to below half that of neighbouring Lozère, mountainous and still Catholic. Bishops' pastoral visits were greeted with *charivaris*. A local saying claimed that 'if our Saviour returned to earth, it is the people of the Biterrois who would crucify him again'. The clergy saw their countryside 'perverted' by the anticlerical *Petit Meridonal*, by café owners, republican state employees and by teachers. Some clergy attempted to defend the *langue d'oc* as a last-ditch barrier to the Voltairean tide. Whether laic teachers were a major force in spreading anticlericalism is debatable. Cholvy argues that in the Languedoc uplands they attempted no frontal assault on religion and sought a *modus vivendi* with clergy and populations in a still-Catholic area. Yet undoubtedly, as a body, teachers had bitter memories of the years of humiliating subordination to the clergy during the *Loi Falloux*, were on the offensive in the battle for village prestige – and may have helped disseminate through the schools the leftist myth of medieval Albigensianism as the true religion of Languedoc until persecuted by the church and its northern royalist allies.

In parts of central France such as the Yonne, or the middle-Loire valley, anticlericalism came to be the distinguishing feature of a rural republicanism from which the 'socialist' tinge of 1848–51 had been exorcized. Such areas were on 'the left' in 1848 and 1869, but drifted to the centre by 1900. What then differentiated the politics of the Blésois or the Gâtinais from areas further west like Anjou was, precisely, religious practice, which was at least four times higher in the latter. In terms of literacy or land-holding patterns the Blésois and Anjou were very similar. But the former had a 'blue' republican tradition as a part of its consciousness, passed on by family tradition, expressed in loyalty to the laic school. Vocations were low. Howling mobs of schoolchildren pursued village *curés*, the 'black crows', making crowing noises! Conversely Anjou expressed its fidelity to its past by high religious practice and support for Catholic schools. In the Midi, however, hit by the wine crisis, republicans attempted to use anticlericalism as a 'revolution on the cheap', to divert peasant protest away from socio-economic issues.

Mesliand's analysis of the Vaucluse bourg of Pertuis presents a graphic local study of this phenomenon. Pertuis participated in the

1851 insurrection, deeply resented its imposed clerical-Bonapartist mayor. In the 1870s national politics found their local expression in the battle for a girls' laic school. As the republic triumphed, *Marianne*'s bust replaced Jesus in the courthouse, civil funerals spread, church processions were banned. By being the party of anticlericalism in a bourg where barely ten men in a population of 5000 attended Mass, Radicalism delayed any swing to the left which the wine crisis might have produced. Fifty per cent of marriages were civil, 20 per cent of children unbaptized. When the socialist party finally grew in the 1900s, winning 23 per cent of the poll and championing peasant cooperatives, it was forced to play the anticlerical card, denouncing the Radicals for excessive leniency towards the church after the separation and excessive tolerance towards church processions.

V Class Conflict in the Countryside?

The 'modernization' of rural France was not a process of conflict-free peaceful economic and cultural change. Issues of national politics, such as religion, education, conscription, tariffs and taxation, affected peasant electors. As Tony Judt warns, it is absurd to view the 'real' history of the French countryside as a chronicle of love, festival and death with political conflict excluded, equally misleading to portray rural France as an homogeneous unity with common interests to defend against an alien or urban world. Class conflict, open or latent, persisted in the countryside. By 1914 eight of the twelve departments which gave more than 20 per cent of their votes to the *SFIO* were rural. There was much continuity here with areas of *Dem-Soc* penetration in 1848–51, though mountain departments like the Ariège had drifted to the right as the young emigrated, and central departments like the Loiret or the Yonne were now middle-of-the-road, republican and anticlerical. Rural protest took a variety of forms, ranging from the strikes and syndicalism of woodmen and day labourers, through the demands of sharecroppers for improved lease-terms, to cooperative ventures of small peasant properietors. These grievances were, belatedly, espoused by socialists in the 1890s and enshrined in their party programmes.

A number of general factors encouraged rural socialism. As in the 1840s, agrarian depression had followed a period of relative prosperity and rising expectations, facing peasants who had acquired land before 1875 with crop failures, falling prices and indebtedness. Traditions of temporary migration facilitated the transmission of urban ideology to the countryside. The Limousin countryside, whose building-worker migrants had been killed in the Commune, showed little sympathy for the conservative republic. The socialism of Carmaux miners influenced the Tarn peasantry from which they were recruited just as Montluçon industrial militancy may have spilled into the Allier countryside – though it is possible that in Languedoc hitherto quiescent Catholic miners may have been radicalized by the example of local *vignerons*. Possibly the role of village artisans as culture-brokers declined. Barrel-makers, cork-workers and shoemakers, the cadres of Var militancy in 1851, were fast disappearing in the changing Provençal economy of the 1880s, although Judt may underestimate their role in the revival of leftist politics. Villages were becoming 'peasantized', yet still succeeded in generating a militant response to agrarian crisis. As single-class communities they confronted adversity with some degree of solidarity. Provençal wine growers felt exploited by middlemen, wine merchants, governmental tax and tariff policies which trapped them in a subordinate position in the market-economy. The credit situation as Rinaudo shows, had eased during the wine boom, but the phylloxera crisis made 'usury' an issue again. Twenty-six per cent of the wealth in Var inheritances above 20,000 francs came, in 1900, from money-lending. Families like the Trucs of les Arcis built up extensive vineyards on the large profits from usury. In lower Languedoc, R. Pech estimates, 15 per cent of the income of the bourgeoisie in wine areas came from this source.

Politics and economics became interlinked in the villages. Men who ran wine cooperatives sat on municipal councils, which in turn supervised communal fertilizer purchases. Unable to use the strike weapon, such threatened petty producers were less tempted into 'economism' than urban workers, and were forced to seek political solutions to their problems. The left tended to do best in areas of low religious practice, but where, as in the Var, de-Christianization was a 'fact' and where religion had ceased to be the focus of local conflict. As in 1849 there seems little simple correlation between the rural left and literacy levels, while its success in the Morvan hills, or the scattered Allier hamlets, cast doubt on any firm generalizations about its necessary connection with regions of concentrated habitat.

Lumbermen played a key vanguard role in central France. Forests had always provided a refuge for social rebels, poachers, deserters, and been a symbol of a certain independence to sedentary peasants. Lumbermen had traditions of solidarity, of fixing wages collectively in work-teams, which provided a foundation for trade unionism. Rail-building had fostered a boom, but the late nineteenth century saw coal ousting wood fuel, shipbuilding switch to iron-steel for construction, growing Norwegian imports and the labour pool swell with peasants seeking lumber work to offset falling crop prices. Wage rates fell and employers attempted to erode 'customary rights' of workers to a proportion of wood for their own use. A wave of strikes in the Cher won successes, and a trade union claimed 6000 members by 1892, before employers' use of blacklegs, and police arrests of militants broke the initial momentum. A second upsurge in 1899, coordinated by the Bourges *Bourse de Travail*, secured the application of accident compensation laws to forestworkers. By 1914 their National Federation claimed 170 branches in fifteen departments, enforced a closed shop and envisaged nationalization of forests under workers' control. Conservatives denounced 'union tyranny' in central France, as lumbermen's militancy spread socialism in the Cher, Allier and the Nièvre.

Among those influenced by their example were the Allier sharecroppers, a group hitherto maintained in a position of a deferential subordination to absentee landowners and rapacious estate managers – *fermiers-généraux*. The evolution of share-cropper consciousness was accelerated by economic change, as the railways brought market contacts and cash-crop production. Some sharecropper sons were tempted to migrate away from their extended family, increasing reliance on expensive wage-labour. Faced with falling crop prices, owners shortened leases and increased rents, accentuating old fears of eviction at St Martin (11 November). Cash-crop farming exposed sharecroppers to market fluctuations, while the lumbermen's militancy provided local evidence of the potential of unionization. By 1900 their *Fédération des Travailleurs de la Terre* (*FTT*) which grew to 1800 members, was agitating for longer leases, compensation for farm improvements, and the abolition of the arbitrary *impôt colonique*. The indifference of local Radicals pushed them towards the *SFIO*, which championed their cause in parliament.

This belated awakening of precarious militancy was evoked in the novels of Guillaumin, himself an Allier sharecropper. Hitherto rural novels had oscillated between the rustic idylls of Georges Sand, and portraits of peasants as coarse, greedy savages in Balzac or Zola. Eugene Le Roy's novels of the Périgord countryside had mixed an interest in local folklore custom with an awareness of class conflict but Le Roy was a romantic 'Jacobin' whose concentration on quaint patois vocabulary and melodramatic acts of rural revolt could not disguise his lack of experience of the real world of peasant toil. By contrast Guillaumin saw class conflict in the countryside as real, yet usually latent, marked by the occasional refusal or strategem. His *Vie d'un Simple* is a slow saga of grinding toil, poverty, small problems, minor conflicts. He rejected fascination with patois and folklore as urban outsiders' obsession with the quaint and the picturesque. Bad weather or the death of a horse are disasters in his world. The toil of the sharecropper causes him to resent the *fermiers-généraux* as parasites. Inability to speak proper French is a source of growing humiliation, as bourgeois children mock the peasants' patois. Marriage is neither a Rousseauesque idyll nor Zola's animal coupling, but a matter of economic necessity. Women are silent, sullen, fatalistic, impassive – yet capable of tenderness to a sick child or tears at the departure of a son to the army. Poverty makes sharecroppers harsh to the unproductive old. Economic subordination forces them into deference to the *fermier-général* – wives do laundry for him, cheese and poultry have to be supplied, caps have to be tipped to '*not*' maitre'.

Guillaumin's personal experience as an activist in the *FTT*, adviser to its leader Martin Bernard, and secretary to its newspaper *Travailleur Rural*, gave him the material for a second novel, *Le Syndicat de Bougignoux* a 'miniature rural *Germinal*,' written with careful restrained passion. The hero's father retains 'no tenderness for the past' of 'emptiness in the pit of one's stomach' and appreciates a present which offers bacon soup, white bread and occasional wine. He rejoices in the chance to send his son to school. A lifelong republican, he subscribes to a republican paper despite his own illiteracy. In this sense there is progress in the countryside. Yet the relative position of the peasantry has changed little. After three decades of the republic, one sharecropper remarks, 'we are still treated as dogs.' The dream that the republic would mean a new world has not been realized. Local Radical politicians are viewed with increasing cynicism. The radical doctor in *Vie* is a 'red' who grows paler with the years, apes the tastes of aristocrats he professes to despise, ignores his peasant patients, and is a harsh landlord. Trochu, the local mayor is a republican wine merchant, enriched by the spread of wine-drinking. He courts popularity by writing letters for peasants and allowing them time to repay bills. Yet his children go to Catholic colleges, one marries an industrialist, and he buys up aristocratic estates. His prefectoral contacts ensure that the railway goes through his bourg, to the benefit of local traders and hotel owners. His response to the hero's announcement of the formation of the trade union is one of outrage. Beneath the town-hall bust of *Marianne* he claims that 'no one is a slave today', contracts are freely entered into, anyone dissatisfied is free to seek work elsewhere. 'I am a worker, too, am I not?'

The hero's revolt stems from his father's republicanism, his own literacy and widening of horizons through military service, and daily experience in a village where two owners control two-thirds of the land and sharecroppers, after paying the *impôt colonique* for their home and garden are left with barely one-quarter of their harvest crop. One habitually deferential sharecropper is evicted for daring to protest 'we are not in the army', when reprimanded because a bourgeois hunter has tripped over an obstacle on his land. Contact with a lumbermen's trade union inspires the founding of the sharecroppers' organization and the hero writes a propaganda brochure recounting the history of centuries of feudal oppression and denouncing the *fermier-général* as the new seigneur; an interesting example, *pace* Weber, of the way in which the peasantry's collective memory could be tapped for 'modern' political mobilization. Better lease terms are demanded, and fertilizer and wine co-ops established. Yet the venture is precarious. The father is alarmed at his son's move from verbal protest to action. The hero's wife, from a pious Catholic family, resents the time wasted on the union. Literate local branch organizers prove scarce. Habits of deference run deep – one union member crawls to local *notables* by reminiscing about the 'good old days' when seigneurs whipped their serfs. A local Catholic paternalist sets up a rival 'mixed' *Syndicat Agricole*, uniting owners and sharecroppers. The rightist press portrays the hero as an ambitious half-educated *déraciné*, undercutting local traders by dumping 'Jewish' produce in his cooperative store. Middle-class students disturb his farming in their search for thesis topics. The union is wracked by divisions between sharecroppers and day-labourers, and between those, like the hero, who favour a gradualist syndicalism based on cooperatives and self-education, and militants who flirt with revolutionary syndicalist direct action. After an abortive day of action the hero resigns, to return to life on his plateau farm, a wife who accepts his evening reading as an inoffensive distraction, and utopian dreams of a future where the local château will be a clinic and old people's home, agricultural machinery will relieve peasant toil, and village assemblies will make local decisions. The peasants have been mobilized sufficiently to vote socialist and displace mayor Trochu, but the trade union collapses.

It would be wrong to see Guillaumin as 'typical'. One letter to the *Travailleur Rural* warned him that 'though a peasant, you don't know how to speak to peasants. You make them mistrustful by speaking of solidarity, raising of the moral level. All this means nothing to the young peasants round here.' Yet his study group at Ygrande did attract hundreds. The sharecroppers were not necessarily the most militant group in the Allier. Their farms were large – in 1920 they made up 20 per cent of the rural population, yet farmed 50 per cent of the land. Their social position as employers of wage-labour was ambivalent, and led to some suspicion from other trade unions. Though by 1914 Allier had the highest percentage of socialist voters in France, many of these were lumbermen and peasant proprietors. Sharecroppers were always limited by fear of eviction, the difficulty of a 'strike' which could harm their own livestock, and by the dispersed habitat of north Allier which made organization difficult. The *FTT* collapsed in 1912. Sharecropping could also, despite its critics, prove an economically efficient combination of capitalist investment and peasant inolvement. Productivity could be high – and prices and profits rose after 1900.

In general sharecropping regions were not on the left. In the Var it was the low percentage of tenants and sharecroppers, (18 per cent in contrast to a national average of 38 per cent), which made peasants less open to landowner pressure and permitted the emergence of one of the *SFIO*'s rural bastions. Tenant areas of the

Var tended to remain conservative. By 1902 the Var had four socialist deputies, by 1914 giving over one-third of its votes to the *SFIO*. The nature of this 'socialism' has been much debated. Judt denies the standard claim that it was an amorphous, undoctrinal, reheated Radicalism. Peasants took more notice of the contrast between socialism and Radicalism than historians have done, he claims. Socialism provided reasoned policy to defend specific interests. As early as 1883 the Radical candidate in Cuers was denounced for not being a socialist. *SFIO* deputy Allard defended small peasant farms, but preached a collectivism as the only remedy for the economic decline of a department where phylloxera destroyed 60 per cent of vineyards by 1889, wine prices fell 85 per cent between 1886 and 1905, cork, shoe and olive sectors collapsed, and the population fell by over 10 per cent. State action was clearly necessary to halt economic collapse. The *Cri du Var* denounced bourgeois reformism and the 'mushy spirit of '48', and urged collectivization of big capitalist wine estates, held responsible for overproduction.

Though the tradition of the Second Republic nurtured the left, it cannot be used as a blanket explanatory factor. Some Radical strongholds were never converted to the *SFIO*, while Carces, socialist in 1900s had been royalist in the 1870s. Indeed, until the 1900s, socialism faced a serious rival in the all-class *Syndicats Agricoles*, patronized by royalist *notables* like Villeneuve-Flayosc, which enrolled some 30 per cent of the peasantry. By 1914, however, an extensive network of 35 socialist cooperatives helped store up to 16 per cent of the department's wine and avoid quick sales on depressed autumn market, as well as aiding bulk fertilizer purchase, insurance and marketing. Strong, communal tradition, and sociability of large wine villages allowed collectivist post-capitalist doctrines to take root, which makes a nonsense of Weber's argument that 'leftist' peasants were 'really' conservatives defending old communities. Peasant-family needs for the labour of their sons fed antimilitarism and resistance to the conscription laws. The department was de-Christianized but its economic problems made anticlericalism a minor feature of local politics, and Radicalism lost ground by ignoring the wine crisis and overplaying the Dreyfus issue.

VI The 'Révolte du Midi'

The most violent explosion of rural discontent occurred in lower Languedoc in the 1900s. The *révolte du Midi*, triggered by the wine-price collapse, produced a crisis for Clemenceau's government, already shaken by syndicalist strikes and resistance to inventories. The exact nature of this 'revolt' is difficult to define, for those involved were socially and politically heterogeneous – ranging from vineyard labourers and small wine growers to large landowners, from socialists to *Action Française* royalists and southern regionalists.

During the phylloxera years the wine industry had recourse to the twin expedients of north African imports and 'sugaring' of wine to increase its alcohol content. The rebuilding of the vineyards with American roots then produced an overproduction crisis as yield per hectare rose 75 per cent between 1896 and 1907. Land values fell by two-thirds in the Biterrois. However only the socialist and syndicalist left analysed the crisis in terms of overproduction by the big capitalist estates. The widely accepted myth in the Midi, fostered by large-owners, royalists and local Radicals, was that 'sugaring' by northern sugar-beet growers was the key to the glut. A 1905 law permitting bulk sugar sales was seen to facilitate fraud, and fuelled anti-parliamentary feelings.

The fraud myth directed attention away from class tensions. The phylloxera crisis had proletarianized thousands of small *vignerons* and weakened the position of those who remained – still one-third of the landed population. Large 'industrial' wine estates, owned by absentee nobles and bourgeois took over the best land in the coastal plain. In the Béziers I constituency half the area was owned by 3.4 per cent of owners. The estates were run by managers, paternalism had collapsed and absentee owners were large conspicuous spenders. 163,000 (56 per cent) of the rural work force in four departments were day-labourers. Their militancy derived from bitterness at recent expropriations, from the tradition of 1851, from the quasi-independence of the 62,000 who owned small wine plots and from their social contacts with surviving small-owners and barrelmakers. The large villages of the coastal plain had study societies and *libre-pensée* groups. The overpopulation crisis led to

30 per cent wage cuts, and unemployment among agricultural labourers and barrel-makers. In 1903–4 the *CGT* helped coordinate two strike waves for restoration of wage cuts and shorter hours to reduce unemployment. The focus of the local labour movement shifted from the towns, and from socialism still embedded in the *Bloc des Gauches*, to a rural syndicalism, coordinated by the *Bourses de Travail (BT)* in Béziers, Montpellier and Narbonne. In 1905 the *SFIO* candidate for Béziers was the Guesdist Cachin, urging collectivist solutions and reminding the Midi that it could not subsist on the radical diet of anticlericalism alone.

Recent village monographs have illuminated the mentality of rural militancy. In Coursan (Aude) the pre-phylloxera *vignerons* had been a labour-aristocracy, owning their own plots of land and hiring themselves to the big estates in work-gangs (*colles*). The pruning and grafting work was skilled. Wages had doubled in 1850–80. The big estates were determined to stage high-productivity/low-cost operations to recoup their heavy investments in American vines, chemicals and new wine presses after the phylloxera. As wages fell by nearly 70 per cent between 1870 and 1900 the workforce, disillusioned with the manoeuvrings of the reformist socialist deputy Ferroul, mayor of Narbonne, moved to direct action led by the syndicalist Cheyton, a future secretary of the Narbonne *BT*. In the 1904 strike red flags hung from the church, an estate manager shot two demonstrators and troops were used as strikebreakers – increasing the appeal of Cheyton's antimilitarism and advocacy of sabotage. In Cruzy (Hérault) the proportion of rural labourers rose from 9 per cent to 46 per cent in 1876–1911, as *vignerons* were proletarianized. Imposition of tight labour-controls, foremen and timesheets on the big estates eroded the job control of 'artisan' vine-dressers. Cheap and docile upland and Spanish migrants were imported. It was this experience, and the memory of the lost 'golden age' of the 1870s, rather than urban-based propaganda which radicalized them. Work became more unhealthy as new plants were treated with toxic chemicals. The pace of work quickened. The 1904–5 strikes received *CGT* support and the socialist municipality employed strikers on roadworks. In 1906, when the wine company imported docile upland migrant labour, there was a near insurrection led by the anarchist Calmette, in which workers took over the village, blockaded roads, set up cooperatives, crèches and collective kitchens.

The overproduction crisis threatened the remaining small *vignerons* faced with the perennial problem of selling wine in the autumn at rock-bottom prices. Bankruptcies grew. Fifty-three plots came up for sale on one day in March 1906 in Fontes (Hérault). Land values plummeted. A whole way of life appeared threatened by 'the vine which is dying'. An *SFIO* militant, Elie Cathola, in the Biterrois established cooperatives – the first at Maraussan, a village decimated by the repression of the 1851 insurrection. This had 300 members, secured prices 20 per cent above the departmental average, and acted as an inspiration to nearby villages.

However the strike setbacks of 1904–5 allowed other groups to seize the initiative. To divert labour militancy, big landowners and the press invented 'fraud' as the monster devouring the Midi and focused attacks on 'northern' governmental and sugar interests. The aim was to create an all-class movement of regional unity to 'defend the vine'. Tax boycotts and collective municipal resignations were threatened until the government eradicated fraud. Workers were promised higher wages once wine prices rose. Royalists helped finance the campaign of republican café owner Marcellin Albert whose paper *Le Tocsin* stressed the all-class, all-party nature of the crusade of the vine against the northern beetroot.

Local legitimists, weakened by the decline in religious practice and by the class conflicts of the coastal plains, seized the movement as a diversion from the strikes and as a weapon against the Radical government. They stepped up their regionalist-decentralist rhetoric, aided by a clergy who had come to act as the defenders of local patois and culture against the French language and the culture of the 'Jacobin' secular republic. *Action Française* militants set fire to the Perpignan prefecture, and Mgr de Cabrières allowed demonstrators to sleep in his Montpellier cathedral. The crisis exposed the weakness of the so-called Felibrige movement, led by the Provençal poet Mistral. 'Mistralism' had been an essentially bourgeois movement encouraging the preservation of southern culture. It had rallied to the defence of bullfighting in 1895 but in the face of a real regional revolt it lacked political perspectives and simply dithered.

Yet alongside this ultra-right exploitation of the crisis there existed a strand of 'red' federalism, influenced by Proudhonist anarchism, reflecting a hostility to the northern centralizing-capitalist state. Intellectuals like Xavier de Ricard had stressed the traditions of Albigensian resistance to northern Catholicism and this anticlerical myth may have been spread via the schools by those laic teachers on whom the republic relied to achieve national unity. It is true that many peasants and workers in the Midi welcomed the teaching of French and the erosion of patois, viewed as a symbol of their backwardness. Yet the chants and banners of the angry demonstration of 1907 testify to strong latent regionalist sentiment and hostility to the north. The most influential 'red' regionalist was Dr Ferroul, the enigmatic mayor of Narbonne. Feroul was a regionalist yet a patriot, a Guesdist who urged an all-class Midi wine lobby. His admirers interpreted his strategy as an attempt to stage a decentralist challenge to Clemenceau's centralism. Yet his rhetoric disturbed may of his left-wing allies with its insistence that 'the interest of rich and poor are not separate' and its claim that 'we are no longer Opportunists, Radicals, socialists. We are merely southerners demanding the right to live.'

The *CGT* and *SFIO* voiced justifiable alarm at Ferroul's strategy, yet the size of the 1907 demonstrations suggested that he touched a deep local chord, and local labour leaders were forced to swim with the tide. Wine villages, feeling an instinctive suspicion of a 'northern' government accepted the 'fraud' thesis. While socialists participated in the mass demonstration with their own banners calling for collectivization of big estates, these were swamped by anti-northern, anti-deputy and anti-fraud slogans.

The crisis climaxed in 1907 as Clemenceau sent in the troops. Six demonstrators were shot in Narbonne, three-quarters of Hérault municipalities resigned in protest at government policy, and southern troops of the 17th Regiment entered local folk-memory by their mutiny at Agde. Before such conflicts could escalate, Clemenceau defused tension by passing an anti-fraud law (29 June), taxing sugar and requiring a declaration of grape harvest. He negotiated a settlement with the newly formed *Confédération Générale des Viticulteurs du Midi* (*CGVM*) an all-class wine lobby including Ferrouⁱ and big landowners. The *CGVM* promised unemployment aid to labourers and insisted on its 'patriotism' and refusal to act as an agent of Catalan or Irish-style autonomism. Wine prices rose slowly till the poor harvest of 1910, when they soared to 36 francs a hectolitre, six times the level at the depth of the crisis.

What were the consequences of this crisis for the Midi? The *SFIO* had been uneasy at the all-class nature of the crusade, denounced the *CGVM* as an employers' front organization and called for collectivism of the wine estates, seen as the real causes of local overproduction. The interpretation which sees the crisis as marking a major swing from Radicalism to socialism needs careful qualification. If the *SFIO* vote grew from 13 per cent to 15 per cent in the four lower Languedoc departments between 1906 and 1910, the Radicals progressed from 25 per cent to 28 per cent. Local Radical politicians had flirted with the 1906–7 crusade to control its 'excesses'. Radicals were able to play on local popular anticlericalism in a region where workers and *vignerons* saw the church as the ally of the legitimist estate-owners. Lafferre, the radical deputy for Béziers, adopted a populist programme by calling for income tax, profit-sharing and cooperatives in order to fight off the socialist electoral challenge. Yet Radicalism had become the party of the local status quo, attracting law-and-order voters, backed by wine merchants and commercial bourgeoisie of towns like Béziers, using its administrative links to pressure electors. In the Hérault its vote rose by 50 per cent between 1906 and 1914.

Yet the crisis *did* both increase socialist support and shift local socialism to the left. The strike wave and calls for estate nationalization moved the party away from its anticlerical and pro-Bloc stance of 1899–1904. The agricultural workers union (*FTAM*) had lost 85 per cent of its 15,000 members between 1905 and 1907, but revived by 1908 as workers became disillusioned with the all-class *CGVM*, denounced by the CGT as 'yellow'. Rising living costs sparked a fresh strike wave in 1910–11 as workers tried to secure their share of rising wine prices. Harvey Smith argues that these strikes were largely reformist and wage-orientated and that the 'artisan' vine-dressers' aspirations to job control had faded as the new workforce accepted the rules of the capitalist game. Such a conclusion is too pessimistic. P. Ader, the *FTAM* leader, was a syndicalist who had argued that '1907' might prove a useful example of the potentialities of direct action once workers saw through the employers' manipulation of the *CGVM*. The most militant *Bourses de Travail* in lower Languedoc (Béziers, Mèze etc.) kept a higher membership than reformist ones. Over one-third of Hérault wine villages were unionized, despite large fluctuations in annual membership. The 1910–11 strikes were well-organized by strike committees, municipalities set up soup kitchens, red flags were flown. Police reported that in Marsillargues (Hérault) only expropriation of the big estates would satisfy strikers. In Coursan (Aude) the syndicalist Cheyton led three strikes, recruited female workers and spread antimilitarist propaganda.

The significance of the Midi crisis is difficult to assess. The *CGVM* succeeded in diverting the 1906–7 crusade away from class-war or regionalist separatism. The Midi's reliance on the French market for its sales inhibited separatism, labourers and *vignerons* saw *oc* as the language of their subjection and French as the symbol of emancipation. When Jaurès spoke to Languedoc villagers he began in *oc* to please their localism – then spoke in French to flatter them that he knew that they now understood it. In 1914 Midi conscripts complied with the military mobilization with the resigned acceptance shown elsewhere in France. And yet these years saw a genuine syndicalism among day-labourers, the mobilization of anxiously vulnerable *vignerons*, deep-seated antinorthern feelings. The mutiny of the 17th Regiment was celebrated in local songs. The regiment's commander saw the mutineers as 'natives of a region where one is involved in politics from the cradle'. The three-year conscription law met barrack protests. Integral nationalists came to be suspicious of the loyalty of the Midi. An internal racism grew ('the southerner, there is the enemy!') which viewed the man of the Midi as anticlerical, unpatriotic, 'red'. The *révolt du Midi* provides strong evidence that the 'modernization' of rural France engendered more conflict than some historians have suggested.

VII The Peasantry and the Bourgeois Republic

The hegemony of bourgeois republicanism over the peasantry was, thus, not monolithic. In the 'accepted hierarchies' of the west and central Massif royalist *notables* still dominated deferential Catholic tenants. In the centre and the Midi class-conflict occurred as sharecroppers, lumbermen, vine labourers and small-winegrowers contested capitalist control of the countryside. Regionalist protests emerged in peripheral areas. Yet the republic came to secure support or acquiescence from wide areas of rural France. A few strikes among day-labourers and market gardeners failed to disturb the capitalist hierarchies in the commercial farming regions of the north and the Paris basin. Politically 'neutral' areas like Calvados (Normandy), prospering on livestock farming, shifted quietly from Bonapartism to conservative republicanism which offered order and stability. Anticlericalism attracted the peasants of the Charentes or the Gatinais to the laic republic, while in the 'rural democracies' of lower Burgundy, the Vendée plain or southern Jura, republican middle-peasants rejected socialist and clerical extremes. Mountain regions like the Basses-Alpes, 'red' in 1849, lost the vitality of their young men through migration and came to rely on influential deputies to secure favours from centrist governments. Many areas of small-peasant Catholicism such as the Bièvre (Isère) or Pays de Léon (Finistère) came to prefer republicanism to royalist clericalism.

Shrewd propaganda won the republicans their 1870s triumphs. In his *New Letters to the Peasants* (1871) Joigneaux insisted that for an adult people like the French, who had cut their teeth, to revert to being wet-nursed by a divine right monarch would cause the rest of Europe to die of laughter. To those who argued that the republic meant the 1793 Terror, he retorted that monarchism meant a return to the tithe, the *corvée* and the bad old days when peasants beat the ponds to stop frogs croaking to disturb aristocrats' sleep. Peasants and urban dwellers were not enemies but shared mutual interests, the more the latter consumed, the more the former sold. A royalist victory would mean internal chaos, leading to an economic slump, and foreign war to restore the pope's Temporal Power at a time when France was still burdened by the indemnity to the Prussians and still to recover her own lost territory. He promised that a republic would mean progressive income and profits tax, to relieve small men and place a proper share of taxation on large landowners, together with a secret ballot, to reduce the threat of electoral pressure from landlords, bailiffs, tax collectors, clergy and rural police.

The First Republic gave the land, the Second the vote, the Third now offered peasants schools, railways, cheaper freight rates, tariffs. Village democracy was assiduously courted. As agrarian depression caused some *notables* to quit the land, peasants appeared on municipal councils, from which mayors were now elected, rather than being government appointees. In 1889 and 1900, at the height of the Boulangist and Dreyfus crises, 20,000 village mayors came to official banquets in Paris. Within village *mairies* busts of *Marianne* presided over the advent of the rural *nouvelles couches* to municipal control. Class-collaborationist *Syndicats Agricoles* were sponsored by the regime, offering cheap credit and bulk-purchase, and came to flourish in the Charentes, lower Normandy and the Pas-de-Calais as official rivals to Catholic organizations or leftist unions and co-ops.

R. Goujon has analysed the ways in which the rural bourgeoisie came to dominate and manipulate the associations and communal life of wine villages in Saône-et-Loire. Doctors, lawyers, bourgeois landowners and wine merchants, whose own *cercles* had often been the focus of republican politics since the mid-century, succeeded in replacing religious *confréries* and choirs with a network of republican organizations. Over two-thirds of choral groups became secular. Mayors patronized shooting clubs, whereas once the *curés* had blessed the targets in shooting competitions. Gym clubs were used to control adolescent sociability between school and conscription. Physical fitness and marksmanship were lauded as essential for 'future defenders of *La Patrie*'. These organizations all starred in the ceremonies of 14 July. The crude, vulgar, coarse, anarchic elements of the old youth culture were combatted, youths fined or dismissed for unpunctuality or indiscipline. Visits were arranged to nearby Le Creusot to teach admiration for France's industrial achievements.

Dupeux's study of Loir-et-Cher can serve as a model for a rural France of the 'satisfied centre'. Here, as elsewhere, republican lawyers and doctors seized the initiative in the 1870s by playing on peasant fears of war, neo-feudalism and clericalism in a department of few religious vocations, where religious practice fell 50 per cent between 1850 and 1900. The depression hit cereal and wine growers and rural traders, while landowners reacted to price decline by attempts to shorten leases and raise rents. Noisy but incoherent rural protest resurfaced against taxes, high rail freight rates, middlemen. Cereal growers urged higher protectionism while wine growers complained that tariffs raised their food bills. The republicans' share of the vote fell from 54 per cent to 33 per cent between 1881 and 1889, with the right and radical-socialist left making gains. Socialists, fighting on issues of income tax, ·cheap credit, anticolonialism, attracted lumbermen, Vendômois wine growers and small shopkeepers in the 1890s, but was over-reliant on a few urban-based militants. Bourgeois hegemony was restored in the 1900s. Rural exodus removed potential militants among day-labourers, rural artisans and small wine growers – who left behind a department where small-medium property was the norm. Indeed in France as a whole the number of smallholdings below five hectares fell 50 per cent between 1890 and 1929, while holdings of 10 to 20 hectares were consolidated.

By 1910 the republicans held all four parliamentary seats in Loir-et-Cher. Their deputies were lawyers and landowners, socially conservative men with firm support from the prefect. They built up a rural clientele by arranging advantages for their supporters, fixing promotions or dismissals among teachers and postal workers, secured tobacco-licences or conscription delays. Tassan, the 'god of Loir-et-Cher' manipulated anticlericalism for 25 years, yet arranged a rapid deal with Catholics in 1906 to thwart a potential republican rival. He played off the peasantry against 'idle' urban workers. 'The republican establishment owes its security to the present day to this division, carefully maintained by our omnipotent bourgeoisie,' lamented one local socialist.

Conclusion

The France of 1914

In 1914 Frenchmen mobilized with little internal dissent in defence of the republican *patrie*. It is tempting to view this *Union Sacrée*, encompassing the Guesdist left and the nationalist right, as symptomatic of the success of the republican bourgeoisie in consolidating its hegemony over French society. Yet, as J. J. Becker emphasizes, such a conclusion may be erroneous. National unity, engendered by a belief that France was the innocent victim of unprovoked Teuton aggression, proved fragile and ephemeral. The *Union Sacrée* was a temporary truce in deep-seated political and class conflicts, not proof that such conflicts had evaporated.

I The Path to War

The standard post-1918 view that the war was the logical and inevitable product of a profound national obsession with revanche for the loss of Alsace-Lorraine is misleading. Certainly the anti-German bellicosity of Déroulède in the 1880s was echoed in the novels of R. Bazin and Barrès two decades later. Yet these reflected neither official policy nor public mood. From Gambetta onwards republican politicians were pragmatically aware of the risks of revanchism. The *Quai d'Orsay*, while anxious to seek European allies, gave Alsace-Lorraine a low priority. The impeccably patriotic republican historian Lavisse emphasized that any war would trap the Alsatian population dangerously in the crossfire. Until 1901 there was some hope that a compromise deal, involving perhaps Alsatian autonomy, could be made with the Reich. Laic school textbooks expressed sadness at the loss, and kept memories alive by colouring Alsace in a distinct shade on their wall-maps. Yet they made no mention of imminent plans for recovery of the lost provinces. Within Alsace-Lorraine itself the population concentrated on securing rights within the reich, while the journals of

Alsatian *emigrés* in France were cultural rather than bellicose or irredentist. Public attitudes on the issue were ritualistic rather than obsessive. When Germanophobia revived in the 1900s, its emphasis was frequently economic and colonial.

For two decades France remained diplomatically isolated. Rapprochement with Britain would have necessitated an anti-Russian stance in the near and Far East. Tsarist distaste for republicans was so deep that only the disintegration of Russo-German relations in the late 1880s pushed Russia, reluctantly, towards the French alliance. This alliance, gradually cemented between 1892 and 1894, was widely welcomed in France by all except the left, understandably dubious at *Marianne*'s flirtation with Europe's most reactionary ruler. Financiers jumped at the chance to invest in Russia. By 1914 25 per cent of French foreign investment was in Russia, including a rapidly increasing volume of industrial investment. Twenty per cent of the investment income of French government ministers in the 1900s came from Russian holdings. Loans were increasingly tied to French heavy industry and arms exports. The French army enthused at the prospect of trapping Germany into a war on two fronts, and French investments speeded the building of Russia's strategic railways. Critics of the alliance became 'unpatriotic'. Clemenceau, who opposed it in 1891, maintained it after 1906 despite his professed sympathy with the 1905 revolution.

Yet for several years the alliance did not function as a firm anti-German front. The tsar, unwilling to be dragged into a revanchist crusade, advised Frenchmen to 'wait with dignity' for a solution to the Alsace problem. French reluctance to support Russia's Balkan and near eastern aspirations mirrored Russian's lack of enthusiasm for France's colonial ventures. Only in 1910 did France give Russia a virtual Balkan *carte blanche* in return for stronger guarantees against Germany.

Colonial expansionism, conceived by Ferry as a strategy to boost French self-confidence and economic and military strength while avoiding immediate conflict with Bismarck, was initially condemned by nationalists and neo-Jacobins as a senseless diversion from the 'real' German issue, which would play into German hands by embroiling France in rivalries with other imperialist powers. Indeed the Tunisian annexation pushed Italy into the Triple Alliance and triggered a prolonged tariff war. French resentment at British annexation of Egypt, a traditional French cultural preserve, augmented existing Anglo-French trade rivalries in West Africa, souring relations for two decades. British resistance to French expansionism in the upper Nile, culminating in the 1898 Fashoda incident, increased Anglophobia to the point where a delighted German ambassador in Paris reported that Frenchmen had forgotten Alsace. London purported to view French policy in Laos as a threat to her position in Siam, and French-financed Russian railways in central Asia as a challenge to India. Between 1894 and 1898 Foreign Minister Hanotaux toyed with the idea of a Franco-German consortium for joint colonial exploitation. France shared Germany's distaste for British policy in South Africa.

Delcassé, who kept open the option of an anti-British stance until 1901 before deciding that the German regime was too volatile and unpredictable to be trusted, eventually chose an entente with a Britain increasingly alarmed by German economic and naval power. There was mutual recognition by Britain and France of their respective Egyptian and Moroccan spheres of influence. But as Delcassé sought to extend French economic penetration of Moroccan mineral resources towards political control he clashed with the reich which resisted such unilateral expansionism. With Germany the new colonial rival, revanchists like Barrès became belated converts to colonialism. Germany was anxious to prove to France that the British entente was useless, and that colonial expansion necessitated a *modus vivendi* with the Reich. Unwilling to risk war in 1905, at a point when army-republican relations were at their nadir, and when Russia was in chaos after the Japanese debacle, the government was forced to jettison Delcassé. However, British support for France at the Algeciras conference of 1906 showed that the crisis had cemented rather than undermined the entente.

Though Franco-German relations remained tense from 1906–10, and though the tone of the French right-centre press was increasingly belligerent, successive governments made some attempts to achieve a *modus vivendi* with Germany. Rouvier had close contacts with financial groups who argued for a joint German-French consortium to exploit colonial resources. Clemenceau (1906–9), though firmly hostile to the kaiser's 'domineering' and 'aggressive' attitudes and convinced that a war was inevitable, was aware that a war over obscure Moroccan or Balkan conflicts would alienate not only the *SFIO* but left-radicals. With Russia still weak and Britain's military commitment still nebulous he, therefore, sought to control the impatience of the military to occupy Morocco and concluded an agreement with Berlin, in which the rights of German traders in Morocco were guaranteed in return for German recognition of French predominance.

When Berlin responded to French military occupation of Morocco with a show of force in 1911 Caillaux was able to defuse the immediate crisis by offering Germany the *quid pro quo* of concessions in the Congo. A reluctant parliament accepted this compromise but, with anti-German sentiment whipped up by the right-wing press, Caillaux was immediately overthrown, replaced by the tough, nationalistic Lorrainer Poincaré determined to prepare France for 'inevitable' war.

Was the 1914 war caused by Franco-German imperialist economic rivalries? Existing evidence is often ambiguous, and the question still awaits a French Fritz Fischer. Caillaux represented a sector of French finance which, fearing the consequences of war, placed their hope in joint Franco-German financial exploitation of the underdeveloped world. Poidevin and Guillen have emphasized the joint Franco-German investments in northern African minerals and have suggested that a series of compromises over the Morocco (1909), the Congo (1911) and Ottoman Railways (1914) suggest that imperial conflicts were waning by 1914. *Disconto* and *Paribas* invested jointly in Roumania; German firms invested in metropolitan France. Meanwhile France retained fears of British control of Arab oil and of Russian designs on Turkey. However, Guillen's thesis remains implausible. French business interests in central Africa resented German penetration of the Congo and designs on Portuguese Angola. Morocco was viewed, like Algeria, as 'naturally' French, for the Mediterranean flowed through France like the Seine through Paris. By 1914 Bethmann-Hollweg was expressing intense German anger at the, only partly successful, attempts to close French colonial markets to German trade. Arms giants Schneider and Krupps were involved in bitter export feuds in the Balkans and Latin America. With the *Bourse* and the banks increasingly tying foreign loans to demands that recipients import French goods, the cliché that financiers were less economically chauvinistic than heavy-industrialists became suspect. Alarmed at

German import penetration of French markets, French capitalists got tariffs increased (1910), propagandized against German imports and tried to limit Thyssen's investments in Lorraine ores, on which, as Gatzke argued, German industrialists had begun to cast envious eyes.

The links between imperialism, industry and politics are epitomized by E. Étienne, leader of the colonial lobby. He had shares in the Congo, links with Pinot of the *Comité des Forges*, was president of the Paris bus monopoly. He was, also, a director of the cable, electric and aluminium giant *Tréfileries et Laminoirs du Havre*, which had numerous interlocking directorships with major colonial banks and colonial railways. Étienne emphasized that the *TLH*'s future lay in a *mise en valeur* of the empire via rail and port developments. In 1913 Étienne was war minister.

Major conflict centred, above all, on Asia Minor where German economic and cultural intrusion threatened French hegemony. German Catholic missionaries threatened a French role of *fidei defensor* whose hypocrisy had been exposed by the separation conflicts. The financial power of France in the Ottoman lands was buttressed by an extensive school network, in which pupils were taught that one example of the usage of the verb 'prefer' was 'I prefer France to Germany'! France clearly preferred informal economic empire to direct colonial rule, but in face of German challenge and the danger of Ottoman collapse they had developed plans, encouraged by the *Comité d'Asie Française* for annexation of Syria and surrounding territory. French banks blocked the efforts of Germany to raise loans on the Paris finance market for the Berlin-Baghdad railway. Leninists might cite this as a classic instance of imperialistic economic rivalry.

If there is little direct evidence that capitalists planned war, nevertheless chambers of commerce supported Poincaré's conscription bill, rearmament meant full order books for heavy-industry, and French economic leverage in Russian railways and industry was an obvious element in Berlin's encirclement paranoia.

The Moroccan crisis accentuated fears of German bellicosity which fuelled a real, if limited, 'nationalist revival' incarnated by Poincaré. The regime mended its fences with the military, put over 520,000 men into the army. The 1913 conscription law was justified on the grounds of the German 1912–13 military build-up. As Porch argues, the legacy of the radical-army feud persisted, officer recruitment had fallen steadily since 1900. Morale, efficiency and discipline had all suffered. However the high command was now reorganized, France began to spend 36 per cent of her budget on arms – as against 25 per cent in 1872 – and Joffre planned an offensive war-strategy. The Triple Entente, by allowing France to concentrate on her fleet in the Mediterranean, permitted a firm anti-German stance in the near East.

Undoubtedly, *pace* Krumeich, there was an element of internal political calculation in this militaristic tub-thumbing. Poincaré was neither the first nor last modern capitalist politician to attempt to defeat the left and avoid internal fiscal and social reform by whipping up chauvinism. It was highly convenient to brand Jaurès, with his *SPD* contacts and his calls to replace the army with a citizens' militia, as a tool of Berlin. If Poincaré did not, perhaps, desire war, he regarded it as inevitable – and feared that if it were to be delayed too long a leftist government might dismantle the conscription law. Hence this pragmatic heir of Ferry became an exponent of brinkmanship, making little effort in his July 1914 trip to Russia to diffuse the Serbian crisis by urging caution on his tsarist ally.

A wave of chauvinism was encouraged by military parades in provincial towns, Joan of Arc ceremonies designed to achieve a synthesis of republican, nationalist and Catholic patriotism – of Briand, Barrès and de Mun. Squabbles over whether Joan was an authentic saint who really heard voices, or a sturdy French peasant who imagined them, declined. Becker emphasizes both the reality of the wave of bellicose verbiage which polluted French intellectual discourse, though also its social and geographic limits. The *Action Français* had 13,000 members, sold 30,000 copies of its paper, was strongest in Paris and among students and urban middle-bourgeois groups – though it had, too, a sizeable audience of provincial Catholic fellow-travellers. Paris lycée students expressed their taste for anti-intellectual, anti-pacifist patriotism by booing leftist teachers. Lyautey, who received an ovation at the *École Libre des Sciences Politiques*, declared: 'What I like about the youth of today is that they have no fear of war, of the word, of the thing itself.' Psichari, in *L'Appel aux Armes* (1912), argued that peace meant decadence, pacifism was a noxious illusion, war alone offered a chance to show courage and initiative and his fellow-Catholic Claudel welcomed 'that beautiful word of deliverance and adventure: *Krieg!*' One should, perhaps, emphasize that these effusions of rightist intellectuals and the reported sentiments of an elite of bourgeois students are not, necessarily, symptomatic of the entire national mood, any more than Barrès's Alsace novels necessarily prove the dominance of revanchism in French politics after 1905.

Indeed the left's failure to present a coherent antiwar strategy in July 1914 has overshadowed their real achievement in the general election of that year in halting the right's bellicose bandwagon. The *SFIO* had used epidemic deaths in overcrowded barracks to increase populist anticonscription feeling, and demanded a negotiated Alsace settlement. With Caillaux at his head, the Radical party responded to the anticonscription sentiments of its peasant clientele and the feeling that escalating military expenditure demanded a more equitable tax-structure. The two parties won 342 of 602 parliamentary seats, though perhaps some 60 of the Radical deputies supported the conscription law. The left attracted an anticonscription majority in 39 departments.

This was all too little and too late to halt the military juggernaut. The *CGT*, a shadow of its former self after the collapse of the syndicalist offensive, was able to organize sizeable antiwar demonstrations on 29 July but, feeling that an antiwar general strike would be suicidal, thereafter attempted to coordinate its strategy with the *SFIO*. Most socialists accepted the necessity of national defence, though ideally with a democratic citizens' militia. The *SFIO*'s naive hope that a pacific general strike in conjunction with the *SPD* might halt war foundered on the Reich's ability to persuade German workers of the peril from reactionary tsarism. Their antiwar strategy, premised on the notion that here was just another Balkan crisis, was overtaken by the speed of the slide into the abyss, while Jaurès made the mistake of assuming the pacific intentions of the French establishment, including Poincaré. Any remote prospects of organized worker resistance to mobilization were undercut by ostentatious government attendance at Jaurès's funeral and by Jouhaux's funeral oration, emphasizing that the dead hero would have defended the republic against reactionary Kaiserism. The left-centre cabinet of Viviani, which was divided on the conscription issue, wisely refrained from creating working-class martyrs by implementing the *Carnet B* plans for mass arrests of militants.

The August 1914 mobilization occurred with neither the peasant indifference of 1870 nor the violent proletarian antimilitarism which the authorities feared. Barely 2 per cent of conscripts failed to respond to the call-up. However few reports of the mobilization mention revanchist enthusiasm. Pro-war demonstrations were rare – though there were assaults on such 'German' businesses as the Swiss Maggi stores and the shop of an unfortunately named M. Allemand. Brave patriots beat up a deaf-mute whose vocal utterances were interpreted as German phrases!

Dutiful resignation reigned. The republic was seen as the innocent victim of a bullying kaiser. Aggrieved injured innocence mingled with astonishment, for incessant war-scares since 1905 had not prepared many for war. It was assumed that the church bells were tolling to warn of impending thunderstorms. Tearful women registered sad fatalism more than bellicose enthusiasm. Working-class strongholds like Carmaux were calm. Atavistic Jacobin patriotism taught the old Blanquist-communard Vaillant that France, motherland of revolution, was worthy of protection. One Saône-et-Loire miner militant jailed for antimilitarism in 1912, and a communist leader by 1920, went unhesitatingly to the trenches. Yet underlying working-class resentments did surface. Red flags waved in Narbonne; in Limoges the mood was sullen, workers were jailed for stating loudly in public that the army was capitalism's guard-dog, that Germans were fellow workers. Six Aube workers were jailed for singing the *Internationale* in a café. An Auvergnat peasant advise troops to shoot their officers and behead Poincaré. Several hundred such incidents suggest that the *Union Sacrée* was not unanimous, yet such minority voices of sanity were crying in a wilderness.

Yet the *Union Sacrée* was limited and fragile, a brief party truce, like feuding neighbours uniting to fight a forest fire. Guesde entered the war cabinet, rail-companies reemployed strikers sacked in 1910, Barrès attended Jaurès's funeral. However, the conflicts which were to divide French society after 1917 soon appeared. Socialists emphasized that war only strengthened the need for socialist internationalism to succeed. Republicans claimed that war justified the three-year conscription law. The right argued that their peculiar values of heroism, authority, discipline would alone ensure victory against the 'ferocious' teutonic race. There were, *pace* the *SFIO*, no good Germans. Anti-Dreyfusard officers, persecuted by a corrupt republic, were now 'saving civilization'. Catholics, encouraged by an ephemeral increase in mass attendance, cited the dedication of army chaplains and nun-nurses as proof of the need to repeal the laic laws. By 1912 as antiwar feeling grew, *Union Sacrée* rhetoric became merely a part of the rhetoric of bourgeois ideology.

II The Consolidation of Bourgeois Hegemony?

During the nineteenth century the dominance of the French bourgeoisie was subject to periodic threat from aristocratic-clerical, petty-bourgeois, peasant or working-class movements. By 1914, however, parliamentary politics appeared to be dominated by centrist parties which accepted the bourgeois republic's consensus. This was possible, it has been suggested, because of a fortunate 'staggering' of crisis points. The bourgeois revolution was consolidated by 1830. The problems of adjustment to universal suffrage, which forced the capitalist elites to resort to authoritarian rule for two decades, came only after 1848. The pace of industrialization was sufficiently gradual to 'spread out' the inevitable resulting social dislocation. Despite the severity of the 1873–96 Great Depression there was no major economic catastrophe to threaten the broad strata of petty producers with immediate collapse. Eventually, shrewd manipulation of the 'democratic' rhetoric of 1789 against residual but declining clerico-aristocratic elites allowed 'progressive' republican capitalists to form a broad alliance with rural and urban petty producers, cushioned by protectionism and imperialism, which achieved a certain stability not attained by contemporary 'liberal' elites in Spain or Italy, although a stability threatened in the 1880–90s by economic crisis which pushed marginal petty producers towards socialist or proto-fascist 'extremism'.

By 1910 the challenge from the intransigent anti-parliamentary right, whether royalist, Catholic, nationalist or proto-fascist, appeared to have faded. Barely 20 of the 70 rightist deputies were hardline opponents of a republic still labelled by them as '*la guese*' ('the slut'). The *Action Française* flirtation with syndicalism was a minor cul-de-sac of French politics. Maurras encouraged diehard Catholic rejection of *laicité* and separation, yet Catholic youth organizations, the *Sillon*, *abbés démocrates* and Catholic white-collar organizations were prepared to work within the republic. Aristocratic royalism had largely retreated to a few rural bastions, though the old *notables* retained powerful influence on peasant *Syndicats Agricoles* in some regions. Small-trader grievances, which had fuelled proto-fascism in the 1880s, had been channelled into respectable conservative anti-collectivist organizations.

The challenge from the revolutionary left had, similarly, waned. Blanquism was dead; Guesdism had failed to sustain its initial dynamism beyond its major Nord bastion. Syndicalism's challenge had faded in the face of tough governmental and employer repression and the erosion of the skilled craft-groups, the bedrock of nineteenth-century labour protest, by technological change. The new semi-skilled proletariat of Lorraine or the Paris *banlieu* lacked organization and traditions of militancy. Jouhaux symbolized a new bread-and-butter pragmatism within the *CGT*, while the 'revolutionary' groups in the *SFIO* provided a Marxist fig leaf for the drift towards reformism.

In the countryside the economic distress which had fuelled peasant protest had receded. Agrarian depression had accelerated the exodus of village artisans, day-labourers and marginal smallholders, leaving many regions to a relatively secure 'middle-peasantry' capable of profiting from the post-1900 price rise, loyal to the centrist republic which had emancipated them from 'feudalism' and offered tariff protection. Despite a certain peasant unease at the erosion of village community life by rural exodus, and despite genuine class-conflict in some areas, Weber's trinity of railway, schools and barracks had clearly achieved a degree of 'integration' of the peasantry into the capitalist market economy and national culture. Illiteracy had fallen to 4 per cent. One-sixth of the Provençal villages studied by Agulhon boasted official municipal busts of *Marianne*.

Post-1896 economic growth had, clearly, dulled the edge of social protest. Despite real weaknesses in foreign trade and shipping, the growing 'underdevelopment' of regions like the south-west, the restrictive effects of demographic stagnation on internal demand and the potentially serious consequences for metropolitan industrial investment of the level of capital export, the industrial growth rate of 3.56 per cent per annum was close to the German level. Unemployment fell and, despite the 1910–14 price inflation, real wages rose. The grinding monotony of semi-skilled industrial labour represented unprecedented security for many rural migrants to the cities.

The steady acceptance of colonialism helped consolidate bourgeois hegemony. The widespread and heterogeneous anti-colonialism of the 1880s, declined. Radical politicians became ensnared in colonial bureaucratic careers. Catholics welcomed the opportunity to extend Christian mission activity, and pro-colonialism was the one sentiment shared by Catholic and laic school textbooks. The reluctance of small investors to buy colonial shares gradually declined. Café-concert songs sang the praises of colonial troops. As Olivesi shows, the Marseille left found difficulty in sustaining its courageous anti-colonialism of the 1890s, when socialist municipal councillors boycotted receptions for returning colonial troops and denounced colonialism for wasting resources, better spent on the metropolitan economy, to promote the interests of capitalist elites. By 1906, with thousands of the city's citizens flocking to the Colonial Exhibition, and 25 per cent of its trade with the empire, *SFIO* protest became muted, restricted to urging governments to limit colonial activity to France's 'natural' Mediterranean sphere. The Jacobin-assimilationist myths persuaded some socialists of the civilizing role of French colonialism; the poverty of Marxist thought in France deprived the *SFIO* of a coherent analysis of imperialism. Paul Louis, a rare militant anti-imperialist, lamented that workers were malleable dupes on the colonial issue, antimilitarism reflected hostility to strike-breaking and conscription more than internationalism. Even well-meaning militants saw the role of 'generous' Frenchmen as teaching French to 'primitive' Arabs rather than encouraging anti-imperialist revolt. And anti-colonial movements among the native populations were, as yet, only a cloud on the horizon, for the 'Young Tunisian' movement was smashed in 1911–12, and Vietnamese revolts had been reduced to sporadic terrorism.

The *grande-bourgeoisie* survived the transition to 'democracy' remarkably unscathed. The Popular Front assult in the 1930s on the '200 families' who controlled the French economy reflected a legend about the power of the bourgeois dynasties with a basis in reality. Thirty per cent of Parisian wealth was controlled by 1 per cent of the population in 1830, by 0.4 per cent in 1914. The average wealth of a Parisian merchant or banker increased 650 per cent between 1820 and 1914, that of a small shopkeeper by a mere 65 per cent. The diffusion of industrial shares among small 'passive' investors failed to shake the dominance of a small class of very rich. Forty per cent of the profits of the *Comptoire de l'Industrie Linière* went to four directors. Profit levels rose steadily from the 1850s, despite the brief hiccup in the 1880s. Profits of 35 per cent were achieved in the chemical sector. While 38 per cent of Frenchmen left nothing at death, 70 per cent of inherited wealth was controlled by 3 per cent of the population. Fifty-five per cent of state revenue came from indirect taxes, under 20 per cent from taxes on income, while the 1893 and 1901 laws taxing share-profits and inheritances were systematically evaded. Access to local elites became restricted. Intermarriage between mercantile *grand-bourgeois* and shopkeepers, not infrequent in Rouen in 1850, was unknown by the 1900s, J. P. Chaline claims. Entry to the bureaucratic elite required higher education, money and 'connections'. Under 5 per cent of pupils in 1920, as in 1870, received secondary schooling, while university education cost 3000 francs per year. Terry Shin notes only a marginal 'democratization' of the *École Polytechnique* after 1880. Access to the *grandes écoles* remain monopolized by a few posh lycées. The *École Libre des Sciences Politiques*, established by Emile Boutmy in the 1880s, with support from leading business republicans like J. Siegfried, to produce a trained elite to check democratic 'excesses', inculcated a deeply conservative ethos derived from a *mélange* of de Tocqueville, Le Play and Anglophile laissez-faire. Its pupils dominated the diplomatic corps and the upper-bureaucracy. Estèbe has emphasized that, despite a degree of change with the post-1899 Radical cabinets, leading republican politicians remained men of financial standing. One-third of ministers in 1871–1914 died with over one million francs, 80 per cent were drawn from the richest 2 per cent of the population, four-fifths married women wealthier than themselves. In all they derived two-thirds of their income from stocks-and-shares, and were linked with the dynamic capitalist sectors. Few put their savings into woollen socks!

Through an expanding network of chambers of commerce, employers' associations, cartels and parliamentary lobbies, economic elites successfully guided state policies. As J. Jeanneney emphasizes, 'hidden money' had a powerful, if inevitably incalculable, capacity to secure favours from politicians and the press. The judiciary, despite the purge of 'royalists' in 1881, remained an elite preserve, for *juges suppléants* required a private income to tide them over until the belated arrival of their first salary cheques. Until 1907 the bourgeoisie monopolized juries, which consistently regarded property as more sacred than life. Eighty-four per cent of unskilled working-class defendents were convicted between 1855 and 1907, 81 per cent of property offenders, 70 per cent of those accused of violence, and a mere 61 per cent of bourgeois suspects accused of fraud or white-collar crime. Murderers were much more likely to face conviction if suspected of property-crime too.

The dominance of narrow elites relied inevitably on their ability to disseminate capitalist values to broad middle strata of society, a process facilitated by the transition of the Radicals from a party of populist protest to a governing party denying class-realities. Herriot, radical mayor of Lyon, insisted: 'I refuse to believe the theory of class and class-conflict for a country like France, where the variety of conditions is so great.' While 190,000 Frenchmen had incomes, in the 1890s, above 10,000 francs, 1.3 million 'earned' from 2500 to 10,000 francs. 1.7 million persons payed the '*patente*' (business-tax), there were 500,000 rentiers, and shareholders trebled to 2 million between 1850 and 1914. Protectionism, a stable franc and negligible income tax cushioned such strata, the sober bulwark of bourgeois stability with their decent, unostentatious dress, careful budgeting and Russian bonds. Technical and commercial education courses and a trickle of scholarships nurtured their faith in the republic as a socially mobile meritocracy. Over one-third of lycée teachers, generally a conservative, conformist group, were recruited from offspring of the peasantry and petty bourgeoisie. The growth of salaried middle-strata in an expanding bureaucracy helped offset the relative decline of the economic petty bourgeoisie.

In the new world of seaside holidays, bicycles and an anodyne conformist mass press, epitomized by the *Petit Journal*, the department store stood out as a potent symbol of bourgeois values. The ascent of a Joseph Rémond from commercial clerk to shop-magnate nurtured the self-made rags-to-riches mythology. The *Bon Marché*, with 4500 employees the world's premier store, was a monument to bourgeois culture. It became a *Société en Commandité par Actions* in 1880, permitting the Boucicart family to retain control while having access to outside capital. Specializing in price-cutting sales, utilizing advertizing catalogues, economies of scale and division of labour, it proves that the equation between 'family firm' and 'inefficiency' is unreliable. Such huge shops raised disquieting moral and socio-economic dilemmas for bourgeois society. Hostility to large competitors fuelled small-shopkeeper protest in the 1880–90s. Despite demands for higher taxes on large stores, *Bon Marché* paid only 10 per cent profits tax in 1913. Zola's fascination with the bustling vitality of such stores was mixed with regret at the way in which their standardized products, made by sweated labour, undercut artisan crafts. Moralists expressed disquiet both at a new consumerism, which hypnotized bourgeois wives into overspending and kleptomania, and at the fine clothes and loose social and sexual mores of salesgirls who, disturbingly, seemed neither proletarian nor bourgeois. Department stores disclosed alarming contradictions in bourgeois ideology, which claimed to prize efficiency and dynamism yet, equally, to respect quality, family, thrift, deferred gratification, honesty. The Boucicarts, however, synthesized these values by joining efficiency to family paternalism. *Bon Marché*, with its motto 'Loyalty makes my Strength', became a 'Big Happy Family', epitomizing the 'true socialism' of capital-labour collaboration. Pictures of happy, smiling craftsmen emphasized that the store sold 'quality' goods to 'faithful clients'. The *Bon Marché* portrayed itself as being as French as Notre Dame, 'a humanitarian institution'. Its tidy, courteous assistants were a far cry from nasty, unwashed proletarians. Their petty-bourgeois aspirations were flattered by well-publicized courses on etiquette and music, so that 'today the people of the *quartier* raise their daughters to enter the *Bon Marché*'. As Miller emphasizes the store's mixture of managerialism and paternalism, its flaunting of appearances, its celebration of materialism and leisure, its strike-free workforce and its encouragement of petty-bourgeois consumerist fantasy make it a potent symbol of the bourgeois hegemony of the *Belle Époque*.

Sport, too, played a role in national and social integration. Courbertin's introduction of athletics and rugby was a conscious attempt to manufacture a virile ethos which could synthesize old and new elites, just as English public schools welded together sons of Tory gentry and non-conformist industrialists. Sport would inculcate teamwork, discipline, leadership and fitness for a new suntanned muscular elite. By 1899 two-thirds of lycées in the south-west had rugby teams. The promotion of the *Tour de France* as the national fête emerged from both commercial and nationalistic motives. Its founder, H. Desgranges, used it to emphasize French unity, briefly duping the gullible German authorities to allow it to pass through Alsace. The *Tour* created a new image of Frenchmen as tough and hardy, well suited to an age obsessed with racial hygiene.* Cycling also boosted the sales of an expanding sports press, epitomized by Desgrange's *L'Auto*, and of cycling and tyre firms like Michelin which sponsored urban stadia. Urban audiences were frequently violent and xenophobic, jeering a black American cyclist carried concussed from the track after being deliberately unseated by the French champion. Dreams of cycling stardom filled the fantasy-world of adolescent workers. The rapid growth of gymnastic and shooting societies suited patriotic demands that France's future soldiers should acquire some 'muscle'. Chauvinistic crowds at Parc des Princes rugby internationals tried to lynch the referee, an ironic reflection on earlier claims that codified sport would reduce the 'anarchic' violence of traditional village pastimes! Sports clubs encouraged the machismo and 'male-bonding' of petty-bourgeois bachelors. Soccer's popularity in the north prompted employers to sponsor works' teams to promote company loyalty, while Lille industrialists financed cock-fighting arenas.

Yet sport had obvious limitations as an opium for the masses, frequently reflecting rather than obscuring political and class-divisions. A Catholic sports federation developed its own muscular Christianity, ran a separate Catholic national soccer team, and clashed frequently with local laic clubs. The Catholic-royalist elite of the Midi, hoping to emulate Andalucian *hacienda*-owners, sponsored bull-fighting to emphasize Barrèsian virtues of courage and brutality against their effete, humanitarian, Protestant-republican Dreyfusard opponents. Sport frequently emphasized rather than helped break down class barriers. In Batignolles the petty-bourgeois clerks of the *Union Cycliste* refused to share a table with their proletarian cycling opponents. As Holt comments,

---

*The emergence of child-welfare groups, campaigning against wet-nursing, developed from similar racial obsessions. Child-protection became a 'truly national task . . . which touches the well-being of thousands of little beings destined to become soldiers of France'. With child-welfare laws France 'might not have lost Alsace-Lorraine'.

Liberté, Egalité, Fraternité was best left, where it belonged, on official monuments.

Indeed unresolved tensions persisted even at the heart of the bourgeois family itself. Opportunist politicians had attempted to extend the republican concensus by extending laic primary schooling for girls and by establishing secular lycées, to provide liberal training for future bourgeois wives and mothers, though the church continued to control much girls' education. The Sée law had not envisaged female access to bourgeois careers, and had not offered a full baccalauréat course for girls. Nevertheless, by the 1900s, 600 girls were studying annually for the baccalauréat, 2500 were in higher education. Eight per cent of dentists, 3 per cent of doctors were women. Women compromised a growing proportion of the expanding tertiary sector, 20 per cent of postal employees, 40 per cent of commercial personnel. There were 50,000 female primary schoolteachers. Expanding career opportunities for middle-class and petty-bourgeois women were accompanied by a few minor legal reforms, such as the right of married women to control their own wages (1908). However the path towards sexual equality was strewn with major educational, legal and cultural obstacles. Article 213 of the Code required wives to obey until 1938. Women had to seek their husbands' permission to take employment, were obliged to live where their spouse chose. A growing, vociferous, feminist movement, recruited largely from the tertiary sector, demanded reform. Yet 'official' feminism, sponsored by the Gambettist-freemason Leon Richer, remained tactical, limited, paternalistic, patronized by wives of opportunist *notables* such as Mme J. Siegfried. Deep-rooted fears of the 'clericalism' of women prompted fears that 'if women had the vote the republic would not last six months' (Richer). If republicans did not wish to see women in the church, they were happy to confine them to children and the kitchen. The republic's true security lay in the family remaining a kingdom, with the republican-anticlerical husband as king. Doctrines of 'separate spheres' persisted. Man, the thinking head, was worker and citizen. Woman, the feeling heart, was wife and mother. Sexual double-standards persisted, so that L. Blum's suggestion that bourgeois girls should sow a few wild oats was greeted with horror. Husbands could shoot adulterous wives or have them jailed. The reverse did not apply. Wives, like property, were to be purchased unsoiled and intact. The insistence that, by contrast, the husband should be 'experienced' necessitated a vast prostitution industry. Prostitutes, recruited from the metropolitan lower-classes and from colonial immigrants, played a key role in bourgeois society in protecting the purity of wives and daughters. Sexual initiation in the brothel was a rite of passage for lycée students. Prostitution was legalized, carefully policed, marginalized to brothels in red-light districts. Tight medical controls, however, failed to halt the spread of VD. Fourteen per cent of deaths in France in 1900 may have been from syphilis, a scourge equal in bourgeois thought to that of socialism, viewed with alarm by nationalists as a threat to the racial stock, treated with irony by moralizing novelists as the symbolic revenge of proletarian girls on their bourgeois oppressors. The fact that one-third of Paris prostitutes in the 1880s were servants accentuated fears that sexual diseases might infiltrate the sanctuary of the bourgeois home.

E. Shorter has claimed that sexual gulfs within the family were being narrowed. He argues that couples began to marry for love and practised birth control to have fewer children. Yet these children were now loved and cared for as mothers began breast-feeding, accelerating the decline of the Morvan wet-nursing industry. Manuels like J. Droz's *Monsieur, Madame et Bébé* suggested a new playful sexuality in bourgeois marital relations. Educational equality made marriages 'concomitant' partnerships of affection. It would, certainly, be a mistake to regard all bourgeois wives as passive victims. Many managed household budgets and servants, disciplined children, chose schools. Yet the idea of a sexual-marital revolution remains dubious. Marriage remained a property transaction. Catholic training taught girls to suffer sex in dutiful silence, to submit to their husbands and think of France. Gynaecological problems made sex painful for many women. The age and culture gap between the laic bourgeois husband and his younger Catholic wife remained a major source of family tension.

And, indeed, many of the nineteenth-century conflicts persisted unresolved. The consolidation of a French conservative party remained uncompleted. Catholic school history textbooks continued to praise the Middle Ages, regard Jews as deicides, Protestants as heretics and '1789' as the satanic result of Voltaire's wickedness. They emphasized a providential history in which God sent cholera in 1830 to punish France for overthrowing the Bourbons. The Ferry laws were denounced as atheistic and costly to the taxpayer. A similar vision of the French past, equally hostile to the republic, flowed from the popular history of *Action Française* writers like Bainville. As Kuisel emphasizes, some business groups, critical of French economic performance, were impatient with parliamentary government, and yearned for a technocratic authoritarianism, while Jesuit-trained industrialists in the Nord retained corporatist and anti-republican preferences. If the post-1896 boom dulled the edge of urban petty-bourgeois extremism, the economic marginality of many small businesmen made it probable that any future economic recession would revive anti-semitism and proto-fascism. In the countryside large Catholic landowners in the west and north had little love for the republic, had powerful influence on peasant *Syndicats Agricoles*, and espoused a rural corporatism with strong 'agrarian' anti-urban tendencies.

Regionalist tensions persisted despite the republic's success in 'integrating' peripheral areas. Certainly no organized, coherent regionalist movement with a clear ideology and programme appeared before 1914. Many peasants viewed the transition from patois to French as a symbol of their social emancipation. 'Mistralism' in Provence, or embryonic Breton nationalism, remained essentially cultural protest movements of declining local elites, lacked political perspectives or mass support. Breton peasant migrants looked to Paris for employment, just as the Midi relied on sales of its wine to the north and to bureacratic jobs for its surplus sons. Republican parties, having flirted with decentralist rhetoric until 1871, set their face firmly against any devolution of power to the regions, arguing that regionalism was a tool of reactionary royalists in the Midi, or of dubious clerical politicians like Abbé Lemire in Flanders.

Yet, even within the Radical party, local deputies from the Midi or the south-west expressed unease at excessive centralization. C. Beauquier, from Franche-Comté, voiced regionalist sentiments at party congresses, while areas like Aquitaine felt neglected, as their old industries died and rapid industrialization in northern and eastern France widened the gulf between developing and underdeveloped regions. Novelists like E. Le Roy and Gullaumin expressed anxiety as the new urban, mechanized society supplanted the rural culture of their regions, which they saw as the heartlands of the true France. As Elegoët claims, the suppression of the Breton language could create a sense of alienation comparable to that experienced by artisans in face of division of labour and erosion of their skills. French was an instrumental language, a tool of social and geographic mobility, yet one which failed to register and sustain Breton collective memories and culture. Nor did the process of centralization and national-building eliminate the strand of 'internal racism' within France. Taine and Barrès both viewed the population of the Midi as 'racial mongrels', congenitably frivolous, lazy, unproductive, insubordinate and unpatriotic. With the memory of the mutiny during the Midi revolt of 1907 still vivid, army officers in 1914 were quick to accuse southern conscripts of cowardice and lack of patriotic enthusiasm, citing the alleged remark of one conscript that the Midi had its own frontier, and that if the northerners wanted to defend theirs they should get on with it themselves.

Much of the peasantry still felt, despite decades of republican schooling and the spread of railways and conscriptions, subordinate and manipulated. Many were exploited by middlemen, wine and grain merchants, money-lenders and fertilizer salesmen. They were saddened by a rural exodus which weakened the solidarities of the village community. Many small-owners remained potentially vulnerable to any future agrarian depression. As we have seen, such peasant grievances had generated left-wing traditions in parts of the countryside. In the interwar years the communist party was to establish bastions in departments like the Corrèze and the Allier. Indeed in 1920 the communists were more successful in attracting peasant-smallholders in the Allier than in winning over industrial workers in Montluçon. One interesting hypothesis advanced to explain the strength of communism in twentieth-century France does, indeed, claim that it has its roots in deep-seated patterns of rural protest and left-wing rural penetration. This plausible thesis does, however, require careful qualification. One could argue that much of the rural 'socialism' of the Midi emphasized cheap credit and cooperatives, feeding most naturally into the domination of lower Languedoc in the interwar years by the reformist *SFIO*. The notion that peasants already radicalized in the villages, became converts to communism once they migrated to the cities needs qualification. The Guesdist-Marxist Nord bastion of the 1890s was built up among a workforce recruited from the Catholic and politically conformist peasantry of Flanders. The Paris *banlieue*, which became *the* communist stronghold after 1920, drew heavily on migrants from Catholic Brittany. Equally the idea, suggested by sociologists like Giddens, that the survival of neo-feudalism in the nineteenth-century countryside produced rural protest which, in turn, facilitated peasant socialism is, at best, a partial truth. For 'feudal' strongholds in the west remained Catholic-royalist fiefs, while resistance to clericalism and fear of the tithe frequently drove peasants, as in Burgundy, into the arms of anticlerical republicans.

Others have argued that the strength of French communism derives from the 'revolutionary tradition', perpetuated by the 1848 and 1871 insurrections, and embodied in Blanquism, Guesdism and syndicalism. While there is a strong element of truth in this, various qualifications must, again, be made. Lenin himself insisted that, by 1914 the *SFIO*, though 'lightly coloured with a revolutionary tint', was 'reformist in practice'. Jaurès, who became an increasingly dominant figure, emphasized that workers should utilize republican democracy, with its legal freedoms and educational opportunities. In 1920 Loriot, who supported the new communist party, lamented the hold of bourgeois-democratic ideology on workers' perspectives. 'Whatever we do, we cannot avoid the fact that in France, over 50 years of bourgeois democracy has created within the masses amongst whom we work . . . an entirely distinctive mentality. . . . People here are still convinced that we have a patrimony of liberties to defend. The whole of our mental formation is based on a revolutionary tradition, skilfully manipulated by our bourgeois democracy.'

Indeed one could argue that each of the main 'revolutionary' traditions of late-nineteenth century France exhibited particular weaknesses. Blanquism, sometimes interpreted as a precursor of Leninism, did not necessarily provide a very suitable preparation for future communist penetration. Blanqui's economic analysis, with its emphasis on parasitic usury, was crude and anachronistic. His elementary class analysis, with its contrast between one million exploiters and 30 million exploited, placed little emphasis on the role of the industrial proletariat. Even at its peak, in 1868–71, Blanquism had only a few thousand militants, and failed to sustain any effective alliance between the elite revolutionary party and the wider labour movement. Blanquism's violent anticlerical spirit caused the *CRC*, when it did capture power in St Denis in the 1890s, to waste its energies on futile attacks on the local clergy, while its Jacobin patriotism led some mavericks into Boulangism in the

1880s and Vaillant himself into the *Union Sacrée* in 1914. It has been suggested that this patriotism would have made Blanquism, had it survived, an obstacle to Leninism in France, although one could argue that French communism's strength has lain, precisely in its ability to channel anti-German sentiment in the 1940–4 period, anti-Americanism thereafter.

Guesdism too, did not *necessarily* provide fertile soil for post-1918 communism. Guesde's own Marxism was vulgar. His party tended to ignore or despise strike activity, and made its major gains in the 1890s when it adopted a reformist-municipalist strategy. Its strength in the rural Midi was based on support for peasant cooperatives. Above all it was weak in Paris, where the communist party built its bastion, powerful in the Nord which was to remain an *SFIO* stronghold.

Finally, the link between syndicalism and the post-1918 revolutionary left is unclear. Syndicalism, although it *had* recruited among the unskilled, had relied essentially on craft-groups who were already in sharp decline before the rapid mechanization of World War I. The communist party was to recruit heavily among the semi-skilled proletariat of the Parisian *banlieue* who had been untouched by syndicalism, and the communist-dominated bureaucratic, centralized unions were the antithesis of nineteenth-century decentralized craft-unions, and proved anathema to the surviving syndicalist veterans, who joined the *PC*, only to quit in disgust.*

Yet if the evidence for discontinuity between the pre-1914 left and the twentieth-century *PC* is strong, one could still argue that certain *general* characteristics of French society before 1914 did encourage the persistence of deep-seated alienation of the working class from the bourgeois state. For all its ability to manipulate the myth of 1789, the bourgeoisie ran the risk of having its rhetoric of liberty, equality and fraternity turned against it. Political dialogue in France was less couched in the obfuscatory mumbo-jumbo of constitutions and religion than was the case in Britain. 1789 and 1830 were sufficiently close at hand to make obvious that the bourgeoisie had come to power via the violent, revolutionary overthrow of the feudal elites – a fact decently obscured by the mists of time in Britain. France possessed a peculiarly intransigent

---

* This discussion owes much to the analysis of Duncan Gallie at the University of Warwick.

patronat which, in order to control wage levels to maintain international competitiveness, delayed trade-union legalization till 1884 and continued thereafter to refuse to recognize or negotiate with unions, regarding strikes as mutinies. The willingness of the governing elite, from Guizot via Thiers to Clemenceau, to utilize troops against strikers, to mobilize state violence rather than to make concessions, reminded workers in their daily experience that the state was the right arm of the employing class. The annual processions to Père Lachaise cemetery served to keep alive the memory that the republic had been born amid the mass slaughter of the Parisian working class. Despite minor social reforms, and some improvements in real-wages and diet, the workers remained a pariah class, poorly-housed, insecure, trapped into a rigid class-structure with little upward social mobility. Despite the republic's calculated utilization of social imperialist strategy after the 1880s, imperialism came too late to play the role it did in Victorian Britain. Kith-and-kin ties were fewer, pride in empire less pervasive and less corrupting.

Bibliography

Abbreviations

ACNSS	*Actes du Congrès National des Sociétés Savantes*
AHR	*American Historical Review*
AJS	*American Journal of Sociology*
AESC	*Annales: Économies, Sociétés, Civilisations*
AM	*Annales du Midi*
AHRF	*Annales Historiques de la Révolution Française*
ASR	*Archives de Sociologie des Religions*
BIHR	*Bulletin of the Institute of Historical Research*
CH	*Cahiers d'Histoire*
CHIMT	*Cahiers Historiques de l'Institut Maurice Thorez*
CHR	*Catholic Historical Review*
CSSH	*Comparative Studies in Society and History*
EcHR	*Economic History Review*
EHR	*English Historical Review*
ESR	*European Studies Review*
FHLMR	*Fédération Historique de Languedoc-Méditerranéen et de Roussillon*
FHS	*French Historical Studies*
HJ	*Historical Journal*
HR	*Historical Reflections*
HS	*Historical Studies*
IH	*Information Historique*
IRSH	*International Review of Social History*
JSS	*Jewish Social Studies*
JCH	*Journal of Contemporary History*
JEBH	*Journal of Economic and Business History*
JEH	*Journal of Economic History*
JEEH	*Journal of European Economic History*
JHI	*Journal of the History of Ideas*

JIH	*Journal of Interdisciplinary History*
JMH	*Journal of Modern History*
JPS	*Journal of Peasant Studies*
JPE	*Journal of Political Economy*
JSH	*Journal of Social History*
MS	*Mouvement Social*
NRS	*Nouvelle Revue Socialiste*
PP	*Past and Present*
PH	*Provence Historique*
REP	*Revue d'Économie Politique*
RE	*Revue Économique*
RFHOM	*Revue Française d'Histoire d'Outre-mer*
RFSP	*Revue Française des Sciences Politiques*
RHES	*Revue d'Histoire Économique et Sociale*
RHM	*Revue d'Histoire Moderne*
RHMC	*Revue d'Histoire Moderne et Contemporaine*
RH	*Revue Historique*
RN	*Revue du Nord*
Rom	*Romantisme*
SH	*Social History*
SHR1848	*Société d'Histoire de la Révolution de 1848*
SS	*Science and Society*
SSH	*Social Science History*
TS	*Theory and Society*

General Works

The following books cover the entire period.

Economy and Society
T. Kemp, *Economic Forces in French History* (1971)
P. O'Brien, *Economic Growth in Britain and France* (1978)
A. Armengaud, *La population française au XIXᵉ siècle* (1971)
F. Braudel and E. Labrousse (eds.), *Histoire Économique et Sociale de la France*: vol. III, *1789–1880* and vol. IV, *1880 à nos jours* (1976)
G. Dupeux, *French Society 1789–1970* (1976)
P. Sorlin, *La Société Française*, vol. I (1969)
A. Daumard, 'L'évolution des structures sociales de la France' (*RH 1972*)

A. Daumard, *et al.*, *Les fortunes françaises au XIXe siècle* (1973)

Education
A. Prost, *L'enseignement en France 1800–1967* (1967)
J. Moody, *French Education since Napoleon* (1978)

Culture and Society
M. Crubellier, *Histoire culturelle de la France Contemporaine* (1974)
J. Cruikshank (ed.), *French Literature and its Background*: vol. IV and vol. V (1969)
C. Bellanger (ed.), *Histoire-générale de la Presse Française*: vol. II, *1815–71* and vol. III, *1871–1940* (1972)

Army
R. Girardet, *La société militaire dans la France contemporaine* (1959)

Religion
A. Dansette, *Religious History of Modern France*. 2 vols. (1961)

Politics
R. Remond, *The Right Wing in France* (1966)
M. Branciard, *Société française et luttes de classes 1789–1914* (1967)

Rural Society
G. Duby and A. Wallon (eds.), *Histoire de la France Rurale*, vol. III, *1789–1914* (1976)

General Surveys
T. Zeldin, *France 1848–1945*, 2 vols. (1973; 1977)
G. Wright, *France in Modern Times* (1962)

Chapter 1

The best studies of the Restoration remain G. de Bertier de Sauvigny, *The Bourbon Restoration* (1966), sympathetic to the regime; J. Vidalenc, *La Restauration* (1968); and the still-useful F. Artz, *France under Bourbon Restoration* (1931). A. Jardin and A. Tudesq, *La France des Notables 1815–48* (1973), vol. VI of *Nouvelle Histoire de la France Contemporaine* (*NHFC*) is excellent.

The survival of the nobility is discussed by R. Gibson, 'The French Nobility in the Nineteenth Century' in J. Howarth and P. Cerny (eds.), *Élites in France* (1981); R. Forster, *PP 1967*; T. Beck, *JSH 1981*; D. Higgs, *ESR 1971*; A. Tudesq, 'Les survivances de l'Ancien Régime' in D. Roche and C. Labrousse (eds.), *Ordres et Classes* (1973); and Soutade-Rouger, *RHES 1960*. A. Soboul, *AESC 1968* and P. Masse, *AHRF 1958* and *1965* discuss the survival of 'feudalism' in the countryside.

The nobility's western bastions are studied in C. Tilly, *The Vendée* (1964); J. Meyer, *La noblesse bretonne* (1972); and in the important thesis of M. Denis, *Les royalistes de la Mayenne et le monde moderne* (1977). P. Bossis studies noble landholding in the Vendée in *ACNSS 1972* (97e Congrès), and R. Lagrée and R. Gildea debate the determinants of political attitudes in Ille-et-Vilaine in *EHR 1979*.

Midi ultraroyalism is studied by D. Resnick, *The White Terror* (1966), but placed more adequately in socio-economic context by G. Lewis, *The Second Vendée* (1978), complemented by his articles in *AHRF 1964* and *PP 1973*, and the thesis of B. Fitzpatrick, *Catholic Royalism in the Gard 1815–51* (Warwick University PhD). Useful regional studies include D. Higgs, *Ultraroyalism in Toulouse 1789–1830* (1973); R. Forster, *The House of Saulx-Tavanes* (1971), a study of one Burgundy dynasty; and C. Brélot, *La noblesse de Franche-Comté 1789–1808* (1972).

Ultraroyalist ideology is analysed by J. Oechslin, *Le mouvement ultraroyaliste sous la Restauration* (1960) and N. Hudson, *Ultraroyalism and the French Restoration* (1935). N. Richardson emphasizes aristocratic colonization of the bureaucracy in *The French Prefectoral Corps 1814–30* (1966). A. Spitzer discusses prefects and police in *CSSH 1966*. D. Cohen stresses the anti-capitalist rhetoric of de Bonald in *JMH 1969*. C. Pouthas shows the discrepancy between decentralist rhetoric and policy in *RHM 1926*. J. Vidalenc, *Les émigrés français 1789–1825* (1963) and D. Greer, *La Restauration et les biens des émigrés*, 2 vols. (1928) discuss the fate of exiled nobles. G. de Bertier de Sauvigny, *Un type d'ultraroyaliste: le Comte F. de Bertier* (1948) exposes the ultraroyalist 'congregation' secret society. J. Fourcassie, *Villele* (1964) is a useful biography, as are V. Beach, *Charles X* (1971) and J. Cabanis, *Charles X* (1972).

Religious politics are analysed by A. Dansette, op. cit., vol. I and E. Sévrin, *Les missions religieuses en France sous la Restauration*, 2 vols. (1948; 1959). Diocesan studies include M. Lagrée, *Mentalités, Religion et Histoire en Haute Bretagne* (1977) and C. Langlois, *Le diocèse de Vannes 1800–1830* (1974). S. Hartman in *JMH 1972* assesses the Sacrilege Law. T. Zeldin, 'The Conflict of Moralities' in Zeldin (ed.), *Conflicts in French Society* (1970) helps explain growing anticlericalism.

The one recent synthesis on '1830' remains D. Pinkney, *The French Revolution of 1830* (1972), stronger on detail than interpretation. In *FHS 1963*, *AHR 1964* and *RHMC 1965* he discusses popular activity in the revolution, as does R. Price, *ESR 1971*. *RHM 1931* has articles on the provinces. J. Merriman (ed.), *1830 in France* (1975) is a collection of useful essays. M. Agulhon analyses the 'liberty' which 1830 introduced in *Rom 1980*.

The role of the army in the opposition to the regime is assessed in D. Porch, *Army and Revolution* (1974) and R. Holroyd, *HJ 1971*. J. Vidalenc,

Les demi-solde (1957) studies Bonapartist veterans and L. Girard, *La Garde Nationale 1815–71* reveals petty-bourgeois discontent. Carbonarist plots are uncovered by A. Spitzer, *Old Hatreds and Young Hopes* (1971), while P. Pilbeam, *HJ 1982*, J. Newman, *JMH 1974*, and J. Merriman's essay on Limoges in Merriman (ed.), *French Cities in the Nineteenth Century* (1981) discuss the liberal opposition. The liberal press is the subject of C. Ledré, *La presse à l'assaut de la monarchie 1815–48* (1960) and D. Rader, *Journalists and the July Revolution in France* (1973), while S. Mellon, *The Political Uses of History* (1958) illustrates the utilization of history as propaganda. Liberal ideas are discussed in E. Harpez, *L'école libérale sous la Restauration* (1968). P. Gonnet, *RHES 1955* describes the economic crisis.

Among the best of the few regional monographs are P. Leuilliot, *L'Alsace au début du XIXe siècle*, 3 vols. (1960); J. Vidalenc, *Le départment de L'Eure: 1914–48* (1952); and M. Agulhon, *La vie sociale en Provence intérieure au lendemain de la Révolution* (1970).

Stendhal's novel *Scarlet and Black* is essential reading.

Chapter 2

The essential works are A. Tudesq, *Les grands notables en France 1840–49*, 2 vols. (1964) and J. Lhomme, *La grande bourgeoisie au pouvoir 1830–80* (1960). A. Daumard, *La bourgeoisie parisienne 1815–48* (1963) exhibits the strengths and weaknesses of a quantitative-statistical approach. Useful studies of the bourgeoisie include R. Pernoud, *Histoire de la Bourgeoisie en France*, vol. II (1962); F. Ponteil, *Les classes bourgeoises et l'avènement de la démocratie* (1968); C. Morazé, *The Triumph of the Middle Classes* (1966); and L. Bergeron, *Les capitalistes en France 1780–1914* (1978). E. Beau de Loménie, *Les responsabilités des dynasties bourgeoises*, 3 vols. (1943; 1947; 1954) is a stimulating polemic. The nature of the Orleanist elite is debated by D. Pinkney, 'The Myth of the Revolution of 1830' in T. Ropp (ed.), *Festschrift for F. B. Artz* (1964); A. Cobban, *FHS 1967*; and L. O'Boyle, *AHR 1966*.

Regional studies include J. Lambert-Dansette, *Quelques familles du patronat textile de Lille-Armentières* (1954); P. Barral, *Les Périers dans L'Isère* (1964) and *La Bourgeoisie Alsacienne* (1967); and O. Voillard, *Nancy au XIXe siècle* (1971).

M. Agulhon discusses bourgeois sociability in *Le cercle dans la France bourgeoise 1810–48* (1977), and B. Smith bourgeois wives in *Ladies of the Leisure Class: Bourgeoises of Northern France in the Nineteenth Century* (1981).

In addition to the works of Kemp and O'Brien cited in the general section, E. Labrousse, *et al.*, *Histoire Économique et Sociale de la France*, vol. III, *1789–1880* (1976) is fundamental. Other important works are A. Dunham, *The Industrial Revolution in France 1815–48* (1955); R. Price,

The Economic Modernization of France: 1750–1870 (1975); G. Palmade, *Capitalisme et Capitalistes français au XIXᵉ siècle* (1961); and B. Gille, *Recherches sur la formation de la grande entreprise capitaliste: 1815–48* (1959). Assessment of French economic performance can be found in F. Crouzet, *History 1974*, and M. Lévy-Leboyer, *AESC 1968*, who in *MS 1974* questions the myth of the 'Malthusian' entrepreneur propounded by D. Landes in *JEH 1949*. C. Johnson, 'The Revolution of 1830 in French Economic History' in J. Merriman (ed.), *1830 . . .*, op. cit. stresses the modernizing ethos of bureaucrats. D. Sherman in *JEEH 1977* emphasizes anxieties about rapid industrialization. P. Stearns in *JMH 1965* discusses attitudes towards British industry and in *Paths to Authority* (1978) analyses labour control policies. B. Ratcliffe in *JEEH 1978* surveys tariff reform, while C. Fohlen discusses attitudes towards laissez-faire in *RE 1956*.

Studies of particular regions include P. Léon, *La naissance de la grande industrie en Dauphiné*, 2 vols. (1954) and G. Thuiller, *G. Dufaud et les débuts du grand capitalisme en Nivernais* (1959). Coal-mining is studied in R. Geiger, *The Anzin Coal Company 1800–33* (1974); P. Guillaume, *La Compagnie des Mines de la Loire* (1966); and M. Gillet, *Les charbonnages du Nord de la France* (1973). On banking B. Gille, *La Banque et le Crédit en France* (1959) and M. Lévy-Leboyer, *Les banques européennes et l'industrialisation internationale* (1964) are essential, to be complemented by A. Tudesq, *RH 1961*. D. Landes, *The Unbound Prometheus* (1969) discusses textiles; G. Lefranc, *JEBH 1930* railways; and B. Gille, *Les origines de la grande industrie métallurgique en France* (1948) metallurgy.

The best introductions are P. Vigier, *La Monarchie de Juillet* (1969) and A. Jardin and A. Tudesq, op. cit. D. Johnson, *Guizot* (1963) remains essential. V. Starzinger, *Middleingness* (1963) compares the Orleanists to the Whigs.

Parliamentary politics are illuminated by L. Girard, *et al.*, *La Chambre des Députés en 1837–39* (1976); T. Beck, *French Legislators 1800–34* (1974); S. Kent, *Electoral Procedure under Louis Philippe* (1937); and P. B. Higgonet, *RH 1968*. The decline of Guizot's system is discussed by P. B. and T. Higgonet in *FHS 1967*; R. Koepke in *ESR 1979* and *FHS 1973*; and in A. Tudesq's essay in *Administration et Parlement depuis 1815* (1982). F. Julien-Laferrière, *Les députés fonctionnaires sous la Monarchie de Juillet* (1970) discusses the civil-servant/deputy phenomenon.

For foreign policy consult C. Pouthas, *La politique étrangère de la France 1815–48* (1948).

Among contemporary memoirs those of C. Remusat, *Mémoires de ma vie*, vols. III and IV (1960; 1962) and A. de Tocqueville, *Recollections* (1948) are revealing.

In addition to R. Remond, *Right . . .*, op. cit. and A. Dansette, *Religious . . .*, op. cit., A. Tudesq's *Les grands notables*, op. cit., vol. I is fundamental. R. Price in *HJ 1974* and J. Vidalenc in *ACNSS 1964* (88ᵉ Congrès) discuss legitimist resistance after 1830. J. B. Duroselle, *Les débuts du Catholicisme Social en France* (1951) analyses Catholic criticism of laissez-faire, as does P. Droulers, *Action Pastorale et problèmes sociaux sous la Monarchie de Juillet chez Mgr D'Astros* (1954). The regime's strained relationship with the clergy is illustrated by A. Dansette, op. cit., vol. I; Y. Hilaire, *Une chrétienté au 19ᵉ siècle? Le diocèse d'Arras* (1977); and by M. Gontard in *PH 1977*. Liberal Catholicism is discussed by J. Moody's essay in E. Acomb and M. Brown (eds.), *French Society and Culture since the Ancien Régime* (1966), and P. Stearns, *Priest and Revolutionary: Lamennais and the Dilemma of French Catholicism* (1967).

R. Giraud, *The Unheroic Hero* (1969) and C. Grana, *Modernity and its Discontents* (1967) analyse the distaste of intellectuals for Orleanism's ethos. An element of socio-political protest is discerned in popular literature by J. S. Allen, *Popular French Romanticism* (1981), D. Evans, *Social Romanticism in France 1830–48* (1951) and in *Romantisme et Politique: 1815–51* (1966). Generational and student protest is analysed by L. O'Boyle in *JMH 1970*; M. Esler, 'Youth in Revolt' in R. Bezucha (ed.), *Modern European Social History* (1972); J. Gallaher, *The Students of Paris* and *The Revolution of 1848* (1980). G. Lukács, *European Realism* (1950) remains a key Marxist analysis of major novelists.

In the absence of a modern study of republicanism G. Weill, *Histoire du parti républicain 1814–70* (1928) remains useful. A. Faure discusses working-class republicanism in *MS 1974*. R. Aminzade, *Class, Politics and Early Industrial Capitalism* (1981) studies Toulouse republicanism. Anti-Orleanist caricature is discussed by R. Passeron, *Daumier* (1981), and *Art and Politics in France* (Open University: Age of Revolutions Units 29–30) (1972).

Chapter 3

There is no adequate modern synthesis. W. Sewell, *Work and Revolution: the Language of Labor from Ancien Régime to 1848* (1980) emphasizes the continuity between artisan guild ideas and socialism. P. Kessel, *Le Prolétariat français avant Marx* (1968) is a useful survey by a journalist. B. Moss, *The Origins of the French Labor Movement* (1976) analyses cooperative socialism.

L. Chevalier, *Labouring and Dangerous Classes in Paris* (1973) remains stimulating but needs to be corrected by G. Rudé, 'Cities and Popular Revolt' in J. Bosher (ed.), *French Government and Society 1500–1850* (1973).

Strikes are analysed by J. Aguet, *Les grèves en France sous la Monarchie de Juillet* (1954) and P. Stearns, *AHR 1965*. F. Manuel, *JMH 1938* discusses Luddism. Textile workers are the subject of J. P. Courtheaux, *RE 1957*; W. Reddy, *PP 1977*; and A. Lasserre, *La situation des ouvriers de l'industrie textile dans la région lilloise* (1952). C. Johnson's essay in J. Merriman (ed.), *Consciousness and Class Experience* (1979) compares Lodève weavers and Parisian tailors. P. Guillaume in *MS 1963* analyses Loire miners' strikes.

Silk-weavers' revolts are studied by F. Rude, *L'insurrection Lyonnaise de 1831* (1969 ed.) and R. Bezucha, *The Lyon Uprising of 1834* (1974). L. Strumhinger, *Women and the Making of the Working Class: Lyon 1830–70* (1979) discusses female silk-workers, while M. McDougal in *JSH 1978* emphasizes community solidarities in Lyon.

Useful studies of artisans also include W. Sewell, *PP 1974* on Marseille; M. Agulhon, *Une ville ouvrière au temps du socialisme utopique: Toulon* (1970); Y. Guin, *Le mouvement ouvrier nantais* (1976); and R. Aminzade, op. cit. (1981) on Toulouse. C. Johnson, *Icarian Communism in France, 1839–51* (1974), together with articles in *IRSH 1966* and *AHR 1971*, are important studies of Cabetism.

Workers' newspapers are analysed by A. Cuvillier, *Un journal d'ouvriers: 'L'Atelier'* (1954) and E. C. Altman, *The Emergence of a Workers' Newspaper Press in Paris 1830–48* (PhD thesis Brandeis University, Mass. 1974). A special edition of *MS 1966* discusses working-class anticlericalism, as does F. Isambert in *ASR 1958*. Proudhon's anticlericalism is studied by P. Haubtmann, *Genèse d'un antitheiste* (1969).

Among the rare worker autobiographies M. Nadaud, *Mémoires de Léonard* (1976 ed.); J. Benoît, *Confessions d'un prolétaire* (1968 ed.); and A. Perdiguier, *Mémoires d'un compagnon* (1964 ed.) are all of interest.

G. Lichtheim, *Origins of Socialism* (1968) is an introduction to pre-Marxist socialism. F. Manuel, *The Prophets of Paris* (1962) is interesting on Fourier and St Simon. R. Fakkar, *L'influence de St Simon* (1968) analyses Marx's debt to St Simon. P. Ansart, *Naissance de l'anarchisme* (1970) and R. Hoffmann, *Revolutionary Justice* (1972) are sympathetic to Proudhon. L. Loubère, *Louis Blanc* (1959) and A. Spitzer, *The Revolutionary Theories of L. A. Blanqui* (1957) are both lucid and useful.

J. Maitron, *Dictionnaire biographique du mouvement ouvrier français* contains invaluable biographies of hundreds of militants. H. Rigaudis-Weiss, *Les enquêtes ouvrières 1830–48* (1936) is still valuable.

J. Vidalenc, *Le Peuple des Campagnes 1815–48* (1970) is an interesting survey, while E. Weber, *Peasants into Frenchmen* (1976) emphasizes 'archaism' in rural society. A. Jardin and A. Tudesq, 'La France des Notables' in *NHFC* vol. VII contains useful information on the regions. G. Cholvy, *IH 1974* provides a short analysis of peasant society and culture.

H. Clout, *French Agriculture on the Eve of the Railway Age* (1980) surveys agricultural productivity, as does Newell in *JEH 1973* and J. Toutain, *Le produit physique de l'agriculture français*, vol. II (1961).

Impressive regional studies include A. Corbin, *Archaisme et Modernité en Limousin 1845–80*, 2 vols. (1975); A. Armengaud, *Les populations de l'est Aquitaine 1845–71* (1961); G. Désert, *Les paysans du Calvados 1815–95*, 3 vols. (1975); R. Laurent, *Les vignerons de la Côte d'Or*, 2 vols. (1958); and P. Vigier, *La Seconde République dans la région alpine*, vol. I (1963).

Rural religiosity and anticlericalism are analysed by Y. Hilaire, *IH 1963*;

G. Cholvy, *Religion et Société au XIXᵉ siècle: le diocèse de Montpellier*; C. Marcilhacy, *Le diocèse d'Orléans au milieu du XIXᵉ siècle* (1964); *ASR 1958*; and J. Faury in *ACNSS 1977* (102ᵉ Congrès).

A. Soboul emphasizes 'feudal' survivals in *AESC 1968* and the threats to the village community in *PP 1956*. Forest rights conflicts are discussed by F. Baby, *La guerre des 'demoiselles' de l'Ariège* (1972), by J. Merriman's essay in J. Merriman (ed.), *1830 . . .*, op. cit. and L. Clarenc in *AM 1965* and *1967*. J. Merriman discusses rural arson in *FHS 1976*. Food riots are the subject of L. Tilly, *JIH 1971*, while Y. Bionnier analyses the Indre troubles of 1846–7 in *Cahiers Médiévaux* (1978). J. Vila studies vineyard strikes in the Midi in his essay in *Droite et Gauche en Languedoc de 1789 à nos jours* (1975). J. F. Soulié discusses 'usury' in Pyrénées in *AM 1978* and it is the theme of H. de Balzac's *Les Paysans*, ed. J.-H. Donnard (1964). A. Corbin in *RH 1971* and A. Chatelain, *Les migrants temporaires 1800–1914* (1976) discuss temporary migration. P. Vigier's essay in *La France au XIXᵉ siècle: Mélanges C. Pouthas* (1973) stresses the importance of the widening of the municipal franchise after 1831, while P. Jones, *ESR 1980* sees southern Massif 'politics' in terms of local feuds.

D. Fabre and J. Lacroix, *La vie quotidienne des paysans de Languedoc au XIXᵉ siècle* (1973), though weak on chronology, offers stimulating insights from two social anthropologists.

Chapter 4

R. Price, *The French Second Republic: A Social History* (1972); P. Vigier, *La Seconde République* (1967); and M. Agulhon, *1848 ou l'apprentissage de la République* (1973) are all good recent introductions. R. Price, *Revolution and Reaction* (1975) is a collection of essays. G. Duveau, *1848* (UK, 1968) is interesting but impressionistic.

K. Marx, *The Class Struggles in France* and *The 18th Brumaire of Louis Bonaparte* remain essential reading, alongside A. de Tocqueville, *Recollections* (1971 ed.) and G. Flaubert, *Sentimental Education*. E. Gargan, *De Tocqueville: The Critical Years* (1955) and S. Drescher, *De Tocqueville and the Dilemma of Democracy* (1968) are both excellent.

The impact of the economic crisis is explored in E. Labrousse (ed.), *Aspects de la crise 1846–51* (1956); for Paris by Markovitch, *RHES 1965*; for the Loire by P. Guillaume, *RHMC 1963*.

C. Jennings, *France and Europe in 1848* (1973) discusses the republic's failure to take up the Jacobin heritage. G. Fasel studies the April election in *FHS 1974* and analyses republican strategy in *FHS 1974*. Radicalism is discussed by P. McPhee, *HS 1974*; A. Calman, *Ledru Rollin* (1980 ed.); and M. Dessal, *Delescluze* (1952). R. Gossez studies peasant tax-revolt in *SHR 1948: Études XV* (1953). A. Cobban analyzes the role of teachers and clergy in the April elections in *France since the Revolution* (1970), while J. Droz (ed.), *Réaction et suffrage universel 1848–50* (1963) discusses attitudes to universal suffrage.

See also the works cited in chapter 3, by Sewell, Moss, Johnson, Agulhon, Aminzade, Strumhinger and Guin.

R. Gossez, *Les ouvriers de Paris* (1967) is a mine from which useful information can be hewn. W. Sewell analyses workers' revolutionary discourse in *CSSH 1979*. G. Fasel discusses provincial workers in *IRSH 1972*. D. McKay, *The National Workshops* (1933) has not been superseded. T. Christofferson in *FHS 1980* discusses provincial workshops. P. Amann, *Revolution and Mass Democracy* (1975) assesses the role of Parisian clubs. Blanqui's strategy is discussed by T. Denholm in E. Kamenka (ed.), *Intellectuals and the Revolutions of 1848* (1979). W. Sewell and T. Christofferson analyse Marseille conflicts in *MS 1971* and *The Historian 1974*, while J. Merriman studies Limoges workers in *Societas 1974*, and R. Leibman repression of militancy in Lyon in *SSH 1980*.

The June Days are the subject of C. Tilly and E. Lees in R. Price (ed.), op. cit.; G. Rudé, *The Crowd in History* (1964); R. Gossez, *EG 1956*; and M. Traugott, *AJS 1980*, while the '*garde mobile*' is analysed by P. Caspard, *RHMC 1974* and M. Traugott, *TS 1980*.

A. Tudesq, *Les grands notables*, op. cit., vol. II is indispensable for the elites. F. de Luna, *The French Republic under Cavaignac* (1969) attempts to salvage the general's reputation. Bonapartism is analysed by A. Tudesq, *L'élection présidentielle de Louis Napoléon* (1965) and in *RH 1957*; F. Bluche, *Bonapartisme, naissance d'une tradition de droite 1800–50* (1980); and A. Dansette, *Louis Napoléon à la conquête du pouvoir* (1961).

P. Pierrard, *1848: Les pauvres, L'Évangile et La Révolution* (1977) discusses the role of religion in the revolution. The dilemmas of liberal Catholicism are analysed by M. Gabbert in *FHS 1978* and *CHR 1978*. M. Hebert and A. Carnac, *La Loi Falloux* (1953) summarizes the education debate.

The problems of the Party of Order are discussed by M. Cox, *FHS 1968* and M. Huard in *Droite et Gauche en Languedoc*, op. cit. J. Merriman, *The Agony of the Republic* (1978) and T. Forstenzer, *The French Provincial Police and the Fall of the Second Republic* (1981) present contrasting views on the efficacy of bureaucratic repression.

See also the works of Corbin and Weber cited for chapter 3.

T. Margadant, *French Peasants in Revolt* (1979) is now, despite its questionable 'modernization' thesis, the definitive general study. M. Agulhon's brilliant *La République au Village* (1970) studies the Var. Important regional studies include P. Vigier, *La Seconde République dans la région alpine*, vol. II (1963); L. Loubère, *AHR 1968* on lower Languedoc; and P. Goujon, *Le vignoble de la Saône-et-Loire 1815–71* (1975). Older but useful studies include J. Dagnan, *Le Gers sous la Seconde République*, 2 vols. (1929); G. Rocal, *1848 en Dordogne* (nd); and E. Reynier, *La IIe République dans L'Ardèche* (1947). C. Marcilhacy studies the Loiret in *RHMC 1959* and A. Bergerat radicalism in the Allier in *CHIMT 1978*.

The 1849 election is analysed by J. Bouillon in *RFSP 1956* and the left's rural propaganda by M. Agulhon in *PH 1960*; R. Magraw, *FHS 1978*; and A. Zevaès in *La Révolution de 1848* (1934–5). The politicization of peasant culture is explored by P. McPhee in *JPS 1978* and by T. Clark's outstanding *Image of the People* (1973). J. Gaillard emphasizes the credit question in peasant politics in *SHR 1948: Études XVI* (1954). The role of radical teachers is assessed by M. Gontard in *PH 1977*. J. Martinet, *Clamécy et ses flotteurs* (1976) shows the 'vanguard' position of wood-floaters, and R. Huard, *AM 1971* discusses protests against the 1850 electoral law. E. Weber in *FHS 1980* and Y. Bercé, *Croquants et Nus-Pieds* (1974) emphasize peasant 'archaism'.

M. Agulhon discusses interpretations of the 1851 insurrection, while V. Wright in R. Price (ed.), *Revolution*, op. cit. assesses the nature of the repression. Much of the recent historiography is summarized by P. Vigier in *AHRF 1975*.

Chapter 5

Recent general studies of the regime include A. Plessis, *De la fête impériale au mur des fédérés* (1973) and J. Bury, *Napoleon III and the Second Empire* (1965). S. Campbell, *The Second Empire Revisited* (1978) is a stimulating analysis of historians' assessments of the regime, for which one can also consult A. Spitzer, *FHS 1961–2*.

The works of Kemp, R. Price, Palmade, Lhomme and Pernoud cited for chapter 2 are valuable. Rail policy is discussed in L. Girard, *La politique des travaux publics du Second Empire* (1952). For banking, consult J. Bouvier, *Le Crédit Lyonnais* (1961); D. Landes, *RHMC 1956*; and R. Cameron, *JPE 1955*. C. Fohlen, *L'industrie textile du Second Empire* (1956) and B. Gille, *La sidérurgie française au XIXe siècle* (n.d.) discuss major industries.

C. Freedman, *Joint-Stock Enterprise in France 1800–67* (1980) emphasizes relaxation of controls on companies. F. Wallin in *Studies in Modern History in Honour of F. Palm* (1956) illustrates counter-cyclical interventionism. J. Gaillard, *Paris la Ville* (1977), D. Pinkney, *Napoleon III and Rebuilding of Paris* (1958), and C. Leonard, *Lyon Transformed* (1961) discuss urban renewal. P. Cayez, *Métiers Jacquards et hauts fourneaux* (1978) studies the Lyonnais. For the free-trade issue consult A. Dunham, *The Anglo-French Treaty of 1860* (1930); M. Rist, *REP 1956*; and P. Bairoch, *RE 1970*. R. Cameron (ed.), *Essays in French Economic History* (1970) contains useful articles. R. Locke studies 'corporate business' in *FHS 1977*.

T. Zeldin, *The Political System of Napoleon III* (1958) attempts a Namier-ite approach. G. Boilet discusses the emperor's ideas in *La doctrine sociale de Napoléon III* (1961). The bureaucracy is analysed by H. Payne, *The Police State of Louis Bonaparte* (1966); V. Wright, *Le Conseil d'État sous le Second Empire* (1972); B. Le Clère and V. Wright, *Les* *préfets du IIe Empire* (1973); and V. Wright, *RH 1968*. L. Girard and A. Prost emphasize the influence of *notables* in *Les Conseillers Généraux en 1870* (1967).

Among the more useful studies of individual ministers are J. Maurain, *Baroche* (1936); R. Schnerb, *Rouher* (1949 ed.); H. Farat, *Persigny* (1957); and J. Rohr, *Duruy* (1967).

J. Maurain, *La politique écclésiastique du Second Empire* (1930) remains essential for church-state relations. The regime's failure to rally the Catholic-royalist elites is emphasized by A. Gough, 'The Conflict in Politics' in T. Zeldin (ed.), *Conflicts . . .*, op. cit. (1970); M. Denis, *Les royalistes de la Mayenne*, op. cit.; G. Cholvy, *Religion et Société*, op. cit.; and M. Brown, *Louis Veuillot* (1977). Nord *notables* are discussed by B. Menager, *IH 1979*.

R. Anderson, *Education in France 1848–70* (1975) analyses educational conflicts. D. Baker and P. Harrigan (eds.), *The Making of Frenchmen: Current Directions in the History of Education in France* (1979) contains useful essays. P. Harrigan, *Mobility, Elites and Education* (1980) should be qualified by R. Anderson's review in *SH 1982*. R. Oberlé, *L'enseignement à Mulhouse 1789–1870* (1961) is a good local study, while Catholic colleges are the subject of J. Bush, *FHS 1975*; P. Harrigan, *Societas 1976*; and J. Padberg, *Colleges in Controversy* (1969).

P. Vigier's essay in *Le Bonapartisme: Phénomène Historique et Mythe Politique* (1977) suggests a framework. In addition to the regional studies already cited for chapters 2 and 3 by Armengaud, Loubère, Goujon, Laurent, Désert and Corbin, one can consult G. Dupeux, *Aspects de l'Histoire Sociale et Politique du Loir-et-Cher 1848–1914* (1962); G. Garrier, *Paysans du Beaujolais et du Lyonnais* (1973); and E. Constant, *Le département du Var sous le Second Empire* (Aix thesis 1977).

J. Darmon, *Le colportage de librairie en France* (1972) discusses rural culture. R. Price and P. Hohenberg debate rural labour supply in *EcHR 1975* and *1979*. R. Magraw in T. Zeldin (ed.), *Conflicts . . .*, op. cit. and C. Marcilhacy, *Le diocèse d'Orléans sous . . . Mgr Dupanloup* (1962) analyse peasant anticlericalism. Rural election conflicts are studied by L. Girard (ed.), *Les élections de 1869* (1960) and M. Vigneux, *RHMC 1978*. E. Zola's novel *The Earth* (*La Terre*) (Penguin ed. 1980) offers a vivid portrait of peasant attitudes.

The works by Moss and Aminzade cited for chapter 3 are useful. G. Duveau, *La vie ouvrière en France sous le Second Empire* (1946) is brilliant if idiosyncratic. P. Pierrard, *La vie ouvrière à Lille sous le Second Empire* (1965) and Y. Lequin, *Les ouvriers de la région Lyonnaise 1848–1914*, 2 vols. (1977) offer local studies.

D. Kulstein discusses workers' attitudes to Bonapartism in *FHS 1962* and *IRSH 1964*, as does B. Ménager, *RH 1981*. L. Berlanstein studies adolescent apprenticeships and delinquency in *JSH 1979* and *FHS 1980* and D. Pinkney migrant workers in *JMH 1955*.

G. Sheridan discusses Lyon silk-workers in *FHS 1979* and M. Moissonnier studies the rise of the worker opposition in the city in *CH 1965*. P. Léon, *RHMC 1954* and F. L'Huillier, *La lutte ouvrière à la fin du Second Empire* (1957) discuss strikes. J. Gaillard discusses metalworkers in *MS 1960–1* and producer cooperatives in *MS 1965*. D. Poulot in A. Cotterau (ed.), *Le Sublime* (1980) is essential for Parisian militancy.

G. Duveau, *La pensée ouvrière sur l'éducation* (1947); F. Charpin, *Pratique religieuse et formation d'une grande ville: Marseille* (1964); and A. Gough in E. Kamenka (ed.), *Paradigm for Revolution* (1971) discuss worker attitudes to education and religion.

The regime's decline is described by T. Zeldin, *Ollivier and the Liberal Empire* (1963) and M. Jeloubovska, *La chute du Second Empire* (1954). For foreign policy consult P. Renouvin, *La politique extérieure du Second Empire* (1947); N. Barker, *The French Experience in Mexico* (1979); L. Case, *French Opinion on War and Diplomacy* (1954); M. Howard, *The Franco-Prussian War* (1967); and M. Emerit, *RHMC 1969* on the Spanish crisis.

S. Elwitt, *The Making of the Third Republic* (1975) and *FHS 1969*, and K. Auspitz, *The Radical Bourgeoisie* (1982) analyse the republican revival. L. Girard, *Les élections de 1869* (1960) can be complemented by articles in *CH 1956, 1961, 1962* and *RHES 1963*. D. Gordon's essay in J. Merriman (ed.), *Cities in Nineteenth-Century France* (1981) discusses republican industrialists. R. Williams, *H. Rochefort* (1970) studies a radical journalist.

The Parisian working-class revolutionary mood is discussed by A. Faure, A. Dalotel and J. C. Freiermuth, *Aux Origines de la Commune* (1980); M. Dommanget, *Blanqui et l'opposition révolutionnaire . . .* (1960); and J. Bruhat, *E. Varlin* (1975).

K. Marx, *The Civil War in France* (1872) remains essential. The best synthesis in English is S. Edwardes, *The Paris Commune* (1971). E. Schulkind, *The Paris Commune: The View from the Left* (1972) is a collection of documents. Of the countless French studies the most stimulating include J. Rougerie, *Le procès des Communards* (1964) and *Paris Libre* (1971); C. Rihs, *La Commune de Paris* (1955); H. Lefèbvre, *La proclamation de la Commune* (1965); and J. Bruhat, *et al.*, *La Commune de 1871* (1960).

J. Leith (ed.), *Images of the Commune* (1977) offers interesting essays. E. Thomas, *The Women Incendiaries* (1967) studies women militants. M. Dommanget, *L'enseignement, l'enfance et la culture sous la Commune* (1964) discusses education. R. Toombs, *The War against Paris* (1981) analyses the military repression.

R. Wolfe studies the Montmartre revolutionary club in *PP 1968*. R. Price discusses communard ideology in *HJ 1971*. Waldmann in *SS 1973* describes the branding of communards as criminals. G. Wright studies internal opposition in *FHS 1977* and J. Roberts right-wing interpretations in *EHR supplement 1973*. E. Schulkind in *FHS 1960* emphasizes the role of popular organizations.

The provincial response is analysed by L. Greenberg, *Sisters of Liberty* (1971); J. Gaillard, *Communes de Province* (1971); Olivesi, *La Commune de Marseille* (1950); J. Archer, *MS 1971*; and R. Aminzade, op. cit.

Chapter 6

S. Elwitt, *The Making* . . ., op. cit. is essential. J. Mayeur, *Les débuts de la IIIᵉ République* (1973) and R. Anderson, *France 1870–1914* (1977) provide sound general studies. P. Barral, *Les fondateurs de la IIIᵉ République* (1968) contains documents.

A. Mitchell, *The German Influence on France after 1870* (1979) is not entirely convincing. J. Bouvier in *RH 1953* and *RHMC 1958* analyses the political response of capitalist groups, and R. Schnerb, *RH 1949*, Thiers's fiscal policy. R. Gouault, *Comment la France est devenue républicaine 1870–75* (1954) studies by-elections, and J. Joughhin, *The Paris Commune in French Politics 1871–84* discusses the amnesty issue.

Among biographical studies J. Bury, *Gambetta and the Making of the Third Republic* (1973) and *Gambetta's Final Years* (1982) are sympathetic to their subject. S. Ashley, *FHS 1975* analyses Gambetta's ministry. P. Sorlin, *Waldeck-Rousseau* (1966) is essential. P. Bertocci, *J. Simon* (1978); M. Schmidt, *A. Ribot* (1977); and Albrecht-Carrié, *A. Thiers or the Triumph of the Bourgeoisie* (1977) are useful. A. Siegfried, *Jules Siegfried 1836–1922* (1946) discusses a republican business *notable*.

Education policy is analysed by K. Auspitz, *The Radical Bourgeoisie* . . ., op. cit.; E. Acomb, *The French Laic Laws* (1941); L. Legrand, *L'influence du positivisme dans l'oeuvre scolaire de J. Ferry* (1961); F. Mayeur, *L'enseignement secondaire des jeunes filles en France* (1977) and *L'éducation des jeunes filles* (1979). M. Maingeunau, *Les livres d'école de la République* (1979) analyses textbooks.

The works by Kemp, Palmade and Cameron cited above remain useful. E. Labrousse (ed.), *Histoire Économique et Sociale de la France*, vol. IV (1976) is essential.

C. Trebilcock, *Industrialization of the Continental Powers* (1981) is 'pessimistic'. E. Carter, *et al.*, *Enterprise and Entrepreneurs in Nineteenth-Century France* (1976) contains important essays.

M. Lévy-Leboyer in *MS 1974* refuses to blame 'Malthusian' entrepreneurs for the economic slow-down analysed in *RHES 1971*. M. Smith, *Tariff Reform in France 1860–1900* (1980) defends tariff protectionism as useful for the elites.

J. Bouvier, *Un siècle de banque français* (1973) discusses financiers. C. A. Michalet, *Les placements des épargnants français* (1968) studies investment patterns and A. White, *The French International Accounts* (1933) calculates the balance of payments.

F. Caron, *La compagnie des chemins-de-fer du Nord* (1973) studies a major railway, while R. Gonjo analyses the Freycinet Plan in *RH 1972*. F. Crouzet assesses the locomotive industry in *RHES 1977* and the armament sector in *RH 1973*. M. Gillet in *RN 1971* and D. Lemenuvel in *RH 1981* discuss the coal industry, while J. Laux, *In First Gear* (1976) is enthusiastic about the car industry.

R. Fox and G. Weisz (eds.), *Organization of Science and Technology in France* (1981) emphasize the 'modernization' of higher education, as does T. Shinn, *L'école polytechnique* (1980).

Business lobbying is discussed by H. Peiter, *JSH 1975*; R. Prioret, *Les Origines du Patronat Français* (1963); and M. Rust, *Business and Politics in the Third Republic* (Princeton PhD 1974).

H. Brunschwig, *French Colonialism* (1966) sees economic empire as a 'myth'. C. Ageron, *France coloniale ou Parti Colonial* (1978) emphasizes the limited popularity of empire. J. Ganiage, *L'expansion coloniale de la France* (1968) describes expansionism. C. Andrews and A. Kanya-Forstner, *France Overseas* (1981) offers an assessment.

For imperialist ideology consult R. Girardet, *L'idée coloniale en France* (1972); R. Betts, *Assimilation and Association in French Colonial Thought* (1960); and C. Ageron, *L'anticolonialisme en France* (1973). M. Astier-Loutfi, *Littérature et Colonialisme* (1971) analyses colonial novels.

Studies of particular regions include J. Ganiage, *Les origines du protectorat français en Tunisie* (1959) and A. Kanya-Forstner, *The Conquest of Western Sudan* (1969).

For economic imperialism see J. Bouvier, *MS 1974*; S. Elwitt, *SS 1967*; J. Laffey, *FHS 1969* and *HR 1974*; Lagana, *RFHOM 1979*; T. Hara, *RHES 1976*; R. Johnson in R. Owen and B. Sutcliffe (eds.), *Studies in the Theory of Imperialism* (1972); P. Guillen, *RI 1974*; M. Brugière, *RHD 1963*; R. Thobie, *Intérêts économiques et imperialisme français dans l'Empire ottoman* (1977); and C. Coquery-Vidrovitch, *Le Congo au temps des grandes compagnies concessionnaires* (1972). S. Persell in *HJ 1974* and *HR 1981* discusses the '*Parti Colonial*' and the business ties of the colonial lobby are emphasized by L. Abrams and D. Miller in *HJ 1976*, denied by C. Andrews and A. Kanya-Forstner in *HJ 1971* and *1976*.

M. Réberioux, *La République Radicale 1898–1914* (1973) is stimulating. There is no satisfactory party history, but J. Kayser, *Les grandes batailles du Radicalisme* (1962) and J. Nordmann, *Histoire des Radicaux* (1974) are useful. J. Ellis's psycho-history, *The Early Life of G. Clemenceau* (1980) complements D. Dawson's sober *G. Clemenceau* (1976). L. Loubère studies radicals' socio-economic policies in *IRSH 1962*, *FHS 1963*, *RHES 1964* and J. Hayward analyses solidarism in *IRSH 1959, 1961, 1963*, as does M. Ruby, *Le Solidarisme* (1971). M. Vandenbussche studies Nord radicalism in *RN 1965*.

On Caillaux consult J. C. Allain, *Caillaux; le défi victorieux* (1978) and F. Seagar, *FHS 1979*.

Chapter 7

E. Weber, 'France' in E. Weber and H. Rogger (eds.), *The European Right* (1965); R. Girardet, *Le Nationalisme français* (1966); and R. Anderson, *Conservative Politics in France* (1974) are general surveys. D. Shapiro (ed.), *The Right in France 1890–1919* (1962) contains useful essays.

Royalist decline is analysed by R. Locke, *French Legitimists* (1974); S. Osgood, *French Royalism since 1870* (1970); M. Brown, *The Comte de Chambord* (1967); J Rothney, *Bonapartism after Sedan* (1969); and A. Bonafous, *RH 1965*.

For aristocratic politics consult M. Denis, *Les royalistes*, op. cit.; J. Bécarud, *RFSP 1973*; and D. Halevy, *La Fin des Notables* (1972 ed.).

Religious politics are discussed by J. McManners, *Church and State in France* (1972); J. Gadille, *La pensée et l'action des évêques français 1870–83*, 2 vols. (1967); A. Sedgewick, *The Ralliement in French Politics* (1965); and M. Larkin, *Church and State after the Dreyfus Affair* (1974). J. Mayeur discusses the inventories' disputes in *AESC 1966*.

B. Martin, *Count Albert de Mun* (1978) studies a key lay Catholic. B. Ménager, *La laicisation des écoles communales dans le Nord* (1971) illustrates conflicts over the laic laws, while J. Freyssinet-Dominjon, *Les manuels scolaires de l'École libre* (1969) analyses Catholic school textbooks.

Aspects of social Catholicism are covered by H. Rollet, *L'action sociale des Catholiques en France*, 2 vols. (1948; 1957); J. Mayeur, *L'abbé Lemire* (1968); R. Talmy, *L'Association Catholique des Patrons du Nord* (1962); C. Molette, *L'Association Catholique de la Jeunesse Française* (1968); and J. Caron, *Le Sillon et la Démocratie Chrétienne* (1967). On Catholic trade unions see T. Caldwell, *IRSH 1966* and M. Launay, *MS 1969*.

R. Griffiths, *The Reactionary Revolution* (1966) analyses Catholic literature.

Z. Sternhell, *La Droite Révolutionnaire en France* (1978) seeks to link proto-fascism with the left. For Boulangism consult F. Seagar, *The Boulanger Affair* (1967); J. Néré, *Le Boulangisme et la presse* (1964); and P. Hutton, *FHS 1971*. Déroulède is assessed by P. Rutkoff, *FHS 1974* and Z. Sternhell, *JCH 1971* and Barrès by Z. Sternhell, *M. Barrès et le Nationalisme Français* (1972); R. Soucy, *Fascism in France* (1972); and C. Stuart Doty, *From Cultural Rebellion to Counter-revolution* (1976).

Crowd theory is the subject of S. Barrows, *Distorting Mirrors* (1981) and R. Nye, *Origins of Crowd Psychology* (1975).

Small-trader grievances are discussed by M. Réberioux and P. Nord in *MS 1981*. S. Wilson, *Ideal and Experience: Anti-semitism in France at the Time of Dreyfus* (1982) supersedes R. Byrnes, *Anti-semitism in Modern France*, vol. I (1950). S. Wilson's articles in *JCH 1975* and *HJ 1973* remain useful. Catholic anti-semitism is explored by P. Sorlin, *La Croix et les Juifs*

(1967); P. Pierrard, *Juifs et Catholiques Français* (1970); and J. Verdès-Leroux, *Scandale Financier et Antisémitisme Catholique* (1969). V. Glasberg analyses socialist anti-semitism in *JSS 1974*. P. Albert, *The Modernization of French Jewry* (1979) and M. Marrus, *The Politics of Assimilation* (1971) study the Jewish community.

The Dreyfus Affair is explored by R. Kedward, *The Dreyfus Affair* (1965) and D. Johnson, *France and the Dreyfus Affair* (1967). D. Ralston, *The Army of the Republic* (1967) and P. Porch, *The March to the Marne* (1981) assess the role of the military. F. Bédarida emphasizes officer royalism in *RH 1964*, A. Mitchell the role of spy-fever in *JMH 1980*. J. Ponty discusses press coverage of the Affair in *RHMC 1974*, and an issue of *RFSP 1959* the role of intellectuals. M. Burns, *HR 1978* assesses the Affair in rural France.

E. Weber, *Action Française* (1962); E. Tannenbaum, *The Action Française* (1962); and L. Thomas, *L'Action Française devant l'Église* (1965) analyse the post-Dreyfus right. P. Mazgaj, *The Action Française and Revolutionary Syndicalism* (1979); J. Roth, *The Cult of Violence: Sorel and the Sorelians* (1980); G. Mosse, *JCH 1972*; and R. Griffiths, *JCH 1978* discuss rightist wooing of the workers.

For the pre-1914 period consult E. Weber, *The Nationalist Revival in France* (1959); Sumler, *FHS 1970*; R. Sansom, *RHMC 1973*; A. Olivesi, *PH 1957*; and Beneton, *RFSP 1971*.

Chapter 8

M. Réberioux's contribution to J. Droz (ed.), *Histoire Générale du Socialisme*, vol. II, *1875–1918* (1975) is an excellent introduction. International comparisons are made by P. Stearns and H. Mitchell, *Workers and Protest* (1971) and D. Geary, *European Labour Movements* (1981), and C. Willard, *Socialisme et Communisme Français* (1970) provides a short survey. G. Lefranc, *Le mouvement socialiste sous la IIIe République* (1963) and D. Ligou, *Histoire du Socialisme en France* (1962) are standard accounts. A. Noland, *The Founding of the French Socialist Party* (1956) and J. Fiechter, *Le socialisme français de l'Affaire Dreyfus à la Grande Guerre* (1965) cover the 1893–1914 years. Useful interpretative articles include D. Baker, *HR 1974*; L. Derfler, *RHMC 1963*; M. Réberioux, *AESC 1964*; and A. Kriegel, *Le Pain et les Roses* (1968).

L. Portis, *Workers and Bourgeois Culture* (N. Illinois University PhD 1975) discusses attempts to 'integrate' workers. H. Hatzfield, *Du pauperisme à la sécurité sociale* (1971) discusses social welfare policy.

Marxist thought is analysed by G. Lichtheim, *Marxism in Modern France* (1966) and T. Paquot, *Les faiseurs de nuages* (1981) and the Marxist movement discussed by C. Willard, *Les Guesdistes* (1965); C. Landauer, *IRSH 1961*; D. Baker and L. Derfler in *IRSH 1967*; and P. Hutton, *FHS 1971*.

Blanquism is discussed by P. Hutton, *JMH 1974*; J. Howarth, *MS 1970* and *NRS 1975*; and M. Dommanget, *E. Vaillant* (1956). D. Stafford, *From Anarchism to Reformism* (1971) studies Brousse, while M. Winock, *MS 1971* explains Allemane's break with possibilism. H. Goldberg, *The Life of Jean Jaurès* (1964) needs to be complemented by *Jaurès et la classe ouvrière* (1981). L. Derfler, *Millerand* (1979) is a sound study. Municipalist socialism is analysed by M. McQuillan, *The Development of Municipal Socialism in France* (University of Virginia PhD 1972); J. Scott in J. Merriman (ed.), *Cities . . .*, op. cit.; and J. Brunet, *St Denis: la ville rouge* (1979).

J. Maitron, *Le mouvement anarchiste en France*, 2 vols. (1975) is a definitive study of anarchism. Useful articles include J. Maitron, *MS 1973*; J. Masse, *MS 1969*; and J. Polet, *RN 1969*, while N. Fleming, *The Anarchist Way to Socialism: E. Reclus* (1979) is a biography of an anarchist militant.

P. Stearns, *Lives of Labor* (1975) has information on living standards. J. Rougerie and J. Lhomme analyse wage-trends in *MS 1968*. M. Perrot discusses factory discipline in J. Merriman (ed.), *Consciousness . . .*, op. cit. (1979). M. Mottez analyses employer strategies in *Systèmes de salaires et politiques patronales* (1966) and M. Moutet discusses Taylorism in *MS 1975*.

General studies of unionism include G. Lefranc, *Le mouvement syndical en France*, vol. I (1967); V. Lorwin, *French Labor Movements* (1954); and R. Brécy, *Le mouvement syndicaliste en France* (1963). M. Perrrot, *Les ouvriers en grève*, 2 vols. (1974) and C. Tilly and E. Shorter, *Strikes in France 1830–1968* (1974) are two major quantitative studies of strikes, to be supplemented by the articles by Tilly and Shorter in *MS 1971*; Y. Lequin, *CH 1967*; J. M. Flonneau, *MS 1970*; J. Bouvier, *MS 1964*; and E. Andréani, *Grèves et fluctuations économiques* (1968).

Miners are studied by R. Trempé, *Les mineurs de Carmaux*, 2 vols. (1971) and *MS 1968*; L. Loubère, *JSH 1968*; J. Michel, *RN 1973* and *MS 1974*; J. Julliard, *MS 1964*; M. Gillet, *RN 1957*; D. Reid, *FHS 1981*; and M. Perrot, *MS 1963*. For railmen see L. Ceplain, *French Railroad Workers and the CGT 1890–1922* (Wisconsin PhD 1973); F. Caron, *MS 1965*; and G. Thuillier, *MS 1969*. R. Cazals, *Avec les ouvriers de Mazamet* (1980) studies wool-workers. J. Scott, *The Glassworkers of Carmaux* (1974) is an important book, as is M. Hanagan, *The Logic of Solidarity* (1980), a study of Loire engineering and glass-workers. C. Gras studies Paris 'metallos' in *MS 1965* and *1971*, while car-workers are the subject of J. Laux, *MS 1972* and M. Fridenson, *Histoire des Usines Renault*, vol. I (1972). M. McMechan, *The Building Trades of France 1907–14* (Wisconsin University PhD 1973) is an important thesis. For semi-skilled workers see Berlanstein, *JSH 1981* and for immigrants see J. C. Bonnet, *CH 1971* and S. Bonnet, *JSH 1968*.

The unionization of women workers is analysed by M. Guilbert, *Les femmes et l'organisation syndicale* (1966) and M. H. Zylberberg-Hocquard, *Féminisme et syndicalisme* (1978). *MS 1978* has an edition on women's work. J. Scott and L. Tilly, *Women, Work and the Family* (1978) compares France and Britain. T. McBride, *The Domestic Revolution* (1976) and P. Guiral and G. Thuillier, *La vie quotidienne des domestiques en France* (1978) present contrasting views on servants. T. McBride studies shop-workers in *FHS 1978*, M. Boxer artificial-flower makers in *FHS 1982*, while L. Tilly discusses female workers in J. Merriman (ed.), *Cities . . .*, op. cit. (1982) and women strikers in C. Tilly (ed.), *Class Conflict and Collective Action* (1981). C. Sowerwine discusses feminism and socialism in *MS 1975*.

General interpretations of syndicalism include P. Stearns, *Revolutionary Syndicalism and French Labor* (1971); H. Dubief, *Le Syndicalisme Révolutionnaire* (1969); F. Ridley, *Revolutionary Syndicalism in France* (1970); R. Brécy, *La grève générale en France* (1969); and M. Collinet, *L'ouvrier français; esprit de syndicalisme* (1951). On Pelloutier consult J. Julliard, *F. Pelloutier* (1971); A. Spitzer, *IRSH 1963*; and A. Baker, *F. Pelloutier* (UCLA PhD 1973). Government and employer repression is analysed by P. Stearns, *JMH 1968*; J. Julliard, *Clemenceau, briseur des grèves* (1965); and A. Calhoun, *The Politics of Internal Order* (Princeton PhD 1973). For syndicalist strikes see G. Désiré-Vuillemin, *AM 1971* and *1973* on Limoges, G. Baal, *MS 1973* on Brest, Y. Guin, *Le mouvement ouvrier nantais*, op. cit. (1976), J. Julliard, *MS 1968*, J. M. Flonneau, *MS 1970* and Y. Lequin, *Les ouvriers*, op. cit. (1977). The *Bourses de Travail* are discussed by P. Schöttler, *MS 1981*. For Pouget see E. Fitzgerald, *E. Pouget* (Yale PhD 1973) and for the drift to reformism B. George, *et al.*, *L. Jouhaux*, vol. I (1962).

On antimilitarism and the approach of war see S. Kriegel and J. J. Becker, *1914: la guerre et le mouvement ouvrier français* (1964) and J. J. Becker, *Le Carnet B* (1973).

Working-class education is discussed by M. Ozouf, *MS 1963*, and in *Niveaux de culture et groupes sociaux* (1967).

Chapter 9

E. Weber, *Peasants . . .*, op. cit. and R. Barral, *Les Agrariens Français de Méline à Pisani* (1968) are the two best general studies. *MS 1969* contains a special edition on the peasantry.

E. Weber, *AHR 1982* discusses the 'politicization' of the peasantry. C. Tilly questions Weber's chronology in J. Merriman (ed.), *Consciousness and Class Experience*, op. cit. P. Barral, *RH 1967* discusses rural electoral sociology.

In addition to the regional studies of Corbin, Dupeux, Désert and Garrier already cited, P. Barral, *Le département de l'Isère* (1962) and R. Hubscher, *L'agriculture et la société rurale dans le Pas-de-Calais 1848–1914* are important and A. Siegfried, *Tableau Politique de la France de l'Ouest* (1913) remains a flawed classic.

A. Chatelain, *Les migrants temporaires 1800–1914* (1976) is reviewed by

J. Vidalenc, *RH 1978*. P. Hohenberg, *AESC 1974* also discusses migration. P. Hohenberg studies landed income in *RH 1971*, C. Mesliand peasant wealth in *AESC 1967*.

Among village monographs are J. Lehning, *The Peasants of Marlhes* (1980); L. Wylie, *Chanzeau* (1966); and E. Ackermann, *FHS 1977*.

A. Sylvere, *Toinou, le cri d'un enfant auvergnat* (1980) is an evocative peasant autobiography.

M. Gontard, *Les écoles primaires de la France bourgeoise 1833–75* (nd) and *L'oeuvre scolaire de la IIIe République* (1967) and R. Thabault, *Education and Change in a Village Community* (1971) are essential. F. Furet and J. Ozouf, *Lire et Écrire*, 2 vols. (1977) refuse to correlate literacy with education legislation. J. Ozouf, *Nous les maîtres d'école* (1967); M. Ozouf, *L'école, l'église et la République* (1963); P. Meyers, *JSH 1975*; and B. Singer, *JCH 1977* discuss the teachers. G. Cholvy studies the clergy-teacher conflict in *AM 1975* and P. Goujon laic village associations in *CH 1981*.

The impact of education in the west is discussed by B. Singer, *FHS 1977*; P. Hélias, *The Horse of Pride* (1978); F. Elegöet, *Nous ne parlions que le breton et il fallait parler français* (1978); and G. Désert in D. Baker, *et al.* (eds.), *The Making of Frenchmen*, op. cit. (1980). The Breton problem is analysed by J. Reece, *Bretons against France* (1977) and the peasantry by J. Berger, *Peasants against Politics* (1972) and T. Brekilien, *La vie quotidienne des paysans bretons* (1966).

G. Cholvy, *Religion et Société au XIXe siècle*, op. cit. (1973) is summarized in *IH 1973*. His article in *FHLMR 1976* (46e Congrès) on the Narbonnais is excellent. J. Faury, *Cléricalisme et Anticléricalisme dans le Tarn* (1980) is important. *CH 1969* has an issue on de-Christianization. J. Silver studies the Vendômois in *JSH 1980*; C. Mesliand the Vaucluse in *ASR 1960*; B. Peyrous the Bordelais in *AM 1975*.

P. Gratton, *La lutte des classes dans les campagnes* (1971) and *Les paysans français contre l'agrarisme* (1972) offer a general view. H. Goldberg, *IRSH 1957* and C. Landauer, *IRSH 1961* discuss socialist peasant policy.

Var socialism is analysed by T. Judt, *Socialism in Provence 1871–1914* (1979); *HJ 1975*; *SH 1976*; and by Y. Rinauldo, *Les paysans du Var* (1980), *PH 1870*, *AM 1980* and *MS 1980*.

For peasant socialism in central regions see S. Derruau-Bonniol, *CH 1957*; R. Braque, *MS 1963*; P. Pigenet, *et al.*, *Terre de Luttes*, 2 vols. (1976–7); C. Pennetier, *Le socialisme dans les départements ruraux français* (1979); A. Kriegel, *Le Pain et les Roses* (1968); and S. Sokoloff, *ESR 1980*. E. Guillaumin, *La Vie d'un simple* (1904) and *Le syndicat de Bougignoux* (1912) can be supplemented by P. Vernois, *Le roman rustique* (1962); R. Mathé, *E. Guillaumin* (1966) and *Le Centenaire d'Emile Guillaumin* (1975).

For the Midi, L. Loubère, *Radicalism*, op. cit. offers an overview. J. Sagnès, *Le mouvement ouvrier en Languedoc* (1980) and *MS 1978* are essential. R. Pech, *Entreprise viticole et capitalisme en Languedoc* (1975) studies the big estates. C. Warner, *The Winegrowers of France* (1960) analyzes government policy. Vineyard labourers are studied by R. Harvey Smith, *JIH 1975* and *PP 1978* and L. Frader, *CHIMT 1978*. P. Guidoni, *La cité rouge: Narbonne 1871–1921* (1979) studies a socialist stronghold.

For regionalism see Andréani in *AM 1978* and *RHMC 1973* and J. M. Cabasse, *X de Ricard* (1977).

FHLMR annual editions contain many useful articles.

Conclusion

On foreign policy see P. Renouvin, *La politique extérieure de la III*ᵉ *République* (nd); E. Carroll, *French Public Opinion on Foreign Affairs* (1931); and R. Challenor, *French Theory of the Nation in Arms* (1955).

Franco-German problems are discussed by P. Renouvin, *Les relations franco-allemandes 1871–1914* (1952); H. Contamine, *La revanche* (1957); and C. Digeon, *La crise allemande de la pensée française* (1959). F. Seager discusses Alsace in C. Warner (ed.), *From Ancien Régime to Popular Front* (1969). R. Poidevin, *Les relations économiques et financières entre la France et l'Allemagne 1898–1914* (1969) is important. P. Guillen discusses Franco-German relations before 1914 in *RH 1972*.

The Russian alliance is the subject of W. Langer, *The Franco-Russian Alliance* (1929). R. Girault, *Emprunts russes et investissements français en Russie* (1973) analyzes economic ties, as do articles in *RHMC 1966* and *1969* and *RN 1975*, while in *RH 1975* Girault assesses Balkan policy.

C. Andrew, *Delcassé and the Making of the Entente Cordiale* (1968) and S. Williamson, *The Politics of Grand Strategy* (1969) discuss relations with Britain.

Imperialist economic rivalries are discussed by P. Guillen in *RH 1963*, and *RD 1965* for Morocco, and by J. Thobie, *MS 1974* and *RH 1968* and W. Shorrock, *ESR 1974* for the Ottoman Empire.

J. Becker, *1914* (1977) and his article in *RH 1980* and G. Krumeich, *Aufrustung und Innenpolitik in Frankreich vor dem ersten Weltkrieg* (1980) discuss the domestic build-up to war.

The conclusion to M. Réberioux, *La République Radicale*, op. cit. is suggestive. F. Codaccioni, *Lille 1850–1914* (1971) emphasizes economic inequalities. The tax system is discussed by J. Bouvier in *Mélanges: Charles Pouthas*, op. cit. and by M. Frajerman and D. Winock, *Le vote de l'impôt sur le revenu* (1973). For profits consult J. Bouvier, *et al.*, *Le mouvement des profits en France* (1965) and for bourgeois wealth A. Daumard (ed.), *Les fortunes françaises au XIX*ᵉ *siècle* (1973). J. Jeanneney, *L'argent caché* (1981) discusses money and politics, J. Estèbe, *RHES 1976* ministerial fortunes and J. Donovan, *JSH 1981* bourgeois control of the jury system.

M. Miller, *The Bon Marché* (1981) is a fine study of bourgeois culture. E. Weber, *AHR 1971* discusses sport and society.

For the impact of colonialism on the workers see Olivesi, *MS 1963* and F. Bédarida, *MS 1974*.

Recent studies of French women include J. McMillan, *Housewife or Harlot?* (1981); A. Corbin, *Les filles de noce* (1978) on prostitution; and R. Phillips, *Family Breakdown in Late Nineteenth-Century France* (1981) and B. Smith, *Ladies of the Leisure Class* (1981).

Index

Index